CONSERVATIVE
ECHOES
IN
FIN-DE-SIÈCLE
PARISIAN
ART
CRITICISM

Michael Marlais

CONSERVATIVE ECHOES IN *FIN-DE-SIÈCLE* PARISIAN ART CRITICISM

The Pennsylvania State University Press
University Park, Pennsylvania

Library of Congress Cataloging-in-Publication Data

Marlais, Michael Andrew.
    Conservative echoes in Fin de siècle Parisian art criticism /
  Michael Marlais.
          p.   cm.
    Includes bibliographical references (p.   ) and index.
    ISBN 0-271-00773-7 (acid-free paper)
    1. Art criticism—France—Paris—History—19th century.
  2. Symbolism in art.   3. Idealism in art.   I. Title.
  N7476.M37   1992
  701'.18'094436109034—dc20   91–8370
                                                              CIP

It is the policy of The Pennsylvania State University Press to use acid-free paper for
the first printing of all clothbound books. Publications on uncoated stock satisfy the
minimum requirements of American National Standard for Information Sciences—
Permanence of Paper for Printed Library Materials, ANSI Z39.48–1984.

CONTENTS

List of Illustrations   vii

Acknowledgments   ix

Introduction   1

1   Antinaturalism   5

2   Idealism and Symbolism in the Criticism of Art   25

3   Symbolism Divided: Félix Fénéon and the Defense of
       Modernism   77

4   Symbolism Divided: Albert Aurier's Traditionalism   105

5   Symbolism Divided: Conservatives Among the Modernists   149

6   Maurice Denis's Conservative Modernism   185

Conclusion   221

Selected Bibliography   225

Index   241

LIST OF ILLUSTRATIONS

1. Auguste Toulmouche, *Forbidden Fruit* (Salon, 1865). Collection unknown

2. P.-A.-J. Dagnan-Bouveret, *Wedding at the Photographer's* (1878–79). Lyon, Musée des Beaux-Arts

3. P.-A.-J. Dagnan-Bouveret, *Pardon in Brittany* (1889). New York, Metropolitan Museum of Art, Gift of George F. Baker, 1931

4. Jean-Charles Cazin, *Tobias and the Angel* (1880). Lille, Musée des Beaux-Arts (photo: Giraudon/Art Resource, New York)

5. Jean-Charles Cazin, *Hagar and Ishmael* (1880). Tours, Musée des Beaux-Arts (photo: © Photo R.M.N.)

6. Georges Moreau de Tours, *A Stigmatization in the Middle Ages* (1885). Nantes, Musée des Beaux-Arts (photo: Ville de Nantes, Musée des Beaux-Arts, Patrick Jean)

7. Edmond Aman-Jean, *St. Julian the Hospitator* (1882). Carcassonne, Musée des Beaux-Arts

8. Edmond Aman-Jean, *St. Genevieve Before Paris* (1885). Brest, Musée Municipal (photo: © Photo R.M.N.)

9. Maurice Denis, *Catholic Mystery* (1889). Saint-Germain-en-Laye, Musée du Prieuré (photo: © Photo R.M.N.)

10. Jean-Jacques Henner, *Nymph by a Fountain* (1880). Paris, Musée National J.-J. Henner

11. Georges-Antoine Rochegrosse, *The Knight Among the Flowers* (1894). Paris, Musée d'Orsay (photo: © Photo R.M.N.)

12. Alexandre Séon, *Holiday* (1889). Courbevoie, Hôtel de Ville, Salle des Mariages

13. Alexandre Séon, *The Despair of the Chimera* (1890). Paris, Charbonnier Collection (photo: R. Turnbull, Fontainebleau)

14. Alexandre Séon, *Portrait of Joséphin Péladan* (1891). Lyon, Musée des Beaux-Arts

15. Alexandre Séon, *The Return Home* (1913). Saint-Étienne, Musée d'Art Moderne

16. Maurice Denis, *The Exaltation of the Holy Cross* (1898), in place at the Collège de Saint-Croix, Le Vésinet (photo: Private Collection, Saint-Germain-en-Laye)

17a. Maurice Denis, *The Exaltation of the Holy Cross*, upper panel. Paris, Musée d'Orsay (photo: © Photo R.M.N.)

17b. Maurice Denis, *The Exaltation of the Holy Cross*, central panel. Paris, Musée d'Orsay (photo: © Photo R.M.N.)

17c. Maurice Denis, *The Exaltation of the Holy Cross*, far left panel. Paris, Musée d'Orsay (photo: © Photo R.M.N.)

17d. Maurice Denis, *The Exaltation of the Holy Cross*, left center panel. Paris, Musée d'Orsay (photo: © Photo R.M.N.)

17e. Maurice Denis, *The Exaltation of the Holy Cross*, right center panel. Paris, Musée d'Orsay (photo: © Photo R.M.N.)

17f. Maurice Denis, *The Exaltation of the Holy Cross*, far right panel. Paris, Musée d'Orsay (photo: © Photo R.M.N.)

18. Maurice Denis, *Sunlight on the Terrace* (1890). Paris, Musée d'Orsay (photo: Giraudon/Art Resource, New York)

19. William-Adolphe Bouguereau, *The Annunciation* (c. 1888). Collection unknown

20. Maurice Denis, *Homage to Cézanne* (1900). Paris, Musée d'Orsay (photo: © Photo R.M.N.)

21. Maurice Denis, *Dessert in the Garden* (1897). Saint-Germain-en-Laye, Musée du Prieuré

22. Maurice Denis, *Our Lady of the Schools* (1903). Brussels, Musées Royaux des Beaux-Arts de Belgique (photo: © Musées Royaux des Beaux-Arts de Belgique)

The paintings by Maurice Denis are reproduced by permission, © ARS, N.Y./SPADEM.

ACKNOWLEDGMENTS

Research for this project was made possible through grants from the University of Michigan and Colby College, as well as a Travel to Collections Grant from the National Endowment for the Humanities. In France my work was greatly facilitated by the generous assistance of Isabel Fonseca. Jacques Vilain, in charge of French Provincial Museums, made it possible for me to see far more art than I might have without his kind offices. Professor Gabriel Weisberg and his wife Yvonne were invaluable in providing contacts, moral support, and companionship in Paris. Professor Weisberg later gave generously of his time in reading this manuscript at various stages. Phylis Floyd offered much information concerning the mechanics of research in Paris. Patrick Vazeilles, archivist at the Mairie du Vésinet, helped locate photographs of Maurice Denis's work in that city and Isabelle Olivares at the Bibliothèque du Vésinet was most generous with information concerning the town itself. Claire Denis kindly offered her time and knowledge in discussing her grandfather's work. I owe a special debt of gratitude to Marie Amélie Anquetil, curator of the Musée de Prieuré, and to Marie El Caidi, Musée du Prieuré archivist, for their assistance with my research.

Dr. James Kearns, at the University of Exeter, kindly provided a photograph of Alexandre Séon's *Despair of the Chimera*. Professors George Mauner at The Pennsylvania State University, Paul Archambault at Syracuse University, and Patricia Mathews at Oberlin College read early versions of this manuscript and provided helpful commentary. Professors Diane Kirkpatrick, Victor Miesel, and Stephen Tonsor at the University of Michigan all read early versions of the manuscript and were very supportive. Joel Isaacson consistently offered cogent and detailed criticism, and the very form of my research owes much to his advice. At Colby my colleagues David Lubin, Hearne Pardee, and Gina Werfel have offered much in the way of support and advice. Kirsten Wallace and Grace von Tobel typed the manuscript in various stages. Philip Winsor, senior editor at Penn State Press, was both encouraging and expeditious in seeing this manuscript to publication. Cherene Holland and Betty Waterhouse deserve special mention for their expert editorial work. My wife, Marianne Doezema, diligently edited my writing, offered extensive commentary on its contents, and helped, through lengthy discussion and occasional coaxing, to develop the thesis contained in these pages. Finally, I would like to dedicate this book to my father, Andrew Marlais, with much respect and gratitude.

INTRODUCTION

This book is about the conservative tendencies in much symbolist art criticism and the shared goals of avant-garde and conservative camps in Paris at the end of the nineteenth century. The differences between two slim volumes of art criticism, one published in 1886, the other in 1896, serve well as introduction to the theme expounded herein. Although Félix Fénéon's *Les Impressionnistes en 1886* and André Mellerio's *Le Mouvement idéaliste en peinture* were both intended as timely summaries of contemporary events in painting, they also mark a sharp difference in attitude, a difference emphasized in the very titles each author chose. Fénéon's *Les Impressionnistes en 1886* is specific. By dating his study in the title he turned a very general term into a precise qualification. The reader today understands that the subject at hand is of historical import: impressionism as it was in the year 1886. Fénéon's contemporaries would have derived a feeling of currency from the title, an up-to-the-minute look at a movement most Parisians already knew. Mellerio's *Le Mouvement idéaliste en peinture* is more general. The implication is that idealism was to be found in many areas of French cultural life in 1896 and that contemporary events in painting could be linked to other idealist manifestations. Fénéon excludes, while Mellerio includes.

Each author's commentary follows suit. Fénéon's language and the boundaries of his discussion are precise and targeted. His French is concise, surgical in its brevity. He carefully confined his comments to descriptive analyses, drawing certain conclusions about style from the available physical evidence of specific paintings in specific exhibitions during the year 1886. Mellerio, on the other hand, is a good deal more general. He offers a long introduction to the concept of a revived idealism and then connects many artists, members of the establishment and newcomers as well, with idealist tendencies. He rarely mentions specific paintings and never analyzes them, preferring generalized descriptive adjectives and quotations drawn from various sources. Mellerio's is the overview, the grand scheme, as it were, over and against Fénéon's analytical frame of mind.

Stated another way, one might contend that Fénéon's purpose was more literally avant-garde than Mellerio's, if one understands the term as referring to a select, limited group of "advanced" tastes. He distinguished the nugget of neo-impressionism from the wider impressionist movement, itself an isolated phenomenon in French painting. Mellerio was more concerned with sweeping inclusions, gathering various factions—indeed artists as diverse as Paul Gauguin, Georges Seurat, Puvis de Chavannes, and Vincent van Gogh—into the idealist camp. Furthermore, any reader versed in even the outlines of advanced art during the last decades of the nineteenth century would have recognized Mellerio's use of a term that was anathema to avant-garde impressionist circles. Although he did not refer to the crusty idealism of the past, Mellerio's very mention of "idealism" would have struck many as a return to a concept abandoned by the naturalist avant-garde of the 1860s and 1870s. Today it can serve as indication of the general conservative tendencies that permeated the symbolist generation of the eighties and nineties.

Suggesting that the symbolist generation sought a return to certain traditional values is not new. In the 1890s Maurice Denis invented the term *néo-traditionnisme* to describe the artistic mood of the period. Writing in 1931, Robert Rey spoke of *La Renaissance du sentiment classique dans la peinture française à la fin du XIXe siècle*. Contemporary art historians have long been aware that the last two decades of the nineteenth century witnessed a revival of idealist tendencies. The avant-garde aspects of that revival have been documented often in studies of the development of modernism. But no careful chronicle of the conservative mood of French art criticism in the 1880s and 1890s exists. This book is meant to fill that gap by detailing some parts of the mechanism through which the naturalist avant-garde of the early 1880s evolved into a late symbolist conservatism. The reader should be warned that what is offered here is not meant as a comprehensive history of either the symbolist movement or symbolist criticism itself. My concern is with certain aspects of symbolist art criticism, not an overview.

It will become apparent quickly enough that one overriding phenomenon dominates the following discussion. That phenomenon is antinaturalism. The reaction against naturalism was, perhaps, the most vital artistic fact of the late nineteenth century in France. It was certainly one of the most interesting. This book is about the ways in which various aspects of antinaturalism were made manifest in the art criticism of the time, both symbolist and conservative, and its first task is an explanation of the historical and intellectual context of these phenomena and a discussion of antinaturalism itself. Chapters 1 and 2 are meant to provide some sense of the intellectual ambiance of the 1880s and 1890s. Chapters 3 through 6 focus on some, not all, individual symbolist critics as examples of various conservative attitudes. Taken by itself this book offers a viewpoint, a way of understanding one aspect of the cultural climate in Paris at the end of the nineteenth century. It is meant to complement as much as challenge earlier studies of the period and, indeed, will be most appreciated by those who have already absorbed the literature on the development of modernism in France.

1

ANTINATURALISM

It has long been understood that the symbolist movement in France grew out of a broader intellectual reaction against the naturalist movement.[1] The fundamental opposition between the naturalism of the 1860s and 1870s and the antinaturalism of the *fin de siècle* is of major import because it ran so deep, crossing boundaries between art and society, culture and politics.[2] Thus, to the extent that the naturalist age can be

1. See, among many other examples, such widely separate sources as André Barre, *Le Symbolisme* (Paris: Jouve, 1911), 7–8; Robert Goldwater, *Symbolism* (New York: Harper and Row, 1979), 1; and Robert Delevoy, *Symbolists and Symbolism* (Geneva: Skira, 1978), 12.

2. It should be noted that some scholars have challenged certain assumptions regarding the relationship between naturalism and symbolism. Recently, to note an author dealing with many of the same critical sources cited in the present book, Richard Shiff has argued that the goals of the impressionists—held by many to be basically naturalists—were quite close to those

seen as positivist, realist, modernist, and progressive, the antinaturalism of the eighties and nineties was antipositivist, idealist, traditional, and, in some quarters, conservative. To be sure, such generalizations are dangerous. The naturalist period was as much a time of empire as it was of progressive republicanism and the antinaturalist *fin de siècle* saw the consolidation of the Third Republic. If naturalism gave rise to the avant-garde art of Manet and the impressionists, it also produced the conservative styles of Jules Breton and Bastien-Lepage. If antinaturalism informed the conservative style of Puvis de Chavannes, it was also the impetus for Gauguin's avant-garde art. Yet the generalization remains true enough as long as one uses such terms as "conservative," "idealist," and "tradition" gingerly. What we mean by such terms today is not always the same as what they stood for in late nineteenth-century France. Nor, for that matter, did every Frenchman living in the 1890s define them in exactly the same manner. The word "tradition," for example, had a special meaning for Maurice Denis—a meaning very different from that which the old impressionist Camille Pissarro associated with the term.

Antinaturalism will be used here as a blanket concept referring to an intellectual mood that saw naturalism's fondness for the quotidian, the factual, the real, and the ordinary as wrongheaded. Both symbolism— first in literature and then in the visual arts—and a revival of idealism grew out of antinaturalism and might in fact be seen as two sides of the same coin. Accordingly, the first would be the avant-garde reaction to naturalism and the second a more conservative reaction. However, terms like "conservative" and "avant-garde" are confusing in that the former has come to have a pejorative connotation, while the latter is associated with such other terms as "advanced," "progressive," "modern." While I am well aware of the arguments behind these distinctions, I wish to avoid the good/bad connotations attached to them. As will be seen in the discussions that follow, some of the more "advanced" artistic

---

of the symbolist painters. His analysis of impressionism is cogent and provocative but not meant to address the fundamental opposition between naturalism and symbolism, which, to my thinking, is indisputable. See Shiff, "The End of Impressionism," in the exhibition catalogue, *The New Painting, Impressionism 1874–1886* (San Francisco: Fine Arts Museums of San Francisco, 1986), 61–89. This essay is a revised version of arguments originally printed elsewhere: "The End of Impressionism: A Study in Theories of Artistic Expression," *Art Quarterly*, n.s. 1 (Autumn 1978), 338–78; and *Cézanne and the End of Impressionism* (Chicago: University of Chicago Press, 1984).

ideas of the period had a conservative, traditionalist edge. Conversely, in a period that had institutionalized a progressive, modernist attitude—as the materialist, naturalist age had—a conservative, traditional sensibility could seem quite new.

One might well be better advised at times to abandon definitions of movements and instead think in terms of tendencies. In criticism, symbolist and idealist tendencies abounded during this antinaturalist period; yet it is difficult to define, or even encounter, the "perfect" symbolist or idealist critic. To speak of tendencies, as opposed to offering categorical, defining labels is, to the skeptic, merely a way of avoiding an argument. It also makes the student's job harder. But labels are, in themselves, mere conveniences that avoid the real-life complexities of any period. Symbolism and idealism were fluid concepts, defined in individual cases in individual manners. Thus artists as far apart as Gauguin and Gustave Moreau can be called symbolist, and critics as far apart as Albert Aurier and Ferdinand Brunetière can be associated with idealism. That Aurier, for one, tended to be both symbolist and idealist serves to confuse as well as demonstrate the issue, and antinaturalism is the key concept for understanding how.

THE ANTINATURALIST PROGRAM

In June 1889, the writer, moralist, and sometime philosopher Paul Desjardins published a short article in the *Revue bleue* on the occasion of the reception of his friend and colleague Eugène Melchior de Vogüé into the Académie française.[3] While he was highly skeptical of the motives behind his friend's acceptance into the august body, Desjardins took this opportunity to define the antipositivist intellectual position of the Marquis de Vogüé and to offer a brief synopsis of the recent generation of French intellectual thought. In so doing he presented a relatively complete picture of the reaction against naturalism. He complained that what had befallen France was "a simultaneous invasion of positivism in thought, of naturalism in art, of mechanism and analysis in criticism, of realism and *the hoax* in literature, of agnosticism and indifference in

3. Paul Desjardins, "Sur M. E. Melchior de Vogüé, a propos de sa réception académique," *Revue bleue*, xxvi (8 June 1889), 713–19.

religion, of practical sense in life."[4] He then named some of the men responsible for this situation: Claude Bernard, the physician now known as the founder of experimental medicine; the historian and critic Hippolyte Taine; the writers Dumas, Flaubert, and Champfleury; and finally Charles Darwin himself. Desjardins was careful not to deny the many accomplishments of the scientific generation but suggested that "it sinned . . . on one point: it believed that its results embraced everything which exists."[5] This admission was followed by a deluge of complaints and a description of the young generation's reaction against the scientific age. He wrote of painting's being reinvigorated, as if in a "nouvelle Fiesole," and cited the art of Gustave Moreau and Puvis de Chavannes as examples. He noted the revival of idealist philosophy and of poetry and the renewed interest in the Catholic church, citing among others the doyen of the symbolists, Paul Verlaine.

In all, Desjardins's short article read as a sweeping indictment of the naturalist age and a heady prediction for a more humanistic and idealistic future. His summary of antinaturalism, coming as it did in 1889, was one of the earliest insightful characterizations of the movement. Indeed, it was in this year that the young symbolists Georges Vanor, Charles Morice, and Jean Moréas each came out with their now-famous treatments of the development of French symbolism.[6] The centennial of the French Revolution was a time for taking stock in the world of politics, the arts, and literature as well as philosophy. What is remarkable is that Desjardins, who wrote for the establishment *Revue bleue* and *Journal des débats,* who founded the *Union pour l'action morale* in 1892, could outline a position that was so close in principle to the symbolist viewpoint of both Moréas and Morice. It is important to understand that Desjardins's antinaturalist stance was by no means a backward step into an old idealism. It was meant to represent a new attitude among the young generation, a reaction against the old-line rationalist viewpoint of the academy. The symbolists were saying similar things earlier in the de-

4. Ibid., 714. (". . . une invasion simultanée du positivisme dans la pensée, du naturalisme dans l'art, du méchanisme et de l'analyse dans la critique, du réalisme et de *la blaque* dans la littérature, de l'agnosticisme et de l'indifférence dans la religion, de sens pratique dans la vie.")

5. Ibid., 715. (". . . elle a péché cependant en un point: elle a cru que ses résultats embrassaient tout ce qui existe.")

6. Jean Moréas, *Les Premières armes du symbolisme* (Paris: Vanier, 1889); Charles Morice, *La Littérature de tout à l'heure* (Paris: Perrin, 1889); Georges Vanor, *L'Art symboliste* (Paris: Vanier, 1889).

cade, but their writings had been concerned almost exclusively with literature and lacked the comprehensive nature of Desjardins's statement. Desjardins attacked determinist history, positivist philosophy, naturalist literature and art, scientism, rationalism, and agnosticism while proclaiming the revival of idealism, religion, imagination, and poetry in literature, the visual arts, and music as well.[7]

Antinaturalism included, most obviously, the rejection of naturalism in literature and painting. It was also fed by a reaction against positivist philosophy and against the scientific movement that accompanied positivism. To the extent that naturalism itself could be allied politically with a republican, socialist-leaning philosophy, antinaturalism could be linked with a rejection of democracy and a reactionary position. Idealism and religious subject matter were both largely rejected by naturalism and revived, in varying forms, by antinaturalism. Before considering how each of these aspects of antinaturalism was manifested in art criticism of this period, it is important to offer a brief synopsis of how philosophy, theology, and to a certain extent politics also demonstrated an antinaturalist bias.

FROM ANTIPOSITIVISM TO NEO-CATHOLICISM AND REACTIONARY POLITICS

Positivism, in its most basic form, was a philosophical system based on information gleaned empirically from scientific facts and natural phenomena. It was concerned only with the knowable and specifically excluded idealism and metaphysics. Auguste Comte was the father of positivism in France and, after him, Emile Littré. But positivism in France was not monolithic and, for a supposedly rational and scientific way of thinking, was difficult to pin down on certain specifics. Comte himself gave in to the temptation to make of positivism a sort of religion toward the end of his life. Littré, while following Comte, differed with him on

7. Joséphin Péladan, *La Décadence esthétique, L'Art ochlocratique, Salons de 1882 et de 1883* (Paris: Camille Dalou, 1888; hereafter referred to as *L'Art ochlocratique*), outlined a similar program as early as 1882, but then it was more in the form of a giddy but accurate prophesy of what was to come than a summation of what had happened.

many points. Indeed, the historian Hippolyte Taine, also considered a positivist, admitted that he had only read Comte's definitive *Cours de philosophie positive* after he had formulated many of his own ideas.[8]

Thus, it is important to differentiate positivism itself from ideas about it. Popularly it was associated with a kind of pure materialism, an anti-religious rationalism, that was not necessarily part of the writings of the important positivist philosophers. But it is the way in which positivism was popularly understood that is of greatest importance to this discussion. And in this respect it is the essential modernity of the positivist position that must be emphasized. No matter how vaguely understood, positivism was seen to be an attack on the traditional schools of philosophy. Here was a rational, scientific explanation of things, a rejection of the ancient modes of philosophy. Positivism accentuated the progress that science had made and suggested that the more society trusted science, the sooner it would progress. Indeed, it was this belief in progress that would most popularly come to represent positivism in the public mind. If positivism was seen as an attack on crusty forms of philosophical thought, it was also either applauded or scorned as an attack on traditional religious values. A concomitant of the positivist viewpoint was a cosmopolitan agnosticism that dominated intellectual circles during the Second Empire. It became unfashionable to be a believer.[9] In the popular mind positivism gave rise to a belief that science would also cure the ills of society. Science, democratic in its blindness to everything but facts, would provide a new future in which all sections of society would enjoy its fruits.

Given the rationalist, progressive image positivism projected, it is not difficult to imagine how carefully critics approached the movement. To attack such an enlightened and esteemed movement could appear very reactionary in a world infatuated with science, modernity, and progress. Just so, the first new critics of positivism in philosophy were extremely careful in their arguments. It should be noted that our concern here is with "new" criticism of positivist thinking. There had always been an old-line idealist opposition to positivism, but this was of little influence

8. Donald Geoffrey Charlton, *Positivist Thought in France During the Second Empire, 1852–1870* (Oxford: Clarendon Press, 1959), 135.

9. Richard Griffiths, *The Reactionary Revolution: The Catholic Revival in French Literature, 1870–1914* (London: Constable, 1966), 6, talks of the positivist reign at the Sorbonne, when no one believed that a person could be both intelligent and Catholic.

against the hegemony of rationalist thought during the Second Empire. The present discussion will deal with what has been termed the renaissance of idealism.[10]

Alfred Fouillée's *Le Mouvement idéaliste et la réaction contre la science positive*, originally published in 1896 by the Librairie Félix Alcan, known for its serious offerings in the field of philosophy, is a case in point.[11] While he spoke of an insurrection of the heart against the intelligence, Fouillée also rejected any tendency toward mysticism or organized religion, and he specifically rejected symbolism. He understood how attractive religion, mysticism, and symbolism had become in some circles, noting that "the general need for beliefs has resulted in a recrudescence, sometimes exaggerated, of metaphysical speculation. Some have fallen into the overly subtle and recondite; like literature, philosophy has had its symbolists and decadents."[12] But throughout Fouillée's study it becomes more and more evident just how far the idealist movement of his title was from symbolism or any of the more outspoken reactions against positivism. Fouillée's new idealism retained a profound respect for science and endeavored to provide a marriage of science and philosophy. Ultimately he rejected only scientism, the belief that science can answer everything and can deal in realms that do not involve facts. His "reaction" against positivism was as rational and scientific as any positivist tract and was ultimately of a family with positivism.

Henri Bergson's *Essai sur les données immédiates de la conscience* (1889) provides another example of how cautiously philosophy challenged positivism at this time. In spite of the far-reaching implications of Bergson's work and in spite of claims that he attacked the hegemony of science and reason, one is most struck when reading the *Essai* by its care and respect for the scientific method. The first chapter of the *Essai* constitutes an attack on psychophysics and its attempts at measuring sensation, yet the attack is presented in such a way that it reads like one of the new tracts on perceptual psychology. Bergson does not reject science

10. By the conservative critic Ferdinand Brunetière, *La Renaissance de l'idéalisme* (Paris: Librairie de Firmin-Didot, 1896).

11. Alfred Fouillée, *Le Mouvement idéaliste et la réaction contre la science positive* (Paris: Félix Alcan, 1913). All further quotes are from this edition.

12. Ibid., vi. (". . . le besoin de croyances générales a produit une recrudescence, parfois exagerée, des spéculations métaphysiques. On est tombé dans le subtil et dans l'abscons; comme la littérature, la philosophie a eu ses symbolistes et ses décadents.")

so much as he challenges it on its own ground, and he continually demonstrates a respect for science that belies any antiscientific prejudice on his part.

Similarly, the philosopher Elme Marie Caro, in a series of articles and books, presented an antipositivist position, but he did so in the context of intense studies of the doctrines of positivism itself. As early as 1882 Caro painted a grim picture of what would happen to a world "under the influence of the positivist faith, a hard generation, practical, solid, calculating, positive in excess." And in opposition to this he even raised the possibility of a renewal of religious fervor: "It will be thus right up to the day when some brave thinker will realize that there is something beyond physics and chemistry, and by an unexpected stroke of genius will discover the soul and God."[13] What Caro ultimately attacked, however, was the "positivist faith," the corruption of positivism that made of it a new religion. Much like Alfred Fouillée, Caro argued for a world in which science and faith could live together, and he advocated the dominance of neither.

Across the board the French philosophical community of the eighties and nineties was timid in its reaction toward positivism. Thus, the philosophical reaction against positivism lacked the fervor necessary to be a forceful movement. However, fervor was not what much of the religious writing on positivism lacked. Polemic was a mainstay of religious commentary on positivism, and it was there that the antipositivist reaction gained the power of a vital movement. And one of the most violent and sustained attacks on positivism came, not surprisingly, from the Catholic church.[14]

13. Elme Marie Caro, "Le Prix de la vie humaine et la question du bonheur dans le positivisme," *Revue des deux mondes*, LII (August 1882), 520. (". . . sous l'influence de la foi positive, une génération dure, pratique, solide, calculatrice, *positive* à outrance." / "Il en sera ainsi jusqu'au jour où quelque penseur hardi s'avisera qu'il y a quelque chose au-delà de la physique et de la chimie, et par un coup de génie inattendu découvrira l'âme et Dieu.")

14. Catholicism was of course not the only religion to manifest a great antagonism toward positivism. Helena Petrovna Blavatsky, *Isis Unveiled: A Master Key to the Mysteries of Ancient and Modern Science and Theology* (New York: J. W. Bouton, 1877), 73–78, fiercely attacked Comtean positivism. The connections between Theosophy and symbolism have been considered by Filiz Eda Burhan, "Vision and Visionaries: Nineteenth-Century Psychological Theory, the Occult Sciences, and the Formation of the Symbolist Aesthetic in France" (Ph.D. dissertation, Princeton University, 1979). I concentrate on Catholicism here because it was a far more pervasive influence on its time than was the peripheral world of the occult.

The history of the Catholic church in France, as in other European countries, often revolved around the twofold problem of the authority of the pope and the relationship between church and state. An oversimplified, but useful, division can be made between Gallicanism on the one hand and ultramontanism on the other. The basis of Gallicanism, which in the nineteenth century represented a relatively liberal attitude, was a challenge to the authority of the pope, while ultramontanism, which had become highly conservative by this time, upheld papal authority. It perhaps goes without saying that the word "liberal" should be used qualifiedly in reference to Catholicism during this period, and both factions condemned positivism until late in the century. But it should be noted that the ultramontane faction of the church dominated from the late 1850s through the early 1880s. This domination came in the form of the papacy of Pius IX, who reigned from 1846 to 1878.

Although hailed as a liberal when he first assumed the throne of Saint Peter, Pius IX was to become radically conservative. At first he was reactionary only in religious matters, but he soon tempered his political position as well. He came to believe that the French Revolution had destroyed traditional values as well as the social, moral, and religious order. From 1848 he supported reactionary politics in Europe and fulminated against modern society. One could not think of a poorer leader for the church in the age of the Industrial Revolution, for the thrust of his papacy was to leave the church isolated in a positivist world. On 8 December 1854 the pope defined the doctrine of the Immaculate Conception, but it was ten years later, to the day, that his most influential doctrine was published: the famous, or infamous, *Syllabus of Errors*.

The *Syllabus of Errors* was a sweeping indictment of modern society. In ten sections, containing eighty separate theses, the pope condemned, among other "evils" of the modern world, pantheism, absolute and moderate rationalism, liberalism, communism, and socialism. The final thesis condemned the proposition that the pope should reconcile himself to modern society. It was a stunning and powerful decree that would be crowned in 1870 with the ultimate ultramontane statement. In that year Vatican Council I adjourned, having added its denunciation of rationalist society to that of the *Syllabus*, and having offered the world the irrevocable doctrine of papal infallibility. It was a great victory for reactionary forces within the church.

The reactions of lay governments in Europe were as strong as the *Syllabus* itself. In England, *Punch* of 7 January 1865 presented a cartoon ridiculing the "Pope's Mad Bull."[15] The French government, very much concerned at the time with separating the powers of church and state, forbade promulgation of the encyclical. However, the French Catholic church, if sometimes curiously, rallied to support the pontiff.

The support of the French church was curious in that, at least as far as the more liberal factions of the Catholic community were concerned, the *Syllabus* was clearly an embarrassment. Monsignor Dupanloup, the bishop of Orléans, escaped the government restriction against promulgation of the encyclical by writing a pamphlet explaining it. But the very fact that he felt the necessity of an explanation demonstrated just how far the pope had gone. In answer to the eightieth thesis of the *Syllabus*, which condemned the proposition that the pope should reconcile himself to modern society, Dupanloup suggested the pope did not need to do this as he always stood for the good in the modern world and against the bad. This was a circuitous and lame argument that benefited the author little; he was condemned on both sides for having hidden the true meaning of the *Syllabus*.[16] But whatever the feelings of liberal Catholics in France, the *Syllabus* won the day. There was a great tide of ultramontane support for the pope. The ultimate thrust of the *Syllabus* and the reign of Pius IX was to send the French Catholic church into a period of deep conservatism and reactionary policies from which it would not emerge until the very end of the century. Not until well into the reign of Leo XIII (1878–1903), who was in many ways the opposite of Pius IX, was the church to make real strides in bringing itself into the modern world.

Given the French church's reactionary position and its fierce promotion of a traditional religious view, we can well imagine with what fury it would attack positivism. Indeed, Msgr. Dupanloup resigned from the French Academy under protest in 1871 when the "atheist" Littré was elected. He sharply criticized Littré, Hippolyte Taine, and one other author in whom the French Catholic church was to see the veritable Satan of the age. This man was Ernest Renan, and it is in criticism of Renan in particular that we can best observe the virulence of the Catholic position toward positivism.

15. Reproduced in Damian McElrath, O.F.M., *The Syllabus of Piux IX, Some Reactions in England* (Louvain: Bibliothèque de l'université, Bureau de la Revue, 1964), frontispiece.

16. Vytas V. Gaigalas, *Ernest Renan and His French Catholic Critics* (North Quincy, Mass.: Christopher Publishing House, 1972), 37. This book is an excellent source of Catholic anti-positivist statements and served as a reference for much of what follows on Renan.

Outside studies in French culture of the nineteenth century, Ernest Renan is not much spoken of today. This was not always so. From the 1860s through the end of the century Renan was one of the most influential thinkers of his time. Renan's rejection of his church and his romantic attachment to its ritual were familiar themes to most Frenchmen in the last part of the nineteenth century. His poetic musings on such themes as his Jesuit training, Brittany, and the future were well known during his lifetime—in fact a good deal better known than his more scholarly pursuits. For many he became the paradigm of the thoughtful, positivist agnostic. Most readers in France were familiar with his *Vie de Jésus* of 1863, the first work in his monumental study of the origins of Christianity, in which he argued against the divinity of Christ. The book was a sensation, its rationalism considered anathema by the church, and it was violently attacked in the Catholic press. Msgr. Dupanloup accused Renan, along with Littré and Taine, of trying to destroy Christianity; Dupanloup warned that Renan was a wolf in sheep's clothing, sounding at times like a Christian but undermining the foundations of the church.

Louis Veuillot, reactionary polemicist and editor of the ultramontane *Univers*, said that Renan was "uglier than toad and scorpion." He compared Renan to a rat, gnawing away at the Gospels, and associated him with "Judas, heretics, atheists, light-minded Frenchmen, clumsy Germans, shrewd Jews, positivist Englishmen and all those who had attempted to destroy the temple of God and told them that Jesus must die."[17] Charles de Bussy, a Catholic historian, continued the anti-Semitic note, accusing Renan of trying to please Jews and comparing him to a rabbit with "the snout of a usurer."[18]

In literary circles Jules Barbey d'Aurevilly, the late romantic writer and staunch Catholic, devoted considerable effort to discrediting Renan. In 1863 he reviewed the *Vie de Jésus* for the *Nain jaune*, delivering a diatribe accusing the scholar of indecency and insolence, calling his arguments "ridiculous monstrosities, wretched and imbecile."[19] Barbey d'Aurevilly was well aware of Renan's great reputation and noted that many were cowed by the erudition of the historian, but he found the

---

17. Both quotes from Veuillot come from Gaigalas, *Ernest Renan*, 47–48.

18. Ibid., 63.

19. Jules Barbey d'Aurevilly, *Philosophes et écrivains religieux et politiques* (Paris: A. Lemerre, 1909), 152. (". . . ces ridicules monstrueux, abjects et embécilles.")

reputation utterly unwarranted and dismissed Renan as totally unimportant. Others may have seen Renan as the Antichrist, but not Barbey:

> I vow that, for my part, I do not find him very grandiose. I vow that I do not recognize in Renan the frightening, apocalyptic notion. . . . Antichrist! Him! No! Not even as a joke, because he is insipid and boring! I do not allow . . . application of this grand and terrible name of Antichrist to this little critic who nibbles at history the way a mouse nibbles lace.[20]

Some twenty years later Barbey was no less spiteful in his condemnation of everything that Renan wrote. In a review of Renan's *Dialogues philosophiques* he compared the author to a reptile, "a very supple, very subtle, very tricky reptile which has laboriously crept into all the systems and philosophies of the time."[21] Barbey suggested that Renan was of insufficient intelligence to be a philosopher, then compounded the calumny by intimating that philosophy was incapable of discovering absolutes anyway. Only the Catholic church was apprised of absolute knowledge. In its insularity and absolute rejection of anything but the Catholic position, Barbey's argument is clearly inherited from the spirit of Pius IX and the *Syllabus of Errors*. His violent and irrational polemic was not the reasoned attack of the idealist movement in philosophy. It was the emotive outcry of a believer—the sort of writing that instilled antipositivist feeling in a way that dry philosophical discourse could never match. For all of its intractable sensationalism, Barbey's writing was a powerful weapon in the struggle against the hegemony of positivism.

Another literary figure, Léon Bloy, whose writing style was a tour de force of uncontrolled invective, was easily Barbey d'Aurevilly's equal as a fanatical Catholic polemicist. In Rodolphe Salis's *Chat noir* of 1 September 1883, Bloy presented a "review" of Renan's *Souvenirs d'enfance et*

---

20. Ibid., 143. ("J'avoue que, pour ma part, je ne le trouve pas très grandiose. J'avoue que je ne reconnais pas dans Renan l'effrayante notion apocalyptique. . . . L'Antéchrist! lui! Non! pas même pour rire, car il est fade et ennuyeux! Je ne permets pas même a l'Epouvante d'appliquer ce grand et terrible nom d'Antéchrist à ce petit critique qui ronge l'histoire comme une souris ronge une dentelle.")

21. Jules Barbey d'Aurevilly, *Les Philosophes et les écrivains religieux* (Paris: Quantin, 1887), 110. (". . . un reptile très souple, très subtil, très rusé, qui a laborieusement rampé dans tous les systèmes et les philosophies du temps.")

de jeunesse.[22] Not atypically, Bloy's "review" made no mention of Renan's autobiographical account of youthful struggles with loss of faith. Instead Bloy described to the reader a fantasy, a vision of himself sitting in on Renan's course at the Collège de France, noting that he wanted to see the man to get "one more idea of this mellifluent sophist who has disconcerted and overworked the imagination in the opposite direction of moral splendor and all true grandeur." On this premise Bloy launched into a devastating verbal caricature of Renan himself. He compared the portly Renan to an old friar with a glabrous face, "distributing the fruits of the tree of science to three or four generations," and describes in detail the "fat double chin," the eyes, the ears, "M. Renan's dirty grey-brown hair, rare at the summit of the cranium and unskillfully combed." In all, it is a merciless satire meant to profane the august academician with its invective rather than to convince the reader by reasoned argument. Renan's course, he adds, is always the same old thing, based on some obscure bit of text, from which the historian derives a long and fruitless argument against Christianity: "It is always the same conjectural argument, a supposed annihilation of complete certitude accompanied by a misericordia of pity for the poor little people ignorant of philosophy who hold to good sense and tradition."[23]

Bloy's emotional appeal did not pretend to argue rationally with positivism but rather sought to demolish it through invective. It was a reactionary holding to Christian dogma that, like the *Syllabus of Errors* itself, eschewed the rationalist dialogue of the modern world from which it only sought retreat, not rapprochement.[24] As such, Bloy's writing fit well into the Catholic mentality of the time. What is surprising is that such a profession of staunch Catholicism should appear within the pages of the *Chat noir*.

The *Chat noir*, launched in 1882 by Rodolphe Salis, owner of the

22. Léon Bloy, "A propos de *Souvenirs d'enfance et de jeunesse* de M. Renan," *Le Chat noir*, II (1 September 1883), 134.

23. Ibid. (". . . une idée de plus sur ce sophiste mellifluant que déconcerte et surmène l'imagination en sens inverse de la splendeur morale et de toute vraie grandeur." / ". . . distribué les fruits de l'arbre de la science à trois ou quatre générations." / ". . . double menton gras . . ." / ". . . les cheveux de M. Renan, rares au sommet du crâne et malhabilement ramenés . . . d'une nuance châtain-gris sale." / ". . . c'est toujours le même argument conjectural dans un néant supposé de toute certitude accompagné de miséricordieuse pitié pour les petites gens sans philologie qui s'en tiennent au bon sens et à la tradition.")

24. Indeed, Bloy called himself "un catholique de *Syllabus*," Ernest Seillière, *Léon Bloy, psychologie d'un mystique* (Paris: Editions de la nouvelle revue critique, 1936), 127.

Montmartre cabaret of the same name, was meant to advertise the cabaret and to serve as a vehicle for the bohemian community in Montmartre. A spirited journal, the *Chat noir* published articles by many of the most advanced critics and authors of the period. It was thoroughly up-to-date, insightful, and often highly satirical, hardly an organ of the hard-line Roman Catholic faction. Thus it may seem surprising that Bloy would publish there. That Bloy and Salis were close friends provides the simplest answer but does not explain what a bohemian like Salis and a fanatical Catholic like Bloy would have in common. Nor does it fully explain why Bloy's writing would be welcome in this irreverent journal. Nor, for that matter, does it explain Bloy's other friendships among the literary avant-garde; he was, for example, close to J.-K. Huysmans, with whom he carried on a lively correspondence until they had a personal falling-out in 1889.

In essence the radical, reactionary, Catholic movement and the avant-garde had something in common at this time, namely their hatred for the Academy and for the French scientific/positivist establishment. Throughout the fifties, sixties, and seventies, positivism had represented the most progressive, modern approach. But by the early 1880s positivism itself was firmly installed in the sacred halls of the French establishment. In their attack on positivist science, Catholic writers found themselves, in spite of their underlying conservatism, flying in the face of that establishment. It was because of their defiance that their writing could well serve the purposes of an irreverent bohemian publication. Given the rationalist, scientific basis of much in French thought until this time, it now became, paradoxically, modern to be reactionary. Léon Bloy, in what might be termed his refreshingly fanatical style, represents an important fact of intellectual life in France from the early 1880s right through the turn of the century—the confluence, no matter how temporary, of the avant-garde and reactionary conservatism. It would be, of course, a marriage of convenience—a coming together of disparate factions for a single purpose. But, as we shall see, the confluence of conservative and avant-garde thought would have important implications for the criticism of art.

To be sure, the official position of the Catholic church did not remain totally reactionary once Pius IX died. His successor, Leo XIII sought to reconcile the church with the modern world and with science. He advocated the study of astronomy and the natural sciences. In 1891 his encyclical *Rerum Novarum*—which sought to bring the church in line with contemporary social theories by supporting the rights of labor—constituted a major step in the emergence of the church into the modern world. But there remained a reactionary faction that resisted every attempt at modernization within the church. It was this facet of Catholicism, rather than the official church's belated and somewhat weak attempts at reconciliation with the modern world, that generated a veritable revival of Catholicism in intellectual and literary circles. The *renouveau religieux,* as this revival of Catholicism in the literary community has been called, was a reactionary revolution.[25]

Studies of late nineteenth-century French literature have long established the revival of Catholicism among some of the most important writers of the period. The list of literary notables who either converted or were already fierce advocates of Catholicism is a long one. Included are such important authors as Léon Bloy, J.-K. Huysmans, Barbey d'Aurevilly, Léon Daudet, Adolphe Retté, Ferdinand Brunetière, and Paul Claudel. Richard Griffiths, in his excellent discussion of the literature of the Catholic revival, noted some features of this phenomenon that demonstrate its reactionary nature. One of these has already been alluded to, that is, the nonintellectual nature of much of the Catholic writing of this time. To a large degree the Catholic literary revival strongly upheld revelation and tradition in opposition to science, progress, and thought itself. For these writers intellectualization was considered out of place in reference to religion. Religion was not a thing to be discussed and argued about as if it were capable of rational explanation. Religious truth was to be believed, fiercely.

Paul Verlaine, the poet whose work was so important to the symbolist generation and whose deep Catholicism is often overlooked, offered an example of the anti-intellectual attitude of the new Catholic writers in a poem from his *Liturges intimes:*

> Little Jesus, whom it is necessary for us to be like
> If we want to see God the Father,
> Grant us to be reborn
>
> As pure babies, naked, with no more shelter
> Than a stable, and with no more company
> Than an ass and ox, humble pair;

---

25. Two excellent sources on this subject are Elizabeth M. Fraser, *Le Renouveau religieux d'après le roman français de 1886 à 1914* (Paris: Société d'édition "Les belles lettres," 1934); and Richard Griffiths, *The Reactionary Revolution.*

> To have the infinite ignorance
> And the immense, complete weakness
> With which humble childhood is blessed.[26]

This is far indeed from Thomist scholasticism. It is an unquestioning, unthinking, deeply felt Christianity. It is also far from the attempts at reconciliation with the modern world sponsored by Leo XIII. It is, in short, exactly the sort of pure, devotional Catholicism so longed for by Pius IX.

One result of this desire for simplicity in belief was a feeling of empathy for the French peasant and antipathy toward the middle class. Here, the Catholic writers felt, was an example of pure piety for all to follow. The hated bourgeoisie had corrupted Catholicism, and the peasant attitude was seen as the only hope for a true Catholic. Léon Bloy expressed this feeling in his absolute hatred of modern, "mediocre" Catholics. Bloy's marvelous polemic style is so entertaining—he once referred to Protestant Denmark as a "frigidarium of souls"—that it is possible at times to overlook his fierce hatreds. But above all else his antagonism toward "modern" Catholics surfaces throughout his writings. In no uncertain terms Bloy fulminated against the lax attitude of bourgeois Catholics who felt no real devotion to their religion:

> They are not necessarily eunuchs, nor wicked, nor fanatics, nor hypocrites, nor insane imbeciles. They are neither egotistical with assurance nor cowards precisely. They don't even have the energy to be skeptical. They are absolutely nothing. But the

26. Verlaine, *Liturges intimes,* as quoted in Griffiths, *The Reactionary Revolution,* 57.

> (Petit Jésus qu'il nous faut être,
> Si nous voulons voir Dieu le Père,
> Accordez-nous d'alors renaître
>
> En purs bébés, nus, sans repaire
> Qu'une étable, et sans compagnie
> Qu'une âne et qu'un boeuf, humble paire;
>
> D'avoir l'ignorance infinie
> Et l'immense toute-faiblesse
> Par quoi l'humble enfance est bénie.)

earth is at their feet and everything appears quite simple to them.[27]

The final word on bourgeois Catholics for Bloy was what he called "the surpassing horror, it is that they are MEDIOCRE."[28] It was this mediocrity, this lack of any zeal, that resulted from attempts to intellectualize Catholicism. What the church needed was a pure and simple faith, a faith uncluttered with thought, driven by devotion. For Bloy and for others the perfect example of faith was to be found in the French peasantry, or in the fervent Christianity of the Middle Ages.

For Bloy the medieval period was "the time of love and enthusiasm for Christianity!"[29] The Middle Ages were "an immense church such as one will no longer see until the day when God returns to earth."[30] J.-K. Huysmans, both before and after his conversion, had spoken of the purity of faith in the High Middle Ages.[31] Paul Verlaine, in *Sagesse*, offered a comment on the seventeenth century in praising the Middle Ages:

> No. It was Gallican, this century, and Jansenist! It is towards the Middle Ages, enormous and delicate that my heart must navigate.[32]

Léon Bloy struck a cord that became increasingly common at this time —that the Renaissance had destroyed the true Catholic world represented by the Middle Ages:

> Under the name of the Renaissance an intoxicating paganism came over Christ's people. Great forces of change were operative in Europe, unprecedented displacements of civilization menaced

27. Léon Bloy, *Le Désespéré*, Paris, 1887, as quoted in Sister Mary Rosalie Brady, *Thought and Style in the Works of Léon Bloy* (Washington, D.C.: Catholic University of America Press, 1945), 70. ("Ils ne sont, nécessairement, ni des eunuques, ni des méchants, ni des fanatiques, ni des hypocrites, ni des imbéciles affolés. Ils ne sont ni des égoïstes avec assurance, ni des lâches avec précision. Ils n'ont pas même l'énergie du scepticisme. Ils ne sont absolument rien. Mais la terre est à leurs pieds et cela leur paraît très simple.")

28. Ibid., 74. (". . . la surpassante horreur, c'est qu'ils sont MEDIOCRES.")

29. Ibid., 82. (". . . le temps de l'amour et de l'enthousiasme pour le christianisme!")

30. Ibid. (". . . une immense église comme on n'en verra plus jusqu'à ce que Dieu revienne sur terre . . .")

31. Griffiths, *The Reactionary Revolution*, 240.

32. Ibid., 241. (Non. Il fut gallican, ce siècle, et janséniste! C'est vers le moyen âge, énorme et délicat. Qu'il faudrait que mon coeur en panne naviguât . . .")

> the universal security and made one fear for the seamless robe of
> the papacy. Constantinople had just succumbed and Luther was
> about to be born. The most triumphant purveyor of heresy, the
> printing press, had been discovered.[33]

Bloy conveniently forgot that the Middle Ages were filled with heresy,
and his condemnation of printing again shows his intransigent attitude
toward any product of the modern world. Just so, he and other writers of
the Catholic revival hated those other products of the modern world,
democracy and the French Revolution.

I have already noted how Pius IX believed that the French Revolution
had destroyed Catholic values and the sense of order that resulted from
the Catholic tradition. The writers of the Catholic revival took up this
cry in the extreme. For them order, hierarchy, and tradition were to be
upheld against the individualism, equality, and antitraditionalism of democracy. Many advocated a return to the monarchy, where at least order and hierarchy were honored, but all agreed that democracy and the
idea of equality were destroying Catholicism.[34]

One of the most widely read Catholic writers of the period, Edouard
Drumont, echoed this view in warning that "the clearest result of the
revolution has been to make more difficult the plight of the little man
and, on the other hand, to strengthen the position of the great and the
rich by delivering them from all moral responsibility."[35] Such concern
for the downtrodden did not make Drumont, or any of the reactionary
Catholics, turn to social liberalism. They felt that the monarchy, and only
the monarchy, could save the poor, and their position was both antiso-
cialist, antidemocratic, anticapitalist and, very often, anti-Semitic.
Drumont's incredibly fanatical *La France juive* (1886) stands as a long
indictment of modern society and the end of traditional French values,

33. Bloy, *Révélateur de globe*, Paris, 1884, as quoted by Brady, *Thought and Style*, 83. ("Sous
le nom de Renaissance, un paganisme enivrant s'abattait sur les peuples de Jésus-Christ. De
grands changements s'opéraient en Europe, des déplacements inouïs de civilisation menaçaient
la sécurité universelle et faisaient trembler pour la robe sans couture de la Papauté. Constan-
tinople venait succomber et Luther allait naître. La plus triomphante pourvoyeuse de l'Hérésie,
l'imprimerie était découverte.")

34. See Griffiths, *The Reactionary Revolution*, 268–69.

35. Edouard Drumont, *Testament d'un anti-sémite*, as quoted in Griffiths, *The Reactionary
Revolution*, 277. (". . . le résultat le plus clair de la Révolution a été de rendre plus dure la
situation des petits et de fortifier au contraire la situation des grands et des riches en la déli-
vrant de toute responsabilité morale.")

all of which the author attributes to Jewish control of every facet of French life. For Drumont, "France, thanks to the principles of '89, cleverly exploited by the Jews, has fallen into dissolution."[36] Drumont's anti-Semitism, though not unpopular, may not have been shared by all the writers of the Catholic revival, but his hatred of democratic society was. For them the words "tradition" and "hierarchy" carried great weight and in those terms only could the hope of society be placed.

It must be understood that these writers were not just backward in their thinking. They were actively reactionary and provided a good deal of the most vibrant and violent polemic against everything that positivist, rationalist, scientific society stood for.[37] And, for a short time at any rate, their conservatism won the day in France. These were the years of great antirepublican stirrings in French political life, a time when a coalition of monarchists, radical Catholics, workers, military, and other malcontents almost managed to bring General Georges Boulanger to power. Antipositivist sentiment was capable of turning, through contact with the Catholic revival, into a strange mixture of conservatism and revolt. In certain respects the most reactionary factions of French culture became the most active. It was a lean and hungry group, not a fat and satisfied conservatism, that led the revolt against the rationalist, positivist, democratic establishment in France.

Up to this point, then, it has been noted that the last two decades of the nineteenth century in France were dominated by a reaction against naturalism. Just as naturalism itself involved more than literature or the visual arts alone, the reaction against it was not limited to these spheres. It was a broad reaction, with philosophical, religious, and political, as well as cultural, implications. Further, antinaturalism tended toward a

36. Edouard Drumont, *La France juive, essai d'histoire contemporaine* (Paris: Librairie Blériot, 1887), 23. (". . . la France, grâce aux principes de 89 habilement exploités par les Juifs, tombait en dissolution.") Drumont's work originally appeared in a two-volume set published by E. Dentu, Paris in 1886.

37. Edmond de Goncourt saw this vibrancy even in Drumont, noting on 5 January 1886: "at the Spartiate dinner today Drumont officially announced the forthcoming publication of his book attacking the Jews—that book written for the personal satisfaction of hatred by a Catholic and reactionary in the midst of the complete and insolent triumph of republican Jewry. If he is unbearable and even a little despicable sometimes because of the narrowness of his ideas on everything, at least Drumont has the valiance of spirit of a man of another age and almost an appetite for martyrdom." Edmond de Goncourt, *Paris and the Arts, 1851–1896: From the Goncourt Journal,* ed. and trans. by George J. Becker and Edith Philips (Ithaca: Cornell University Press, 1971), 229–30.

reactionary position in response to the general liberal views of the naturalists. Finally, the antinaturalist conservatism of the 1880s was an aggressive, new movement, not a staid, tired one. We shall see that a similar situation obtained in the antinaturalist art criticism of this period as well. The world of art also had an actively, even pugnaciously, reactionary side. Perhaps no single statement is more indicative of this than Joséphin Péladan's famous opening to his Salon of 1883: "I believe in the Ideal, in Tradition, in Hierarchy."[38] Péladan's voice was, to be sure, extreme, but he offered a forceful statement—one that would have increasing echoes in French art criticism of the 1880s.

38. Joséphin Péladan, *L'Art ochlocratique*, 45. ("Je crois à l'Idéal, à la Tradition, à la Hiérarchie.")

2

IDEALISM AND SYMBOLISM IN THE CRITICISM OF ART

Idealism and symbolism were the two important forces behind the reaction against naturalism in art. This has been recognized often enough in the scholarly accounts of symbolism in painting. Robert Goldwater described a difference between avant-garde, symbolist painting, and what he termed "thought painting."[1] He outlined a distinction between the traditional, allegorical efforts of Salon "thought painters," who sought to go beyond naturalism, and the more "unified" and "successful" efforts of "advanced" painters such as Gauguin. Goldwater was well aware that both "thought painters" and symbolists were equally concerned with going beyond naturalism, with offering an art of ideas. However, he felt the former achieved this through well-worn allegorical or literary means

1. Goldwater, *Symbolism*, 1–72.

that shared little with the stunning formal achievements of symbolism's gifted artists. Goldwater's is an instructive and intelligent comparison, one that, excepting its modernist bias, works well enough for painting. However, his distinction applies less effectively to art criticism. Idealist—for so the critical concomitant of "thought painting" should be termed—and symbolist criticism are not so easily separated into opposing camps. These two sides shared a great deal. For all their differences, symbolist critics often sounded like their idealist counterparts and vice versa, so much so that it is often difficult to know where their ideas originated. Many of the thoughts that symbolist art critics so fervently expounded in their writings were part of the general cultural ambience of the 1880s and 1890s. It was the artists to whom the symbolists applied these ideas that distinguished them from the idealists. For instance, many critics from this period, both conservative and progressive, can be found espousing an art of nuance and suggestion over and against objective realism. No idealist, however, would have applied such thoughts to the art of Paul Gauguin, as many symbolist critics did. Both idealists and symbolists advocated changing nature for expressive purposes, but no idealist espoused the radical deformations of nature central to a symbolist like Albert Aurier. I shall not be concerned here with further differences between symbolist and idealist art criticism, differences more easily noted in individual cases. My purpose in this chapter is to demonstrate several of the ways in which they were similar, and this is best achieved by noting some of the most cherished notions of the anti-naturalist generation.

REACTION AGAINST THE NATURALIST MOVEMENT IN LITERATURE

The core of the general intellectual mood that I have defined as anti-naturalism was a rejection of the literary naturalism of Emile Zola and his followers. The main concern of the critics who upheld an anti-naturalist line was literary, and the criticism of the time was filled with attacks on Zola and his group. Painting often entered the discussion only as a sidelight.

The opposition to Zola came from two sides: conservative and avant-garde. A large part of the reaction against Zola and literary naturalism came from within, through defections from the naturalist movement itself. Many of the first-generation symbolists had been naturalists themselves. The early symbolist periodicals, such as *La Revue indépendante* or *La Vogue*, often published naturalist works alongside the budding symbolist poetry. The first novels of J.-K. Huysmans and Paul Adam, both of whom played important roles in the development of literary symbolism, were naturalist. It is not surprising, therefore, that the most virulent criticism of Zola and his group came from conservative, idealist critics and not from the symbolists.

Thus the idealist Ferdinand Brunetière, literary critic for the staid but highly influential *Revue des deux mondes,* attacked Zola directly throughout the 1880s. Indeed, a good deal of Brunetière's reputation was made on his long-standing opposition to naturalism.[2] In an important review from 1887 of Zola's *La Terre*—a review entitled "La Banqueroute du Naturalisme"—Brunetière said that he had avoided reviewing Zola's work for some time because it was "always the same M. Zola."[3] He berated naturalism for being out-of-date and noted that Zola's group was being depleted by defections from within.[4] Brunetière accused Zola of "vaudevillism," of creating caricatures rather than real people, and of not being faithful to reality.

The reaction of symbolist critics to Zola's naturalism was less argumentative than Brunetière's attack. Charles Morice, for example, writing his history of the first years of the symbolist movement, was careful to praise Emile Zola, Stendhal, and Edmond de Goncourt, whom he called "masters" of naturalism.[5] Morice distinguished between the work of these masters, on the one hand, and all of the followers and imitators of the naturalist style, on the other. It was for such latecomers that he saved his sharpest criticism. Noting that Zola was quite capable of going beyond mere objective description he stated:

2. See, for instance, F. Lefranc, "Le Naturalisme contemporain d'après une conférence de M. Brunetière," *L'Art,* xlviii (1890), 201.

3. F. Brunetière, "La Banqueroute du naturalisme," *Le Roman naturaliste* (Paris: Calmann-. Levy, 1893 [article first published in 1887]), 345. (". . . mêmes Rougon-Macquart, mêmes procédés, même absence aussi de sens moral, c'était toujours le même M. Zola.")

4. Ibid., 346–47. ("On peut prévoir enfin le temps où M. Zola, dans cet abandon de tous les siens, n'aura plus pour lui que le seul M. Albert Wolff.")

5. Charles Morice, *La Littérature de tout à l'heure,* 69.

> But the file of followers don't go beyond anything. The imitators are more faithful to the Formula than the masters. These young Naturalists—indeed they are already old—copy nature so closely that a blind person could almost see it. . . . Laboratory and Document! Indeed, these poor young people must bore themselves. No doubt they only write when they are in a bad humor. To be sure, if they have any "poetic moments," they are playing baccarat or smoking cigars during those moments.[6]

Morice's reaction to what he saw as the negative side of naturalism was as violent as Brunetière's, perhaps more so, but he refrained from open invective against Zola himself. Moving in advanced literary circles, Morice could not bring himself to decry the work of an author who only a few years earlier had been such a hero to the avant-garde. Brunetière, associated with conservative circles where Zola had never been accepted, felt no need to exclude Zola from his general criticism of naturalism.

Significantly, although Brunetière and Morice applied their criticism to different writers, they both found naturalism to be severely limited, and for very similar reasons. For them, naturalism lacked imagination as well as morals and was alienated from the religious traditions of the past.[7] They saw naturalism as a product of the modern, materialist society they both rejected, at least in part. Indeed, in their search for something beyond materialist society, both Morice and Brunetière would turn to religion.[8] For all of the differences in their cultural positions, the one an established conservative and the other a young symbolist, their arguments concerning naturalism are similar. Indeed, a case was made in 1890—and might plausibly be made today—that Brunetière was really

6. Ibid., 169. ("Mais la *queue* ne dépasse rien: les imitateurs sont plus fidèles à la Formule que les maîtres. Les jeunes Naturalistes—ils sont déjà bien vieux!—copient patiemment la nature à peu près tel qu'un aveugle la verrait. Eux, ils ne transigent pas: plus d'âme décidément et pas la moindre issue dérobée par où pourrait pénétrer le Rêve. Laboratoire et Document! Ces pauvres jeunes gens doivent bien s'ennuyer. Ils n'écrivent, sans doute, que lorsqu'ils sont de mauvaise humeur. A coup sûr, s'ils ont des 'instants de Poëte', ils jouent au baccarat ou fument des cigares, dans ces instants-là.")

7. Ibid., 1–70, for Morice. Brunetière's feelings on religion and morals are noted in John Clark, *La Pensée de Ferdinand Brunetière* (Paris: Nizet, 1954), 43–48. His thoughts on naturalism are noted on pages 29–36.

8. Morice already had by 1889 and Brunetière would in 1895.

the first to carry on an effective campaign against naturalism.[9] This idealist critic, writing for the conservative *Revue des deux mondes* in the early 1880s, anticipated symbolism's reaction against naturalism by several years.[10] No one would argue that there were not wide differences in what Morice and Brunetière offered as critics, but their mutual reaction against naturalism served to mitigate that distance. So, too, with the critical camps they represented. In 1891, Jules Huret published his *Enquête sur l'évolution littéraire*, a series of interviews with many of the leading figures in literature and philosophy of the time.[11] Included were both conservatives and modernists. It was readily apparent that the single theme that united them all—indeed, Huret's central concern in forming this particular *Enquête*—was their antagonism toward naturalism.

Perhaps this coming together of diverse factions in terms of their opposition to naturalism was one reason for symbolism's rapid debut in conservative journals. As early as 1887 the *Nouvelle revue* published an article on the new movement.[12] In 1888 Jules Lemaitre, Ferdinand Brunetière, and Anatole France, all well-established writers, offered commentary on symbolism.[13] These articles were by no means favorable toward the new movement, especially in the case of Anatole France and Jules Lemaitre. They chided the symbolists for the obscurity of their prose and generally saw them as youthful radicals. However, throughout the articles there is a tacit assumption that symbolism was a serious movement, deserving of consideration. These literary conservatives also

9. F. Lefranc, "Le Naturalisme contemporain."

10. See, for instance, Brunetière, "Les Petits naturalistes," *Le Roman naturaliste*, 321–44 (article first published in July 1884); "Le Faux naturalisme," *Revue des deux mondes*, XLIX (15 February 1882), 932–43; and "Les Origines du roman naturaliste," *Revue des deux mondes*, XLVII (15 September 1881), 438–50.

11. Jules Huret, *Enquête sur l'évolution littéraire* (Paris: Charpentière, 1891).

12. Maurice Peyrot, "Symbolistes et décadents," *La Nouvelle revue*, XLIX (November–December 1887), 122–46.

13. These were noted by Jacques Lethève, *Impressionistes et symbolistes devant la presse* (Paris: Armand Colin, 1959), 209ff., who also noted the phenomenon under discussion here. Anatole France's article originally appeared in *Le Temps*, in August 1888; Lemaitre's in the *Revue bleue*, January 1888; and Brunetière's in the *Revue des deux mondes*, in November of the same year. Brunetière's article was republished in his *Nouvelles questions de critique* (Paris: Calmann-Levy, 1890), 304–29. Anatole France had actually published commentary about symbolism as early as 1886, also in *Le Temps*, in an exchange of letters with Jean Moréas concerning the latter's famous symbolist manifesto. The exchange of letters was republished in Moréas, *Les Premières armes du symbolisme* (Paris: Vanier, 1889), 45–58.

noted symbolism's rejection of naturalism, which they applauded. Brunetière also praised the young writers for reviving the art of poetry, long neglected by naturalist writers. Brunetière and the symbolists were generations apart; yet he wrote an objective and intelligent study of the new movement, a study that often reads like the work of a symbolist rather than the literary critic of the *Revue de deux mondes*. Charles Morice recognized this when, a year after Brunetière's article, he included the conservative among the established critics whose ideas he had appreciated.[14] By the early 1890s symbolism was accepted in all but the most conservative circles. In a very short time symbolism went from being a radical, avant-garde literary movement to one enjoying widespread recognition and respect. There were many reasons for this development but one of the most important was that both symbolist writers and idealist critics shared a distaste for naturalism. Just so, the reaction against naturalism in painting served to bring together idealist and symbolist.

REACTION AGAINST THE NATURALIST MOVEMENT IN PAINTING

Although the main thrust of the reaction against the naturalist movement was literary, there was also a strong contemporaneous critical reaction against naturalism in painting. This reaction took two forms. The first was a hatred of the photographic and anecdotal naturalism that dominated the annual Salons by the early 1880s. Second, there was a rejection of impressionism and, to a lesser extent, the heritage of Courbet. Essentially the difference was between the reaction against conservative and that against avant-garde naturalism, although critics of both kinds of naturalism did not necessarily coincide with corresponding sides of the conservative/avant-garde dichotomy. Consider, for instance, the reaction against Salon naturalism.

During the last half of the nineteenth century there grew up in the annual Parisian Salons a kind of painting which might best be described as a popularized response to Baudelaire's famous call for paintings of modern life. The trend was marked by lighthearted subjects from con-

14. Morice, *La Littérature de tout à l'heure*, 263–64.

temporary life. Romantic or mildly erotic overtones predominated in paintings executed in an almost photographic, trompe l'oeil manner. A painting called *Forbidden Fruit* by Monet's cousin, Auguste Toulmouche, typifies the genre (Fig. 1), with its sharp-focus realism, accent on contemporary fashion, and insipid subject matter.[15] Even a painter such as P.-A.-J. Dagnan-Bouveret, who was capable of better and more serious efforts, fell prey to the temptation to work in this anecdotal and popular manner. His *Wedding at the Photographer's* (Fig. 2) was a great success at the Salon of 1879.[16] Indeed, many serious Salon naturalists found it convenient to work occasionally in what was evidently a salable genre.

As widely popular as this anecdotal naturalism was, it was just as despised by symbolist critics. Avant-garde critics unanimously reviled artists using this style, whom they saw as pandering to low commercialism. In an article of 1884, J.-K. Huysmans mercilessly attacked this anecdotalism, which he connected with the sentimentality of café-concert entertainment. He noted ironically that these students of the Ecole des Beaux-Arts, while repudiating the subject matter of their teachers, had nevertheless remained true Beaux-Arts products, "drawing the romances of the café-concert with the pencil of Cabanel and Gérôme."[17] Suggesting that these students, "sons of workers and of the very low bourgeoisie," could not transcend the mentality of the "obtuse people of their heredity," he noted how, in the tradition of the café-concert, they created "little childish women who cry on the shoulder of a man whose conventional grimace attests to his resolve."[18] Few writers could carry off such a vehement attack with such style. "Never," Huysmans added, again in reference to the similarity between these artists and the café-

15. It might be suggested here that this painting, submitted to the Salon just one year before Monet began work on his *Women in the Garden*, influenced the later painting. There is a similarity in emphasis on fashionably dressed women in various stances. Of course Monet rejected the anecdotalism of his cousin's painting. Perhaps he was offering a better version of a typical Salon style.

16. On Dagnan-Bouveret see Gabriel P. Weisberg, "P.A.J. Dagnan-Bouveret and the Illusion of Photographic Naturalism," *Arts Magazine*, LVI (March 1982), 100–105; and "P.A.J. Dagnan-Bouveret, Jules Bastien-Lepage, and the Naturalist Instinct," *Arts Magazine*, LVI (April 1982), 70–76.

17. J.-K. Huysmans, "La Genèse du peintre," *La Revue indépendante*, I (May 1884), 25. (". . . dessineront avec le crayon de Cabanel et de Gérôme des romances de café-concert.")

18. Ibid., 22, 25, 26. (". . . fils d'ouvriers et de très bas bourgeois" / ". . . la bêtise peuple de leur hérédité" / ". . . femmes bébêtes qui pleurent sur l'épaule d'un monsieur dont la grimace convenue atteste la force d'âme.")

concert, "no, never, you understand, has there been a transposition of one art into the other more faithfully and completely!"[19]

Félix Fénéon, easily Huysmans's equal in irony, made reference to the popular and prolific romantic novelist Paul de Kock in parodying artists who "supply Pauldekocklike jokes, arranging droll anecdotes, put together in the manner of a rebus, which reverberate in the catalogue in puns: to make the belly of the sly bourgeois shake is their noble dream, a dream realized."[20] In a later Salon review he complained of the new infatuation of Salon painters with photographic reality, citing their belief, "like Saint Anthony 'in the reality of things'; their obsequious, adulatory reverence for the mannequin of the true."[21] Noting that these artists had the "good temperament of statisticians and catalogers," he complained that all they offered were "works of photography that they quite unduly take pride in as being real."[22]

Echoing the sentiments of J.-K. Huysmans, Albert Aurier satirized, in an 1888 review, the painter Gustave Curtois, "who finds the means to charm us, through art, while singing the old dramatico-sentimental romances of the café-concert."[23] A few years later, in a more original passage, he chided Salon artists who held to "this stupid belief that to reproduce nature servilely, by all of its most known aspects, that is to say the most trivial, is to make a work of art."[24] Aurier continued, noting that in their work, "the banality is not even relieved by the interpretation, which remains, I repeat it, photographic. Try, if you can, to count the newsy items, the anecdotes involving concierges, the plays on words of traveling salesmen, the sets of kitchen utensils laid out in

19. Ibid., 26. ("Jamais, no jamais, vous entendez, transposition d'un art dans un autre n'a été plus fidèle et plus complète!")

20. Félix Fénéon, *Oeuvres plus que complètes* (Geneva: Librairie Droz, 1970), 77. (". . . machinent des facéties pauldekocasses, combinent des anecdotes drôlatiques, agencent des façons de rébus qui se répercutent dans le catalogue en calembours: faire tressauter la bedaine du bourgeois malin est leur noble rêve, rêve réalisé.")

21. Ibid., 152. ("Ils crurent comme saint Antoine 'à la réalité des choses'; leur obséquieuse révérence adula le mannequin du vrai.")

22. Ibid. ("Beaux tempérament de statisticiens et de catalogueurs" / ". . . des travaux de photographie qui très indûment se targuèrent de réalisme.")

23. Marc d'Escaurailles [Albert Aurier, pseud.], "Le Salon de 1888," *Le Décadent*, iii (1–15 June 1888), 11. (". . . qui trouvent moyen de nous charmer en chantant, avec art, de vieilles romances dramaticosentimentales de Café Concert.")

24. Aurier, *Oeuvres posthumes*, 357. (". . . cette stupide croyance que reproduire la nature servilement, par ses côtés les plus connus, c'est-à-dire les plus triviaux, c'est faire oeuvre d'artiste.")

golden frames this year."[25] Clearly, symbolist circles were unanimously disgusted by what they saw as the most debased form of naturalist painting. Progressive critics, however, were not alone in their attacks on anecdotal Salon painting, nor were they the first to criticize this popular style openly.

As early as the 1860s both Charles Blanc and Hippolyte Taine had flatly renounced photographic imitation of nature: such was not the goal of art and could only result in inferior work.[26] Eugène Véron, who was very much a champion of the academic naturalism of the 1880s, also condemned the idea of photographic representation of nature as reducing the artist to a copyist.[27] Joséphin Péladan, who was anything but friendly toward avant-garde art, as early as 1882 decried the artistic situation in which "inspiration has flown away, procedure alone remains, and anecdote, genre, and still life reign."[28] In 1883 he railed against both the commercial and "journalistic" quality of contemporary painting and singled out the Salon naturalist Jean Béraud as inferior.[29]

The intelligent, conservative critic André Michel, writing the Salon review for *L'Art* in 1884, spoke of how public taste had come to dominate the Salons: "the greater part [of the Salon audience] only sees the subject of a painting, interesting or boring, pleasing or sad, and they get the same pleasure there as from a vaudeville entertainment or a sentimental romance."[30] Continuing in the same vein—and voicing a criticism rather similar to that of Huysmans—Michel noted:

> A whole class of painters—those that are called *genre*—have found in this taste a great outlet and disastrous encouragement.

25. Ibid. (". . . la banalité n'est même pas relevée par l'interprétation, qui reste, je le répète, photographique. Essayez, si vous pouvez, de compter les faits-divers, les anecdotes de concierge, les jeux de mots de commis-voyageur, les batteries de cuisine serties en des cadres d'or, cette année.")

26. Charles Blanc, *Grammaire des arts du dessin* (Paris: Librairie Renouard, 1883), 488. Hippolyte Taine, *Philosophie de l'art* (Paris: Hachette, 1893), 28.

27. Eugène Véron, *L'Esthétique* (Paris: C. Reinwald, 1878), xxiii. Véron, who was editor of *L'Art*, also took up the campaign against photographic realism in his "Salon de 1885," *L'Art*, XXXVIII (1885), 194–95.

28. Joséphin Péladan, *L'Art ochlocratique*, 17. (". . . l'inspiration s'envole, le procédé seul demeure, et l'anecdote, le genre et la nature morte règnent.")

29. Ibid., 45 and 87.

30. André Michel, "Le Salon de 1884," *L'Art*, XXXVI (1884), 163. ("La plupart ne voient dans un tableau que le sujet, intéressant ou ennuyeux, plaisant ou triste; et ils y prennent le même plaisir qu'à un vaudeville amusant ou à une romance sentimentale.")

> It is necessary, in effect, for a busy and superficial society to have an art easy to house and easy to understand because apartments are small and business absorbing. . . . amusing and decorative painting are very much on the march and one could say that it is the least artistic part of the public that exercises the most considerable influence on artistic production.[31]

For all of his conservatism, Michel adamantly opposed the anecdotal style of Salon naturalists, as did Huysmans, Fénéon, and Aurier.

In truth, the picture of the advanced critic in the 1880s, struggling in isolation against the banality of anecdotal naturalism in the Salon, is a false one. Few serious critics were willing to praise such a commercial and highly popular art. Henry Houssaye, who in his 1884 Salon offered modest praise for the "pretty" efforts of some anecdotal genre painters, was careful to note that the work of an artist such as Jean Béraud was meant only for the amusement of the public.[32] Just as in the world of literature there was a general dislike—conservative or avant-garde—for the minor naturalist followers of Emile Zola, so too the minor naturalism of anecdotal Salon painting was generally reviled. The artists to whom the criticism applied varied greatly. Henry Houssaye blamed the whole trend on impressionism while Fénéon saved his sternest criticism for Dagnan-Bouveret.[33] Avant-garde critics like Fénéon discerned the differences between impressionism's and anecdotal naturalism's use of modern subject matter. But the criticism remained the same. For the majority of critics in the 1880s the greatest sin of naturalism was this tendency toward photographic realism and anecdotal genre subjects. This virtually universal cry against a debased form of naturalism, however, was not the

31. Ibid. ("Toute une classe de peintres—ceux qu'on appelle de *genre*—a trouvé dans ce goût de larges débouchés et des encouragements désatreux. Il faut, en effet, à une société affairée et superficielle, un art facile à loger et facile à comprendre, car les appartements sont étroits et les affaires absorbantes; et, comme ce goût des arts est un des articles nécessaires du luxe moderne, comme le salon de tout millionnaire doit être décoré d'un certain nombre de tableaux et que même la vanité contemporaine est sur ce chapitre exigeante au point de décider de braves gens à *louer* pour une soirée les croûtes qu'ils ne peuvent acquérir en toute propriété,—la peinture amusante et *décorative* est cotée très haut sur le marché, et l'on peut dire que c'est la partie la moins artiste du public qui exerce sur la production artistique la plus considérable influence.")

32. Henry Houssaye, "Le Salon de 1884," *Revue des deux mondes*, LXIII (1 June 1884), 579.

33. Houssaye, "Le Salon de 1882," *Revue des deux mondes*, LXI (1 June 1882), 516ff. Fénéon, *Oeuvres*, 152.

only sign of antinaturalism in the criticism of painting. Impressionism, the advanced side of naturalism, also came under heavy fire.

As might well be expected, the most vocal criticism of impressionism came from conservative circles. Thus, in 1882, Henry Houssaye accused the impressionists of having led the French school to the point where it was about to "fall, on the threshold of the 20th century, into all manner of trivialities."[34] Joséphin Péladan accused the impressionists of "the desperate artifice of a decadent."[35] This sort of attack was not, however, part of the old-line conservative reaction toward the movement. Impressionism's newest antagonists found themselves struggling against a general trend toward acceptance of the movement; indeed, impressionism was invading even academic circles by the mid-1880s. As early as 1879 Charles Tardieu, writing for *L'Art*, remarked how the movement was gaining ground at the Salon, noting, "Impressionism? It's cleaning itself up, it's putting on its gloves. Soon it will dine in the city. Academicism? It is in complete retreat."[36] Although many critics at this time really did not understand exactly what impressionism was—some saw Jules Bastien-Lepage as an impressionist, others, Jean-Jacques Henner— it was no longer possible to look down upon this painting as a temporary manifestation. The movement had arrived and was very much a part of the total artistic picture in Paris. Conservative circles required a new method of attack.

Thus Joséphin Péladan admitted the importance of Manet in an 1883 article published in *L'Artiste*. He argued that Manet should be included in the state exhibition of that year, but his support was anything but friendly: "Oh, I don't like Manet! He is mistaken. Local color and plein-air are errors, but he belongs to the history of art, like a schism belongs to the history of religions."[37] While recognizing that impressionism could

34. Houssaye, "Le Salon de 1882," 564. (". . . tomber au seuil du XXe siècle dans toutes les trivialités.")

35. Péladan, *L'Art ochlocratique*, 55. (". . . un artifice désespéré de décadent.")

36. Charles Tardieu, "La Peinture au Salon de Paris, 1879," *L'Art*, xviii (1879), as quoted by Lionello Venturi, *Les Archives de l'impressionnisme* (Paris: Durand-Ruel, 1939), 338. ("L'impressionnisme? Il se nettoie; il met des gants. Bientôt il dînera en ville. L'Académisme? Il est en pleine retraite.")

37. Joséphin Péladan, "L'Esthétique à l'exposition nationale des beaux-arts," *L'Artiste*, liii (October 1883), 260. ("Oh! je n'aime pas Manet, il s'est trompé, le ton local et le plein air sont des erreurs; mais il appartient à l'histoire de l'art, comme un schisme appartient à l'histoire des religions.")

not be dismissed, Péladan at the same time condemned the movement. He sounded the old argument that impressionist painters offered only sketches, but he also attacked what he saw as their decadent concern with technique.[38] Because Péladan also hated any art that dealt with contemporary life and felt that imitating nature could never be the goal of art, to him the subject matter of impressionism was also anathema. Péladan's comments on impressionism were those of a defender of tradition who felt the great French ideal was in danger, yet his criticisms also show the respect of someone who knows the power of the enemy.

Georges Lafenestre, career member of the Ministry of Fine Arts, took a similar position in the *Revue des deux mondes* of 1887. He was well aware that the new preoccupation of Salon painters with "generalities . . . exterior effects . . . phenomena of light" would lead in painting to "a transformation much more serious than all of those which we have seen."[39] Lafenestre feared that these new ideas would bury the traditional French concern for "the reflective science of balanced and significant composition, the precision and suppleness of drawing, the intelligence of grace and of beauty."[40] As for tradition, he declared, "our duty is to defend it."[41] By the 1880s a new urgency and seriousness had entered into conservative commentary on the impressionist movement; this criticism generally tended to decry impressionism and its Salon counterpart for destroying the French school of painting. The only answer was a return, as Péladan had noted it, to the Ideal, to Tradition, to Hierarchy. Interestingly, avant-garde critics of the period could, in their own way, offer a somewhat similar solution to the "problem" of impressionism.

It must be understood first of all that no avant-garde critic in Paris during the 1880s ever attacked impressionism outright. Impressionism still stood for independence from the establishment Salon and represented the paradigm of intransigence for the young generation. But in spite of its mildness, the reaction against impressionism in advanced circles was considered and purposeful. Much has been written about this reaction. Indeed, George Heard Hamilton calls the period "anti-impres-

38. Péladan, *L'Art ochlocratique*, 55.

39. George Lafenestre, "Le Salon de 1887," *Revue des deux mondes*, LXXXI (1 June 1887), 605. (". . . réalités générales . . . effets extérieurs . . . phénomènes lumineux . . . une transformation beaucoup plus grave que toutes celles auxquelles nous avons pu assister.")

40. Ibid., 606. (". . . la science réfléchie de la composition équilibrée et significative, la précision et la souplesse du dessin, l'intelligence de la grâce et de la beauté.")

41. Ibid. ("Notre devoir, à nous, est de le défendre.")

sionist" in his survey of modern art.[42] While noting that artists such as Gauguin and Redon owed a good deal to impressionism, students of the period have long been aware that Gauguin believed the impressionists neglected "the mysterious centers of thought," while Redon spoke of the "rather low-vaulted edifice of Impressionism."[43] While such comments might well be seen as representing no more than the natural transition from one artistic generation to another, it is interesting to note a certain similarity between comments on impressionism among the advanced critics of the 1880s and more conservative ideas on the subject.

Perhaps the most famous "defection" from the impressionist cause was Emile Zola. In 1880, after having defended the movement for years, he finally decided that the impressionists had all been "precusors" and that a true genius had not yet appeared in their ranks, nor had the movement produced any masterpieces.[44] Zola began to see impressionism as a transitional movement, one that would pave the way for great works in the future rather than producing them. Even in his catalogue introduction to the Manet sale of 1884, Zola equivocated as to the position Manet would occupy in the history of art, refusing to see him on the same level as Ingres, Delacroix, and Courbet.[45] It was, of course, a sign of just how far Zola was from a true understanding of impressionism that in 1880 he would suggest that none of them had produced a masterpiece. More important, such a statement demonstrates the extent to which Zola's opinions on art had become more conservative. Perhaps it was this supposed "failure" of impressionism that led Zola away from art criticism after 1884.

Another writer who began as a naturalist and disavowed the naturalist cause in painting was J.-K. Huysmans. Because much of Huysmans's art criticism tended to concentrate on his reaction to individual works it is often difficult to know how he felt about particular movements in general. But his choice of artists and his responses to them are telling. For a critic coming out of naturalist circles he was highly critical of Gustave

42. Hamilton, *Painting and Sculpture in Europe*, 75.

43. Chipp, *Theories of Modern Art*, 65 and 120.

44. Emile Zola, *Le Bon combat* (Paris: Collection Savoir Hermann, 1974), 214–15. ("Ce sont tous des précurseurs, l'homme de génie n'est pas né . . . on cherche en vain le chef-d'oeuvre qui doit imposer la formule et faire courber toutes les têtes.")

45. See George Heard Hamilton, *Manet and His Critics* (New Haven: Yale University Press, 1954), 265ff., who notes the similarity of Zola's criticism to that of the highly conservative critic Albert Wolff.

Courbet, noting that "with Courbet we come back, quite simply, to the most exasperating decay of painting."[46] Huysmans also felt that Manet, while highly important as an innovator, had been surpassed by many painters who followed him.[47] His attitude toward impressionism proper was more positive. Particularly fond of art that dealt with modern life, he enthusiastically praised Degas and Renoir. On the other hand, though he was one of the first to recognize the talent of Cézanne, he remained unmoved by the art of Monet.[48] But it is not Huysmans's expressed attitude toward impressionism or naturalism that reflected his real move away from these styles; rather, it was his promulgation of the art of Redon, Gustave Moreau, and Felicien Rops. Whether a product of his own fierce independence or his desire for an art of more mysterious and meaningful orientation, Huysmans's championing of these three artists constituted a major step away from naturalism.[49] Zola himself had admitted to being seduced by the art of Moreau but ultimately rejected his work.[50] Unfortunately Huysmans did not continue to write about current art throughout this period, and by the end of the 1880s he was no longer intimately concerned with contemporary art criticism. But it is clear that Huysmans was dissatisfied with impressionism and had sought out an art of very different emphasis.

Throughout his writing on the subject, Félix Fénéon remained an intelligent and searching friend of impressionism. He questioned certain less successful works by selected impressionists but always accepted the import and greatness of the movement itself. He did not, however, allow his respect for impressionism to obscure his belief that the movement had become old-fashioned by the mid-1880s. Thus in 1887 he declared that the "great time of Impressionism has lapsed."[51] In 1888 he noted how benign the press now was toward impressionism, while neo-impressionism was the target of adverse criticism. At the same time he

46. J.-K. Huysmans, *L'Art moderne* (Paris: Plon, 1883), 176. ("Avec Courbet, nous revenons tout simplement aux plus exaspérantes vétustés de la peinture.") See also Charles Maingon, *L'Univers artistique de J.-K. Huysmans* (Paris: Nizet, 1977), 35.

47. Huysmans, *L'Art moderne*, 177, and Maingon, *L'Univers artistique*, 39.

48. Maingon, *L'Univers artistique*, 47.

49. For some possible reasons for Huysmans's defection from impressionism see Annette Kahn, *J.-K. Huysmans, Novelist, Poet and Art Critic* (Ann Arbor: UMI Research Press, 1987), 20ff.

50. Zola, *Le Bon combat*, 200–201.

51. Fénéon, *Oeuvres*, 68. ("Les beaux temps de l'Impressionnisme sont périmés.")

specifically criticized Sisley, Monet, Guillaumin, and Gauguin because they continued "in the arbitrary practices of old-time impressionism."[52] These were relatively minor criticisms but they demonstrate that Fénéon, the proponent of neo-impressionism, was not satisfied with impressionism itself. For him neo-impressionism improved on its forerunner by being more scientific and rigorous in its concern with the effects of color. And, finally, when he praised Seurat for his hieratic and summary drawings and compared his static figure arrangements to those of Puvis de Chavannes, Fénéon also suggested that this return to solidity and stasis was another improvement upon older impressionism.

Certainly the clearest anti-impressionist statement made by an avant-garde critic came from Albert Aurier. It is clear that Aurier was not temperamentally in tune with impressionist painting. His commentary on Monet, for instance, could be ecstatic but also curiously inappropriate. He spoke of the painter, glowingly and beautifully, as a worshiper of the sun, of the sun-god Baal, calling him a priest in the temple of the sun.[53] Aurier's ideas about art certainly differed from those of the impressionists and would ultimately lead him to find fault with Monet:

> Without doubt it is permissible to allow certain reservations to slip in, to criticize this work where indeed some of the indispensable elements of perfect beauty are lacking, to establish the rudimentary nature of these instantaneous sketches, often too sketchy and too instantaneous, to censure this constant sacrifice of significant form and this tendency to plunge human beings into these atmospheres so splendidly embracing that they seem to vaporize there; without doubt, also, it is legitimate to wish for an art less immediate, less directly sensorial, an art of dreams more distant, and of the idea.[54]

52. Ibid., 127. (". . . s'obstine dans les pratiques arbitraires de l'impressionnisme des anciens jours.")

53. Aurier, *Oeuvres posthumes*, 221–25.

54. Ibid., 224–25. ("Sans doute, il est permis de glisser des réticences, de critiquer cette oeuvre où manquent bien des indispensables éléments de la parfaite beauté, de constater le rudimentaire de ces pochades instantanées, souvent trop pochades et trop instantanées, de blâmer ce constant sacrifice des formes significatrices et ce parti pris de plonger les êtres dans ces atmosphères si spendidement embrasées qu'ils semblent s'y vaporiser; sans doute, aussi, il est légitime de souhaiter un art moins immédiat, moins directement sensationnel, un art de rêve plus lointain et d'idée.")

Aurier's criticism here was not minor and was reminiscent of what many conservative critics were saying about impressionism in the 1880s. Following an almost standard line, he complained of sketchiness and called for an art less concerned with immediate sensory input. In his famous article on Gauguin, "Le Symbolisme en peinture," Aurier even more clearly stated his case concerning the limits of impressionism. For Aurier, "impressionism is and can only be a variety of realism, a refined realism, spiritualized, dilletantized, but always realism."[55] To this he opposed the new art of symbolists like Gauguin, who, he felt, should disabuse themselves of "this absurd label of 'Impressionists,' which implies, it is necessary to repeat, a program directly contradictory to theirs."[56] Over and against impressionism Aurier posited there was something more painting could offer: an art not limited by reality, an art of dreams and ideas, a more meaningful art. In doing so he not only demonstrated a clearly antinaturalist stance but also offered proof of just how close conservative and advanced viewpoints could come on this subject.

Explaining just why this change in attitude toward impressionism occurred is not simple, but certain inferences can be made. The symbolist criticism of painting was written by men who were imbued with literary ideas first and the mechanics of painting second; consequently, their call for "ideas" in painting. Indeed, the symbolist critic's complaint against naturalism in painting was, ultimately, the same as the symbolist complaint against literary naturalism: the lack of ideas. Naturalist painting, at its best as in impressionism, offered an artist's temperament as demonstrated in a personal technique. It was based on the ability to paint well, on technique, not ideas. Naturalist criticism understood this, but symbolism, in its emphasis on literary ideas, passed over such concerns to call for a revival of ideas in art. To be sure, these were not the same sort of ideas that had dominated academic circles before impressionism, but the very call for more thought and less sensory input in art represented a

---

55. Ibid., 208. ("L'impressionnisme, c'est et ce ne peut être qu'une variété du réalisme, un réalisme affiné, spiritualisé, dilettantisé, mais toujours le réalisme.") Aurier's attitude toward impressionism is discussed in Patricia Townley Mathews, *Aurier's Symbolist Art Criticism and Theory* (Ann Arbor: UMI Research Press, 1986), 110–13; and Margaret Lunn, "G.-Albert Aurier, Critic and Theorist of Symbolist Art" (Ph.D. dissertation, Massachusetts Institute of Technology, 1982), 73ff.

56. Aurier, *Oeuvres posthumes*, 209. (". . . cette absurde étiquette d'"impressionnistes,' qui implique, il faut le répéter, un programme directement contradictoire du leur.")

step closer to the conservative tradition that impressionism had so carefully shunned.

THE NEW IDEALISM IN THE CRITICISM OF ART

By the 1890s idealism, whether in its conservative or avant-garde (symbolist) form, had come to dominate artistic activity in Paris. Idealism was as much in vogue among the Nabis as it was in the Salons—quite unlike the situation in the early 1880s when naturalism dominated. Critics began to speak of a new, revitalized kind of idealism. Because the very word "idealism" conjured up thoughts of the French Academy and "grand" painting of the Salons, one would expect symbolist critics to have been careful to distinguish any "ideal" they might talk about from the one promoted by the Academy and the Ecole des Beaux-Arts. Indeed, they were quite careful.

Albert Aurier called the new art that he advocated *idéiste* to separate it from any association with idealism of the Academy.[57] Charles Henry, referring to the demise of realism and naturalism, stated: "I don't believe in the future of psychologism, or of naturalism, nor in general of any realist school. I believe, on the contrary, in the coming, more or less soon, of a very idealist art, even mystical." Henry was mindful to clarify that this new art would be "founded on absolutely new techniques."[58] Charles Vignier, a writer and intimate of symbolist circles, noted:

> A *fact!* It seems that in literature, in science, in politics, and in life the gross stupidity of materialism, which was the cherished baritone of these last years, sees itself, little by little, pushed back from the scene, back to the wings where a newcomer of a tenor is whispering to itself under the species of a completely smart idealism, completely on the outer fringes, completely spanking new, of an ideal idealism, finally![59]

57. Ibid., 211ff.

58. Huret, *Enquête sur l'évolution littéraire*, 414. ("Je ne crois pas à l'avenir du psychologisme ou du naturalisme, ni, en général, de toute école réaliste. Je crois au contraire à l'avènement plus ou moins prochain d'un art très idéaliste, mystique même, fondé sur des techniques absolument nouvelles.")

59. Ibid., 97. ("*Un fait!* Il semble qu'en littérature, en science, en politique et dans la vie, le

Throughout *La Littérature de tout à l'heure,* Charles Morice proclaimed the importance of the "idée de Dieu" but carefully stipulated that by this he was not advocating a return to organized religion or to a style that was only a mockery of the past.[60] The symbolist writers were quite aware that their desire to move away from naturalism toward an art of ideas might be confused with a desire to return to conservative academic traditions. To be sure, they were very much concerned with linking their art to the best of past traditions, but they were also quick to divorce themselves from the conservative idealism against which naturalism itself had also struggled. In this the symbolists were not alone.

While Joséphin Péladan proclaimed his support for the ideal in art, he made it very clear that the supposed protectors of the ideal in the Academy were not to his liking.[61] In his *La Renaissance de l'idéalisme* Ferdinand Brunetière, while recounting how idealism had gained ground against naturalism throughout the 1880s, carefully noted, "I do not take the word '*Idealism*' here in the precise, technical, and limited sense that the philosophers give it."[62] Eugène Melchior de Vogüé, speaking of the new generation of young writers who were challenging the naturalist school in France, noted that, in spite of their revolt against the materialism of the age, they were not seduced by the old idealist cause as his generation had been.[63] André Michel, in his 1884 Salon review, specifically noted that it would be ridiculous to expect a revival of Greek or Italian ideals in French contemporary art. Michel stated that "it is a more complex and more troubled ideal that emerges from modern hearts and minds."[64]

Thus, not only was the desire for a less materialistic art widespread,

---

gros benêt de matérialisme, qui fut le baryton choyé de ces dernières années, se voit peu à peu repoussé de la scène, et jusqu'à la cantonade où se chuchote la prochaine venue du ténor sous l'espèce d'un idéalisme tout pimpant, tout fringant, tout battant neuf, d'un idéalisme dont on augure des merveilles, d'un idéalisme idéal, enfin!")

60. Morice, *La Littérature de tout à l'heure,* 68, for instance.

61. Péladan, for all of his conservatism, constantly railed against the Salon. At the same time that he found impressionism to be decadent he said the same thing about Salon painting. See, for instance, *L'Art ochlocratique,* 54, 57.

62. Brunetière, *La Renaissance de l'idéalisme* (Paris: Librairie de Firmin-Didot, 1896), 18. (". . . je ne prends pas ici ce mot d'*Idéalisme* dans le sens précis, technique et limitatif que lui donnent les philosophes.")

63. Eugène Melchior de Vogüé, "La Littérature réaliste," *Revue des deux mondes,* LXXV (15 May 1886), 310.

64. Michel, "Le Salon de 1884," 182. He specifically mentions critics who defend "Tra-

crossing conservative and avant-garde boundaries, so too was the feeling that this new spirit had to be distinguished from the old idealism of the establishment. Neither idealist nor symbolist critics wanted to be associated with the idealism of Bouguereau. But when it came to defining the new idealism and showing how it was different from the older variety, meaning became cloudy. Anatole Baju, editor of *Le Décadent*, one of the first of the new literary periodicals, defined the ideal as "physical beauty, the soul of things and moral beauty, this quintessence of the soul"—a statement not essentially different from what Ingres or Bouguereau might have said.[65] In an article on Albert Aurier, Louis Dumur asserted that the new idealism was not a retrogression.[66] But when he defined the ideal he returned to the familiar Platonic thought that the ideal represents the world behind appearances, unknowable in the sense that we know the physical world—a definition, once again, quite close to what any Academician might have offered. For all of his attempts at separating the *idéiste* from the "idealist," Aurier often comes across as essentially linked to the Platonic metaphysics of the past.

The "ideal" was a loaded term for critics and audiences in late nineteenth-century France. The ideal held certain connotations that naturalism and positivism had rejected. The use of the term could be, therefore, at once antinaturalist and inflammatory. Indeed, it still comes as a surprise that the first history of the advanced art of the 1880s and early 1890s in Paris, André Mellerio's booklet, was entitled *Le Mouvement idéaliste en peinture*. Mellerio defined idealism simply as "the tendency of artists searching to escape from contingency through inspiration and the means of expression."[67] By "contingency" he meant dependence upon nature, and for him idealism meant going beyond nature. Finally though, in a footnote, he suggested that the term *idealism* had been around for a long time and he used it for convenience, even though for

---

dition" and the "Ideal," an obvious reference to Péladan. ("C'est un idéal plus complexe et plus troublé qui se dégagera des coeurs et des cerveaux modernes.")

65. Anatole Baju, "Idéal," *Le Décadent*, i (21 August 1886), unpaginated. ("La beauté physique, âme des choses et la beauté morale, cette quintessence de l'âme: voilà l'idéal.")

66. Louis Dumur, "G.-Albert Aurier et l'évolution idéaliste," *Mercure de France*, viii (August 1893), 289–97.

67. André Mellerio, *Le Mouvement idéaliste en peinture* (Paris: H. Floury, 1896), 9. ("La tendance d'artistes cherchant à échapper à la contigence par l'inspiration et le mode d'expression.")

him it had no rational meaning. It is a curious, evasive, but telling statement. The new idealism was often a restatement of older concepts, revitalized in contact with new art; it is this combination of old and new that often marked the symbolist generation and brought it into such close accord with conservative thought.

THE CATHOLIC REVIVAL AND ART CRITICISM

Along with the renaissance of idealism in Parisian circles during the 1880s, and certainly linked to it, was a marked revival of interest in religion. In many cases this meant a resurgence of Catholicism. The social and literary aspects of this situation have already been mentioned briefly in Chapter 1. Now I shall analyze the extent to which the renewed interest in religion influenced art and art criticism.

Undoubtedly the single most important proselytizer for Catholicism in painting was Joséphin Péladan. A truly inspired writer, Péladan offered a stirring call for a new order in art. Especially in the context of the conservative publications in which his first writings appeared, his pronouncements on art are exhilarating. One may not believe him but he made for enjoyable reading at a time when much art criticism was boring. To peruse the many pages of art criticism produced in *L'Artiste* during the 1880s is a frustrating task for the modern reader. Generally the articles are intelligent and well thought out, but pedestrian and usually devoid of controversy. Readers in the nineteenth century must have been just as surprised as we are today to come upon Péladan's entries. He brandished a daring and forceful style, writing about art in an astonishing manner very much against the grain.

It must be remembered that in the early 1880s most of the talk in Salon criticism and in independent circles was about the death of "grand painting" and the triumph of naturalism and contemporary life. Even the *Revue indépendante*, which would become one of the most important organs of symbolist writing, began its first issue with an article that paid homage to materialism as the great new force in the world.[68] In the same issue appeared an article by Edgar Monteil, politician and anticleric. He fiercely attacked Catholicism, which he viewed as antithetical to all

68. [unsigned], "Matérialisme," *La Revue indépendante,* 1 (May 1884), 1–4.

progress.[69] As we have already noted, Catholicism was out of favor in Paris of the early 1880s, which makes Péladan's writing so surprising. Of course Catholicism was not out of vogue in the highly intellectual Lyonnais circles of which Péladan had been a part throughout his youth. But Paris was different and Joséphin Péladan was an anomaly there. However, this did not make him shy. In the tradition of much of the ultramontane writing at this time—indeed his style has many affinities with that of Léon Bloy—Péladan is polemical and dictatorial, dashing off ideas with great aplomb. His very first article in 1882 was a bit of art criticism, a Salon review, and it set the aggressively Catholic tone for the rest of his work. In that initial piece he praised the art of the Italian primitives as the religious ideal and railed against the materialism of the age of Darwin. He haughtily proclaimed:

> There are two irrefragable propositions:
> 1. The masterpieces of art are all religious, even among non-believers.
> 2. For nineteen centuries the masterpieces of art have all been Catholic, even among the Protestants.[70]

It was the kind of criticism meant to draw attention and it did. But Péladan was not alone in his desire for a revival of Catholicism, or at least religious feeling, in art. There were others who took up banners for a renewal of religious art.

In 1886 Eugène Melchior de Vogüé argued that the problem with French literary realism was that it ignored the divine. In his view the pessimism into which France had fallen could be attributed to realism's and positivism's not having fulfilled the great promise held out for them. Russian realist writers, in their adherence to Christian morality, were much superior to their French counterparts.[71] Similarly, Paul Bourget, who would write a novel with the theme that positivism was immoral, noted in an 1881 article on Charles Baudelaire:

---

69. Edgar Monteil, "*Le Manuel d'instruction laïque* et la critique," *La Revue indépendante*, 1 (May 1884), 9–21.

70. Péladan, *L'Art ochlocratique*, 16. ("Il est deux propositions irréfragables: 1° Les chefs-d'oeuvre de l'art sont tous religieux, même chez les incroyants; 2° Depuis dix-neuf siècles les chefs-d'oeuvre de l'art sont tous catholiques, même chez les protestants.")

71. Melchior de Vogüé, "La littérature réaliste," 293ff.

> Slowly, surely, has there not been an elaboration of belief in the
> bankruptcy of nature, [a belief] that risks becoming the sinister
> faith of the twentieth century, if a revival, which could scarcely
> be anything but a religious renaissance, doesn't save an over-
> reflective humanity from the lassitude of its own thought?[72]

Further along Bourget opposed Baudelaire, whose faith was absolute and
real, to the typical modern Catholic whose childhood and childish faith
in God was so often replaced in adult life by a faith in science, socialism, or some other secular ideal.[73] Ferdinand Brunetière also upheld the
rigid Catholicism of seventeenth-century France against what he saw as
the pessimism and self-indulgence of the nineteenth century.[74] Like
Melchior de Vogüé, Brunetière also felt that French realism lacked
moral force.

The critic Charles Bigot, while noting that subjects dealing with contemporary life had taken over the Salon in 1883, lamented the fact that
artists now lacked true faith and that the religious paintings at the Salon
were so devoid of genuine sentiment.[75] Similarly, in André Michel's
view, most contemporary religious painters were not really concerned
with their subject. Michel felt that even in an age of naturalism religious
subjects were allowable, as long as the artist truly felt something for the
subject. A religious painter need not necessarily emulate Fra Angelico in
single-minded devotion, but religious painting did require religious feeling, and he praised only those artists who demonstrated such feeling.[76]
Though lacking Péladan's sense of advocacy, both Bigot and Michel
acknowledged that by the early 1880s religious painting was all but dead
in France. Even while critics were noting the lack of religious convic-
tion in contemporary painting, however, some naturalist painters were
beginning to redress the situation.

72. Paul Bourget, *Essais de psychologie contemporaine* (1881; Paris: Plon, 1901), 13. ("Mais
lentement, sûrement, une croyance à la banqueroute de la nature ne s'élabore-t-elle pas, qui
risque de devenir la foi sinistre du XXe siècle, si un renouveau, qui ne saurait guère être qu'un
élan de renaissance religieuse, ne sauve pas l'humanité trop réfléchie de la lassitude de sa
propre pensée?") On Bourget see Teddy Brunius, *Mutual Aid in the Arts from the Second Empire
to the Fin de Siècle* (Stockholm: Almquist and Wiksell, 1972), 151–53, where the author
discusses Bourget's novel, *Le Disciple,* in which Bourget suggested the lack of morals in positivism.

73. Bourget, *Essais de psychologie contemporaine,* 16.

74. See Edouard Rod, *Les Idées morales du temps présent* (Paris: Perrin, 1911), 215ff.

75. Charles Bigot, "Le Salon de 1883," *Gazette des beaux-arts,* xxvii (1 June 1883), 466ff.

76. Michel, "Le Salon de 1884," 201ff. Also see Michel, "Salon de 1888," *Gazette des
beaux-arts,* xxxviii (July 1888), 21ff.

The first inklings of the return to religious subject matter came in what might be called peasant devotional subjects. This type, owing ultimately to Millet's example, consisted of naturalistic renderings of peasants at worship. Many artists, such as Millet, François Bonvin, Alphonse Legros, Jules Breton, and others had offered such subjects throughout the sixties and seventies.[77] But in the 1880s further interest in peasant devotional subjects—stimulated by the writings of Ernest Renan on Brittany and a general interest in the French peasant tradition coming out of Hippolyte Taine's concern for studying the French national character—resulted in a minor flood of paintings of *pardon* ceremonies in Brittany.[78] Although such paintings at first exhibited a positivist sociological approach they soon took on a more religious cast. While naturalist paintings of contemporary Parisian street life could never exhibit religious overtones, naturalist painters, when working with Breton devotional subjects, tended toward more spiritual meanings. This becomes very clear when a painter like Gauguin takes up such common naturalist subject matter in his Breton paintings, but it is also to be found in the work of a "pure" naturalist like Dagnan-Bouveret. His *Pardon in Brittany* (Fig. 3) for example, while not an object of devotion itself, portrays the pure and simple faith increasingly being called for in certain Parisian circles. Strictly speaking, the subject of Breton *pardon* paintings remained naturalist. But the work of Jean-Charles Cazin, who was extremely popular throughout the 1880s, was sometimes more religious.

Cazin is best known today for his landscapes, but in the 1880s his religious paintings received a good deal of attention. In paintings such as *Tobias and the Angel* and *Hagar and Ishmael* (Figs. 4 and 5), Cazin rendered religious scenes in a straightforward, naturalist style reminiscent of

77. See Gabriel P. Weisberg, *The Realist Tradition: French Painting and Drawing, 1830–1900* (Cleveland: Cleveland Museum of Art, 1980), 107–25.

78. On this subject see Gabriel P. Weisberg, "Vestiges of the Past: The Brittany Pardons of Late Nineteenth-Century French Painters," *Arts Magazine*, LV (November 1980), 134–38. Also see MaryAnne Stevens, "Innovation and Consolidation in French Painting," in Royal Academy of Fine Arts, London, *Post-Impressionism* (London: Harper and Row, 1979–80), 19–25. Fred Orton and Griselda Pollock, "Les Données bretonnantes: la prairie de répresentation," *Art History*, 3 (September 1980), 314–43, offer a challenging treatment of Breton themes in painting. In an excellent recent article Michael Orwicz has shown how naturalist paintings of Breton subjects, specifically two renderings by Dagnan-Bouveret, could be interpreted to fit a conservative political agenda. See Michael Orwicz, "Confrontations et clivages dans les discours des critiques du salon, 1885–1889," in Université de Saint-Etienne, *La Critique d'art en France, 1850–1900*, ed. by Jean-Paul Bouillon (Saint-Etienne: Centre Interdisciplinaire d'Etudes et de Recherches sur l'Expression Contemporaine, 1989), 177–92.

Millet, yet unique. The resulting blend of the real and the mysterious, a natural spirituality, understated and controlled, distinguished Cazin's work from any number of religious paintings inundating the Salons of the 1880s. Throughout the decade religious subjects became more and more fashionable. Miraculous events, the more spectacular the better, painted in a realistic, indeed journalistic, manner came to be the rage.[79] Georges Moreau de Tours's *Stigmatization in the Middle Ages* (Fig. 6) was typical of the genre. Here a concentration on details of late medieval costume and setting were combined with the entranced—and frankly erotic—gaze of the stigmatized woman to produce a striking illusion of reality. In a world not yet used to the wonders of Hollywood period pieces, Moreau de Tours's sensational presentation must have been exciting. Yet it seems frivolous in comparison with Cazin, whose religious works were more timeless, though no less miraculous. Cazin's paintings were naturalistic but never specific. He presented universally understandable images, where feeling and emotion were transmitted by the enchanting intimacy of simple figures in a stark and melancholy setting.

Some critics did object, however, that Cazin's paintings, though beautiful, emotional, and even sentimental, did not convey true spiritual content. Péladan, while citing Cazin's offering to the Salon of 1883 as one of the most interesting works there, specifically stated that it was not religious. Indeed, Péladan warned that too much interest in subtle brush stroke and nuance, as exhibited in Cazin's work, could lead to a decadent art-for-art's-sake mentality.[80] J.-K. Huysmans, while praising Cazin's work, noted that his figures were hardly biblical and their emotion, for him, came not from an old religious story but from their modernity.[81] Inherent in such comments on Cazin was the thought that the naturalist style and religious subject matter were not compatible. Indeed, such thought became common at this time and greatly affected the next phase of religious paintings in the Salons.

A good demonstration of what happened to Salon religious painting

79. It was a type reviled by many critics, among them Gustave Geffroy. For Geffroy's attitude to religious painting at this time see Jo Anne Paradise, *Gustave Geffroy and the Criticism of Painting* (New York: Garland, 1985), 173ff. For an interesting discussion of the role of photography in religious painting see Gabriel P. Weisberg, "From the Real to the Unreal: Religious Painting and Photography at the Salons of the Third Republic," *Arts Magazine*, LX (December 1985), 58–63. It is also intriguing to note that this period saw the publication of many accounts of the lives of various obscure saints.

80. Péladan, *L'Art ochlocratique*, 64.

81. Huysmans, *L'Art moderne*, 156–57.

by the end of the 1880s is the comparing of two works by the same painter, the idealist Edmond Aman-Jean. Aman-Jean's *St. Julian the Hospitator* (Fig. 7) of 1882 is a religious painting very much in the tradition of Cazin. The subject, a medieval legend that had been interpreted in a story by Flaubert, is about a nobleman who accidentally killed both his father and mother. (His wife had given their bed to his parents while he was away on a hunting trip. Upon returning he mistook them for his wife and a supposed lover and killed them.) To atone for his deed St. Julian went off to live in the desert, helping travelers, much in the manner of St. Christopher. What Aman-Jean offered was a realistic rendering, very much in a naturalist style. He concentrated on the idea of thirst in the desert, the sores and odor of the saint, and the curiosity of the small boy who has come upon him. Like many of Cazin's paintings the scene might not be recognized as religious without the halo over the saint. Indeed, the very impact of the picture lies in the realism with which a nominally sacred subject is rendered. It is a naturalist religious painting.

Quite different in conception was Aman-Jean's *St. Geneviève Before Paris* (Fig. 8) of 1885. In three years the painter has moved from a naturalistic style to a much more hieratic one. Geneviève, the patron saint of Paris, holds a white ship, symbol of her reprovisioning of the city. Everything about the painting is meant to remove it from the realm of the real. The saint is presented in conjunction with Notre-Dame and the scene is painted in the flat, decorative manner associated with Puvis de Chavannes, with whom Aman-Jean had been studying by this time.[82] The painting denies the natural in favor of symbolic allegory, instead of trying to present allegory in terms of the natural as had the *St. Julian.* As such it serves as example of the increasing belief in artistic circles that a true religious painting must avoid naturalism. Such an attitude was reflected in the criticism of the period.

The critic Eugène Véron, no friend of idealism in art, still felt that religious art required an abstract style. In his *L'Esthétique* of 1878 he noted that the religious painting of Raphael was effective because his madonnas were so abstract, so unnatural.[83] For this reason Véron felt the time for ideals and for religious art was past. André Michel echoed a

---

82. On the relationship between Aman-Jean, Puvis de Chavannes, and Seurat as well, see my "Seurat et ses amis de l'Ecole des Beaux-Arts," *Gazette des beaux-arts,* cxiv (October 1989), 153–68.

83. Véron, *L'Esthétique,* 339.

similar sentiment in ridiculing Paul-Louis Delance's *The Legend of St. Denis*—one of the more famous examples of the beheaded saint walking along in a realistically rendered suburban scene with his head in hand—as ludicrous in its realism.[84] But Michel and Véron were, at heart, naturalist critics. They did not advocate a return to religious art; they merely noted that naturalism was inappropriate to a religious subject. Others went further, suggesting a more suitable stylistic prototype for religious art.

It was, once again, Joséphin Péladan who vociferously proclaimed the greatness of the Italian primitives as model for religious art. From early on he advocated the purity and deep religiosity of the golden age of Florentine fresco painting. But Péladan was not alone in this interest in a return to a more "primitive" manner. There was a general revival of interest in late medieval painting in France during the 1880s. Puvis de Chavannes spearheaded a large group of painters who turned to a style influenced by the art of the Florentines. To be sure, this revival was not necessarily religious in nature. Much of it was connected with the general revival of idealism during this period. Puvis de Chavannes, for instance, was not particularly noted as a religious painter. But there was a confluence of thinking here, and the return to the more hieratic style of late medieval fresco painting answered the call for both a more idealized art and for a more religious art.

Naturalism had praised the more realistic styles of the past and had eschewed idealism and religious subject matter. The reaction against naturalism produced an interest in much less naturalistic schools of art and a deep concern for the ideal and for religious painting. Soon many began to see the Renaissance—the definitive end of the Middle Ages—as the beginning of the materialism that now dominated the French art world.[85] Just as the Catholic revival itself was inclined toward the Middle Ages, so too was the artistic return to religious subject matter contemporaneous with it. This parallel is hardly surprising. The medieval period was seen as a time of deep pietistic devotion, and any attempt at reviving religious feeling in art would naturally turn in that direction. What is surprising is the way the hieratic manner demonstrated in

84. Michel, "Salon de 1888," 21ff.

85. Aman-Jean himself made such an argument in an article entitled, "Jean Bellegambe (1475–1540)," *L'Art dans les deux mondes* (31 January 1891), 118–20. So did Charles Morice, as noted in Paul Delsemme, *Un Théoricien du symbolisme, Charles Morice* (Paris: Nizet, 1958), 181.

Aman-Jean's *St. Geneviève* did such yeoman's duty, serving as signal for an art of deep meaning whether it be idealist or Catholic. Maurice Denis's painting could be both idealist and Catholic, and symbolist as well.

Maurice Denis's *Catholic Mystery* (Fig. 9) of 1889 still comes as a surprise to those who expect the Nabis to be mere followers of Gauguin. Gauguin may have painted subjects with religious overtones, but his paintings tended to be either observations of the mysterious devotion of others—as in his Breton paintings—or exotic, symbolist musings on the nature of religion. Gauguin always comes across as a painter first, not one of the faithful. Maurice Denis, on the other hand, offered the painted statements of a staunch believer. His *Catholic Mystery*, though certainly not completely orthodox in concept, is about Catholic dogma, about the Annunciation and the continuation of Christ's life on earth through Christian ritual. Its very existence in avant-garde circles demonstrates the extent to which Catholicism had come to be accepted there. Denis himself early on had claimed that he wanted to revitalize Christian painting and affirmed a preference for an abstracted, less realistic manner. He was also intent on a close harmony between the ideas of the symbolists and his own concept of religious painting.[86] But such concerns might only have appeared as a curious personal variation on symbolist themes had not Catholicism penetrated deeply into avant-garde circles. What Denis's *Catholic Mystery* most clearly demonstrates is that by 1889 the intellectual scene in Paris had changed greatly from the beginning of the decade. The Catholic revival had shown that one could indeed be both Catholic and symbolist.

The signs of the confluence of Catholicism and symbolism were many, wholesale conversions among the symbolist writers being not the least. Paul Verlaine, of course, provides the most significant example of a symbolist who was also a very fervent Catholic—and whose Catholicism profoundly influenced his work—but there were many others. By the early 1890s Téodor de Wyzewa, Charles Morice, Adolphe Retté, and J.-K. Huysmans had all shown signs of a turn to Catholicism. Georges Vanor's *L'Art symboliste* of 1889 exhibited a distinctly Catholic tone. As the avant-garde became more open to Catholicism its periodicals began to echo the transformation. The *Revue indépendante* could hold to a strictly materialist line in the early part of the 1880s, but by

---

86. See Humbert, *Les Nabis*, 13, and Maurice Denis, *Du symbolisme au classicisme, théories* (Paris: Hermann, 1964), 72.

the end of the decade *La Plume* was publishing the writings of Léon Bloy. Henri Mazel, publisher of *L'Ermitage*, one of the most active symbolist journals of the 1890s, staunchly defended Christianity against science in one of the first issues of that periodical.[87] By the nineties no one would have been surprised to find Catholic sentiments in symbolist publications. It had become the norm.

Even in the eighties advanced writers had shown an abiding respect for certain aspects of radical Catholicism. J.-K. Huysmans had dedicated *A rebours* to Léon Bloy, "in hatred of the present century," and devoted part of his twelfth chapter to an appreciative discussion of the more venomous writing of several Catholic polemicists. Charles Morice, in *La Littérature de tout à l'heure*, marveled at Bloy's invective but also offered high praise for his style as a writer.[88]

There were, as we have noted, several features of the advanced art criticism of this period that fit well with the new Catholic ideals. One was the general trend toward a higher meaning in art. The way in which symbolist art criticism called for an unintellectual, emotional response on the part of artists also resembles the deep emotional response to Catholicism that was so highly praised during the Catholic revival. Both Catholicism and symbolism were entranced with the art of the late Middle Ages and both saw the abstraction of that period as preferable to and more meaningful than the realism that had dominated French art up to that time.

Each of these features demonstrates a commonality between Catholicism and symbolism that should not go unrecognized. Of course this does not mean that Catholicism and symbolism were the same thing. In essence, the general antinaturalist mood of the *fin de siècle* created the atmosphere in which opposites like avant-garde art critics and Catholic polemicists could come together. Catholics and symbolists were in accord when they spoke of reviving meaning in art, when they proselytized against materialism in painting or called for a new idealism. They could, as it turns out, also agree politically. The reactionary position of the Catholic revival could and did find echoes in the avant-garde. It is now time to discuss that aspect of symbolist art criticism.

87. Henri Mazel, "Le Problème religieux," *L'Ermitage*, 1 (May 1890), 59–69.
88. Morice, *La Littérature de tout à l'heure*, 254.

SYMBOLISM, IDEALISM, AND POLITICS

In the political realm, the symbolist generation has often been associated with the socialist/anarchist movement.[89] While such an association is partially correct it does not offer a complete picture of the politics of the symbolist writers. Not all the symbolists were socialists or anarchists; nor, for that matter, should we expect late nineteenth-century French anarchists and socialists to behave in the textbook leftist manner now understood by the term. Both Edouard Drumont and Léon Bloy, for instance, considered themselves to be socialists for a time. Paul Adam, the young critic associated with the symbolist *cénacle* of Félix Fénéon and Gustave Kahn was certainly, like his friends, drawn to the anarchist movement. In 1892 he wrote a moving elegy after the execution of the anarchist Ravachol.[90] Yet Adam had entered the political arena as a *boulangiste* candidate for deputy; even after abandoning the increasingly rightist following of General Boulanger, he spoke, in elitist fashion, against universal suffrage and for the ascendancy of "the intelligent minority" over the masses.[91] By its very hermetic nature, symbolism showed little concern with the quotidian problems of the urban worker, and the heart of its association with the political left—when such an association was operative—was a shared hatred of the establishment. While the young literary generation did include some who would be quite active politically—Adam, Fénéon, and Anatole Baju, for example—most symbolists merely sympathized with the anarchist desire to tear down contemporary republican society.

French politics at the end of the nineteenth century defy easy summation; however, two salient points pertain. The first is the remarkable fluidity of the period. The rapid change of ministries throughout the Third Republic led to a general mood of political volatility, a feeling not

89. "The symbolists and most of their friends were anarchists," John Rewald, *Post-Impressionism*, 140, noted. Robert Delevoy, *Symbolists and Symbolism*, 76–78, agreed. A good source on this question is Robert L. Herbert and Eugenia W. Herbert, "Artists and Anarchism: Unpublished Letters of Pissarro, Signac and Others," *Burlington Magazine*, cii (November 1960), 473–482; (December 1960), 517–522. See also Eugenia W. Herbert, *The Artist and Social Reform: France and Belgium, 1865–1898* (New Haven: Yale University Press, 1961).

90. Paul Adam, "Eloge de Ravachol," *Entretiens politiques et littéraires*, v (July 1892), 27–30. Ravachol [François Claudius Koenigstein] was guillotined in 1892 for anarchist activity.

91. See ibid., 27. Also see Paul Adam, "Avertissement aux prolétaires," *Entretiens politiques et littéraires*, iii (December 1891), 200.

allayed by the factual longevity of the Republic itself.[92] This, and the shifting allegiances of the Boulanger episode, occurring at precisely the time when the symbolist movement was developing strength, became manifest in the political affiliations of the new literary circles. In 1887 Anatole Baju could, in his *L'Ecole décadente*, complain of the lack of high ideals in naturalist, democratic society and, eight years later, produce a stirring pamphlet in support of the socialist cause.[93]

Even more important is the simple fact that the political establishment under attack by anarchists and symbolists alike was republican. As such, the reaction against it was as likely to come from the right as from the left—and did. Where the political affiliations of literary men hung on a skin-deep antiestablishment position, wavering between rightist and leftist sentiments was not at all uncommon. This, and the overall antinaturalist mood of the period, yielded an ironic situation in art criticism. To a great extent, the republican establishment had associated itself with naturalism in art, and naturalism in turn had always been linked with leftist, or at least liberal, social thinking.[94] Therefore, a reaction against naturalism could very well entail an equal reaction against the political attitudes with which it was associated. On the other hand, staunch conservatives, such as Joséphin Péladan, who might not ordinarily have carried much weight in avant-garde circles, were more influential because they espoused an antinaturalist position. The opposition to naturalism, which was the central focus of the critical community, served to bring together writers of divergent political stripe.

Nor should the power of the political right be underestimated. While the anarchist threat to the established order was certainly real, the republican establishment had a good deal more to fear from such traditional reactionary foes as the ultramontane Catholics. Also, throughout the eighties and nineties the right was growing as an advanced and ac-

92. See, for instance, Theodore Zeldin, *France, 1848–1945*, vol. 1 (Oxford: Clarendon Press, 1973), 570ff.

93. Compare Anatole Baju, *L'Ecole décadente* (Paris: Vanier, 1887) with the same author's *Principes du socialisme* (Paris: Vanier, 1895).

94. On the association of the republican government with naturalist painting see Weisberg, *The Realist Tradition*, 17. For the left-leaning attitude of naturalist art criticism, consider, for instance, comments from Castagnary in Linda Nochlin, *Realism and Tradition in Art, 1848–1900* (Englewood Cliffs, N.J.: Prentice-Hall, 1966), 66 and 68. Also see Joseph Sloane, *French Painting, Between the Past and the Present* (Princeton: Princeton University Press, 1951).

tive force. In opposition to the republican, positivist establishment the right would gain a certain revolutionary aura. In many circles the most up-to-the-minute political stance was reactionary, and art criticism was not unaffected by this situation.

One of the most important expressions of political content in the art criticism of the antinaturalist age was a product of the ongoing debate over the supposed opposition between art and democracy. Téodor de Wyzewa ended his 1886 article "Notes sur la peinture wagnérienne" by praising the few good artists to be found at the Salon.

> There is, through these masters, a splendid flowering of works; as if (before the imminent end of blessed inequalities) the rare DIF-FERENT souls of this time had further refined their differences, to attempt the supreme struggle. When, unbesought, the secular tide of a deluge approaches and mounts, tall men, in order not to be carried away, will right themselves and take refuge on the faraway summits. But soon the invading tide of democracy will attain their refuges: and the sons of these artists, in the equality of necessity, will renounce the vain business of an art henceforth without patronage. The day will arrive when alone will finally dominate the art of Universal Suffrage.[95]

Wyzewa's attack on the Salon was standard fare but his claim that democracy and universal suffrage were responsible for the mediocrity in the Salons is surprising. The naturalist generation had been largely egalitarian, seeking more democratic art not less. Wyzewa was unsympathetic to the needs of the masses and he was not alone.

Just three years before Wyzewa's statement Joséphin Péladan had railed against the effects democracy could have on art. Specifically castigating Proudhon, who had made so much of Courbet's socialism, Pél-

95. Téodor de Wyzewa, "Notes sur la peinture wagnérienne et le Salon de 1886," *Le Revue wagnérienne*, II (May 1886), 113. (". . . c'est, par ces maîtres, une splendide floraison d'oeuvres; comme si (devant l'imminente fin des inégalités saintes) les rares âmes DIFFERENTES de ce temps avaient affiné encore leurs différences, pour tenter les suprêmes luttes. Lorsque s'approche et monte, inimplorée, la séculaire ondée d'un déluge, les hommes de haute taille pour n'être pas emportés se redressent, et se réfugient aux sommets lointains. Mais bientôt l'envahissante marée de la démocratie atteindra leurs refuges: et les fils de ces artistes, dans l'égalité des besoins, renonceront les vains soucis d'un art désormais sans clients. Les jours arrivent où dominera seul, enfin, l'art du Suffrage Universel.")

adan warned of a bourgeois takeover of the arts. Scoffing at the Salon's acceptance that year of 5,000 out of 10,000 submissions, he warned that a wave of mediocrity was overtaking the arts and complained of the "irremediable stupidity" of the bourgeois class.[96] Thus, Péladan and Téodor de Wyzewa were of similar opinions regarding art and democracy. But Péladan voiced his opinions in the highly conservative *L'Artiste* while Wyzewa wrote for the avant-garde *Revue wagnérienne* and was editor of the left-leaning *Revue indépendante.* The art-versus-democracy debate spanned some rather broad social and cultural boundaries.

J.-K. Huysmans also disparaged the effects of democracy on art. Of course *A rebours* consisted of one long diatribe against the banality of modern democratic societies, but Huysmans's art criticism also reflected his view that art was being taken over by the masses. He complained: "The majority of the painting community is made up of sons of workers and the very low bourgeoisie; they have, for the most part, gone through primary school, knowing how to read tolerably, sometimes to write, more often to count."[97] Elsewhere he scoffed at the public for daring to think they could actually understand literature or the visual arts, noting that the ignorant art audience went with equal enthusiasm to view the work of Delacroix or Bastien-Lepage.[98] He complained bitterly that the masses were absolutely incapable of understanding the "high" sentiments of literature and painting. Like Péladan and Téodor de Wyzewa, Huysmans had moved far indeed from the pluralist attitude of early naturalist criticism.

Adolphe Retté, an intimate of symbolist circles and occasional art critic, associated democracy with naturalism and reviled both. In an article warning against the ruinous effects of anarchist/socialist thought on art, he offered a paradigm of the art-for-art's-sake mentality so central to symbolism. Addressing himself to the young generation of writers he noted:

96. Péladan, *L'Art ochlocratique,* 211. ("Cette production est monstrueuse. Le flot des médiocres, qui a déjà submergé tout le reste, submergera l'Art aussi, si l'on n'écrase sous le mépris et l'invective l'hydre de la bourgeoisie—la plus horrible, car elle n'a rien de terrible dans ses millions de têtes—que sa bêtise irrémédiable.")

97. Huysmans, "La Genèse du peintre," 22. (". . . la majorité des peintres est composée de fils d'ouvriers et de très bas bourgeois; ils ont suivi, pour la plupart, l'école primaire, savent à peu près lire, quelquefois écrire, plus souvent compter.")

98. Huysmans, *Certains* (Paris: Tresse and Stock, 1889), 11.

> Either you are sincere anarchists and . . . your writings will be combative prose designed for the people, speaking the language of the people, and, then, you will be militant sociologues—you would not be artists. *Or you are artists and . . . your unique duty is to devote your life to the defense and glorification of Art.* There is no compromise possible. The servants of Art have as exclusive mission to safeguard the tradition of the Ideal, to exalt the unique and integral Beauty, outside of all material contingencies, all social evolutions, all literary distinctions.[99]

For Retté the French Revolution was the beginning of the end for the great ideals of French art and he was intent on preventing a new socialist revolution in literature.

Emile Bernard spoke of democracy as an evil influence on art. Commenting on how he and Louis Anquetin had reacted against impressionism he declared:

> Painting out-of-doors seemed to us to be contrary to art because of its realist tendencies. Carrying the artist away from all concepts, from all interior and personal vision, it could not but add up, according to us, to a deadly and democratic system, reducing artistic production to the monotony of banality.[100]

Although this statement was made in 1932, it typifies the attitude toward democracy and art current in France during the eighties and nineties. Further, by suggesting that realism and painting out-of-doors were

99. The italics are Retté's. Adolphe Retté, "L'Art et l'anarchie," *La Jeune belgique,* xii (March 1893), 104–7. The article originally appeared in Paris—without the italics—in the 1 February 1893 issue of *La Plume.* ("Ou vous êtes des anarchistes sincères et dans ce cas votre devoir est de vous donner entièrement à vos doctrines et de les mettre en pratique, dans la mesure de vos forces jusqu'à leurs plus extrêmes conséquences, y compris la propagande par le fait; vos écrits seront des écrits de combat destinés au peuple, lui parlant sa langue; et alors, vous serez des sociologues militants—vous ne sauriez être des artistes. *Ou vous êtes des artistes et dans ce cas votre devoir unique est de vouer votre vie à la défense et à la glorification de l'Art.* Il n'existe pas de compromis possible. Les servants de l'Art ont pour mission exclusive de sauvegarder la tradition d'Idéal, d'exalter la Beauté une et toujours intégrale, hormis toutes contingences matérielles, toutes évolutions sociales, toutes distinctions d'époques littéraires.")

100. Emile Bernard, "Louis Anquetin, artiste peintre," *Mercure de France,* ccxxxix (November 1932), 594. ("Le plein air nous sembla la contraire de l'art par ses tendances réalistes. Ecartant l'artiste de toute conception, de toute vision intérieure et personelle, il ne pouvait aboutir, selon nous, qu'à un système meurtrier et démocratique, nivelant la production à la monotonie de la banalité.")

to be associated with democracy and banality, Bernard showed how antinaturalism could easily lead to, or align itself with, conservative political views.

Péladan, Téodor de Wyzewa, Huysmans, Retté, and Bernard were not
merely echoing the traditional avant-garde attitude that the general
public is incapable of understanding great new art. Certainly the symbolists in general reiterated such an ivory-tower view, the source of
which was, of course, the elitist aesthetic of Stéphane Mallarmé himself.
But there was a new element here. Now democracy was taking the
blame for the artistic situation. The impressionists, while critical of
bourgeois tastes, had made every effort to capture them as patrons. The
next generation clearly wanted no truck with any but the most refined
aesthetes. This rejection of bourgeois tastes and the implied striving after an aristocracy of artistic sensibilities could and did lead to participa-
tion in the conservative political reaction toward the Third Republic.
Once again, avant-garde and conservative viewpoints coincided. Although it would be difficult to posit an absolute relationship between
conservative politics and art criticism during the 1880s and 1890s, a
circumstantial relationship between the two did exist. As more and
more critics became disenchanted with naturalism they also came to
reject the republican establishment, which they saw as allied with naturalism. Many critics may have turned to leftist politics but many others,
both idealist and symbolist, turned increasingly to the right, and antinaturalism was the catalyst for such a change.

ANTIPOSITIVISM AND ART CRITICISM

Art criticism during the symbolist period in France was not deeply concerned with the fine points of positivist philosophy. Although any intelligent person at the time would have been aware of positivist thought,
the average art critic had no reason to delve deeply into its intricacies.
Basically, idealist and symbolist art critics thought of positivism in terms
of a materialist, pragmatic, scientific approach that, they felt, was not
necessarily appropriate to art criticism. When art critics discussed positivist ideas they usually concerned themselves with one particular writer.
Just as the neo-Catholic writers focused their hatred of positivism on
Ernest Renan, so the art critics saw the evils of positivism as represented

by the historian Hippolyte Taine. This said, it must be carefully noted that while the new Catholics all reviled Renan, Taine was not universally attacked by either symbolists or idealist critics.[101]

Hippolyte Taine was one of the most influential thinkers of the later part of the nineteenth century in France. His writings on literature and painting, which focused on the idea that race, environment, and epoch determined the nature of cultural production, were highly regarded by the youth of the 1880s. Taine was seen as one of the builders of the rationalist, positivist thought that dominated France. His ground-breaking work in the young field of psychology, as well as his historical work, made him a commanding figure in the intellectual life of this period. His lectures on aesthetics and the philosophy of art at the Ecole des Beaux-Arts were highly popular and, as Paul Bourget has noted, his students saw him as the "apostle of the New Faith," a man who would not lie to them and who would never sacrifice his principles.[102] Taine commanded immense respect as a progressive intellectual who thought clearly and without prejudice.

Among the symbolists, Charles Morice praised Taine for his historical researches and for seeing human nature as developing toward a mentality more capable of abstracting and worthy of a more fluid ideal of beauty.[103] H. R. Rookmaaker has noted that Morice may have introduced Gauguin to Carlyle's work through Taine. The title of Gauguin's *"D'où venons-nous? Que sommes-nous? Où allons-nous?"* might well have come from Taine's translation of Carlyle.[104] Taine's studies of English literature and idealism, first published in 1864, were of interest twenty years later to a generation disillusioned with French naturalism. Here were prototypes for a new idealist age, and the symbolists did not fail to take notice.[105]

The painter Maurice Denis also seems to have appreciated Taine's work. In 1896 he noted that the symbolists had "continued on the route indicated by Taine and Spencer"; in mentioning Taine along with Her-

---

101. Hamilton, *Painting and Sculpture in Europe*, 76, and H. R. Rookmaaker, *Gauguin and 19th-Century Art Theory* (Amsterdam: Swets and Zeitlinger, 1972), 110 and elsewhere, both noted that Taine influenced symbolist thinking. Burhan, "Vision and Visionaries," 19ff., also suggested that Taine was not disliked in symbolist circles. Richard Shiff, "The End of Impressionism," *Art Quarterly*, 369ff., noted that symbolists vilified Taine's determinism but appreciated his work in psychological theory.

102. Bourget, *Essais de psychologie contemporaine*, 201. (". . . l'apôtre de la Foi Nouvelle.")

103. Morice, *La Littérature de tout à l'heure*, 262.

104. Rookmaaker, *Gauguin and 19th-Century Art Theory*, 233.

105. Ibid., 40.

bert Spencer he undoubtedly referred to their work in the development of the science of psychology.[106] Taine, in *On Intelligence,* had suggested that all knowledge, all cognition, was subjective. This concept was of great importance to symbolist thought, although it was through German philosophy, particularly that of Schopenhauer, that the subjective was absorbed into symbolist art criticism. But early studies in psychology, Taine's among them, were certainly attractive to some members of the symbolist generation and, at the very least, provided some confirmation for their ideas concerning the subjective.[107]

However much Taine's contributions to the field of psychology and his studies of English literature may have influenced some of the symbolists, most of his work went unremarked in the art criticism of the period. When art critics did discuss Taine—almost exclusively in relation to his *Philosophie de l'art*—he was broadly denounced. Denunciation, however, was not a simple task. Just as it was difficult to condemn positivism itself without seeming reactionary, so too any sharp criticism of Taine required careful consideration for anyone coming of age in rationalist/positivist France. Yet Taine was attacked in both conservative and modernist camps.

The *Philosophie de l'art,* first published in the 1860s but republished often, caused a great stir in the field of art criticism. The book itself—originally presented as a series of lectures at the Ecole des Beaux-Arts—was actually quite staid. Taine defined the work of art in terms reminiscent of academic thought.[108] But his overall approach was inflammatory. Taine proposed to treat the study of art in a purely scientific manner. In his view, race, environment, and epoch combined to determine the creation of art. Taine became associated with the concept of scientific art criticism, and it was against this image that idealists and symbolists both reacted.[109]

Emile Zola, who was otherwise quite appreciative of Taine, was one of the first critics to disavow his theories openly. In an interesting article

106. Burhan, "Vision and Visionaries," 19ff.

107. Ibid., 41.

108. In his *Philosophie de l'art* (Paris: Hachette, 1893), 47, Taine said of the art work: "The work of art has for its goal to manifest some essential or salient characteristic, hence some important idea, more clearly and more completely than real objects." ("L'oeuvre d'art a pour but de manifester quelque caractère essentiel ou saillant, partant quelque idée importante, plus clairement et plus complètement que ne le font les objets réels.") The *Philosophie de l'art* is filled with definitions like this one. They are not particularly conservative, but clearly reflect academic thought.

109. See Brunius, *Mutual Aid in the Arts,* 75ff.

entitled "M. H. Taine, artiste," Zola praised Taine's intelligence and suggested that there was something artistic in the system he had created.[110] But Zola criticized the simplistic nature of the system and chided Taine for not understanding that the great artist is always beyond his time. The critic Emile Hennequin was basically a follower of Taine but ultimately rejected his concentration on race, environment, and epoch.[111] Like Zola, he sought a way beyond Taine's apparent disregard for artistic genius. Soon this became the pattern for attacks on Taine. He was seen as intelligent and challenging but insensitive to the most important aspect of art: personality. Téodor de Wyzewa, while noting that Taine had offered some important theories on artistic production, and while agreeing that artists can reveal a great deal about the culture in which they lived, also rejected Taine's determinism, believing finally that artists were "exceptional souls" owing little to their times.[112] Albert Aurier offered a similar opinion, although he considered Taine much more fully than had Wyzewa. Aurier's "Essai sur une nouvelle méthode de critique" contains a long discussion and refutation of Taine's ideas about art.[113] Like Wyzewa, Aurier chided Taine for disregarding the special qualities of the great artist and ultimately linked Taine to the realist tradition that he himself was so intent upon rejecting.

Zola, Hennequin, and Wyzewa, however, all shared a certain respect for Taine's work. Even Aurier, who argued vehemently against Taine's influence on art criticism, demonstrated respect for the historian's work in the care he devoted to his argument and the length of his treatment of Taine's *Philosophie de l'art*. Other critics were not so considerate.

Félix Fénéon offered a succinct characterization of Taine in his marvelous *Petit bottin des lettres et des arts*:

110. Emile Zola, "M. H. Taine, artiste," *Oeuvres complètes, x, oeuvres critiques* (Paris: Circle de livre précieux, 1968), 139–56.

111. Emile Hennequin, "La Critique scientifique des oeuvres d'art," *La Revue contemporaine*, v (May 1886), 3ff.; also see Enzo Caramaschi, *Essai sur la critique française de la fin-de-siècle: Emile Hennequin* (Paris: Nizet, 1974), 110–13.

112. Téodor de Wyzewa, "Une Critique," *La Revue indépendante*, i (November 1886), 50. ("Analyser une oeuvre d'art pour y découvrir l'histoire d'un temps, est une tâche méritoire, mais qui parait malaisée. Sans doute il serait précieux de retrouver dans la pensée d'un écrivain, par exemple, la peinture complète des pensées d'une époque: M. Taine, jadis, l'a glorieusement essayé. Peut-on croire qu'il y ait réussi; peut-on espérer que d'autres, jamais, y réussiront? Car les âmes des artistes sont des âmes d'exception; à leur temps elles doivent peu, beaucoup à elles-mêmes, et aux qualités anormales de leur tempérament.")

113. Aurier, *Oeuvres posthumes*, especially 176–96. Also see Mathews, *Aurier's Symbolist Art Criticism and Theory*, 97ff.

> TAINE (Hyppolyte). [He] applies to literary history the procedures
> of the science of Agronomy. In a country [he] studies the nature
> of the sun, the topography, the climate, then represents a gener-
> ation of artists as a growth of mushrooms, beets, sycamores, and
> Brussels sprouts.[114]

J.-K. Huysmans attacked Taine in both fiction and criticism. Richard
Shiff has suggested that Huysmans parodied Taine's analytical method in
A rebours.[115] In *Certains*, furthermore, Huysmans claimed:

> The theory of milieu, adapted by M. Taine to art, is correct, but
> correct in a backwards manner when it is a matter of great art-
> ists; because the environment acts on them as by revolt, by the
> hatred that it inspires in them.[116]

For Huysmans, Taine's method applied only to artists who were "sub-
alternate souls . . . whose stay-at-home imagination rivets them to the
present epoch."[117]

Although the above comments were made by critics generally associated with the avant-garde it is important to note that many conservative
critics had similar complaints about Taine's *Philosophie de l'art*. In 1875
A. Bougot, professor at the Lycée Henri IV, argued passionately against
Taine's positivist approach, again asserting that the true artist is always
better than his environment.[118] Paul Bourget, who was very much a follower of Taine through the early 1880s, also criticized his one-sided
determinism. Bourget admitted that there was a certain logic to Taine's
determinist approach but felt that "it is legitimate to hold to a contrary
point of view and to consider works of art no longer as *signifying* but as
suggesting."[119] Ernest Chesneau made a similar point reviewing the *Philos-*

---

114. Fénéon, *Oeuvres*, 548. ("TAINE (Hippolyte). Applique dans l'histoire littéraire les procédés de la science agronomique. D'un pays étudie la nature du sol, la topographie, le climat,
puis se représente une génération d'artistes comme une poussée de cèpes, de betteraves, de
sycomores et de choux de Bruxelles.")

115. Shiff, "The End of Impressionism," 370.

116. Huysmans, *Certains*, 21. ("La théorie du milieu, adaptée par M. Taine à l'art est
juste—mais juste à rebours, alors qu'il s'agit de grands artistes, car le milieu agit sur eux alors
par la révolte, par la haine qu'il leur inspire.")

117. Ibid., 22. (". . . âmes subalternes . . . dont l'imagination casanière se rive à l'époque
actuelle.")

118. A. Bougot, *Essai sur la critique d'art* (Paris: Hachette, n.d. [1875]), 46ff., 359ff.

119. Bourget, *Essais de psychologie contemporaine*, 236. ("Il est légitime de sentir ainsi,

ophie de l'art: "M. Taine is purely objective, which is excellent in matters of science but absolutely erroneous when it is a matter of the arts, where the principle is the expression of individual subjectivity."[120] Comments like these were very common in the literature of the time and were echoed by such critics as Ferdinand Brunetière and Melchior de Vogüé.[121] But Joséphin Péladan was the most virulent of all in his condemnation of Taine's thinking. In 1904 he saw fit to write a "Réfutation esthétique de Taine" in which he suggested that Taine's method made studying art somewhat like studying weeds. For Péladan, who so loved the idea of genius in art, nothing could be worse than Taine, the "grand inquisitor of positivism."[122]

Generally, then, Taine came under attack during the 1880s as the leader in an effort to make the study of art a scientific process. Whether or not these attacks did justice to Taine, it is obvious that fewer and fewer writers were willing to accept his ideas. By the early 1890s Taine had lost much of the respect he had commanded fifteen years earlier.[123]

Aside from the work of Taine, the most important attempt at creating a scientific art criticism came from Emile Hennequin. In 1886 Hennequin published, in *La Revue contemporaine*, a series of articles—later produced in book form—under the general title, "La Critique scientifique des oeuvres d'art."[124] The "Critique scientifique" was an attempt to expand upon Taine's efforts to achieve a scientifically precise criticism of art. Hennequin ultimately rejected Taine's emphasis on the determining influence of environment, but his concentration on the new sciences of psychology and sociology and the general scientific language and thrust of his work reveal his indebtedness to Taine. Unfortunately

---

comme il est légitime de s'en tenir au point de vue contraire et de considérer les oeuvres d'art non plus comme *significatives,* mais comme *suggestives.*")

120. Ernest Chesneau, "Philosophie de l'Art, par H. Taine," *L'Art,* xxx (1882), 260. ("M. Taine fait du pur objectivisme, ce qui est excellent en matière de sciences, mais absolument erroné dès qu'il s'agit des arts dont le principe est l'expression de la subjectivité individuelle.")

121. Brunetière made his comments in a review of Emile Hennequin's writings, "La Critique scientifique," *Questions de critique* (Paris: Calmann-Levy, n.d.), 297–324. Melchior de Vogüé's thoughts on the subject are voiced in "A travers l'exposition, ix, dernièrs remarques," *Revue des deux mondes,* xcvi (1 November 1889), 173ff.

122. Péladan, *L'Art idéaliste et mystique* (Paris: E. Sansot, 1909), 36.

123. Henry Béranger, "L'Art, la science et la démocratie," *Essais d'art libre,* i (February 1892), 2, noted that Taine was outmoded by 1892.

124. Emile Hennequin, "La Critique scientifique des oeuvres d'art," *La Revue contemporaine,* iv (April 1886), 449–88; v (May 1886), 3–39, (June 1886), 197–215. This work was published in book form in Paris, with very slight modifications, in 1888.

the work is filled with oversimplifications and generalizations, its argument never convincing.

In 1888, only a few weeks after publication of his articles in book form, Hennequin died in an accident while swimming in the Seine. He was only thirty years old and, having come on the Parisian literary scene only in 1882, had yet to make a profound mark on his contemporaries. Though known and respected for his erudition, Hennequin ultimately had little influence on the art criticism of his time. He had been a member of the inner circle of symbolists around Stéphane Mallarmé and one of the first critics to recognize Redon. He had produced some excellent individual critical articles, but his cursory leanings toward a theory of scientific criticism were not accepted by most of his contemporaries. His "Critique scientifique"—meant to be a major effort—was not well received in either advanced or conservative circles. Charles Morice wrote a moving eulogy to Hennequin but never mentioned his only published book.[125] Other critics openly derided it.

Georges Lecomte, editor of the symbolist *Cravache parisienne*, reviewed the "Critique scientifique" in 1888. He appreciated the author's efforts but concluded that the work was summary and offered no practical course of action.[126] Lecomte felt that Hennequin's work did not open any new way for criticism and complained that it was pseudoscientific in its use of nomenclature and terminology. Téodor de Wyzewa satirized Hennequin's proclivity for inventing scientific-sounding terms, such as "l'esthopsychologie," and suggested that the author had basically taken a series of rather common thoughts on the role of the critic and dressed them up in a new language.[127] The idealist Ferdinand Brunetière complained that Hennequin's work was full of "completely juvenile generalizations" and demonstrated "an insufficient amount of information, reading and thought." He complained bitterly of the young school that "copies religiously the jargon" of science, and he openly satirized Hennequin's terminology.[128] Albert Aurier, while praising Hennequin personally, found his work to be insufficient and superficial.[129]

125. Morice, *La Littérature de tout à l'heure*, 351–52.

126. Georges Lecomte, "L'Esthopsychologie," *La Cravache parisienne*, no. 359 (15 September 1888), unpaginated.

127. Wyzewa, "Une Critique," 50.

128. Brunetière, "La Critique scientifique," 299, 301. (". . . de généralisation toute juvénile" / ". . . de quelque insuffisance d'informations, de lectures et de réflexions." / ". . . copie religieusement le jargon.")

129. Aurier, *Oeuvres posthumes*, 184–85.

Whether coming from someone relatively close to advanced circles, like Hennequin, or from a more conservative writer, like Taine, the scientific criticism of art was largely rejected by the antinaturalist generation. It is true that the circle of writers who supported neo-impressionism—specifically Félix Fénéon, Gustave Kahn, and Paul Adam—were extremely taken with the use of scientific jargon in their criticism, but their work exhibited little, if any, affinity with the systematic approaches promulgated by Taine and Hennequin. For these writers science represented a style, a fascination, rather than a method for criticism.[130] In general the young critics and artists who concerned themselves with creating an art beyond naturalism—beyond the realities of race, environment, and epoch—could no longer hold to a criticism based upon a materialist/determinist approach. The antinaturalist age was largely unwilling to accept any constraints on the creativity and individuality of its artists.

SCIENTISM AND ART CRITICISM

The reaction against the scientific criticism of art was part of a larger question concerning the relationship between art and science, a subject widely discussed in France during the 1880s. Out of positivism and the general respect with which science had been viewed up to the 1880s there grew a belief that science could not only cure all of the world's problems but that it would also replace other human endeavors, such as art. This phenomenon, scientism, led to a widespread debate over the relative merits of art and science as forms of human investigation. This debate deserves some consideration here, but it must be understood that art critics were much less concerned with attacking science itself than scientism. Few art critics had the temerity to offer any but the most simple comments on scientific knowledge. Indeed, at first it was quite common for critics to welcome the new scientific incursions into the world of art. Only at the end of the decade was there much reaction against scientism.

The art critic of the 1880s had a good deal of scientific writing about art to consult. The work of the chemist Michel-Eugène Chevreul had

---

130. Joan U. Halperin, "Scientific Criticism and *le beau moderne* of the Age of Science," *Art Criticism*, 1 (Spring 1979), 55–71, describes well their fascination with science, noting how it was clearly an affectation.

been available for some time.[131] Charles Blanc's *Grammaire des arts du dessin* of 1867 provided references to the latest knowledge of the fledgling sciences of optics and the physics of color mixture. The work of the American physicist Ogden N. Rood and the Swiss David Sutter were well known in Paris by the early 1880s.[132] The writings of the German physicists Ernest Wilhelm von Brücke and Hermann von Helmholtz had been translated by 1878.[133] Even before Charles Henry's more famous articles on psychophysics, writers like Georges Guéroult had produced long, involved treatises meant to show how science could benefit the arts.[134] In short, scientists seemed greatly tempted and quite willing to offer information to the visual arts. They made careful disclaimers about infringing on the territory of those who made their living on aesthetic investigations, but that did not prevent them from making strong suggestions about the "true" nature of the visual arts. Charles Henry developed a complex scientific aesthetic that was of great interest to Seurat and the neo-impressionists. Georges Guéroult was capable of some rather firm statements on the visual arts. It was only natural that philosophers and critics would respond to this newfound involvement of science with the visual arts; and they did—kindly at first but with increasing hostility.

The general tenor of early commentary on scientific investigations of the visual arts was favorable. Augustin Cartault, reviewing the writings of Brücke and Helmholtz in 1879, began by questioning whether art and science were not harmful to each other, but concluded that scientific studies of the visual arts were useful as long as science did not pretend to encroach on the domain of aesthetics or philosophy.[135] The suggestion

131. Chevreul's *De la loi du contraste simultané des couleurs* was first published in Paris in 1839. A good source on some of the scientific studies about art available at this time is William I. Homer, *Seurat and the Science of Painting* (Cambridge: MIT Press, 1964).

132. Rood's *Modern Chromatics* of 1879 was translated into French in 1881. Sutter, trained in philosophy, mathematics, music, painting, and the physical sciences (see Homer, *Seurat and the Science of Painting*, 275–76) published his *L'esthétique générale et appliquée* in Paris in 1865.

133. E. W. von Brücke, *Principes scientifiques des beaux-arts suivies de l'optique et la peinture par H. Helmholtz* (Paris: G. Baillière, 1878). Helmholtz was available even earlier. Hermann von Helmholtz, *Optic physiologique*, translated by Emile Javal and N. Th. Klein (Paris: V. Masson et fils, 1867).

134. See, for example, Georges Guéroult, "Du role du mouvement des yeux dans les émotions esthétiques," *Gazette des beaux-arts*, xxiii (June 1881), 536–42, and xxiv (July 1881), 82–90; or his "Formes, couleurs et mouvements," *Gazette des beaux-arts*, xxv (February 1882), 165–79.

135. A. Cartault, "Beaux-Arts, l'art et le science dans la peinture, d'après MM. Brucke et

that art and science had their own exclusive territories was common as was the final conclusion that the new scientific approaches to the fine arts could be useful. The philosopher Jean Marie Guyau said as much in 1883. Like Cartault he was worried about the deleterious effects that science might have on the arts, but he was convinced that science could go beyond the limits of pure objective knowledge into the realm of philosophy.[136] He spoke of an ideal future in which science and art would combine to create a better world. Again, this was typical of the early critical reaction to the new scientific literature on the arts. In all, despite hesitations in some quarters, most were confident that art and science could work well together.

It is easy enough to find a parallel in avant-garde artistic circles to the more conservative writers like Guyau and Cartault. The circle of writers who supported neo-impressionist painting were all taken with the work of various scientists. The importance of Charles Henry to the neo-impressionist painters is well known and need not be recounted here.[137] But the critics who supported the neo-impressionists, and who formed one wing of the first symbolist generation, were just as enamored of Henry. Félix Fénéon wrote for a time using a kind of elitist scientific jargon which rendered some of his articles somewhat impenetrable.[138] Gustave Kahn, similarly enthralled with scientific language, produced an article for *La Vogue* called "De l'esthétique du verre polychrome," which is as difficult to decipher as anything by Fénéon.[139]

But if some members of certain symbolist groups were interested in the wonders of science, it should also be noted that neither symbolists nor conservatives were enamored of scientism. They did not believe that science would take the place of the fine arts but rather that art and science would combine to create a better world. Both went beyond a purely positivist belief in materialist science. Paul Adam eloquently at-

Helmholtz," *La Revue politique et littéraire*, VIII (21 June 1879), 1202–8. ("Ces études scientifiques sur les beaux-arts, qui seront nouvelles pour une grande partie des lecteurs, ont leur utilité. Elles ne prétendent pas empiéter sur le domaine de l'esthétique et laissant la philosophie . . . déterminer le but et la mission dernière de l'art.")

136. Jean Marie Guyau, "L'Antagonisme de l'art et de la science," *Revue des deux mondes*, LX (15 November 1883), 356–86. The quote is from page 357.

137. See Homer, *Seurat and the Science of Painting*, and José Argüelles, *Charles Henry and the Formation of a Psychophysical Aesthetic* (Chicago: University of Chicago Press, 1972).

138. This was also noted by Halperin, "Scientific Criticism and *le beau moderne* of the Age of Science."

139. Kahn, "De l'esthétique du verre polychrome," *La Vogue*, I (18 April 1886), 54–65.

tested this fact in his important introduction to Georges Vanor's *L'Art symboliste:*

> The epoch to come will be mystical. And the most astonishing of miracles is that science itself, this famous positivist and materialist science which repudiates orthodoxy, this science itself will come humbly to announce the discovery of the divine principle appearing at the bottom of its crucibles, in the artifices of its prisms, under the undulations of its acoustic cords, in the spasms of its electrified ether.[140]

This is a long way from the positivist notion that art would be rendered superfluous as science made more and more discoveries. Indeed, in spite of their willingness to accept scientific discoveries in the arts, the critics of the early 1880s, whether conservative or modernist, were by no means willing to cede to science the place they felt rightfully belonged to the arts.

Charles Henry spoke to this thought when asked what the future of art would be in a society more and more dominated by science:

> I believe in the future of an art that will be the direct opposite of all logical or historically typical method, precisely because the brain, fatigued from purely rational efforts, will need to be refreshed in completely opposite states of soul.[141]

While in the early 1880s most critics still believed that art and science could combine to create such new "states of the soul," there was an increasing consensus that the two realms were mutually exclusive. Critics began to seriously disparage science's role in the arts and, once again, the criticism came from both conservative and modernist camps.

The symbolist Albert Aurier wrote one of the strongest and most po-

---

140. Paul Adam, preface to Georges Vanor, *L'Art symboliste* (Paris: Vanier, 1889), 11. ("L'Epoque à venir sera mystique. Et le plus étonnant du miracle c'est que la science elle-même, cette fameuse science positive et matérialiste qui renia l'orthodoxie, cette science elle-même viendra humblement annoncer la découverte du principe divin apparu au fond de ses creusets, dans les artifices de ses prismes, sous l'ondoiement de ses cordes acoustiques, dans les spasmes de son éther électrique.")

141. Charles Henry, as quoted in Jules Huret, *Enquête sur l'évolution littéraire*, 415. (". . . je crois à l'avenir d'un art qui serait le contre-pied de toute méthode logique ou historique ordinaire, précisément parce que les cerveaux, fatigués d'efforts purement rationnels, auront besoin de se retremper dans des états d'âme absolument opposés.")

etic arguments against science of any late nineteenth-century critic and his words are worth quoting at length:

> After having proclaimed the omnipotence of scientific observation and deduction for eighty years with childlike enthusiasm, and after asserting that for its lenses and scalpels there did not exist a single mystery, the nineteenth century at last seems to perceive that its efforts have been in vain, and its boast puerile. Man is still walking about in the midst of the same enigmas, in the same formidable unknown, which has become even more obscure and disconcerting since its habitual neglect. A great many scientists and scholars today have come to a halt discouraged. They realize that this experimental science, of which they were so proud, is a thousand times less certain than the most bizarre theogony, the maddest metaphysical reverie, the least acceptable poet's dream, and they have a presentiment that this haughty science which they proudly used to call "positive" may perhaps be only a science of what is relative, of appearances, of "shadows" as Plato said, and that they themselves have nothing to put on old Olympus, from which they have removed the deities and unhinged the constellations.[142]

Aurier's criticism is at its most brilliant here, the impassioned plea of an intellectual fatigued with the intrusions of science into the world of the fine arts. But Aurier was by no means alone in his condemnation of the intrusion of science into the arts.

As early as 1882 Joséphin Péladan had shown a distinct antipathy for the scientific age. He complained that "today they deny the soul in art just as they deny the soul in man. Genius has become a bodily function, the ideal a sham. To the scientific materialism of Darwin corresponds the literary materialism of M. Zola."[143] The idealist painter Edmond Aman-Jean complained bitterly of the intrusion of scientific analysis into the arts. In the following passage he appears the perfect idealist:

142. Aurier, *Oeuvres posthumes*, 293. The translation here is from Chipp, *Theories of Modern Art*, 93–94.

143. Péladan, *L'Art ochlocratique*, 15. (". . . aujourd'hui, on nie l'âme dans l'art! comme on nie l'âme dans l'homme. Le génie est une fonction, l'idéal une balançoire. Au matérialisme scientifique de Darwin correspond le matérialisme littéraire de M. Zola.")

conservative, against science and democracy, and looking for a return to a more traditional conception of art:

> Art is the prerogative of an elite which translates the sentiments of the crowd by means which the crowd does not understand, the truth of the symbol is too great and always escapes those that it symbolizes. From synthetic, which it must be, art has become analytic, more comprehensible to everyone perhaps; but it is a lie to itself and is no longer art. It has followed science instead of preceding it; it has taken in its wings under its head to make a shadow for itself and better see the objective. It has forgotten that it lives on the eternal and that it dies from analysis, that, if it is the eyes that look, it is the heart that sees.[144]

Ferdinand Brunetière saw science as a new superstition and argued that it fell far short of the degree of certitude and objectivity that was supposed of it.[145] In a passage reminiscent of Albert Aurier he stated a firm case against the pretensions of science:

> "There are no longer any mysteries," an illustrious chemist wrote formerly; and to put forward this triumphant cry what moment did he choose? It was the moment when, on all sides, the insufficiency of positivism and of naturalism became obvious even to the most prejudiced. It was the moment when it appeared that all of the questions of origin, of nature and final ends that escaped the pretensions of science are, after all, the principal questions which interest us, and that in vain for one hundred years have they tried scientifically to resolve them.[146]

144. Edmond Aman-Jean, "Puvis de Chavannes," *L'Art dans les deux mondes*, no. 172 (29 November 1890), 10–11. ("L'art est l'apanage d'une élite que traduit les sentiments de la foule avec des moyens qu'elle ne comprend pas, la vérité trop grande du symbole échappant toujours à ceux qu'il symbolise. De synthétique qu'il doit être, l'art est devenu analytique, plus compréhensible à tous peut-être; mais il s'est menti à lui-même et n'est plus de l'art. Il a suivi la science au lieu de la précéder; il a ramené ses ailes au-dessus de sa tête pour se faire de l'ombre et mieux voir l'objectif; il oublie qu'il vit d'éternité et qu'il meurt d'analyse; que, si les yeux regardent, c'est le coeur qui voit.")

145. Brunetière, *Questions de critique*, 318–19.

146. Brunetière, *La Renaissance de l'idéalisme*, 34–35. ("Il n'y a plus de mystères,' s'écriait jadis un illustre chimiste; et, pour pousser ce cri de triomphe, quel moment choisissait-il?

The writer Rémy de Gourmont, who was close to Aurier and certainly one of the leading figures of the later stages of symbolism, carried the campaign against science into the early years of this century:

> Science is the only truth and it is the great lie. It knows nothing and they believe that it knows everything. They slander it. They believe that science is electricity, automobilism, and dirigible balloons. It is quite something else. It is life devouring itself, it is sensibility transforming itself into intelligence, it is the need to know suffocating the need to live, it is the genius of knowledge dissecting, while still alive, the vital genius.[147]

So, there were two sides to the art versus science debate in art criticism. Right through the end of the nineteenth century artists and critics were enamored of science and sought to mix science and the arts—one thinks, for instance, of Paul Sérusier with his interest in mathematics. Just so there were critics who fought heartily against the intrusion of science into the domain of art. For our purposes it is noted that the two sides of the argument did not necessarily represent a conservative/avant-garde split. The debate on the merits of science in the arts crossed such boundaries and again demonstrates how conservative and modernist critics agreed on certain points and how symbolist criticism was deeply rooted in the ideas of its time.

We have also touched here on a problem that needs further discussion. In the 1880s the relationship between science and art was manifested primarily in neo-impressionism, and one of the most important reactions against science in the arts came in the form of adverse criticism of neo-impressionist painting. In Chapter 4 we will discuss this

C'était le moment où, de toutes parts, l'insuffisance du positivisme et du naturalisme éclatait aux yeux même des plus prévenus. C'était le moment où il apparaissait que toutes ces questions d'origine, de nature et de fin, qui échappent aux prétentions de la science, sont après tout les principales questions qui nous intéressent tous; et qu'en vain depuis cent ans avait-on scientifiquement essayé de les résoudre.")

147. Rémy de Gourmont, *Promenades philosophiques* (Paris: Mercure de France, 1905), 128. ("La science est la seule vérité et elle est le grand mensonge. Elle ne sait rien, et on croit qu'elle sait tout. On la calomnie. On croit que la science, c'est l'électricité, l'automobilisme et les ballons dirigeables. C'est bien autre chose. C'est la vie se dévorant elle-même, c'est la sensibilité se transformant en intelligence, c'est le besoin de savoir étouffant le besoin de vivre, c'est le génie de la connaissance disséquant tout vivant le génie vital.")

situation since it can shed light on the way traditionalist, idealist thought came to dominate the symbolist movement by the end of the 1880s. For now one further concept will serve to demonstrate the proximity between advanced and conservative art criticism during the 1880s: the concept of "synthesis."

SYNTHÈSE AND ART CRITICISM

As H. R. Rookmaaker has noted, the term *synthèse* was one of the more popular catchwords used in French art criticism during the 1880s and early 1890s.[148] Like other terms current at this time, such as *symbole, suggestion,* or *idéal,* it was used so frequently its meaning tended to become blurred. Nevertheless, Rookmaaker has shown that *synthèse,* as used among the modernists, did have specific connotations that are of interest as a final example of similarity between idealist and symbolist thinking on art.[149]

Rookmaaker, who limited his discussion to the "synthetist" art theories of the Gauguin circle, basically saw the term as being used in two different but clearly related manners. The term was used, first, to denote a combination or unification of separate elements. This is certainly what Albert Aurier meant when he referred to the work of art as "*a new being . . . which is the very synthesis of two souls, the soul of the artist and the soul of nature.*"[150] In this sense *synthèse* often indicated the opposite of (or next step after) the process of analysis. Analysis was seen as the dissection or examination of objects—taking them apart—and the job of synthesis was to put things together again, to make them whole. Charles Morice saw the duty of the new literature to be the synthesis of all the analytical work of previous schools.[151] Maurice Denis spoke of the "triumph of the spirit of synthesis over the spirit of analysis."[152] The second use of the term was as a distillation or simplification of things in order to get at their essence. In this sense *synthèse* meant the elimination of detail in art in order to concentrate on essentials. It was in this

---

148. Rookmaaker, *Gauguin and 19th-Century Art Theory,* 176.

149. Ibid., 176–86. Also see Vojtech Jirat-Wasiutynski, *Paul Gauguin in the Context of Symbolism* (New York: Garland, 1977), 50–59.

150. Aurier, *Oeuvres posthumes,* 303. (". . . *un être nouveau . . .* qui est même la synthèse de deux âmes, l'âme de l'artiste et l'âme de la nature.")

151. Morice, *La Littérature de tout à l'heure,* 358.

152. Denis as quoted in Rookmaaker, *Gauguin and 19th-Century Art Theory,* 177.

context that Albert Aurier used the term in an article on the painter Jean-François Raffaëlli in which he suggested that Raffaëlli's art lacked the "great synthesis of general forms." This synthesis could be found in an artist like Daumier, whose work was "less *exact*, perhaps, but undoubtedly more *true*."[153]

Rookmaaker concluded his discussion of *synthèse* with the thought that ultimately the term connoted the primacy of the artist over nature. The artist does not merely analyze nature but offers a synthesis of the important elements of nature. The work of synthesis is the prerogative of the artist and as such lies at the very heart of the creative act. It also lies at the very heart of antinaturalism. Just as the generation of the 1880s saw naturalism as the slavish imitation of nature so too they saw synthesis as the artist's dominance of nature and the way beyond the naturalist dilemma. What should be stressed here is that the concept of synthesis was found in both symbolist and conservative circles, and that the symbolists did not invent it. They adapted it to their own use.

The academician Victor Cherbuliez noted in 1891, "to idealize, this is not to embellish things, it is to give them style"; and he defined style as "the spirit of synthesis, which summarizes a crowd of details in a single one that it accentuates and that takes the place of all the others."[154] This use of the term is similar to what Rookmaaker outlined in relation to the Gauguin circle, but we should not interpret this to mean that avant-garde thinking had penetrated academic ranks. The opposite is true: both the term *synthèse* and the concept behind it had been a part of more conservative thinking about art before it became current in modernist art criticism. For instance, as early as 1883 Joséphin Péladan had said that "the first secret of tradition is that art must be a synthesis."[155] He explained how the great artists of the past had offered an expressive synthesis of a particular ideal type and complained:

> But let's leave aside expressive synthesis, contemporary art doesn't even offer a plastic synthesis, it copies the model when it

153. Aurier, *Oeuvres posthumes*, 250. (". . . large synthèse des formes générales" / ". . . moins *exact*, peut-être, mais, indiscutablement, c'est plus *vrai*.")

154. Victor Cherbuliez, "L'Art et la nature," *Revue des deux mondes*, LXI (15 August 1891), 741. ("Idéaliser, ce n'est pas embellir les choses, c'est leur donner du style." / ". . . l'esprit de synthèse, qui résume une foule de détails dans un seul qu'il accentue et qui tient lieu de tous les autres.")

155. Péladan, *L'Art ochlocratique*, 53. ("Le premier arcane de la tradition, c'est que l'art doit être une synthèse.")

> should transfigure it. Because synthesis has as its only object to transfigure the human being, whether one obtains this by the purity of forms, like the Italians, by light like Rembrandt, by the lively accent, like Rubens and Velásquez.[156]

Péladan saw synthesis not only as a central feature of art but also as the artist's method for going beyond nature. Like the symbolists, he praised synthesis over analysis, strongly preferring the "synthetic landscapes of Millet, Rousseau, Daubigny, Corot" over the "analytic landscapes" of more contemporary painters.[157] Charles Blanc also offered a thought very similar to such an understanding of synthesis when he spoke of *le style* as "the imprint of human thought on nature," and noted:

> The painter of style sees the grand side of things, even of little things, the realistic imitator sees the small side, even of grand things. A work has style when objects are represented under their typical aspect, in their primitive essence, disengaged of all insignificant detail, and by that, simplified, aggrandized.[158]

Albert Aurier certainly would have agreed with such an idea.

Clearly, Blanc, Péladan, and Cherbuliez all offer a traditional, academic point of view, handed down from neo-classical art theory. The artist's duty is to change nature, to improve upon it in order to bring out its essence. My suggestion here is that *synthèse*, as used in the art criticism of this period, was not so essentially different from this older tradition. Of course the symbolists did not have the same kind of art in mind when they spoke of synthesis but the idea itself was not new, only the art toward which that idea was directed.

The term *synthèse* was used very early on in discussions of Puvis de Chavannes. As early as 1881 the critic Roger-Ballu saw in Puvis's *Pauvre*

---

156. Ibid. ("Mais laissons là la synthèse expressive, l'art contemporain ne fait pas même de synthèse plastique, il copie le modèle, alors qu'il devrait le transfigurer. Car la synthèse n'a pour objet que d'atteindre à la transfiguration de l'être humain, qu'on l'obtienne par l'épuration des formes comme les Italiens, par la lumière comme Rembrandt, par l'accent vivace comme Rubens et Velásquez.")

157. Ibid. ("paysage synthétique," "paysage analytique")

158. Blanc, *Grammaire des arts du dessin*, 20. (". . . l'empreinte de la pensée humaine sur la nature." / "Le peintre de style voit le grand côté, même des petites choses, l'imitateur réaliste voit le petit côté, même des grandes. Un ouvrage a du style lorsque les objets y sont représentés sous leur aspect typique, dans leur primitive essence, dégagés de tous les détails insignifiants, et par cela même simplifiés, agrandis.")

Pêcheur "a complete synthesis of misery, powerfully expressed by the paintbrush, inexpressible by the pen."[159] In 1884 another conservative critic said of Puvis: "What interests him is not the detail of form, the suppleness of modeling, the anecdotal accidents of life; all of his thoughts turn toward synthesis, all his predilections toward grand spectacles, solemn and tranquil."[160] Indeed, throughout the eighties and nineties there was much discussion of the ways in which Puvis's art deviated from nature and how a synthesis of the objective world was the essential feature of his art. Much of what was said about Puvis was couched in an effort to "explain" why he simplified nature. The approach taken by many conservative critics in regard to his work was to instruct the public, as it were, to teach them that servile imitation of nature was not the object of art.[161] Interestingly, this was very similar to arguments put forward by Albert Aurier concerning the art of Gauguin.[162] Yet many of the critics who supported Puvis's art would not condone Gauguin's synthesis.

Georges Lecomte, who had been editor of *La Cravache parisienne* during the years when the symbolists controlled it, praised Puvis de Chavannes for the power he attained through synthesis and simplification.[163] Yet concerning Gauguin and his followers he said, "under pretext of synthesis and decoration they cover canvases with flat tones that don't reproduce the luminous limpidity of the atmosphere, don't give the surroundings of things, depth or aerial perspective."[164] Speaking of both Puvis and the Gauguin circle, Alphonse Germain said: "the most artistic synthesis of modeling is found in the drawing of Ingres and Puvis

159. Roger-Ballu, "Le Salon de 1881," *La Nouvelle revue*, x (May–June 1881), 451. ("Je vois là toute une synthèse de la misère, puissamment exprimée par le pinceau, inexprimable par la plume.")

160. Michel, "Le Salon de 1884," 183. ("Ce qui l'intéresse, ce n'est pas le détail de la forme, les souplesses du modelé, les accidents anecdotiques de la vie; toutes ses pensées vont à la synthèse, toutes ses prédilections aux grands spectacles, graves et tranquilles.")

161. A typical example is André Michel, "Exposition de M. Puvis de Chavannes," *Gazette des beaux-arts*, xxxvii (January 1888), 37–44.

162. Aurier, *Oeuvres posthumes*, 205–19.

163. Georges Lecomte, "Le Salon du Champ-de-Mars," *L'Art dans les deux mondes*, no. 26 (16 May 1891), 309.

164. Georges Lecomte, "Salon des XX, conférence de M. Georges Lecomte, des tendances de la peinture moderne," *L'Art moderne*, xii (28 February 1892), 66–67. ("Sous prétexte de synthèse et de décoration, on couvre les toiles de teintes plates qui ne restituent point les lumineuses limpidités de l'atmosphère, ne donnent point l'enveloppement des choses, la profondeur, la perspective aérienne.")

de Chavannes—our synthesophile deformers go back to prehistoric techniques."[165] Calling the Gauguin circle *synthesophiles déformateurs* was a clear indication that for Germain they had gone too far in their synthesis, a synthesis he had praised in Puvis de Chavannes.

What was condoned and even praised in the art of Puvis de Chavannes was not tolerated in the work of Gauguin. Why? Style was the key. Most critics were unable to get beyond Gauguin's radically different style to realize that the very concept of synthesis so admired in Puvis was equally applicable to Gauguin. Gauguin and the critics who supported his art accentuated synthesis—"Groupe Impressionniste et Synthétiste" was the label under which Gauguin and his friends exhibited in 1889. The symbolists themselves spoke proudly of the deformations in the art of Gauguin.[166] They took an idea current in conservative circles, an idea very much in the air, and focused upon it. Finally, it was the *art* of painters like Gauguin that was so different and special, not the *idea* of synthesis. Synthesis itself was common coin at this time, shared by conservative and avant-garde alike. As with all of the other concepts discussed in this chapter, synthesis serves to demonstrate the intellectual context of the symbolist criticism of art. Seen in this way the ideas of symbolist critics often appear less radical than they have been portrayed, less innovative and more in tune with the general thought of the age of antinaturalism.

165. Alphonse Germain, "Théorie des déformateurs, exposé et réfutation," *La Plume*, III (1 September 1891), 290. ("La plus artistique synthèse de la plastique se trouve en le dessin d'Ingres et de Puvis de Chavannes,—nos synthesophiles déformateurs recoururent à des technies [*sic*] préhistoriques.")

166. Aurier, *Oeuvres posthumes*, 195. Also see Denis, *Théories*, 118–19, where he speaks of "subjective deformation" and "objective deformation."

3

SYMBOLISM DIVIDED:

FÉLIX FÉNÉON
AND THE
DEFENSE
OF
MODERNISM

One of the most prolific and stimulating art critics of the young symbolist writers, Félix Fénéon published over seventy articles in various periodicals between 1883 and 1896 and edited several of the ephemeral symbolist journals of the period. Indeed, he not only established himself as the definitive voice of neo-impressionism but also as a wry observer of all artistic trends. Recent art history and literary history have rightly praised Fénéon's sagacity and correctly upheld his importance in the development of symbolist art criticism.[1] But no consideration of Fé-

---

1. On Fénéon see Joan U. Halperin, *Félix Fénéon, Aesthete and Anarchist in Fin-de-Siècle Paris* (New Haven: Yale University Press, 1988); and Halperin, *Félix Fénéon and the Language of Art Criticism* (Ann Arbor: UMI Research Press, 1980). Also see her introduction to Fénéon, *Oeuvres*. Other important discussions of Fénéon as art critic may be found in Félix Fénéon, *Au-*

néon's work is complete without some recognition of just how precise—indeed, limited—his admirations were. This chapter, which begins with a few general considerations and then winds its way somewhat circuitously back to Fénéon himself, is meant to expand our understanding of this important symbolist critic and, thereby, of the movement itself.

Who were the major symbolist art critics? Any compilation would certainly begin with someone like Fénéon, or, perhaps, J.-K. Huysmans, or G.-Albert Aurier. Huysmans began writing art criticism in the 1860s but it was in 1883, with publication of *L'Art moderne*, an anthology of articles on impressionist painters, that he was firmly established as a critic of note, albeit still a naturalist critic at that point.[2] *L'Art moderne* was followed by important discussions of Gustave Moreau, Rodolphe Bresdin, and Odilon Redon in both the novel *A rebours* and a second anthology, *Certains*, published in 1889. Here he promoted a highly antinaturalist aesthetic. Throughout the 1880s, Huysmans's art criticism appeared in such important symbolist journals as *La Cravache parisienne*, *La Plume*, and, especially, the *Revue indépendante*.

Albert Aurier began writing art criticism in 1888 and, in spite of his premature death in 1893, achieved prominent status in avant-garde art circles.[3] He not only produced the first article about Vincent van Gogh and the first major study of Paul Gauguin but wrote about many other artists as well. He was founder of one small periodical—*Le Moderniste*—and art critic for the highly influential *Mercure de France*. Of all the critics associated with the symbolist movement, Aurier was the one most concerned with defining symbolism in painting.

A number of other art critics were associated with symbolist circles at one time or another, in one capacity or another. The painter Maurice Denis, for instance, wrote a good deal about art, although much of what he wrote came after the turn of the century in the form of reminiscences about the symbolist generation. The ten articles he produced before 1900 do, however, qualify him as an important symbolist critic. Emile

---

delà de *l'impressionnisme* (Paris: Hermann, 1966); Lövgren, *The Genesis of Modernism* (Bloomington: Indiana University Press, 1971); and John Rewald, "Félix Fénéon," *Gazette des beaux-arts*, XXXII (July–August 1947), 45–62, and XXXIII (February 1948), 107–26.

2. On Huysmans see Annette Kahn, *J.-K. Huysmans, Novelist, Poet and Art Critic*; Maingon, *L'Univers artistique de J.-K. Huysmans*; and Anita Brookner, *The Genius of the Future, Studies in French Art Criticism* (London: Phaidon, 1971), 147–67.

3. On Aurier see Mathews, *Aurier's Symbolist Art Criticism and Theory*; and Lunn, "G.-Albert Aurier."

Hennequin wrote significant early studies of Redon's art and produced some stimulating criticism for the popular and widely read *La Vie moderne*. His attempt at developing an aesthetic theory was, however, as noted in Chapter 2, not particularly well received, and he died too early to have a lasting influence on the symbolist generation. Two young members of the symbolist circle at the *Revue indépendante* and *La Vogue*, Gustave Kahn and Paul Adam, both wrote early appreciations of neo-impressionism although neither focused on art criticism subsequently.[4] Téodor de Wyzewa, founder of the *Revue wagnérienne*, wrote a few studies of painting that show an interest in avant-garde trends but later he disavowed the symbolist camp.

Still other names can be, and indeed have been, associated with symbolist art criticism. Charles Morice, Octave Mirbeau, Edouard Dujardin, the important Belgian critic Emile Verhaeren, and the painter Emile Bernard all produced criticism that might justifiably be called symbolist. A creditable case has been made for calling Joséphin Péladan a symbolist.[5] Finally, one should also not forget such second-generation figures as Camille Mauclair and Alphonse Germain, both of whom will be the focus of a later chapter.

These then are many, if not precisely all, of the writers generally noted as symbolist critics of art. It is a varied and problematic list; problematic precisely because it is so varied. It might be said that all of these men were symbolist critics, but by doing so we risk an implicit assumption that they were part of a single purposeful group of symbolist writers.[6] The opposite was true. Although they often shared certain attitudes, the symbolists just as often argued among themselves, reserving some of their most violent criticism for "in-house" discussions. Not only did sym-

4. On Paul Adam see Paul Smith, "Paul Adam, *Soi* et les 'Peintres impressionnistes': la genèse d'un discours moderniste," *Revue de l'art*, no. 82 (1988), 39–50.

5. See Robert Pincus-Witten, *Occult Symbolism in France, Joséphin Péladan and the Salons de la Rose-Croix* (New York: Garland, 1976).

6. Elizabeth Martin, "The Symbolist Criticism of Painting" (Ph.D. dissertation, Bryn Mawr College, 1948), for example, treats the literary movement from decadence to symbolism to idealism in the 1890s as a linear development of essentially the same goals. On the other hand, Jacques Lethève, *Impressionnistes et symbolistes devant la presse*, 196–204, noted the struggles between various factions of the movement. For more on this subject see my "In 1891: Observations on the Nature of Symbolist Art Criticism," *Arts Magazine*, LXI (January 1987), 88–93. A fine treatment of some of the complexities of Parisian art criticism in the 1890s will be found in Constance Naubert-Riser, "La Critique des années 1890, impasse méthodologique ou renouvellement des modèles théoriques?" in *La Critique d'art en France, 1850–1900*, 193–204.

bolists wrangle among themselves, they also defected in large numbers. Very few of the critics in the list noted above remained symbolists throughout their careers.

The very proliferation of small, short-lived periodicals during the symbolist era stands as witness to the factional character of the movement. As early as 1911 André Barre, in his history of literary symbolism, noted that the very number of symbolist publications indicated a lack of unanimity in the movement.[7] Barre felt that at the period of greatest symbolist activity there were at least four different groups that could lay claim to the name "symbolist." The differences between these groups were, in reality, greater than we might at first think. Even the greatest heroes of the movement were not necessarily respected by all symbolists. Adolphe Retté, who very much considered himself to be a symbolist and wrote one of the earliest memoirs of the movement, was proud to declare in 1903: "I have denounced a hundred times, with a liveliness that some will not pardon, the baleful influence of the deceased Stéphane Mallarmé."[8] While such a denunciation of the single most important influence on the development of symbolism must be seen as an aberration, it demonstrates how stridently these writers maintained their individuality. Symbolism was highly factional, as Gustave Kahn noted in an anecdote concerning the writer and mystic Stanislas de Guaïta. In the preface to a volume of poetry de Guaïta enumerated all the interesting poets he knew of. Then, doubting the inclusiveness of his list, he added: "There are others perhaps, but I don't know them; in any case they don't come to my café."[9] The bitter fight between one particular circle calling themselves decadents and another calling themselves symbolists also illustrates the lack of accord between factions of the new literature.

Historians of symbolism generally agree that before there were symbolists in Paris there were decadents, and that the latter initiated the movement that would become symbolism.[10] There is ample reason for

7. André Barre, *Le Symbolisme*, 96.

8. Adolphe Retté, *Le Symbolisme* (Paris: Vanier, 1903), 7. (". . . j'ai dénoncé cent fois, avec une vivacité que certains ne me pardonnent pas, l'influence néfaste de feu Stéphane Mallarmé.")

9. Gustave Kahn, *Symbolistes et décadents* (Paris: Vanier, 1902), 40. (". . . il y en a peut-être d'autres, mais je ne les connais pas; en tout cas, ils ne viennent pas à mon café.")

10. See, for instance, Noël Richard, *A l'aube du symbolisme* (Paris: Nizet, 1961), and Guy Michaud, *Message poétique du symbolisme* (Paris: Nizet, 1947). An important recent study has suggested that the accepted view of a transition from decadence to symbolism has been over-

such an assessment, both chronological and intellectual. J.-K. Huysmans's *A rebours*—certainly the single greatest exposition of the decadent mentality—predates the use of the term *symbolism* in Paris by two years and yet it embodies much of the essence of symbolist ideas. Indeed, it is a major statement of both decadence and symbolism. Yet the many similarities between these two "isms" should not hide their differences.

Decadence was less a unified movement than a reaction to naturalism. It was generally more negative than symbolism, more concerned with a desire to shock, to oppose the pragmatic, sensible, naturalist/positivist position. The hero of *A rebours*, the duke Jean Floressas des Esseintes, was at once the perfect embodiment of decadence and a main stimulus of the movement. Everything in his character was opposed to the ordinary, the everyday, the natural. Des Esseintes's turtle, encrusted with jewels until it died, his living room into which no natural light was allowed to penetrate, and his incredible recipes for enemas are all allegorical statements of the antinaturalist position at the same time that they are perversions of the natural world. An entire generation of writers grew up in Europe with Des Esseintes as their hero, seeking to emulate his hothouse refinement and his monumental dandyism. But other streams fed the decadent mood as well.

Paul Bourget, in his popular *Essais de psychologie contemporaine* of 1881, offered a definition of the decadent style in art:

> By the word decadence one willingly designates the state of a society that produces too small a number of individuals suited to the labors of the common life. A society should be like an organism. Like an organism, in fact, it may be resolved into a federation of lesser organisms, which themselves are resolved into a federation of cells. The individual is the social cell. For the total organism to function with energy it is necessary that the least cells function with energy, but with a subordinate energy, and for these lesser organisms themselves to function with energy it is necessary that the cells that make them up function with energy, but with a subordinate energy. If the energy of the cells becomes independent, the lesser organisms will likewise cease to subordi-

---

emphasized: see Jean Pierrot, *The Decadent Imagination, 1880–1900* (Chicago: University of Chicago Press, 1981).

nate their energy to the total energy and the anarchy that is established constitutes the decadence of the whole. The social organism does not escape this law. It enters into decadence as soon as the individual life is exaggerated under the influence of acquired well-being and heredity. A similar law governs the development and decadence of that other organism which is language. A style of decadence is one in which the unity of the book is decomposed to give place to the independence of the page, in which the page is decomposed to give place to the independence of the sentence, and the sentence to give place to the independence of the word.[11]

In essence, he defined the decadent style as a self-indulgent one, unconcerned with the "health" of literature itself. Elsewhere in the same essay—an essay on Charles Baudelaire—Bourget suggested that sickness and health were two sides of the natural psychological condition and that, indeed, there was often more of the ideal to be found in sickness than in health.[12] Such comments were as manna to a generation enchanted with decay.

In painting, artists such as Gustave Moreau, with his overrefined, jewel-like visions of the mythology of evil, and Félicien Rops, with his pornographic etchings, were only the most important artists to speak to the decadent mood. In the Salons of the eighties it became fashionable to offer images of "decadent" historical periods. Cabanel's *Cleopatra*

11. Paul Bourget, *Essais de psychologie contemporaine*, 19–20. ("Par le mot de décadence, on désigne volontiers l'état d'une société qui produit un trop petit nombre d'individus propres aux travaux de la vie commune. Une société doit être assimilée, à un organisme. Comme un organisme, en effet, elle se résout en une fédération d'organismes moindres, que se résolvent eux-mêmes en une fédération de cellules. L'individu est la cellule sociale. Pour que l'organisme total fonctionne avec énergie, il est nécessaire que les organismes moindres fonctionnent avec énergie, mais avec une énergie subordonnée, et, pour que ces organismes moindres fonctionnent eux-mêmes avec énergie, il est nécessaire que leurs cellules composantes fonctionnent avec énergie, mais avec une énergie subordonnée. Si l'énergie des cellules devient indépendante, les organismes que composent l'organisme total cessent pareillement de subordonner leur énergie à l'énergie totale, et l'anarchie qui s'établit constitue la décadence de l'ensemble. L'organisme social n'échappe pas à cette loi. Il entre en décadence aussitôt que la vie individuelle s'est exagérée sous l'influence du bien-être acquis et de l'hérédité. Une même loi gouverne le développement et la décadence de cet autre organisme qui est le langage. Un style de décadence est celui où l'unité du livre se décompose pour laisser la place à l'indépendance de la page, où la page se décompose pour laisser la place à l'indépendance de la phrase, et la phrase pour laisser la place à l'indépendance du mot.")

12. Ibid., 11.

Testing Poisons on Prisoners Condemned to Die—whose title is also a description—and Laurens's *Emperor Honorius, the Low Empire*—showing the child on the throne of Imperial Rome—are examples of the genre. On a popular level Parisians became fascinated with images of decadence and delighted in the dubious pleasures of contemplating them. It was only a short step from enjoying the strangely bizarre to cultivating a taste for a decadent style—a step that had been greatly stimulated by Théophile Gautier in his famous preface to Baudelaire's *Les Fleurs du mal.* Written in 1867—but, significantly, published in a new edition in 1883—Gautier's preface offered much of what would later seem so shocking to a wider audience reading Huysmans's *A rebours:* praise of the deliquescent style of dying civilizations, love of the artificial, and "health" in "sickness."[13] Gautier's description of the decadent style— evoking, as it did, a sensitivity to "the subtle whispers of neurosis, the confessions of aging passions which have become depraved, and the bizarre hallucinations of obsession turning to madness"—did not, as Gustave Kahn later noted, fall upon deaf ears.[14]

The decadent mood, far from being something to fear, became a thing to revel in, to seek after as a literary style of infinite refinement. Anatole Baju's preface to the first edition of his *Le Décadent littéraire et artistique* was a case in point worth quoting at length here:

> To hide the state of decadence in which we find ourselves would be the height of insensitivity. Religion, morals, justice, all are in decadence, or rather all submit to an ineluctable transformation. Society is breaking up under the corrosive action of a deliquescent civilization. Modern man is indifferent.
>
> Refinement of appetites, of sensations, of the taste for luxury, of pleasures; neurosis, hysteria, hypnotism, morphinomania, scientific charlatanism, excessive Schopenhauerism, such are the first symptoms of the social revolution.
>
> It is in language above all that the first symptoms are made manifest. New ideas, subtle and infinitely nuanced, correspond

13. Charles Baudelaire, *Les Fleurs du mal, précédées d'une notice par Théophile Gautier* (1868; Paris: Calmann-Levy, 1883).

14. Kahn, *Symbolistes et décadents,* 34. The quote from Gautier is in Baudelaire, *Les Fleurs du mal, précédées d'une notice par Théophile Gautier,* 17. (". . . les confidences subtiles de la névrose, les aveux de la passion vieillissante qui se déprave et les hallucinations bizarres de l'idée fixe tournant à la folie.")

> to new needs. From this the necessity to create unheard vocables
> to express such a complexity of feelings and physiological sensa-
> tions.
>
> . . . We will be the guardians of an ideal literature, the precur-
> sors of a latent transformism that will undermine the superim-
> posed stratas of classicism, of romanticism and of naturalism; in a
> word we will be the madhis eternally proclaiming the elixirific
> dogma, the quintessential word of triumphant decadentism.[15]

Clearly Baju delighted in the very word "decadent." But, for all his
proclamations of a new style, it was not Baju nor those who clung to the
title "decadent" that would create the new literature. It was the symbolists.

The symbolists—and here I refer specifically to the group of writers
who gathered around *La Vogue* and the *Revue indépendante, Le Symboliste,* and *La Cravache* in 1886–88—were concerned with building a new
poetry, under the influence of Mallarmé, on the ruins of naturalist literature. Though they shared many traits and tastes with the decadents
they tended to see decadence as too flamboyant, a short-lived and ultimately unimportant phenomenon. Georges Vanor, for instance, violently attacked the decadents in his *L'Art symboliste* of 1889.[16] Vanor felt
that all of the problems with decadence could be attributed to Anatole
Baju and the group of "hack writers" that he gathered around him at *Le*

---

15. Originally, Anatole Baju, "Aux lecteurs," *Le Décadent littéraire et artistique* (10 April
1886). The quote here is taken from Jacques Lethève, *Impressionnistes et symbolistes devant la
presse,* 188. ("Se dissimuler l'état de décadence où nous sommes arrivés serait le comble de
l'insenséisme. Religion, moeurs, justice, tout décade, ou plutôt tout subit une transformation
inéluctable. La société se desagrège sous l'action corrosive d'une civilisation déliquescente.
L'homme moderne est un blasé.

Affinements d'appétits, de sensations, de goût de luxe, de jouissances; névrose, hystérie,
hypnotisme, morphinomanie, charlatanisme scientifique, schopenhauerisme à outrance, tels
sont les prodromes de l'évolution sociale.

C'est dans la langue surtout que s'en manifestent les premiers symptômes. A des besoins
nouveaux correspondent des idées nouvelles, subtiles et nuancées à l'infini. De là la nécessité
de créer des vocables inouïs pour exprimer une telle complexité de sentiments et de sensations
physiologiques. Nous ne nous occuperons de ce mouvement qu'au point de vue de la littérature. Le décadence politique nous laisse frigides.

. . . Nous serons les vedettes d'une littérature idéale, les précurseurs du transformisme latent
qui affouille les strates superposées du classicisme, du romantisme et du naturalisme; en un mot
nous serons les madhis clamant éternellement le dogme élixirisé, le verbe quintessencié du
décadisme triomphant.")

16. Vanor, *L'Art symboliste,* 13ff.

Décadent. These poets and critics, Vanor felt, had compromised Mallarmé and Verlaine by proclaiming their own subservience to the two older poets.[17] Worst of all he worried that the Parisian public had long confused the two movments of symbolism and decadence, which he felt were seemingly analogous but essentially opposed. He punned that the public stupidly confused the *sornettes,* or nonsense, of René Ghil—a frequent collaborator at *Le Décadent*—with the sonnets of Verlaine.

In the pages of their short-lived review *Le Symboliste,* Gustave Kahn, Jean Moréas, and Paul Adam fervently derided the decadents, in spite of the fact that they had all published in Baju's magazine.[18] Paul Adam in 1886 called the decadents "very young men . . . as unskilled at writing as at thinking."[19] Like Vanor three years later, he worried that the Parisian press confused the two movements, complaining that the critics could not distinguish between the ideas of Moréas and those of the hated Ghil and Baju. The press never tired, according to Adam, of reproducing the "diabolical naïvetés" of *Le Décadent,* while they never delved into the pages of *La Vogue,* "the only admitted periodical."[20]

Anatole Baju, for his part, was no less vehemently antisymbolist. In an article from 1888, meant to set the record straight, he tried to show that decadence was the movement of progress in literature while symbolism was a regression to the thought of the Middle Ages.[21] Baju called the symbolists "pseudo-decadents" and claimed that they merely followed, without adding anything new, the decadent mentality: "Incapable of creating, they [the symbolists] have tried to hoard the work of the Decadents: they are the parasites of an idea."[22]

The general tone of the two groups certainly differed dramatically. Baju's writing, as well as most of what was published in *Le Décadent,*

17. Compromised or not, Verlaine published in *Le Décadent* as did Mallarmé and Paul Adam.

18. Years later Gustave Kahn, *Symbolistes et décadents,* 42, admitted that it may have been a mistake to publish there.

19. Adam, "La Presse et le symbolisme," *Le Symboliste,* i (7–14 October 1886), unpaginated; as reprinted in Moréas, *Les Premièrs armes du symbolisme* (Paris: Vanier, 1889), 59. ("De très jeunes gens . . . inhabiles à écrire comme à penser.")

20. Moréas, *Les Premières armes du symbolisme,* 60. (". . . les diaboliques naïvetés" / ". . . seule revue admis") Charles Morice, *La Littérature de tout à l'heure,* 230–31, makes similar comments.

21. Anatole Baju, "Décadents et symbolistes, "*Le Décadent,* iii (15–30 November 1888), 1–2.

22. Ibid., 2. ("Impuissants à créer, ils ont cherché à accaparer l'oeuvre des Décadents: ils sont les parasites d'une idée.")

tended toward a kind of forced and uninformed dandyism. Within these pages a less than progressive Salon critic called the academic Benjamin Constant's *Justinian* "a superb canvas, full of light, with a magisterial and grandiose allure."[23] Elsewhere Anatole Baju himself informed his readers: "Man subsists by the Ideal. Without the Ideal he will fall like the flower without dew, like the temple without columns, like the universe without God."[24] Such latent conservatism and overblown style could hardly have failed to raise the ire of the intelligent young group of writers— Félix Fénéon, Gustave Kahn, Jean Moréas, and Paul Adam among them—who gathered around the emerging *Revue indépendante, La Vogue,* and *Le Symboliste* in the mid-eighties. These writers, generally staunch supporters of the neo-impressionists, reviled the *retardataire* paintings of such academicians as Constant. If they spoke of the ideal in art it was of a new ideal, not the trite pronouncements of Baju. Thus it is not surprising that these writers would abhor Baju's purposely dilettantish publication and its other writers. More surprising is the manner in which this antagonism seems to have influenced the reaction of the symbolists to the work of J.-K. Huysmans, a much stronger writer than Baju or any of his associates in decadence. Although many modern literary historians would see Huysmans's *A rebours* as both a breviary of decadence and a handbook of symbolism, the symbolists themselves did not necessarily agree.[25]

Georges Vanor's *L'Art symboliste,* published just five years after *A rebours* and purporting to outline the important writers of the young symbolist movement, does not mention Huysmans. In his *Symbolistes et décadents* of 1902 Gustave Kahn was hardly more friendly to Huysmans. Although he agreed that Huysmans had some talent and that *A rebours* was not without value as a curiosity, he felt it had exercised a bad influence on literature and suggested, condescendingly, that the influence

23. Louis Toche, "Le 'Décadent' au Salon," *Le Décadent,* i (9 May 1886), unpaginated. ("Une toile superbe, vivante, pleine de lumière d'une allure magistrale et grandiose.")

24. Baju, "Idéal," *Le Décadent,* i, no. 20 (21 August 1886), unpaginated. ("L'homme subsiste par l'Idéal. Sans idéal il tomberait comme la fleur sans la rosée, comme le temple sans les colonnes, comme l'univers sans Dieu.") Noël Richard, who wrote an excellent account of the decadent movement, suggested, quite rightly, that Baju was not up to the subtle intellectual level of many of his contemporaries and was more suited to polemic. See Richard, *Le Mouvement décadent* (Paris: Nizet, 1968), 120.

25. See Robert Baldick's introduction to the Penguin Books translation of *A rebours:* Joris-Karl Huysmans, *Against Nature* (Harmondsworth, Middlesex: Penguin Books, 1959), 13.

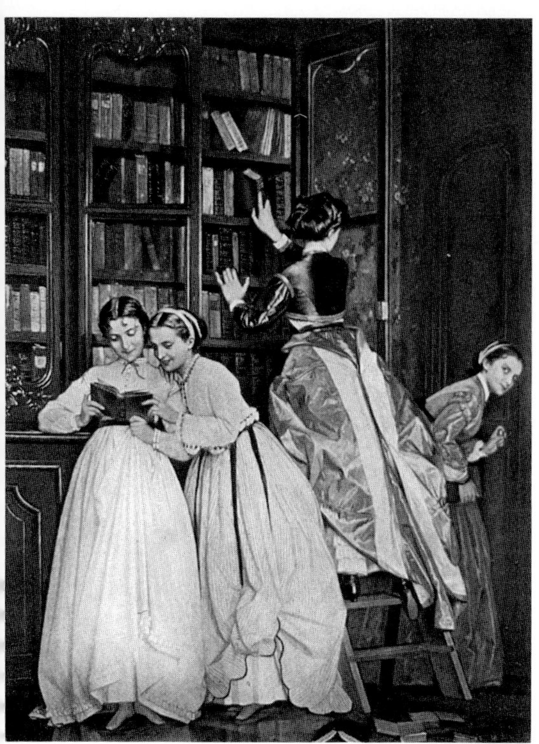

1. Auguste Toulmouche, *Forbidden Fruit* (Salon 1865)

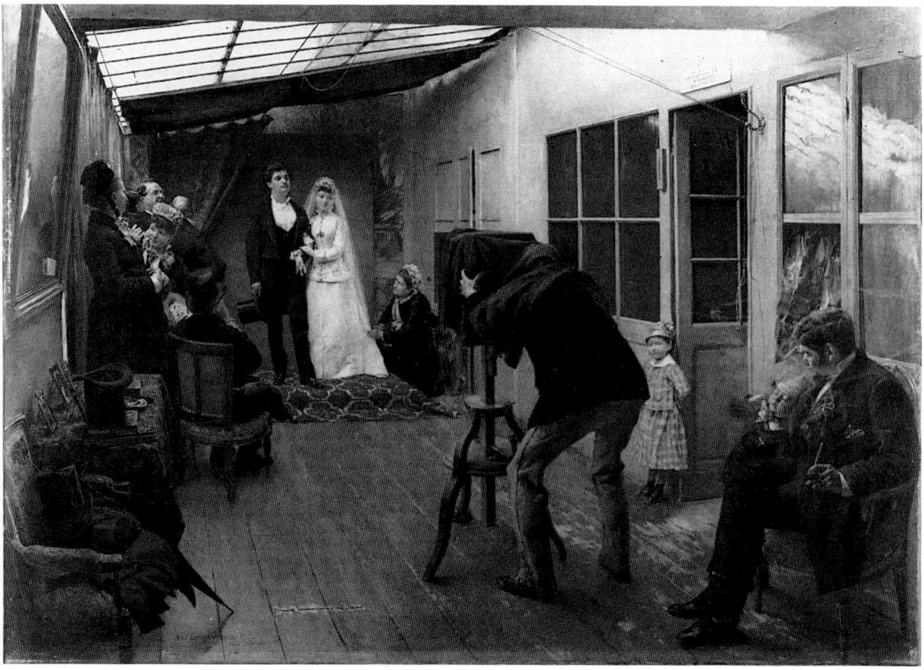

2. P.-A.-J. Dagnan-Bouveret, *Wedding at the Photographer's* (1878–79)

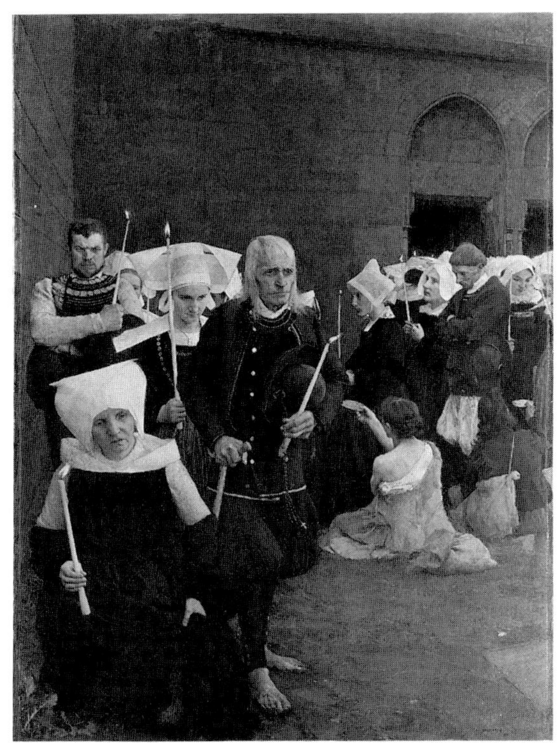

3. P.-A.-J. Dagnan-Bouveret, *Pardon in Brittany* (1889)

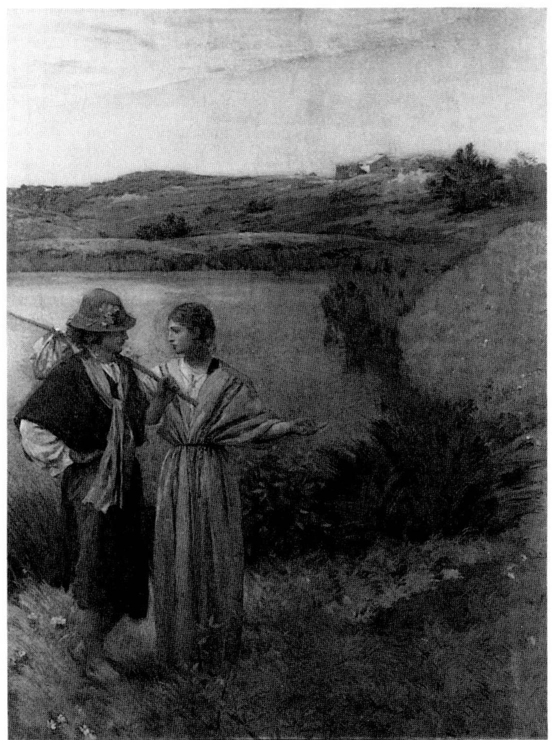

4. Jean-Charles Cazin, *Tobias and the Angel* (1880)

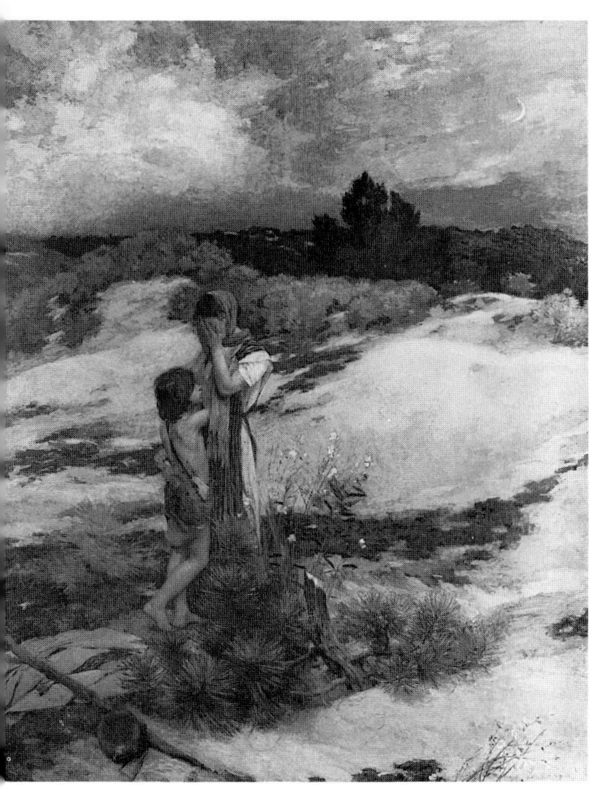

5. Jean-Charles Cazin, *Hagar and Ishmael* (1880)

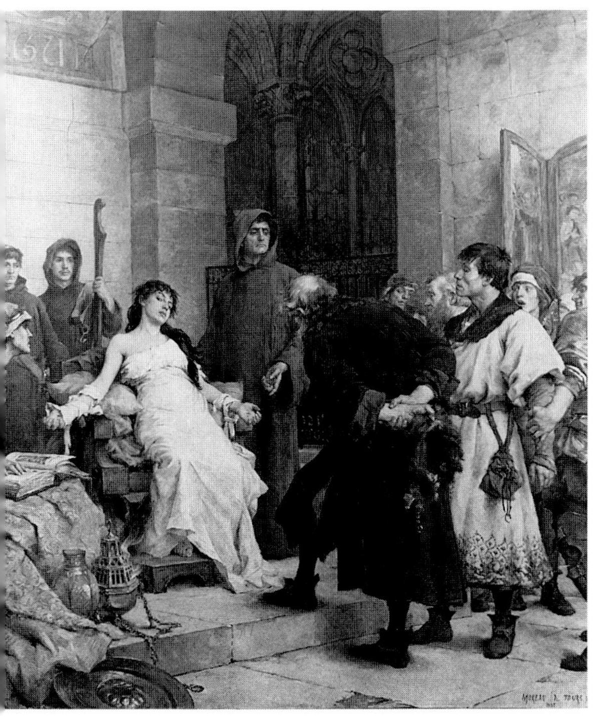

6. Georges Moreau de Tours, *A Stigmatization in the Middle Ages* (1885)

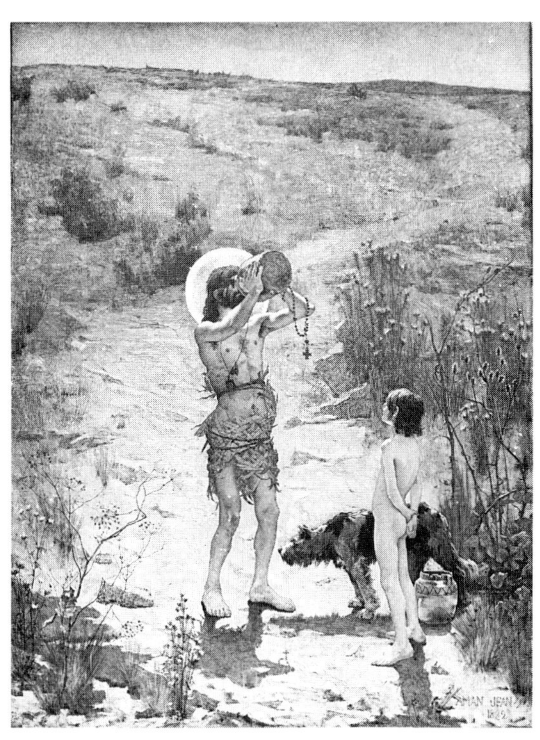

7. Edmond Aman-Jean, *St. Julian the Hospitator* (1882)

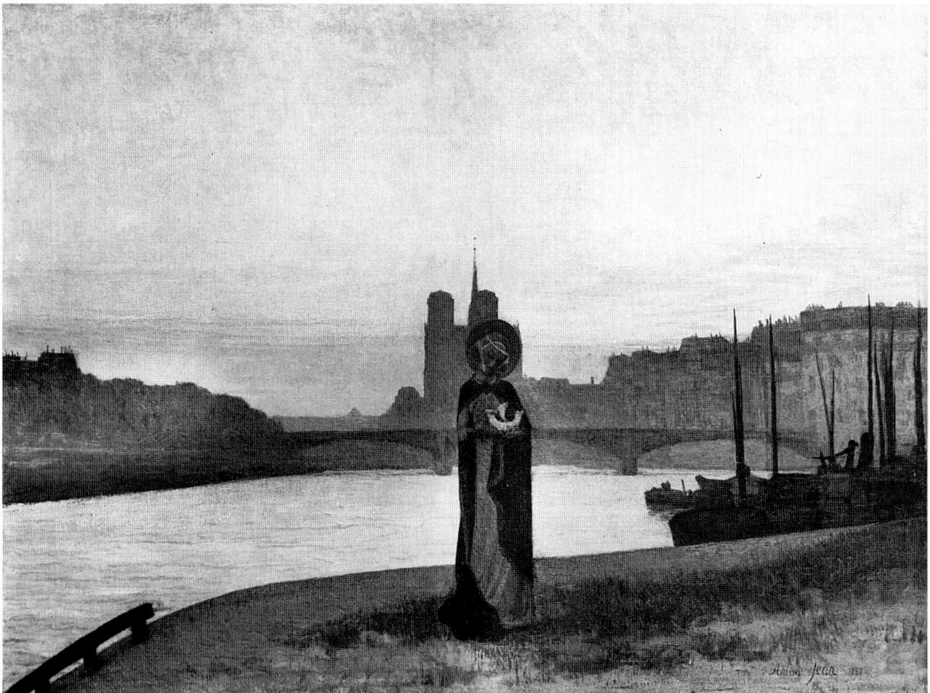

8. Edmond Aman-Jean, *St. Geneviève Before Paris* (1885)

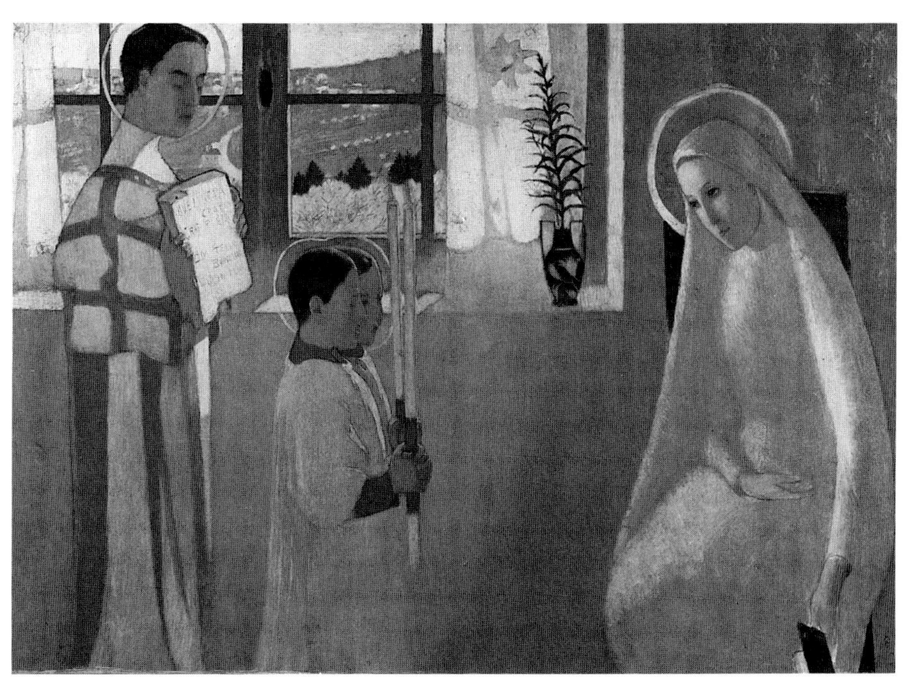

9. Maurice Denis, *Catholic Mystery* (1889)

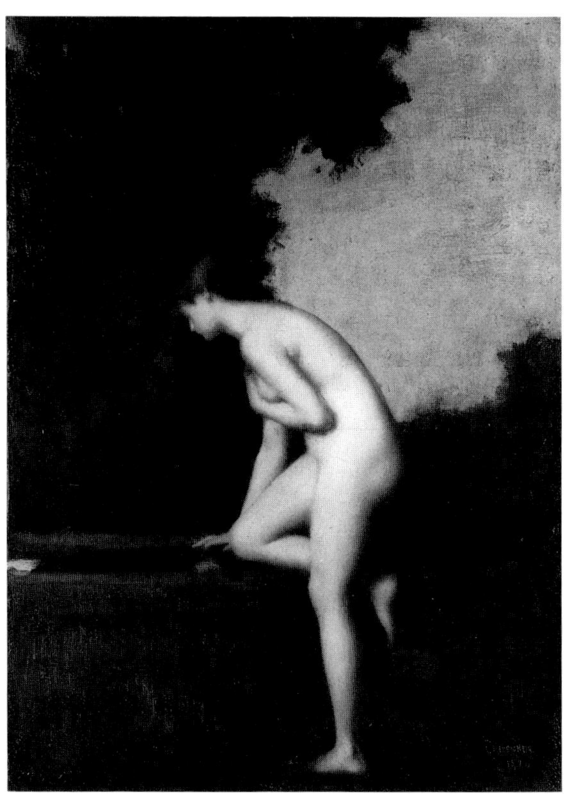

10. Jean-Jacques Henner, *Nymph by a Fountain* (1880)

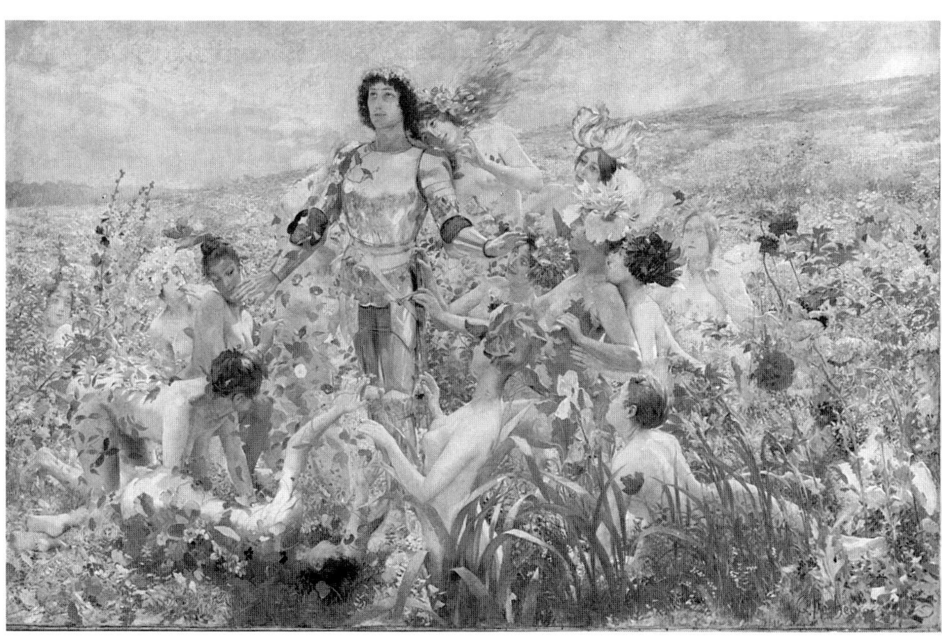

11. Georges-Antoine Rochegrosse, *The Knight Among the Flowers* (1894)

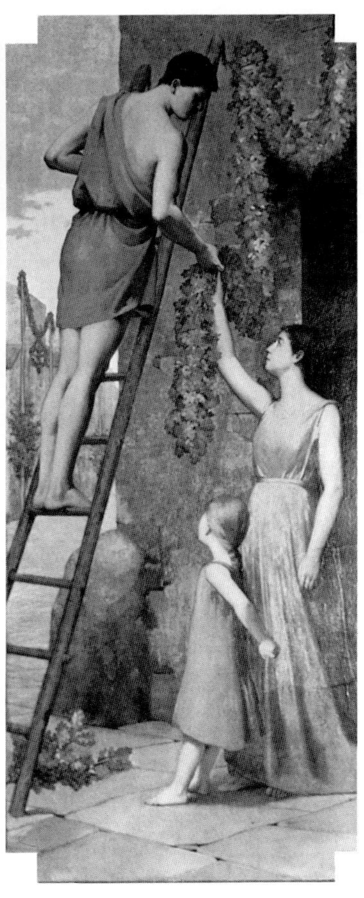

12. Alexandre Séon, *Holiday* (1889)

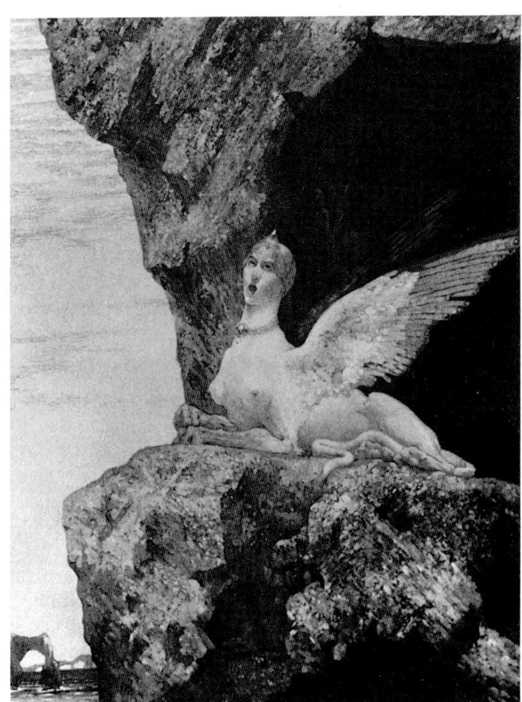

13. Alexandre Séon, *The Despair of the Chimera* (1890)

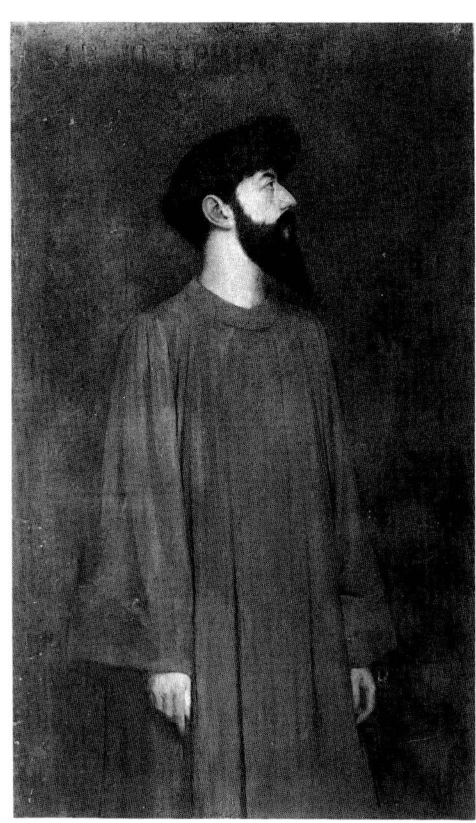

14. Alexandre Séon, *Portrait of Joséphin
    Péladan* (1891)

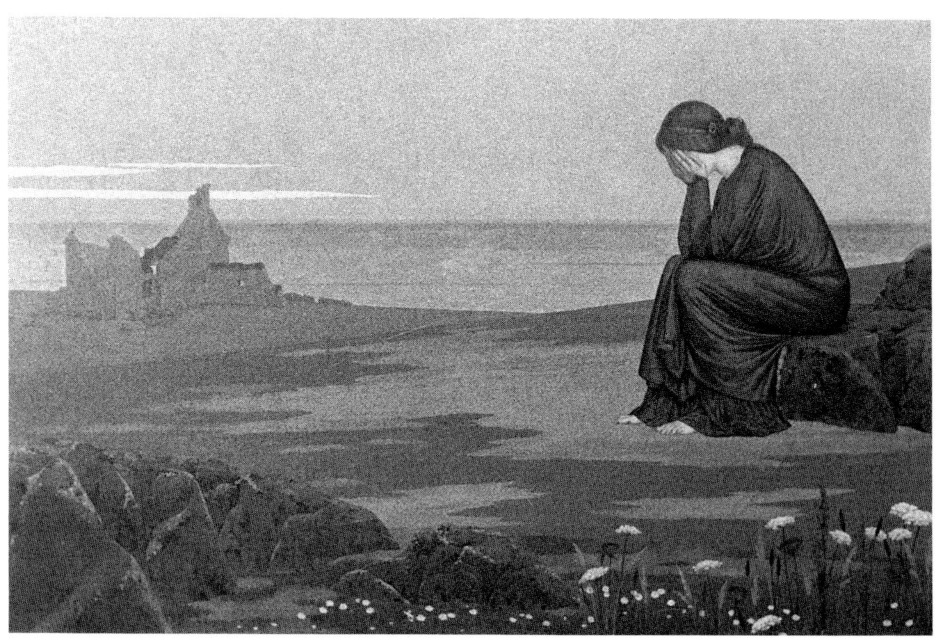

15. Alexandre Séon, *The Return Home* (c. 1900)

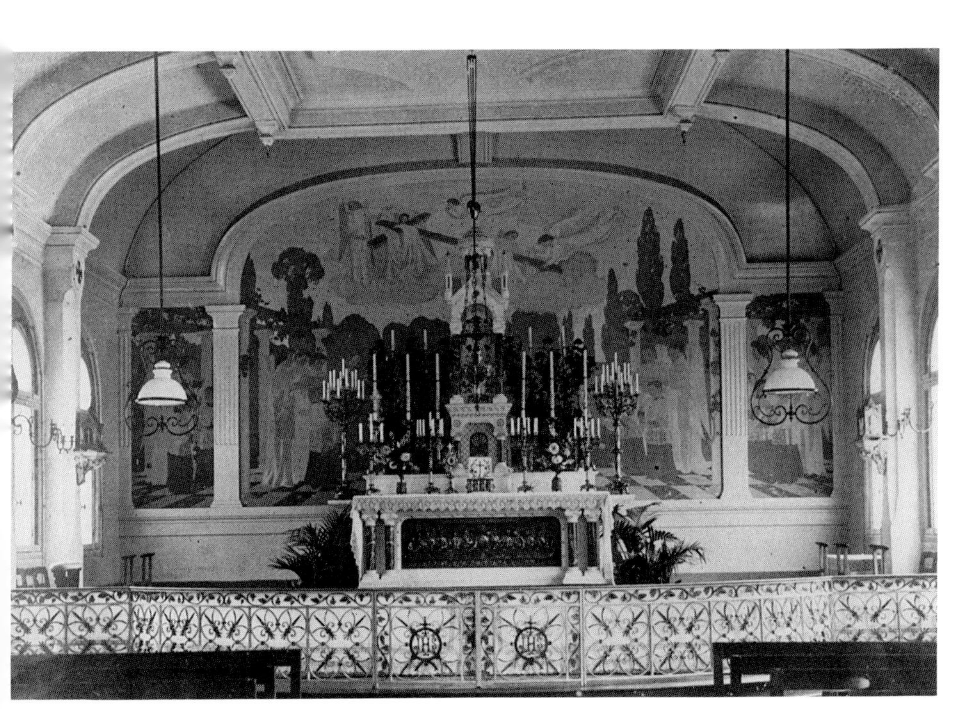

16. Maurice Denis, *The Exaltation of the Holy Cross* (1898), in place at the Collège de Sainte-Croix, Le Vésinet

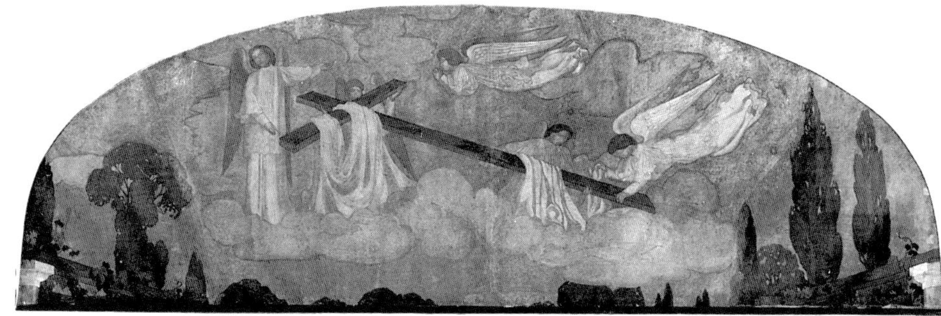

17a. Maurice Denis, *The Exaltation of the Holy Cross*, upper panel

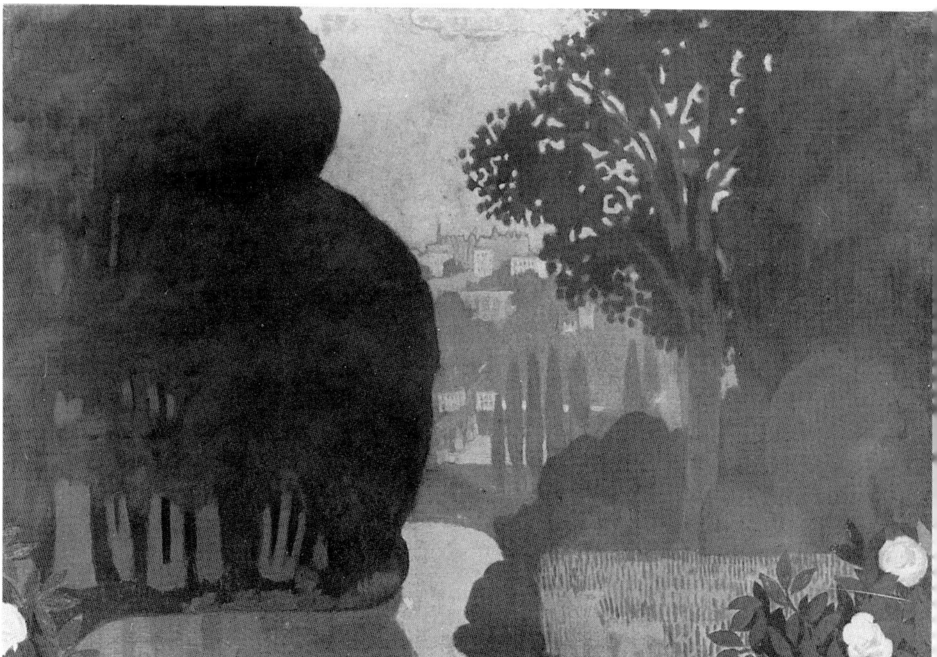

17b. Maurice Denis, *The Exaltation of the Holy Cross*, central panel

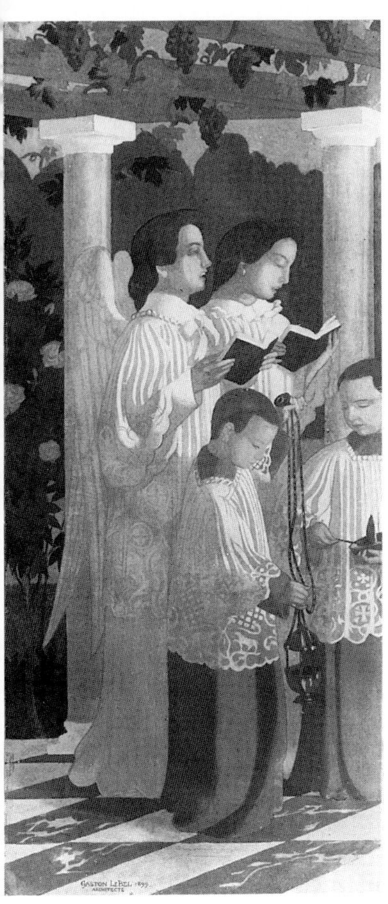

17c. Maurice Denis, *The Exaltation of the Holy Cross,*
      far left panel

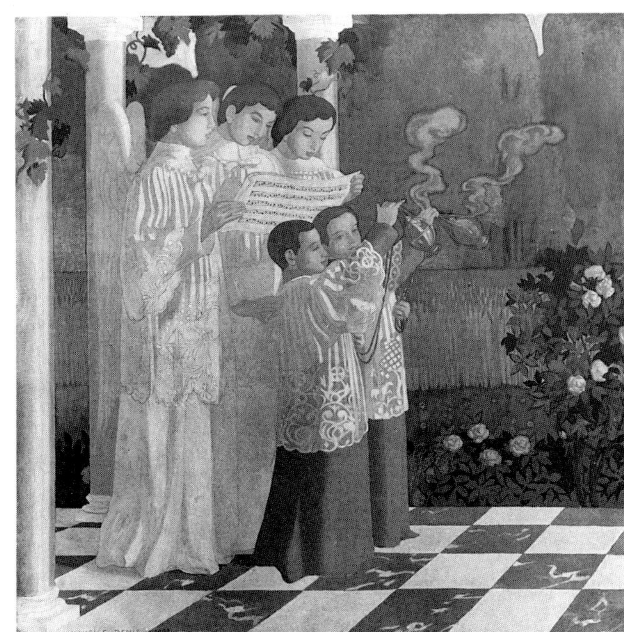

17d. Maurice Denis, *The
      Exaltation of the Holy
      Cross,* left center
      panel

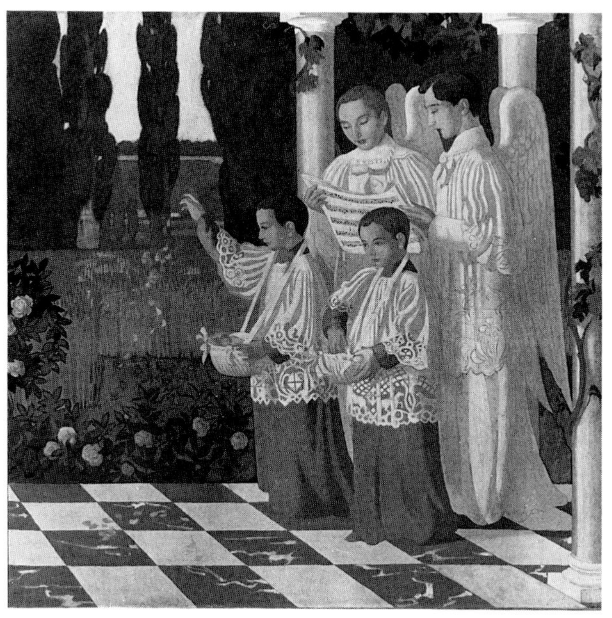

17e. Maurice Denis, *The Exaltation of the Holy Cross*, right center panel

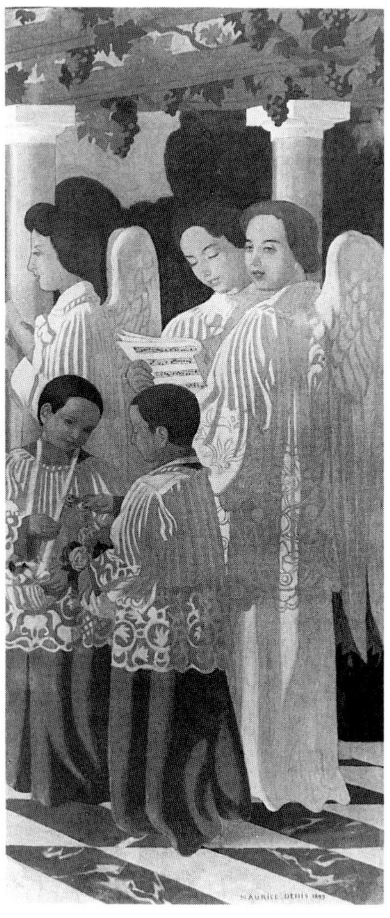

17f. Maurice Denis, *The Exaltation of the Holy Cross*, far right panel

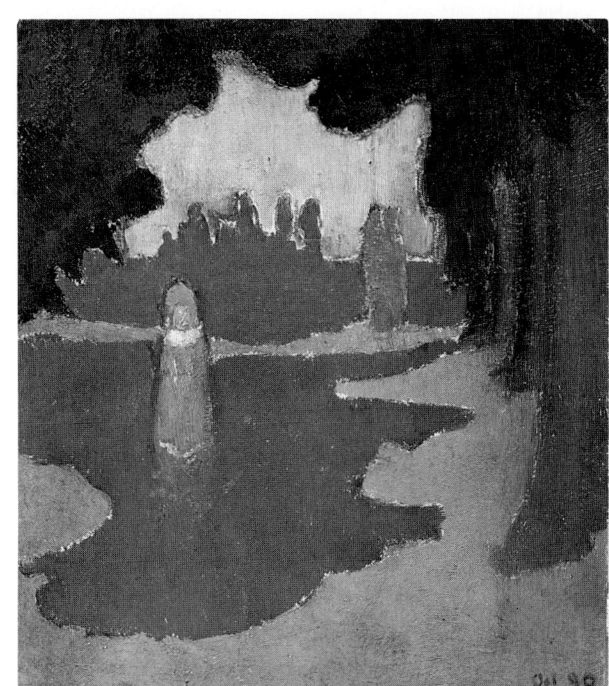

18. Maurice Denis, *Sunlight on the Terrace* (1890)

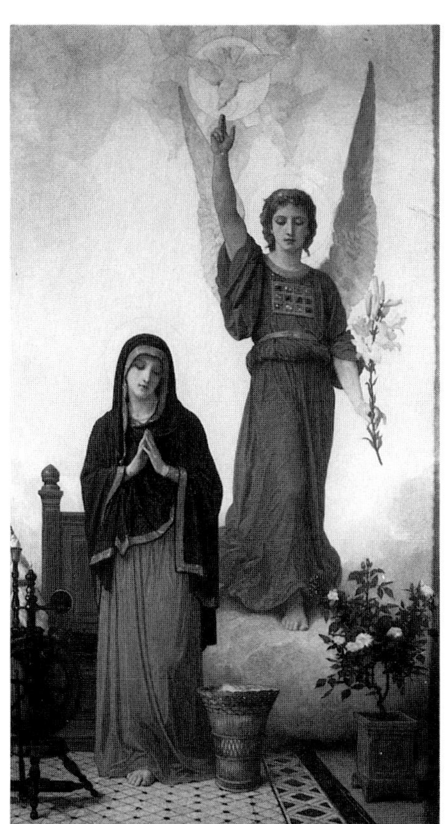

19. William-Adolphe Bouguereau, *The Annunciation* (c. 1888)

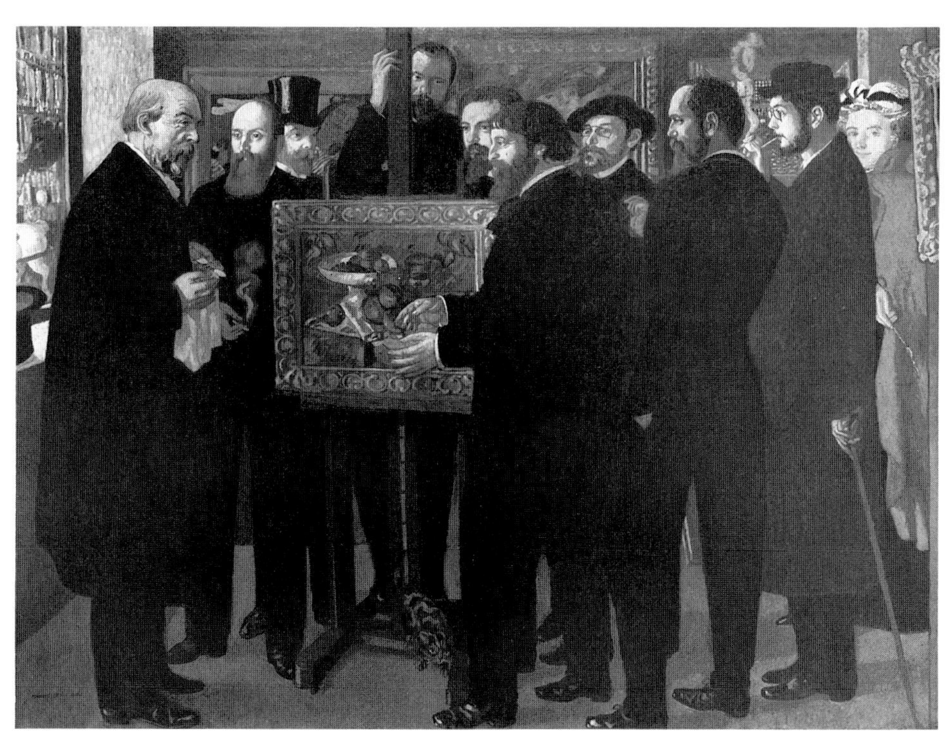

20. Maurice Denis, *Homage to Cézanne* (1900)

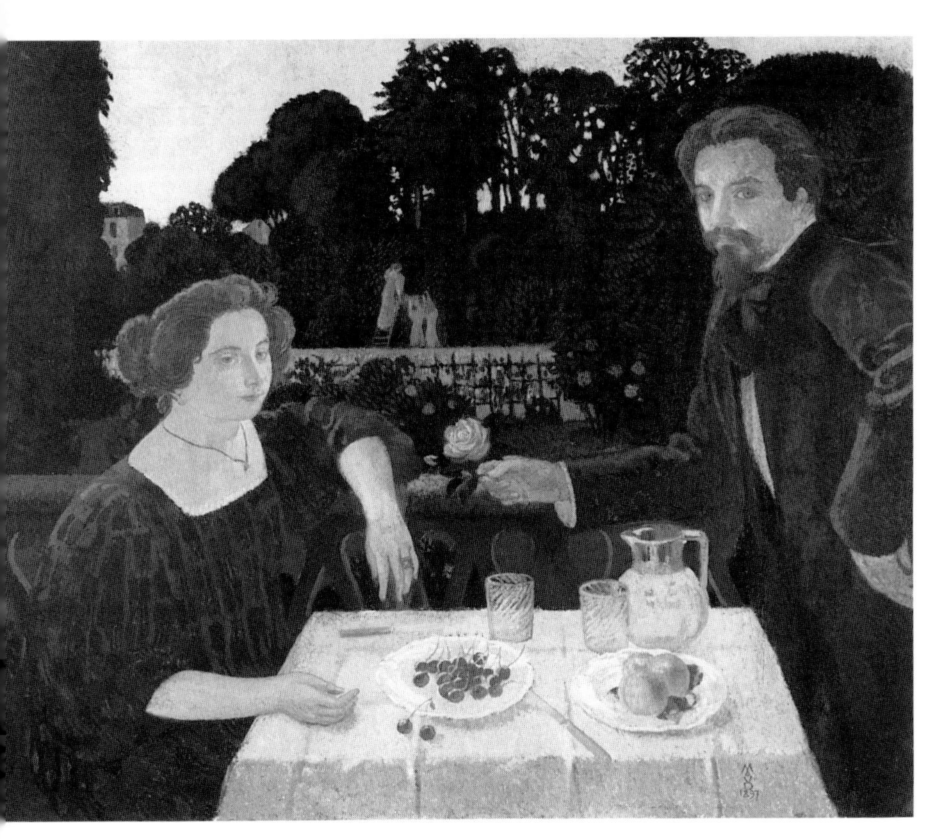

21. Maurice Denis, *Dessert in the Garden* (1897)

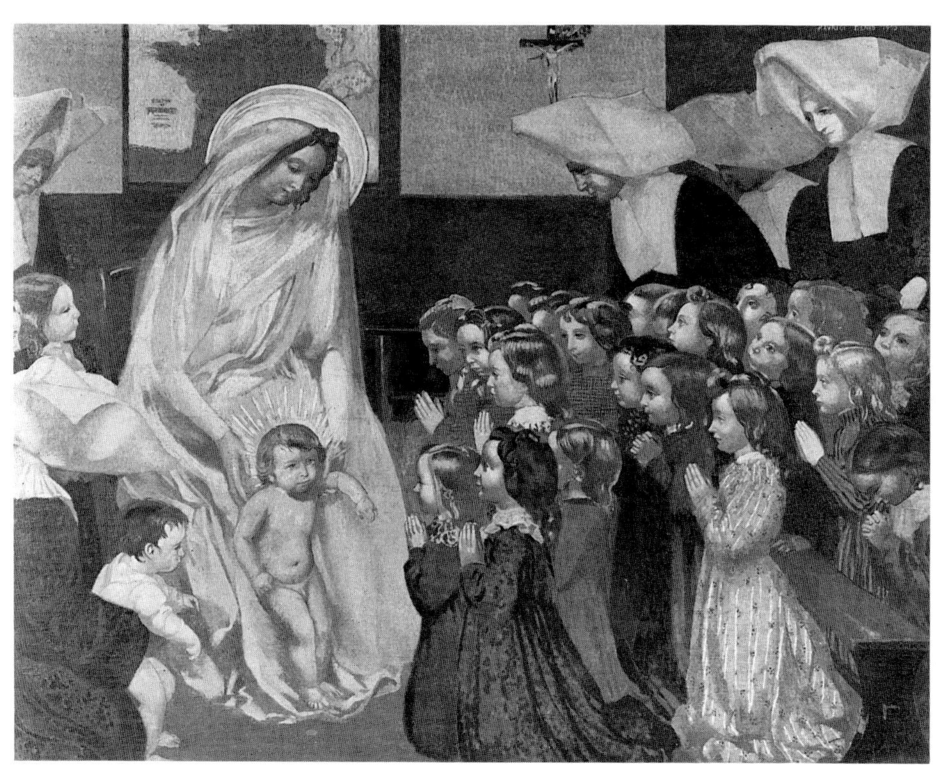

22. Maurice Denis, *Our Lady of the Schools* (1903)

had been limited mainly to Belgium.[26] This antagonism on the part of writers whom one might well have expected to support Huysmans is surprising. More important for our purposes this difference was played out in the art criticism of Huysmans, on the one hand, and Félix Fénéon, on the other. Indeed, the schism between decadents and symbolists in art criticism was as marked as it was in literary theory.

In spite of the fact that they worked together at the *Revue indépendante*—indeed, as editor of the review Fénéon had recruited Huysmans to write art criticism—Huysmans and Fénéon did not necessarily agree on matters of art. Huysmans, for instance, was rather critical of the art of Seurat, whom Fénéon had championed. Huysmans allowed that, like all techniques, Seurat's had both good and bad features and he praised the artist's landscapes. But he specifically criticized Seurat's figurative paintings:

> Strip his figures of the colored fleas with which they are covered, and underneath there is nothing, no soul, no thought, nothing. Nothingness in a body of which only the contour exists. Thus in his picture of the *Grand Jatte* the human armature becomes rigid and hard; everything is immobilized and congealed.[27]

Then, striking a note that was not at all uncommon in conservative discussions of Seurat's painting, he added, "I am decidedly afraid that there is only too much process, too many systems here, and not enough of the flame that ignites, not enough life!"[28]

26. Kahn, *Symbolistes et décadents*, 34–35.

27. Huysmans, "Chronique d'art: les indépendantes," *La Revue indépendante*, iii (April 1887); as quoted in Norma Broude, *Seurat in Perspective* (Englewood Cliffs, N.J.: Prentice-Hall, 1978), 43–44.

28. Ibid., 44. Huysmans was not alone in such comments about Seurat. About seven months earlier the young critic Emile Hennequin—who, like Huysmans, had championed the art of Redon—made a similar critique of Seurat. He too was willing to admit Seurat's talent but made a qualification parallel to that of Huysmans:

> When Monsieur Seurat uses his method to paint Norman seascapes, especially as in that marvelous canvas intitled *Grandcamp*, when he describes the grey arrival of evening, he is excellent. But if, as in the *Grand Jatte*, he attacks the problem of sunlight and the fading figure, he is glaringly unsuccessful, not only because of the absence of light but because of the absence of life in these figures whose outlines have been painstakingly filled in with colored dots as in a tapestry. They are painted Gobelin tapestries, as unpleasant as the originals. (Broude, *Seurat in Perspective*, 42–43)

For his part Félix Fénéon did not specifically give answer to such criticism of his favorite artist, but merely continued to produce thoughtful and intelligent explanations of Seurat's work. There may, however, have been a certain amount of reciprocation in Fénéon's lack of interest in the art of Odilon Redon, whose work Huysmans greatly admired. In 1886 while reviewing the impressionist exhibition of that year, Fénéon barely mentioned Redon's fifteen drawings, considering them "poorly chosen," although he did notice that they were capable of causing anguish to the "prepared soul."[29] Several years later, in 1891, Fénéon was more equivocal in considering Redon's drawings:

> To explain their incredulity the adversaries of the art of M. Odilon Redon say that when M. Odilon doesn't discombobulate form . . . that is to say when he is at his most controlled, he is the most insignificant of draftsmen. However, reply the faithfuls, it would be abusive to conclude from this that he remains a mediocre artist when he monsterizes. Friends and adversaries can, besides, get together on this quaint aphorism that a recent biography of Cézanne attributed to M. Gauguin . . . "Nothing resembles a daub so much as a masterpiece."[30]

This, and the fact that Fénéon rarely mentions Redon in his art criticism seems to confirm the suggestion that he did not number himself among the "faithful." A few years later Fénéon found Redon's nightmares to be overfamiliar.[31] But such minor disagreements would mean little if they did not in fact indicate a deeper gap. That such was the case can be observed in some of Fénéon's comments about Huysmans's art criticism.

Huysmans's statement here is also similar to one made in *Le Décadent* sometime earlier (see note 38).

29. Fénéon, *Oeuvres*, 32. (". . . mal choisis . . . angoissent les âmes préparées.") Was this comment satirical?

30. Ibid., 187–88. ("Pour expliquer leur incrédulité, les adversaires de l'art de M. Odilon Redon disent que lorsque M. Odilon ne bouleverse pas les formes . . . c'est-à-dire quand on a sur son oeuvre d'assez sûrs moyens de contrôle, il est le plus insignifiant des dessinateurs; mais, répliquent les fidèles, il serait abusif de conclure de là qu'il reste un artiste médiocre lorsqu'il tératologise. Amis et adversaires pourront, d'ailleurs, fraterniser sur cet aphorisme à tiroirs qu'attribue à M. Paul Gauguin une récente biographie de Cézanne. . . . 'Rien ne ressemble autant à une croute qu'un chef-d'oeuvre.'")

31. Ibid., 221.

While Huysmans seems never to have written anything about Fénéon, the latter wrote one important bit of criticism of the author of *A rebours*. This was a review of Huysmans's collection of articles, *Certains*, published in 1889.[32] "No one," began Fénéon, "was more perspicacious than M. Huysmans in discovering among the throng a new and strong painter of talent."[33] Fénéon ended by stating that this book, and Huysmans's other collection of essays, *L'Art moderne*, were, "by their certainty of opinion and their solid execution, the only ones on modern art."[34] Between these complimentary lines, however, Fénéon had almost nothing good to say. He asserted that Huysmans followed Théodore Duret in presenting the impressionists to the public and had little to do with the general interest of the young literary set in such artists as Degas. While criticizing Huysmans's style, Fénéon quite correctly noted that the former was more concerned with subject than with form, that in Degas for example he "appreciated the descriptive exactitude and the misogyny more than the abstract beauty of lines."[35] Speaking of Félicien Rops, Fénéon chided Huysmans for being "in rapture before the engravings of M. Rops, which derive from literary preoccupations."[36] Referring to both Huysmans and Camille Lemonnier, who had also supported Rops's art, Fénéon continued:

> On this work, poor in sensations of the pictorial order and which they have preached without seeing that it is strongly imbued with the academic tradition, M. Lemonnier and M. Huysmans have practiced the cruelest of things: their commentary annuls it, being a hundred times more expressive than it is.[37]

32. Ibid., 171–73.

33. Ibid., 171. ("Plus que M. Huysmans nul ne fut perspicace à découvrir dans la cohue un peintre de talent neuf et fort.")

34. Ibid., 173. (". . . pour leur sûreté de verdict et leur ferme exécution, les seuls qui aient été faits sur l'art moderne.")

35. Ibid., 171. (". . . il goûta l'exactitude descriptive et la misogynie plus que l'abstraite beauté des lignes.")

36. Ibid. (". . . en joie devant les planches de M. Rops, dérivées de préoccupations littéraires.")

37. Ibid. ("Sur cette oeuvre, pauvre en sensations d'ordre pictural et qu'ils prônent sans voir qu'elle est foncièrement imbue de traditions académiques, M. Lemonnier et M. Huysmans ont pratiqué les plus cruelles expériences; leur commentaire l'annule, étant cent fois plus expressif qu'elle.") Camille Lemonnier's article, "Une tentation de St. Antoine de Félicien Rops," *La Revue indépendante*, 1 (June 1884), 125–31, was published under Fénéon's editorship.

After insisting that Huysmans's interest in Rops was backward, Fénéon further upbraided the author of *Certains* for being indifferent to the development of neo-impressionism. He wondered if Huysmans was capable of varying the program of his admirations and then cited all the young writers who had lined up on the side of neo-impressionism, asking why Huysmans had dissented. Further, Féneón took issue with Huysmans for promoting the art of Gustave Moreau over that of Puvis de Chavannes. Féneón suggested that it was Moreau and not Puvis whose art was derivative and ultimately "compromised."

The sum of Féneón's criticism of Huysmans was more than just a friendly jibe. There was a distinct tone of mistrust, a genuine fear that Huysmans's tastes were reactionary. Nor was this fear totally unfounded. Huysmans's feeling that Seurat was a better landscape painter than figure painter has a conservative ring to it.[38] It might also be noted that Huysmans's taste for the art of Rops and Moreau had been most vocally and forcefully paralleled in Joséphin Péladan's writings of the early 1880s. Throughout the 1880s Péladan had been the most reactionary of critics, reviling all modern trends in art and calling for a return to the tradition of the ideal. Huysmans too had become increasingly antimodernist. After supporting impressionism in *L'Art moderne*, he increasingly lost interest in modern style and became instead more involved with esoteric subject matter. Like his character des Esseintes, Huysmans came to loathe the modern world, even dedicating *A rebours*, as we noted earlier, to the fanatically antimodern Léon Bloy, "in hatred of the present century."[39] Huysmans developed a taste for things that were, literally, against the grain of modern society. This taste was a general trend in the decadent movement, which is why a critic like Péladan could associate himself with the idea of decadence and did.[40] That Huysmans and

38. Indeed, Louis-Pilate de Brinn Gaubast, conservative critic for *Le Décadent*, had said much the same thing. See his "L'Exposition des artistes indépendantes," *Le Décadent*, 1 (18 September 1886), unpaginated, where he spoke of Seurat "from whom the *Evening, Grandcamp* allows one to judge that he would succeed less badly to daub some landscapes than to set up simple-minded and wooden men in the *Sunday Afternoon on the Island of La Grande Jatte*." ("Seurat, dont le *Soir à Grandcamp* permet de juger qu'il réussirait moins mal à barbouiller des paysages qu'à camper des bonshommes en bois dans *l'Ile de la Grand Jatte, une dimanche*.")

39. See Annette Kahn, *J.-K. Huysmans*, 11ff., for an account of Huysmans's changing critical position. Also see Anita Brookner, *The Genius of the Future*, 157, 159.

40. Péladan's long series of novels was given the title *La Décadence latine* by the author. Elizabeth Martin, in "The Symbolist Criticism of Painting," considered Huysmans and Péladan together in her chapter on "The Decadent View of Painting."

Péladan could have been grouped under the same sobriquet, "decadent," must have rankled a modernist like Fénéon. After all, he had recruited the author of *L'Art moderne* to write criticism for the *Revue indépendante*. What he got was something quite different, the author of *Certains*.

Against Huysmans's aggressive antimodernism, Fénéon and his associates proposed a thoroughgoing modernism. Fénéon had spoken eloquently of neo-impressionism as the newest form of art and praised Seurat as a more progressive Puvis de Chavannes. Fénéon and his young friends espoused the modern aesthetics of the scientist Charles Henry and generally saw themselves as developing along the most advanced lines in both poetry and art criticism.[41] Most of them were politically progressive as well, being either socialists or anarchists. They promoted the new, not the old, and in this they must have seen themselves as defending modernism against the artistically backward thinking they saw in some decadent circles. Fénéon's complaint that Huysmans was more interested in subject than abstract formal qualities in painting reveals his modernist bias. This in turn may have led him to see Huysmans as backward—especially because the latter had not come to appreciate the strictly modern painting of Georges Seurat. A further example of Fénéon's fear of reactionary trends in contemporary art can be found in a rather surprising theme of his art criticism: his treatment of the work of Paul Gauguin.

Since art history has generally, and rightly, asserted the importance of Gauguin and Seurat in the development of modernism, it is not surprising that several art historians have assumed that Félix Fénéon supported not only the art of Seurat but that of Gauguin as well. Sven Lövgren, for instance, felt that Fénéon had been one of the first to recognize Gauguin's talents and had continued to support him throughout the eighties, serving to introduce the painter's work to symbolist literary circles.[42] Werner Haftmann, in his history of twentieth-century European art, similarly tells us that "as early as 1886, the critic Fénéon, one of the leading younger essayists in the Symbolist group, had taken up the cudgels for Seurat and Gauguin in one of the numerous symbolist magazines, *La Vogue*."[43] But in spite of the fact that Fénéon had indeed

41. On this subject see Joan U. Halperin, "Scientific Criticism and *le beau moderne* of the Age of Science," 55–71.

42. Lövgren, *The Genesis of Modernism*, 118.

43. Haftmann, *Painting in the Twentieth Century* (New York: Praeger, 1965), 39.

written about Gauguin as early as 1886 it would be difficult to say that he took up cudgels for him, and it is false, as well, to assert that Fénéon's attitude toward Gauguin influenced that of the literary symbolists; as we will note shortly, Fénéon openly derided Gauguin's connection with literary circles.

The vast majority of Félix Fénéon's writing about Paul Gauguin was offered during the years 1886–91. He never mentioned Gauguin before this period or after 1891, save for a very short notice of an eyewitness description of Gauguin's gravesite, and inclusion of the artist's name in lists of sales and exhibitions. Fénéon first mentioned Gauguin in a review of the eighth impressionist exhibition, published in *La Vogue* and later reprinted in *Les Impressionnistes en 1886*. It is how Gauguin is cited in the beginning of this important article that is interesting. Fénéon saw him, quite properly for Gauguin in 1885–86, as part of the old-line of impressionism while Pissarro, Seurat, and Signac were viewed as innovators.[44] This assessment of Gauguin was a theme Fénéon would repeat on four separate occasions over the following two years.[45] So, from the very beginning Fénéon saw Gauguin as relatively backward in comparison to neo-impressionism. Fénéon then proceeded to a flat, relatively unenthusiastic description of Gauguin's entries to the exhibition.[46] Aside from lists of exhibition participants, Fénéon's next mention of Gauguin came a year and a half later, in January 1888. It appeared in a review of a small exhibition, mounted by Théo van Gogh at Boussod and Valadon in December 1887, of works by Pissarro, Gauguin, and Guillaumin. Gauguin himself commented on the article in a letter to Emile Schuffenecker and he was not pleased.[47] Fénéon noted that Gauguin's style, "without clearing up or getting lighter, is acquiring a certain virile elo-

---

44. Fénéon, *Oeuvres*, 29. The following discussion was part of my doctoral dissertation, "Anti-Naturalism, Idealism and Symbolism in French Art Criticism, 1880–1895" (University of Michigan, 1985). Joan U. Halperin, *Félix Fénéon, Aesthete and Anarchist in Fin-de-Siècle Paris*, 213–37, has dealt with much of the same material. Her interpretation is uniformly excellent, her translations masterly. My transcriptions are in some cases fuller and I have interpreted the strained relationship between Fénéon and Gauguin differently.

45. Fénéon, *Oeuvres*, 66, 82, 116, 127.

46. Ibid., 33. This passage is held up by Lövgren, *The Genesis of Modernism*, 118, as an example of Fénéon's support for Gauguin but there is little here that would suggest that Fénéon was anything but casually interested in Gauguin's work.

47. Lövgren, 122, notes Gauguin's displeasure yet still feels that the article should be regarded as "positive."

quence of line."[48] He described Gauguin's paintings as barbarous, atrabilious, and fine all at once, and characterized his pottery as "baneful and hard" and of an "abnormal and gibbous geometry."[49] Although the text of the article merely notes the presence of these characteristics it is clear enough that Fénéon seems to have liked such features in Gauguin's work. But when, in the same article, he suggested that the artist was above all a potter he was not being complimentary.

Indeed, it was not until May 1888 that Fénéon offered a bit of unequivocal praise for Gauguin. In two sentences he noted the presence of a Gauguin landscape from Martinique at Boussod and Valadon and suggested that an exhibition of his work was in order.[50] Over a year later, in a short review of the famous synthetist exhibition held at the Café Volpini during the 1889 World Exposition, Fénéon again seemed to praise Gauguin:

> Their mysterious, hostile, and rough aspect isolated from their ambiance the works of M. Paul Gauguin, a painter and sculptor of the impressionist exhibitions of 1880, 1881, 1882, and 1886; many details of execution, and the fact that he carved bas-reliefs in wood and colored them, were a sign of a tendency towards archaism; the form of his earthenware vases bore witness to an exotic taste: all characteristics that attain their degree of saturation in recent canvases.[51]

Gauguin was, evidently, proud of this paragraph because he included it years later in his *Cahier pour Aline*.[52] But however much he enjoyed this praise he was also enraged by other comments in the article.[53] Not only did Fénéon suggest that the artist was working toward the same goal as

48. Fénéon, *Oeuvres*, 90. (". . . sans s'éclaircir ni s'alléger acquiert une virile éloquence de lignes.")

49. Ibid., 91. ("De caractère barbare et atrabilaire" / ". . . néfaste et dur" / ". . . d'une géométrie anormale et gobine.") The translation of *gobine* as "gibbous" is from Halperin, *Félix Fénéon, Aesthete and Anarchist in Fin-de-Siècle Paris*, 214.

50. Fénéon, *Oeuvres*, 111.

51. Ibid., 157. ("Leur aspect mystérieux, hostile et fruste isolait de l'ambiance les oeuvres de M. PAUL GAUGUIN, peintre et sculpteur, aux expositions impressionnistes de 1880, 1881, 1882 et 1886; maints détails de facture, et ce fait qu'il taillait dans le bois ses bas-reliefs et les coloriait marquaient bien une tendance à l'archaïsme; la forme de ses vases de grès témoignait d'un goût exotique: tous caractères qui atteignent leur degrè de saturation dans ses toiles récentes.")

52. See Joan Halperin's editorial note in Fénéon, *Oeuvres*, 157.

53. As noted in John Rewald, *Post-Impressionism*, 260–61.

Seurat, thus implying that Gauguin was the follower, he also said that Louis Anquetin probably "had some slight influence" on Gauguin's style. Such suggestions infuriated Gauguin, in spite of the fact that Fénéon was careful to note that the influence was only formal and that Anquetin's paintings lacked the power of Gauguin's.

Up to this point, then, Fénéon seems to have been reticent to discuss Gauguin at all and only in rather equivocal terms. By September 1889 Fénéon recognized Gauguin as the leader of one of the groups dissident from impressionism but focused his attention on the "more numerous" artists who were turning towards neo-impressionism.[54] In his criticism of Huysmans's *Certains*, Fénéon chided the author for being hostile to the early "fauve" pottery of Gauguin, thereby continuing his own insistence on Gauguin's importance as a potter, while neglecting his work as a painter. But it was not until 1891 that Fénéon definitively revealed his true feelings about Gauguin.

Fénéon made no mention of Gauguin from December 1889 to March 1891, a long period of silence considering the important changes occurring in Gauguin's art at that time (precisely, by the way, the period in which Gauguin was getting close to symbolist literary circles). When Fénéon did mention the painter again—actually in reference to the work of Emile Bernard, Maurice Denis, and other followers of Gauguin—his comments were openly derisive of the artist's new style. In a review of the Salon des indépendants, published in the satirical *Chat noir* under Henry Gauthier-Villars's pseudonym "Willy," Fénéon derided the attempts of Denis, Bernard, and others to speak a universal language of art. Fénéon found their employment of this language arbitrary and caricatured.[55] He called Anquetin a painter of "navels and halos" and satirized the symbolist architect Albert Traschel for building "a palace of ecstasy for the hordes of Gauguin, when they are tired of painting."[56] This first blatant attack by Fénéon was enlarged upon just two months later, again in the *Chat noir*, in an article devoted solely to the art of Gauguin:

54. Fénéon, *Oeuvres*, 163. ("plus nombreux")

55. Ibid., 181–82, where Halperin explains the attribution of the content of the article to Fénéon.

56. Ibid., 182. (". . . le peintre savant de nombrils et d'aréoles . . . et l'architecte Trachsel édifie un Palais des extases pour les hordes de Gauguin, quand elles seront lasses de peindre.")

Long neglected, the tradition of Cézanne is today growing thanks to MM. Sérusier, Willumsen, Bernard, Schuffenecker, Laval, Ibels, Filiger, Denis, etc.—M. Paul Gauguin has not been a stranger to the blossoming of these talents. He has some disciples and a public. However his fortunes may prosper in Vaudeville and at the Salon du Champ de Mars the celebrity of his colored wood bas-relief "Soyez amoureuses, vous serez heureuses" is still growing.

Five years ago, at the exposition of the rue Lafitte, his landscapes and his bathers were a bit compromised by the dazzling works of his impressionist companions and by the lucid works of some newcomers. Was M. Gauguin going to fail his destiny? Around this time he met in Brittany a young painter of adventurous and fairly well informed spirit, M. Emile Bernard, who is today perhaps his pupil but who seems to have been his initiator: because M. Bernard first painted, in saturated colors, some upside-down Breton women, delimited by a drawing like leaded-glass windows, enveloped by a scenery without either atmosphere or values. The characteristics of this painting derive partly from the bias of the artist and partly from the clumsiness of the executant. When M. Gauguin came back from out yonder he was all in a literary fervor, he who had, up to that point, with the most paradoxical obstinacy, ignored libraries and ideas in general; and he went beyond the Breton women of M. Bernard but, wise painter, put some logic in their barbarism which, under its wild appearance, was a very controlled barbarism. Later these Bretons and this literature would unite their effectiveness. In 1887 he knew how to see the Antilles with an astonished regard, such as it could have looked to the crew of the Pinta. He sent back some canvases of an evil luxuriance. It was then that he became a prey of the literary set: they affirmed to him that he had charge of souls, that he was invested with a mission (not unlike what happened to that thick Courbet). M. Gauguin terrorizes reality, re-creating lines and shades, annulling the element of depth: he claims all license in expressing himself. So be it, but one waits for more exalted mosaics, more haunting arabesques, and also for more personality. (At the Hôtel Drouot, where thirty of his canvases were reunited recently for the dispersion of a sale, one recognized there some Japanese nudes, there some ground from Monet, there some trees from Cézanne, and his canvases from Arles were from Van Gogh.) Without doubt he has enriched the contemporary soul. But has the asymmetry of his Christs helped them much? And why do his deformations always resolve themselves in an increase of ugliness? M. Gauguin, or the workers of M. Delaherche, or the ceramicists of Takatori know how to incorporate in sandstone some stirring shades. M. Gauguin has drawn from this manner some quite decorative effects. He is more of a statue maker than a painter and one must admire his sculpture; but from concessionary to concessionary one would admire Zapotec funerary pots. And M. Emile Bernard? Ah well, last month he showed, at the Society of Independent Artists, a saintly painting under the somewhat compromising title of *Souvenir*. Memory of what? Of one of those monstrous *criblé* engravings, older even than woodcuts, and of which Holland and Germany dispute among themselves the origins—the *criblé* known by the name of *Jesus aux Oliviers*. The beautiful ideal.[57]

57. Ibid., 192–93. ("Longtemps délaisée, la tradition Cézanne est aujourd'hui en pleine culture, grâce à MM. Sérusier, Willumsen, Bernard, Schuffenecker, Laval, Ibels, Filiger, Denis, etc.—M. Paul Gauguin n'a pas été étranger à l'éclosion de ces talents. Il a des disciples et un public. En Océanie, il cuve une gloire rapidement conquise; cedendant que ses finances prospèrent au Vaudeville et qu'au Salon du Champ de Mars s'accroît encore la célébrité de son bas-relief de bois colorié 'Soyez amoureuses, vous serez heureuses.'

Il y a cinq ans, à l'exposition de la rue Laffitte, ses paysages et ses baigneuses furent un peu mis en désarroi par les oeuvres éclatantes de ses compagnons d'impressionnisme et par les oeuvres lucides de quelques nouveaux venus. M. Gauguin allait-il faillir à ses destinées? Vers ce temps, il rencontre en Bretagne un jeune peintre d'esprit aventureux et assez renseigné, M. Emile Bernard, qui aujourd'hui est peut-être son élève, mais qui paraît avoir été son initiateur: car, le premier, M. Bernard peignit, à couleurs saturées, de chavirantes Bretonnes, délimitées par un dessin en mailles de verrières et enveloppées d'un décor sans atmosphère ni valeurs. Les caractères de cette peinture dérivaient qui du parti pris par l'artiste, qui de la maladresse de l'exécutant. Quand M. Gauguin revint de là-bas, il était tout en ferveur littératurière, lui qui jusqu'alors avait, avec la plus paradoxale obstination, ignoré les librairies et généralement les idées; et il excellait aux Bretonnes de M. Bernard, mais, peintre savant, il mettait de la logique dans leur barbarie, qui, sous des dehors farouches, fut une barbarie très policée. Plus tard ces Bretonnes et cette littérature devaient coaliser leurs efficacités. En 1887, il sut voir les Antilles d'un regard étonné et telles qu'elles purent apparaître à l'équipage de la Pinta. Il en rapporta des toiles d'une luxuriance maléfique. C'est alors qu'il devint la proie des littérateurs: ceux-ci lui affirmèrent qu'il avait charge d'âmes, qu'il était investi d'une mission [pareille aventure était arrivée à ce gros Courbet]. M. Gauguin terrorise la réalité, recrée lignes et teintes, annule l'élément profondeur: il revendique toute licence de s'exprimer à son gré. Soit, mais on s'attendait à de plus exaltés mosaïquages, à des arabesques plus hallucinantes, et aussi à plus de

Much of the article conveys an air of petulance. Although Fénéon could carry such nastiness off better than most writers, he offers some jibes that are less than constructive. Using the word *statuaire* instead of *sculpteur* to describe Gauguin was certainly calculated to be offensive, as was repeating the suggestion that Bernard was responsible for the new style in Gauguin's painting. He further attacked the artist's sensitive ego with the idea that Gauguin was not quite up to the level of the impressionists, that his style was derivative and that his new literary associations were slightly absurd. Such a personal and satirical diatribe may reflect Fénéon's depression over the death of Seurat—whose work he appreciated so much more than Gauguin's—in March 1891, but the very direction of Gauguin's artistic endeavors seem to have upset the critic.

Félix Fénéon's complaints against Gauguin can be reduced to two main arguments. First, he contended that Gauguin was the dupe of the young symbolist literary set, unfairly accusing him of avoiding libraries and ideas until his encounter with the symbolists in Paris. It is of course true that Gauguin had been mixing with a new crowd in the winter of 1890–91, but Fénéon was not just acknowledging new influences on the artist's work. He was attacking them. His descriptions of Gauguin as "invested with a mission" and "in charge of souls" were undoubtedly references to Albert Aurier's famous article on Gauguin, "Le Symbolisme en peinture," published just two months earlier.[58] A bit later, in an article entitled "Quelques peintres idéistes"—the title is another refer-

---

personnalité. [A l'hôtel Drouot, où trente de ses toiles étaient réunies récemment pour la dispersion d'une vente, on reconnaissait, là des nus japonais, là des terrains de Monet, là des arbres de Cézanne, et ses toiles d'Arles étaient du van Gogh.] Sans doute, il a enrichi l'âme contemporaine. Mais l'asymétrie de ses Christs n'a pas dû l'y aider beaucoup. Et pourquoi ses déformations se résolvent-elles toujours en un surcroît de laideur? M. Gauguin, ou les ouvriers de M. Delaherche, ou les céramistes de Takatori savent incorporer au grès d'émouvantes teintes. M. Gauguin tire de cette manière des effets très décoratifs. Il est plus statuaire que peintre, et il faut admirer sa sculpture; mais, de concession en concession, on admirera les pots funéraires tzapotèques. Et M. Emile Bernard? Eh bien, il exposait, le mois dernier, à la Société des Artistes indépendants, un tableau de sainteté, sous le titre peu compromettant de *Souvenir*. Le souvenir de quoi? d'une de ces monstrueuses gravures en criblé, antérieures même aux xylographies et dont Hollande et Allemagne, en d'érudits mémoires, se disputent les actes de naissance,—le criblé connu sous le nom de *Jésus aux Oliviers*. Le bel idéal.")

58. Aurier, *Oeuvres posthumes*, 209. Here the author asserts that painting, like literature, was undergoing an idealist revolution. In his famous article on Van Gogh, ibid., 265, he spoke of the artist's "l'âme d'illuminé." Aurier also spoke of the artist's soul in his "Essai sur une nouvelle méthode de critique," ibid., 186. In his essay on Gauguin, ibid., 219, Aurier stated that in his pottery Gauguin was more a modeler of souls than clay.

ence to Aurier who had coined the term "idéistes"—Fénéon suggested that "today the naissant painters have given over to the Gauguin adventure. It is the impressionism of literary tendencies which seduces them."[59]

Clearly, Fénéon was not happy with the influence of the symbolist literary world on art. He saw any incursion of literature into the visual arts as a backward and antimodern step. Nor was Fénéon alone in such thinking. Others in the neo-impressionist camp were dead-set against such literary influence in painting. Camille Pissarro equated symbolist tendencies in painting with both artistic and political evil:

> The frightened bourgeoisie, astonished by the immense clamor of the disinherited masses, by the insistent demands of the people, feels it necessary to lead the people back to superstitious beliefs. Hence the bustling of religious symbolists, religious socialists, idealist art, occultism, Buddhism, etc., etc. That fellow Gauguin has sensed this tendency.[60]

In 1895, referring to Gauguin, Paul Signac wrote succinctly in his diary, "let us study Delacroix, Corot, Puvis, Manet, and leave those humbugs to their own devices." Elsewhere in the same entry he made fun of the symbolist painters with "leurs merdes mystérieuses" and quoted Octave Mirbeau satirizing the symbolist fondness for lilies, "des lys, des lys . . . de la merde."[61] Georges Lecomte—an early protégé of Fénéon—worried, in an important article from 1892 summarizing all recent trends in the arts, that painting was becoming literary and philosophical.[62] He felt

59. Fénéon, *Oeuvres*, 200. ("Aujourd'hui les peintres naissants donnent dans l'aventure de Gauguin, c'est l'impressionnisme à tendances littéraires qui les séduit.")

60. From a letter to his son Lucien as quoted in Rewald, *Post-Impressionism*, 441. Belinda Thomson, "Camille Pissarro and Symbolism: Some thoughts prompted by a recent discovery of an annotated article," *Burlington Magazine*, cxxiv, no. 946 (January 1982), 14–23, offers an excellent account of Pissarro's antagonism toward symbolism on both the artistic and political level.

61. Paul Signac, "Extraits du journal inédit de Paul Signac, I, 1894–95," *Gazette des beaux-arts*, xxxvi (July–September 1949), 117, 119. ("Etudions Delacroix, Corot, Puvis, Manet et laissons ces bons fumistes se foutre de nous.") Mirbeau used the line in a review published in *Le Journal* (7 April 1895) and reprinted in Mirbeau, *Des artistes, première série, 1885–1896, peintres et sculpteurs* (Paris: Ernest Flammarion, 1922), 212–19.

62. Lecomte, "Salon des XX, conférence de M. Georges Lecomte," *L'Art moderne* (14 February 1892) (21 February 1892) (28 February 1892). The quote is on page 67 of the last section.

that the art of Gauguin and his followers was too much concerned with ideas and too little concerned with plastic beauty and suggested that these ideas would be better worked out in literature.

The second complaint made by Félix Fénéon and others against Gauguin was purely stylistic. Fénéon found Gauguin's style ugly. In his 1891 article on Gauguin Fénéon spoke of "terrorizing reality" and asked why Gauguin's "deformations always resolve themselves in an increase of ugliness."[63] In "Quelques peintres idéistes," Fénéon suggested that the followers of Gauguin had "for rather problematic advantages impover-ished reality—perspective, outline, value," while the neo-impressionists had glorified reality.[64] Georges Lecomte worried that Gauguin and his followers would go too far in their deformation of nature and argued eloquently that the ideal was to be found in nature, not in ideas.[65]

The twofold complaint that Fénéon and others made against Gauguin appears contradictory at first. On the one hand Gauguin was upbraided for a reactionary return to literary values in art. On the other hand there was a reticence to accept Gauguin's deformations of nature—an argu-ment which sounds, at least to modern ears, rather conservative. But although Fénéon's position appears to have been both modern and con-servative, in reality the arguments were not contradictory. Indeed, within the context of naturalism his position was perfectly understand-able. Naturalism had fought against the incursion of literature into the visual arts and for the restriction of the art of painting to the perceivable world. To the naturalist, modern meant the very opposite of the literary and the ideal; Fénéon, though not a naturalist critic, was paying homage to the naturalist heritage in his complaints against Gauguin. Fénéon championed an art that went forward from naturalism, not backwards. Certainly such was the sentiment echoed by Camille Pissarro when he spoke of Gauguin in the following manner:

> I criticize him for not applying his synthesis to our modern phi-losophy which is absolutely social, anti-authoritarian and anti-mystical.—There is where the problem becomes serious. This is

63. Fénéon, *Oeuvres*, 193. ("M. Gauguin terrorise la réalité" / "Et pourquoi ses déformations se résolvent-elles toujours en un surcroît de laideur?")

64. Ibid., 200. ("Bref, pour de problématiques avantages, ils appauvrissent la réalité,—perspective, silhouette, valeurs.")

65. Lecomte, "Salon des XX" (28 February 1892), 66ff.

a step backward: Gauguin is not a seer, he is a schemer who has sensed that the bourgeoisie are moving to the right, recoiling before the great idea of solidarity which sprouts among the people. . . . The Symbolists also take this line! What do you think? They must be fought like the pest![66]

Similarly, an article published in *La Révolte* in June 1891, just two months after Fénéon's *Chat noir* article about Gauguin, viewed symbolism as backwards, specifically in comparison with neo-impressionism. The author of the unsigned article praised neo-impressionism for its modern technique and its modern (i.e., socialist) attitude toward subject matter. Seurat was particularly praised for his depiction of the "debasement of our epoch of transition" and his understanding of the great social exchange between workers and the city of Paris. However, the author specifically excepted from praise the new tendencies of the "symbolist impressionists who, in confining themselves to retrograde subjects, fall into the old errors and forget that art does better to search out the future, so vast, than to exhume the legends of the past, no matter how golden they may be."[67]

It must be remembered, as was noted in the second chapter, that naturalism—in its most modern form, impressionism—was still a viable and powerful force throughout the 1880s. In spite of the reaction against naturalism in the novel and against positivism in philosophy, advanced naturalist ideas in painting still held sway in many circles. This is certainly what Octave Mirbeau meant to be understood from his sharp criticism of Odilon Redon in 1886:

After innumerable battles, all pacific by the way and in which only ink was splattered, everybody agrees that it is necessary for art to approach nature. . . . Among the painters there is hardly

66. Pissarro, *Letters to His Son Lucien,* ed. John Rewald (New York: Pantheon, 1943), 164. Pissarro often attacked Gauguin and the mystical tendencies of the symbolists in the early 1890s. See, for instance, *Letters,* 163, 170, 178, 180, 221.

67. [Paul Signac], "Variétés, impressionnistes et révolutionnaires," *La Révolte,* IV (June 1891), 3–4. The periodical, edited by the famous anarchist Jean Grave, advertised itself as an "organe communiste-anarchiste." An editorial comment at the beginning of the article notes that it came from a "comrade impressionniste." Robert L. Herbert and Eugenia W. Herbert, "Artists and Anarchism," 479, identified the author as Paul Signac. (". . . l'avilissement de notre époque de transition" / ". . . les impressionnistes-symbolistes qui, en se confinant dans des sujets rétrogrades, retombent dans les vieux errements et oublient que l'art consiste beaucoup plus à chercher dans l'avenir, si large, qu'à exhumer les légendes du passé quelque dorées qu'elles soient.")

anybody except M. Odilon Redon who resists the great naturalist current and who opposes the thing dreamed to the thing experienced, the ideal to the truth.[68]

Later Mirbeau drastically changed his opinion of Redon just as he would promote the symbolist art of Paul Gauguin and preach an antinaturalist line.[69] But in 1886 Mirbeau and many others viewed naturalism as concomitant with modernism. To a certain extent Félix Fénéon shared this view.

Of course Fénéon did develop some very specific complaints against naturalism in painting. Fénéon hated Salon naturalism and saw impressionism itself as more and more old-fashioned in comparison with neo-impressionism. But Fénéon never questioned the naturalist assumption that nature was the starting place for art. He also followed the lead of impressionist criticism concerning subject matter. Fénéon concentrated on the style of neo-impressionist painting, not its subject. He took for granted the impressionist focus on modern life or landscape and never challenged it. Indeed, Fénéon's infatuation with science is another example of his grounding in naturalist thought. Finally, his political association with anarchist ideas can be seen as a step beyond, but in the same basic direction as, the naturalist affinity with socialism. Indeed, if it can be said that Fénéon went against naturalism in any way it was more in the form of taking certain naturalist principles to their more or less logical conclusions than in any direct attack on the principles themselves. Rather than antinaturalist, Fénéon's art criticism can at times best be described as postnaturalist.

This point is important because it can explain why Fénéon was so cold toward the art of Redon and so critical of that of Gauguin. Fénéon, whose own attitude toward art criticism involved a rational, logical, and unemotional consideration of style, was deeply suspicious of the emotional and vague criticism that surrounded both Redon and Gauguin. Fénéon preferred a beauty that came from an artist's sensitive treatment of nature, not one based on vague mysteries or Platonic ideals. Thus, in a later criticism of the art at the Rosicrucian Salon of Joséphin Péladan,

68. John Rewald, "Odilon Redon," in *Odilon Redon, Gustave Moreau, Rodolphe Bresdin* (New York: Museum of Modern Art, 1961), 33. Also in Rewald, *Post-Impressionism*, 156.

69. See, for instance, his letter to Redon in Rewald, "Odilon Redon," 37; and his article on Gauguin, first printed in *L'Echo de Paris*, February 1891, and reprinted in *L'Art moderne*, xi (22 March 1891), 92–94.

he noted that "three pears on a napkin by Paul Cézanne are moving and sometimes mysterious, and all the Wagnerian Valhalla is as uninteresting as the Chamber of Deputies when they paint it."[70] Fénéon was deeply critical of the literary nature of Gauguin's painting. To a critic nurtured in a naturalist, modernist environment any return to literary subject matter was a step backward that must be shunned. Although Fénéon was an eloquent proponent of the best in symbolist literature he genuinely feared any incursion of literature into art. To a large extent his fear was not unfounded. During the 1880s, as we have noted, there were many signs that even the most advanced circles were showing affinities with conservative, idealist thought. And it was precisely at the time when Fénéon declared himself opposed to the new tendencies of Gauguin that idealism and conservatism were making their greatest inroads into avant-garde circles.

The years 1888 and early 1889 were witness to the growth of a large right-wing coalition that could have swept General Georges Boulanger into power had the man not been too timid to take up the call. Fénéon, the socialist/anarchist, must have viewed these goings-on with real trepidation. Even worse, the influence of Boulanger found its way into the very heart of symbolist literary circles. In April of 1888 the *Revue indépendante* published an article by Maurice Barrès, one of the earliest supporters of symbolist tendencies in writing, that argued the importance of General Boulanger to the new generation.[71] This must have doubly disturbed Fénéon as he himself had established the *Revue indépendante* as a materialist, rationalist, and left-leaning publication. By the late 1880s, however, the publication was shifting more and more to the right and becoming more idealist. By the early 1890s it had become an organ for idealist tendencies and was publishing articles sympathetic to Joséphin Péladan. Nor was this the only example of a change in the little periodicals that had earlier supported symbolism and neo-impressionist painting.

In 1886 one could have turned to several periodicals for information on the new trends in art and literature. Principal among these were the *Revue indépendante*, the *Revue contemporaine*, the *Revue wagnérienne*, *Le Symboliste*, and *La Vogue*. For a brief time, in 1888, the symbolists con-

---

70. Fénéon, *Oeuvres*, 211. (". . . trois poires de Paul Cézanne sur une nappe sont émouvantes et parfois mystiques, et que tout le Wallahl wagnérien est aussi peu intéressant que la Chambre des députés, quand ils le peignent.")

71. Maurice Barrès, "M. le Général Boulanger et la nouvelle génération," *La Revue indépendante*, VII (April 1888), 55–63.

trolled a tiny publication called *La Cravache*. But by 1889 all of these publications—except the *Revue indépendante*, which was sold in that year—had ceased to exist. In their place an entirely new generation of periodicals appeared. Almost without fail these new periodicals, such as *L'Ermitage* (1890), *La Plume* (1889), *La Revue blanche* (1889), and even the solid *Mercure de France* (1890) were caught up in the new idealist trends sweeping the Parisian art world. By the 1890s idealism was in vogue. Indeed, idealism, conservatism, and their religious concomitant, Catholicism, were taking a toll among the symbolists, and many of Fénéon's former associates were among those to convert.

As I noted in Chapter 2, conversion to Catholicism carried certain specific connotations in late nineteenth-century France. Catholicism at this time was antiscience, stood foursquare against modern society and socialist thought and was, in essence, deeply conservative. Given this it seems incredible that some of the most advanced members of symbolist circles turned to the faith. By the early 1890s, J.-K. Huysmans had converted to a fierce Catholicism that would lead him to a monastery in 1895. Charles Morice, whose *La Littérature de tout à l'heure* was such an important summation of the new literary trends, also moved toward Catholicism. He had indicated an interest in the ideals of the Catholic Church in *La Littérature de tout à l'heure* and published on mysticism in *Le Saint-Graal,* one of the new symbolist/Catholic periodicals of the 1890s, and later converted to Catholicism.[72] Téodor de Wyzewa, whose *Revue wagnérienne* was an important organ of the early symbolist movement and who came to the *Revue indépendante* under Fénéon's editorship, was a third convert from among the young generation. His conversion was particularly fierce; unlike Morice and Huysmans, who continued to remain in touch with advanced circles, Wyzewa completely divorced himself from the concerns of his symbolist days. By 1893 Wyzewa had taken up a thoroughly Catholic, anti-intellectual, and anti-Semitic stance and had joined Ferdinand Brunetière on the staff of the ultraconservative *Revue des deux mondes.*[73] These conversions and the general trend toward Catholicism of this period must have disturbed Fénéon. In the tradition

72. Morice did not definitively convert until the twentieth century, *Lettre à mes amis sur quelques points de durable actualité, I—Le Retour ou: mes raisons* (Paris: Messein, 1913). However, he had thought of religion as central to the artistic experience since the 1880s at least. Also see his *Du sens religieux de la poésie* (Geneva: Eggimann, 1893).

73. See Elga Liverman Duval, "Téodor de Wyzewa: Critic Without a Country" (Ph.D. dissertation, Columbia University, 1960), 90ff. Also see Paul Delsemme, *Téodor de Wyzewa* (Brussels: Presses universitaires de Bruxelles, 1967), 178ff.

of positivist rationalism and socialist anarchism, Fénéon had made his literary debut with a strong attack on religious education; and he never wavered from this position, just as he never revoked his early anarchist/socialist leanings.[74]

Thus Fénéon and the young critics who rallied around his artistic opinions—including Gustave Kahn, Paul Adam, and Georges Lecomte—rejected what they saw as a trend toward the reactionary and the literary in painting. To a large extent this trend was the principal reason for the split between neo-impressionist critics and other critics in the new literary circles. To Fénéon and his friends, enamored with the concept of a modern socialist society, both the decadents and the new "literary" trends in the art of Gauguin represented a reactionary movement. As I have shown, there was already a tendency toward the reactionary and a certain conservatism in much of symbolist art criticism. Fénéon and his associates recognized this and argued against it. Their efforts to defend modern ideas were, however, in vain; the next generation of symbolist art moved in exactly the direction that Fénéon warned against, namely toward Paul Gauguin. This move was, of course, hardly a cause for alarm. But Fénéon felt it was and, from his point of view, concern was justified. Indeed the art criticism of Albert Aurier, the one critic who most vocally supported Gauguin in the early 1890s, exhibited certain conservative leanings. After Aurier's premature death in 1892 the symbolist criticism of art was to take exactly the direction that Fénéon had feared. It became deeply conservative.

74. Fénéon, *Oeuvres*, 885–87. The article, entitled "L'Education Spiritualiste," appeared in the *Revue indépendante* in June 1884. Fénéon may have had something to do with the anticlerical tone of the *Revue indépendante* at that time. Just one month earlier, under his editorship, the journal had published a scathingly antireligious education tract by the famed anticleric Edgar Monteil, "*Le Manuel d'instruction laïque* et la critique," *La Revue indépendante*, i (May 1884), 9–21. It is difficult to be precise concerning Fénéon's attitude toward Catholicism in later years since he rarely talked about it. He did write an appreciation of Léon Bloy, *Oeuvres*, 68–88, in 1887, but his appreciation was of the author's style not his subject matter. Later, *Oeuvres*, 865, he sarcastically found Bloy's ideas "a bit simple-minded." In 1894 he made fun of the new symbolist/Catholic periodical *L'Etoile*, calling it "L'Etoile à matelas," from "toile à matelas" or mattress ticking (*Oeuvres*, 940). Certainly, Fénéon's anarchist sympathies would have put him at odds with the Catholic church, given its right-wing political position at this time. Furthermore, Michael Orwicz, "Confrontations et clivages dans les discours des critiques du salon, 1885–1889," has shown the rightist political implications of Breton subjects in painting. Images of devout peasants were, according to Orwicz, of use to conservative factions. Such an interpretation would have rendered Gauguin's paintings of Breton religious subjects all the more distasteful to Félix Fénéon.

4

SYMBOLISM DIVIDED:

ALBERT AURIER'S TRADITIONALISM

Albert Aurier has long been recognized as one of the most important Parisian art critics of the early 1890s. Indeed, if one were to name a single writer most deserving of the title "symbolist art critic," Aurier would surely be that writer. Unlike the other avant-garde critics of the period, he closely and specifically identified himself with symbolist painting. Because J.-K. Huysmans ceased writing about avant-garde painting by the late 1880s, he left no commentary on the symbolist art of Gauguin or the Nabis. Huysmans was also much more concerned with writing novels than art criticism; furthermore, although he retained a strong interest in the visual arts, his conversion to Catholicism led him to concentrate almost exclusively on religious painting. Félix Fénéon, as we have shown, was antagonistic toward symbolist developments in the art of Gauguin and the Nabis. Aurier not only defended Gauguin, as well as the Nabis, but generally championed symbolism in painting, a concept that he was one of the first to define.[1] Unlike either Fénéon or Huysmans, Aurier also wrote about the role of the critic, producing a long but unfortunately incomplete essay on criticism itself.[2] Even in his own day Aurier was best known as a critic.[3]

Aurier distinguished himself by writing the first study of Vincent van Gogh, as well as major articles on Gauguin, Monet, Renoir, Pissarro, and Eugène Carrière. In spite of the fact that his career in Paris spanned only six years, he established himself as the foremost voice of avant-garde painting by the year of his untimely death, 1892. He wrote art criticism for *La Revue indépendante, La Pléiade, Le Décadent, La Revue encyclopédique, La Vie moderne,* and *La Plume.* In 1889 Aurier established his own weekly magazine, *Le Moderniste illustré.* This publication, which only ran to eight numbers, showed a marked interest in the visual arts, offering several important articles by Aurier himself as well as articles by Emile Bernard and Paul Gauguin. Aurier was also one of the founders of the *Mercure de France* and, from its beginning in January 1890 until November 1892, he formulated the journal's artistic taste. During this three-year period Aurier not only produced ten major articles for the *Mercure* but also wrote its widely read calendar and review section, "Choses d'art." From his position at the *Mercure de France* Aurier was able to exert a good deal of influence. Paul Gauguin courted him to write an article on his paintings. Pissarro knew and often commented on his writings, although by no means always favorably. When, in the early 1890s, Jules Huret of the *Echo de Paris* interviewed the most important figures in the Parisian artistic and literary world concerning the state of the arts, Aurier figured among them. Although he died at only 27 years of age, Albert Aurier had become an established and respected figure in Paris.

Despite Aurier's important position in the art world, little had been written about his art criticism until recently. Both Margaret Lunn and

1. In "Le Symbolisme en peinture: Paul Gauguin," *Mercure de France,* ii (March 1891), 155–65 (reprinted in Aurier, *Oeuvres posthumes,* 205–19); and in "Peintres symbolistes," *La Revue encyclopédique,* ii (April 1892), 474–86 (reprinted in *Oeuvres posthumes,* 293–309).

2. Aurier, "Essai sur une nouvelle méthode de critique," *Oeuvres posthumes,* 175–202.

3. See, for instance, Julien Leclercq, "Albert Aurier," *Essais d'art libre,* ii (November 1892), 203, who says that criticism was the most complete part of Aurier's work. The oration given at Aurier's funeral also stressed his accomplishments as a critic, *Mercure de France,* iv (November 1892), 285.

Patricia Mathews have produced involved studies of Aurier's work and the reader would do well to consult these for a fuller treatment of the critic.[4] This chapter is not meant to offer a complete discussion of Aurier's work but rather to focus on one aspect of that work: its traditionalist bias.

G.-Albert Aurier, born at Châteauroux in 1865, came to Paris in 1883, originally to study law, but he eventually gave this up to pursue a life in advanced literary and artistic circles. He took an apartment in the rue Lepic in Montmartre and began to mingle with the Parisian avant-garde. From his first days in Paris he spent a good deal of time looking at art, first in the Louvre where he especially appreciated the work of the Italian primitives, and later at the annual Salons and in private galleries. His first poems were published in Anatole Baju's *Le Décadent* in 1886, and his first art criticism appeared in that same periodical two years later, under the pseudonym Marc d'Escaurailles.[5] The article, a Salon review, was published just before an encounter that would have a good deal to do with his subsequent interest in the art of Gauguin and Van Gogh. In May of 1888 Aurier met Emile Bernard at St. Briac in Brittany. The two became friends and exchanged letters. Apparently it was Bernard who initiated Aurier into the world of avant-garde painting. For the next four years Aurier steeped himself in contemporary painting, at the same time developing his own critical personality. When he died of typhoid fever on 5 October 1892, he was the strongest active spokesman for symbolist painting in Paris.

To a large degree Aurier's work stands as a perfect example of the

4. See Lunn, "G.-Albert Aurier, Critic and Theorist of Symbolist Art"; and Mathews, *Aurier's Symbolist Art Criticism and Theory*. Also note Carol M. Zemel, *The Formation of a Legend, Van Gogh Criticism, 1890–1920* (Ann Arbor: UMI Research Press, 1980), 59–68, for a good discussion of Aurier's article about Van Gogh. The article itself has been published and translated in Ronald Pickvance, *Van Gogh in Saint-Rémy and Auvers* (New York: Metropolitan Museum of Art, Abrams, 1986), 310–15. Aside from the work of Mathews and Lunn, one might note the following for biographical information: Adolphe Retté, *Le Symbolisme*, 59–66; Julien Leclercq, "Albert Aurier"; the memorial issue of the *Mercure de France* (November 1892); Rémy de Gourmont's introduction to Aurier, *Oeuvres posthumes*; Marcel Coulon, "Une minute de l'heure symboliste, Albert Aurier," *Mercure de France*, cxlv (February 1921), 599–640; Jean de la Baume, "Albert Aurier," *La Revue indépendante*, xxv (October 1892), 130–40; Gaston Couturat and Jules Couturat, "Petites polémiques mensuelles: *Feu*, M. G.-Albert Aurier," *La Revue indépendante*, xxvi (February 1893), 45–66; and Svetozar Rusic, "Biographie d'Albert Aurier," *Dossiers du Collège de Pataphysique*, no. 15 (1961), 47–51.

5. Marc d'Escaurailles [pseudonym of Aurier], "Le Salon de 1888," *Le Décadent*, iii (15–31 May 1888), 9–14 and (1–15 June 1888), 8–12.

confluence of advanced and conservative thinking noted throughout this book. Indeed, Aurier was in many respects the very embodiment of Fénéon's fear that Parisian artistic circles were taking a turn toward a more conservative, "literary" view of painting. Aurier's conservatism can be demonstrated in several ways. My first consideration will be to contrast his criticism with that of Félix Fénéon. Indeed, there was a major split in the thinking of these two important critics.[6]

AURIER VERSUS FÉNÉON

Although Félix Fénéon and Albert Aurier shared positions of leadership among the small group of critics who supported advanced painting in France during the symbolist period, it is the difference between them that dominates any close comparison of their work and personalities. Even their appearance and demeanor emphasized their dissimilarity. Fénéon was a tall, thin man of quiet and meticulous manner.[7] He often wore capes in his younger days and sported a goatee. His air was aristocratic and ironical, yet mannered and courteous. Aurier, on the other hand, was a large man who swaggered through the streets of Paris, as his friend Adolphe Retté noted, "brandishing his right hand like a club, ready to knock his ideas into the insubordinate skulls of the bourgeoisie."[8] An affable individual, Aurier was given to nocturnal rowdiness, such as bellowing like a cow in the streets to disturb both police and sleeping Parisians. On at least one occasion his prankish behavior netted him a night in jail: he was arrested for leading a group of friends from a banquet screaming the music from Wagner's "Ride of the Valkyries" in full voice.

6. Sven Lövgren, *The Genesis of Modernism*, suggests that there was a direct continuity between Fénéon and Aurier; what follows is in opposition to that opinion. A further discussion of the relationship between these critics may be found in my "In 1891: Observations on the Nature of Symbolist Art Criticism."

7. On Fénéon's personality see Joan Halperin, *Félix Fénéon, Aesthete and Anarchist in Fin-de-Siècle Paris*, 5–20. Halperin, 236–37, also notes the differences between Aurier and Fénéon. For more on Fénéon's personality see John Rewald, "Félix Fénéon," 58ff., and *Post-Impressionism*, 140. Also see the introduction by Joan Halperin to Fénéon, *Oeuvres*, xxxi–lxvii.

8. Retté, *Le Symbolisme*, 59. (". . . en brandissant sa main droite comme un battoir destiné à plaquer ses idées sur le crâne réfractaire des bourgeois.")

In spite of the fact that Fénéon was only four years older than Aurier, the two represent different generations of art criticism. The bulk of Fénéon's work as a critic dates from the 1880s, and by 1892 he was approaching the end of his critical output. Aurier's career was really just beginning in the 1890s, and he certainly would have produced criticism throughout the decade had he lived. Fénéon chose to stop writing criticism at that time, perhaps because of the death of Georges Seurat or perhaps because of the increasing reputation of Gauguin and the new ascendancy of more idea-oriented tendencies in general.

Aurier and Fénéon also belonged to rather different groups within the symbolist movement. When Aurier and Gustave Kahn, a close associate of Fénéon, were questioned by Jules Huret about the state of the arts in Paris, each gave a detailed list of the new and important authors. But their lists differed significantly.[9] Indeed, although Fénéon and Aurier both wrote for the *Revue indépendante,* the latter only began to publish there after Fénéon and his friends had left the journal. Most telling is the fact that Aurier made his debut in Parisian literary circles through Anatole Baju's *Le Décadent.* As was noted in Chapter 3, the antagonism that Fénéon's group felt toward this publication was strong, and Aurier's association with Baju's journal could not have stood him in good stead among them. Ultimately, however, all of these facts would be more or less meaningless if they did not reflect more substantial differences between Fénéon and Aurier. While Aurier did not publish any commentary on Fénéon himself, his attitude toward Fénéon is reflected in his views on neo-impressionism, which Fénéon had so ardently defended.[10]

After Aurier's death in 1892, the *Mercure de France* published a memorial issue with a description of the writer's funeral.[11] Included is an

9. See Jules Huret, *Enquête sur l'évolution littéraire* (Paris: Charpentier, 1891), 130–34 and 392–406. Aurier, for instance, praised Jean Moréas, Charles Morice, and Henri de Régnier while Kahn, who took a jocular attitude to the interview, specifically noted that none of these three had any talent. Aurier also mentioned his friends at the *Mercure de France,* such as Julien Leclercq, Rémy de Gourmont, and Adolphe Retté, while Kahn offered praise for virtually no one.

10. Aurier's attitude toward Fénéon may be indicated by the fact that when he mentions the critics of interest in his "Essai sur une nouvelle méthode de critique," *Oeuvres posthumes,* 200–201, he specifically omits Fénéon, who was very well known at the time. He notes that "to be complete" a new orientation of scientific criticism should be discussed but the manuscript is unfinished here. Was he going to talk about Fénéon? Aurier also used the term "to be complete" in reference to neo-impressionists in "Les Peintres symbolistes," *Oeuvres posthumes,* 306.

11. *Mercure de France,* VI (November 1892), 282–83.

accounting of the artists and writers who gathered at the gare d'Orléans to pay their last respects as Aurier's coffin was put on the train for Châteauroux. The list named some of the most important figures in symbolist literary circles, but only a single supporter of neo-impressionism, the painter Charles Angrand. Whether or not this was an intended snub, there was no love lost between Aurier and the neo-impressionists.

Aurier's commentary on neo-impressionism was, significantly, scant. He rarely bothered to discuss the movement or mention the artists associated with it. He apparently planned an article about Seurat, but it is clear enough from his published commentary on the painter that it would not have been entirely laudatory.[12] This attitude is noteworthy considering Aurier's important position in Paris and the dominant position of neo-impressionist painting within the avant-garde from 1886 through the mid-1890s. When he did mention neo-impressionism his remarks were seldom favorable. His kindest comments seem to have emerged out of a vague sense of duty, as in his "Les Peintres symbolistes" of 1892, in which he discussed all of the new movements and grudgingly mentioned Seurat and his followers "to be complete and just."[13] Elsewhere in this article he spoke of the new movement in painting as being called "école symboliste, peintre idéiste, néo-traditionniste" but not neo-impressionist.[14] For Aurier it was Gauguin and not Seurat who was the "incontestable initiator" of the new art.[15]

Furthermore, Aurier often took the few occasions on which he discussed the movement as opportunities for more pointed jibes. Thus, in writing about Camille Pissarro, he plainly preferred the artist's impressionist work to his neo-impressionist paintings.[16] He suggested that the neo-impressionist method rendered the work of art superficial because of its concentration on color and technique. In his famous article on Gauguin he referred to the "harlequinlike vision of the pointillists."[17] In reviewing the second exhibition of impressionist and symbolist painters

---

12. See Mathews, *Aurier's Symbolist Art Criticism*, 116, where the author suggests that Aurier would have criticized Seurat while treating the painter's work in a more symbolist fashion. His opinions about Seurat certainly would have differed from Fénéon's.

13. *Oeuvres posthumes*, 306. (". . . pour être complet et juste.")

14. Ibid., 295.

15. Ibid., 304. ("L'initiateur incontestable.")

16. Ibid., 239–41.

17. Ibid., 207. (". . . l'arlequinesque vision des pointillistes.")

at the gallery of Le Barc de Boutteville, Aurier referred offhandedly to the blinding downpour of multicolored confetti of the neo-impressionists. In a humorous article written in 1891 Aurier spoke of his concierge who, he said, had a "musical painting," a view of a bell tower behind which was a hidden carillon. Tongue in cheek, he continued:

> But a month ago my concierge was—him too—stung by the tarantula of artistic modernism. He had his painting redone by a student of M. Signac. He had the mechanism of the carillon changed. Today the bell tower stands up through a downpour of multicolored sealing wafers and, when the clock marks noon, the new carillon plays the "Ride of the Valkyries." An impressionist painting with Wagnerian music, isn't that the peak of modernity in art.[18]

Such jokes are reminiscent of conversations between Bernard, Gauguin, and their friends at Pont-Aven. There they invented a character named Ripipoint, a neo-impressionist painter, and made up irreverent ditties that they all sang together about him.[19] It is certain that relations were strained between Gauguin and his followers and the neo-impressionists, as was noted in the last chapter. When Gauguin's friends held a farewell banquet before his departure for Tahiti, no neo-impressionist painters or critics attended.[20] As Rewald notes, it seems logical that Aurier, who was introduced to avant-garde art through Bernard, might have picked up Bernard's attitude toward pointillist painting. Adolphe Retté said that Aurier did not like the neo-impressionists and especially "could not brook the pretensions" of Signac.[21] Julien Leclerc, who said that he had been initiated into the wonders of modern art by Aurier, reflected Au-

18. Ibid., 314–15. ("Or, il y a un mois, mon concierge fut, lui aussi, piqué de la tarentule du modernisme-artistique. Il fit repeindre son tableau par une élève de M. Signac. Il fit changer le mécanisme du carillon. Aujourd'hui le clocher s'érige dans une pluie de petits pains à cacheter multicolores, et, quand l'horloge marque midi, le nouveau carillon joue la Chevauchée des Walkyries.

Le tableau impressionniste à musique wagnérienne, voilà, n'est-ce pas, le comble de la modernité en art!")

19. Rewald, *Post-Impressionism*, 274.

20. See the *Mercure de France*, II (May 1891), 318–20, for a description of the banquet. Halperin, *Félix Fénéon, Aesthete and Anarchist in Fin-de-Siècle Paris*, 219–20, notes that Fénéon was on the guest list but also notes that there is no record of his attendance.

21. Retté, *Le Symbolisme*, 62. (". . . ne pouvait digérer les prétentions.")

rier's feelings when he said that Signac was boring and suggested that neo-impressionist researches resulted in vulgarly symmetrical canvases or puerile inventions.[22]

What was the reason for Aurier's antagonism toward neo-impressionism? Was he simply following the tastes of Bernard and Gauguin? Probably not, since Aurier was not necessarily slave to the opinions of anyone and, as will be noted shortly, was quite capable of disagreements with his avant-garde friends. Succinctly put, Aurier was a child of anti-naturalism. Unlike Fénéon, who had been part of naturalist, materialist circles, Aurier began his critical career as a strong opponent of naturalism. For Aurier, neo-impressionism belonged too much to the naturalist/positivist past and it was on this basis that he rejected it. Consider the following.

One of the most persistent notes of Aurier's criticism was his reaction against the incursion of science into the arts. It was Aurier who complained most bitterly against the "puerile" boast that science could unlock all secrets. It was Aurier who scoffed that the experimental method was "a thousand times less certain than the most bizarre theogony, the maddest metaphysical reverie, the least acceptable poet's dream."[23] Some of Aurier's most biting criticism of nineteenth-century society was aimed at the worship of science, and he reserved special hatred not for pure sciences such as mathematics but for what he called "those obtuse bastards of science, the natural sciences."[24]

Considering his feelings about science, it is easy to see how Aurier and the pointillists might clash. Aurier's attitude toward Charles Henry is such a case. Henry was, of course, quite influential in the development of the art of Seurat and among the critics who supported neo-impressionism. According to Adolphe Retté, who was close to Aurier, the critic deplored the "baleful" influence of Charles Henry on Seurat and considered his aesthetic to be absurd.[25] In his own writings Aurier only mentioned Charles Henry once, taking the opportunity to note

22. Leclercq admitted that he learned about art from Aurier, in "Albert Aurier," 202. His comments on neo-impressionism appeared often in the pages of the *Mercure de France* under Aurier's editorship. See, for instance, "Beaux-Arts," *Mercure de France*, i (May 1890), 175, or "Aux indépendants," *Mercure de France*, ii (May 1891), 298.

23. *Oeuvres posthumes*, 292. (". . . a moins de certitude mille fois que la plus bizarre théogonie, que la plus folle rêverie métaphysique, que le moins acceptable rêve de poète.")

24. Ibid., 175. (". . . ces bâtardes obtuses de la science, les sciences naturelles.")

25. Retté, *Le Symbolisme*, 62. (". . . l'influence néfaste.")

that Henry was not attached to the symbolist movement, in spite of his connections with the Fénéon circle. In his commentary he spoke of Henry's experiments as being interesting but too superficial.[26] That was all, but it was clearly unkind to one of the important figures in neo-impressionist theory.

Aurier, like so many of the young antinaturalist generation, argued most vehemently against the concept of scientific criticism. His unfinished "Essai sur une nouvelle méthode de critique" is a long diatribe against the concept of scientific criticism as expressed in the writings of Hippolyte Taine. Aurier deplored the cold, rational method of critics such as Taine and Emile Hennequin and railed against the incursion of experimental sciences into the critic's domain. For Aurier, Taine's criticism was

> marvelously appropriate to the spirit of a skeptical and materialistic epoch that is no longer capable of believing in anything absolute and that makes a career of scoffing at rational proofs and admits only experimental proofs, to an epoch that, not being able to love art any more than believe in a religion, consoles itself by a kind of coquettishness, in loving the history of religions and the history of art.[27]

As a rebuttal to the socioscientific bias of Taine and his followers Aurier advocated a passionate, even mystical, approach to the work of art:

> Yes, without a doubt, it is a matter of mysticism, and it is mysticism that is missing today, and it is mysticism alone that can save our society from brutalization, sensualism and utilitarianism. The most noble faculties of our souls are in the process of atrophying. In a hundred years we will be brutes whose only ideal will be the commodious appeasement of bodily functions. We will have returned, through positive science, to a pure and simple bestiality. We must react. We must recultivate in ourselves

26. *Oeuvres posthumes*, 302.

27. Ibid., 195–96. ("Elle était d'ailleurs merveilleusement appropriée à l'esprit d'une époque sceptique et matérialiste qui n'est plus capable de croire à aucun absolu et qui fait profession de bafouer les preuves rationnelles et de ne plus admettre que les preuves expérimentales, à une époque qui, ne pouvant pas plus aimer l'art que croire à une religion, se console, par coquetterie, en aimant l'histoire des réligions et l'histoire de l'art.")

the superior qualities of the soul. We must become mystics again. We must learn to love again, the source of all understanding.[28]

While Aurier hated the incursion of science into the arts, Félix Fénéon, as we have already noted, showed a marked interest in certain aspects of science. In style his criticism is cool and detached rather than passionate like Aurier's. In a well-known and typical passage Fénéon dryly described Seurat's masterpiece:

> If, in the *Grande Jatte* of M. Seurat, one considers, for example, a hundred square centimeters covered with a uniform tone, one will find on each centimeter of this surface, in a turbulent mixture of tiny spots, all of the elements that constitute the tone. This lawn in the shadows, some touches, the majority, give the local value of the grass; others, orange, thinly scattered, express scarcely felt solar action; others, of purple, bring in the complementary of green; a cyanic blue, provoked by the proximity of a covering of grass in the sun accumulates its siftings toward the line of demarcation, and beyond that point progressively rarifies them.[29]

Nor did Fénéon limit this carefully analytic style to technical discussions. In describing the subject of the painting he was just as aloof, just as coolly rational:

28. Ibid., 201–2. ("Oui, sans doute, c'est là du mysticisme, et c'est le mysticisme qu'il faut aujourd'hui, et c'est le mysticisme qui seul peut sauver notre société de l'abrutissement, de sensualisme et de l'utilitarisme. Les facultés les plus nobles, de notre âme sont en train de s'atrophier. Dans cent ans, nous serons des brutes dont le seul idéal sera le commode assouvissement des fonctions corporelles; nous serons revenus, par la science positive, à l'animalité pure et simple. Il faut réagir. Il faut recultiver en nous les qualités supérieures de l'âme. Il faut redevenir mystiques. Il faut rapprendre l'amour, source de toute compréhension.")

29. Fénéon, *Oeuvres*, 35–36. ("Si, dans la *Grande-Jatte* de M. Seurat, l'on considère, par exemple, un dm^2 couvert d'un ton uniforme, on trouvera sur chacun des centimètres de cette superficie, en une tourbillonnante cohue de menues macules, tous les éléments constitutifs du ton. Cette pelouse dans l'ombre: des touches, en majorité, donnent la valeur locale de l'herbe; d'autres, orangées, se clairsèment, exprimant la peu sensible action solaire; d'autres, de pourpre, font intervenir la complémentaire du vert; un bleu cyané, provoqué par la proximité d'une nappe d'herbe au soleil, accumule ses criblures vers la ligne de démarcation et les raréfie progressivement en deçà.") The translation of dm^2 as a hundred square centimeters comes from Halperin, "Scientific Criticism and *le beau moderne* of the Age of Science," 57.

The subject: under a canicular sky, at four o'clock, the island, boats gliding by its side, moves with a dominical and fortuitous population enjoying the fresh air among the trees, and these forty-odd people are invested with a summary hieratic drawing, rigorously treated, whether from the back or the face or in profile, seated at right angles, stretched out horizontally, rigidly standing: like a modernizing Puvis.

The atmosphere is transparent and vibrates singularly; the surface seems to vacillate. Perhaps this sensation, that one also feels in front of some other paintings in the same gallery, is explained by the theory of Dove: the retina, anticipating the action of distinct groups of light rays upon it perceives, through very rapid alternations, both the disassociated, colored elements and their resultant.[30]

The passage is vintage Fénéon, sparsely sprinkled with inventive adjectives but ending with a distant, almost arrogantly scientific reference to the esoteric work of the German physicist Heinrich-Wilhelm Dove. Aurier's prose style is fiery in comparison. The following section from one incredibly long sentence about the art of Van Gogh serves to illustrate:

. . . it is the troubling exposition of a strange nature, at the same time truly true and quasi-supernatural, of an excessive nature where everything, beings and things, shadows and light, forms and colors, rear up, rise up in a flying rage, howling its essential and unique song, on a most intense, most savagely high-pitched timbre; these trees, twisted like giants in battle, proclaiming through the gesture of their knotty arms that menacingly and tragically give flight to their green manes, their indomitable power, the pride of their musculature, their sap as warm as

---

30. Ibid., 37. ("Le sujet: par un ciel caniculaire, à quatre heures, l'île, de filantes barques au flanc, mouvante d'une dominicale et fortuite population en joie de grand air, parmi des arbres; et ces quelque quarante personnages sont investis d'un dessin hièratique et sommaire, traités rigoureusement ou de dos ou de face ou de profil, assis à angle droit, allongés horizontalement, dressés rigides: comme d'un Puvis modernisant.

L'atmosphère est transparente et vibrante singulièrement; la surface semble vaciller. Peut-être cette sensation, qu'on éprouve aussi devant tels autres tableaux de la même salle, s'expliquerait-elle par la théorie de Dove: la rétine, prévenue que des faisceaux lumineux distincts agissent sur elle, perçoit, par très rapides alternats, et les éléments colorés dissociés et leur résultante.")

blood, their eternal defying of the hurricane, of the thunderbolt, of wretched nature . . .[31]

Aurier writes like an advocate seeking to convince the reader while Fénéon offers dispassionate clarification and information. Fénéon, almost scientifically, one wants to say, concentrates on the physical aspect of painting, on neo-impressionist technique. Aurier concerns himself with technique only where it serves emotional content. Fénéon deals with facts, Aurier with passionate speculation. Indeed, Aurier did not always limit himself to themes with which the artists under discussion might agree. Van Gogh, while appreciating Aurier's interest and admiring Aurier's article enough to send the author a small study, also found the article to be "exaggerated" and wrote a reply in which he warned against its "sectarian spirit."[32] Van Gogh carefully reminded Aurier of the influence of both Monticelli and Gauguin on his art, as well as that of Meissonier, whose painting the critic had disparaged. While Fénéon worked in close association with the neo-impressionists, Aurier could, and to an extent did, make up his own Van Gogh.

This difference in style between Aurier and Fénéon also reflects another of Aurier's arguments against neo-impressionist art and criticism, its materialist bias. Fénéon had argued in favor of a materialist society in the opening issue of the *Revue indépendante*; as an anarchist he was firmly grounded in rationalist thought.[33] Aurier, on the other hand, derided the materialism of the nineteenth century and sought a return to higher ideals. Aurier admitted that rationalist/positivist thought might well be the necessity of the age but he would not allow any narrowly

31. *Oeuvres posthumes*, 258. (". . . c'est l'étalement inquiétant, troubleur, d'une étrange nature, à la fois vraiment vraie et quasiment supranaturelle, d'une nature excessive où tout, êtres et choses, ombres et lumières, formes et couleurs, se cabre, se dresse en une volonté rageuse de hurler son essentielle et propre chanson, sur le timbre le plus intense, le plus farouchement suraigu: ce sont des arbres, tordus ainsi que des géants en bataille, proclamant du geste de leurs noueux bras qui menacent et du tragique envolement de leurs vertes crinières, leur puissance indomptable, l'orgueil de leur musculature, leur sève chaude comme du sang, leur éternel défi à l'ouragan, à la foudre, à la nature méchante . . .")

32. Rewald, *Post-Impressionism*, 343–44. Mathews, *Aurier's Symbolist Art Criticism and Theory*, 122–23, suggests that Aurier's article is close to Van Gogh's painting in several ways. Zemel, *The Formation of a Legend*, 65ff., notes how upsetting the article was to Van Gogh.

33. See the unsigned article, "Matérialisme," *Revue indépendante*, 1 (May 1884), 1–4. Fénéon was editor in chief of the publication from its beginning so one assumes he at least approved of the article if he did not actually write it.

materialist approach to cloud the domain of art.[34] On the contrary, he felt that only art was left as a refuge for those who wished to go beyond the physical world:

> The sensualism of the century has deprived us of seeing in a woman anything more than a chunk of flesh suitable for the appeasement of our carnal desires. The love of woman is no longer permitted us. The skepticism of the century has deprived us of seeing in God anything more than a nominal abstraction, perhaps nonexistent. The love of God is no longer permitted us.
>
> A single love is still allowed us, that of works of art. Let us, then, throw ourselves on this ultimate plank of salvation. Let us become mystics of art.[35]

For Aurier, then, art was to become the new religion, the new passion in a materialist society deprived of both faith and passion. Aurier took his antimaterialism further by questioning the value of the material world itself as subject for art. This approach was quite different from that of Fénéon, who never attacked the impressionist concentration on nature or scenes from everyday Parisian life as artistic subjects. Aurier praised the painter Eugène Carrière for distancing himself from nature, "detestable nature, life, dirty, banal and wretched life."[36] Aurier's ultimate rejection of impressionism came precisely because he saw it as a variety of realism, "an aesthetic based on sensation."[37]

As might be expected, these differences between Fénéon and Aurier were made manifest in their attitudes toward various artists. They differed not only on Seurat and Gauguin but other artists as well. Both reviewed an exhibition of Eugène Carrière's work at Boussod et Valadon in the spring of 1891 and their opinions were in sharp opposition. Fénéon suggested that the sad smiles on Carrière's women and children,

34. *Oeuvres posthumes*, 198.

35. Ibid., 202. ("Le sensualisme de siècle nous a désappris de voir en la femme autre chose qu'un bloc de chair propre à l'assouvissement de nos désirs matériels. L'amour de la femme ne nous est plus permis. Le scepticisme du siècle nous a désappris de voir en Dieu autre chose qu'une abstraction nominale peut-être inexistante. L'amour de Dieu ne nous est plus permis.

Une seule amour nous est encore loisible, celui des oeuvres d'art. Jetons-nous donc sur cette ultime planche de salut. Devenons les mystiques de l'art.")

36. Ibid., 279. (". . . la détestable nature, la vie, la sale et banale et méchante vie.")

37. Ibid., 208. (". . . d'esthétique fondée sur la sensation.")

repeated so many times, became simpering and commercial.[38] He complained that Carrière achieved his effects through an "arrogant" use of shadow rather than through the more difficult language of lines and colors and concluded that his work was for "littérateurs." Aurier, on the other hand, praised Carrière for his antinaturalist style, suggesting that "souls alone interest him."[39] Aurier worked out a complex view of Carrière in which he portrayed the artist as a painter of memories—memories being the very essence of knowledge. Indeed, Aurier was fond enough of Carrière to make the artist the focus of one of his articles in the series, "Les Isolés," which also included Vincent van Gogh.

Concerning another artist whom Aurier praised as an isolated but inventive genius, Jean-Jacques Henner, Fénéon made a sharp reversal of opinion. In 1883 he found Henner's *Andromède* to be "a magistral page, an enthusiastic hymn to the splendor of form."[40] Four years later, after his introduction to neo-impressionist painting, he found Henner and other Salon painters to represent "sordid intellectual destitution, sempiternal rehashing of worn formulas, touching accord between the naïve stupidity of the common herd and the cunning stupidity of the members of the Institute."[41] Interestingly, Aurier also changed his opinion about Henner, but in the opposite direction. In 1888, as the harried reviewer of that year's Salon for *Le Décadent*, he found Henner's work to be repetitive and "worse than other years."[42] One year later, however, he began his "Les Isolés" series with a laudatory article about Henner. This article was written after Aurier's contact with Emile Bernard in the summer of 1888 and his education in the ways of avant-garde painting. As such the article is witness to an important fact about Aurier's criticism, namely, that he was not hesitant to pursue some rather conservative avenues to promote idea-oriented art. Thus, while Fénéon absolutely reviled a painter like P.-A.-J. Dagnan-Bouveret, for example, Aurier was able to find good qualities in his paintings of Breton peasants.[43] Indeed, this

38. Fénéon, *Oeuvres*, 189.

39. *Oeuvres posthumes*, 279. ("Les âmes seules l'intéressent.")

40. Fénéon, *Oeuvres*, 5. (". . . une page magistrale, un hymne enthousiaste à la splendeur de la forme.")

41. Ibid., 78. ("Sordide dénûment intellectuel, sempiternel ressemelage de formules éculées, touchant accord entre la stupidité naïve de la basse foule et la stupidité roublarde des membres de l'Institut.")

42. "Le Salon de 1888" (May 1888), 12. (". . . plus mauvais que les autres années!")

43. Aurier, "Salon de 1889," 63.

ability to go to conservative sources is one of the key differences between Aurier and Fénéon. Fénéon, at most, only passively praised a few select conservative artists, such as Puvis de Chavannes. Aurier actively championed a return to certain traditional values in art. His article on Henner is a case in point.

AURIER'S DEFENSE OF HENNER

Jean-Jacques Henner was by no means a young, isolated artist when Albert Aurier wrote about him in 1889. Born in 1829 in Alsace, Henner had a long and illustrious, even if slow-moving, career in Paris. He won the Prix de Rome in 1858, began showing at the annual Salons in 1863 and continued to show there until his death in 1905. He won medals in 1863, 1865, 1868, and 1872. In 1873 he was made Chevalier of the Legion of Honor. He won first prize at the Paris World's Fair in 1878 and was made Officer of the Legion of Honor. In 1889 he became a member of the Institut de France. He is best known today for portraits and, especially, for his nudes executed in a misty, sfumato technique, works often entitled *Nymph* or *Nymph by a Fountain* (Fig. 10). His work tends to be small in scale and, at its best, conveys an intimate, poetic quality. The greatest complaint about any group of his quiet and unassuming paintings might be that they are repetitive. He was, by no means, a great innovator. What then did a young avant-garde critic like Albert Aurier see in this old academician?

Aurier's article about Henner, which was published in the critic's own periodical, *Le Moderniste*, in April 1889, began with a disclaimer.[44] Noting that Henner had been an academician for two years Aurier stated that one of the most important requirements for entrance into that body was to have invented nothing. He then suggested that Henner did not really belong in the academy and joked that he was elected to keep Gustave Moreau company. Aurier took pains to explain that although Henner had just been made a member of the Institut he was not an academic painter; he was a painter of talent and personality who hated

44. The article "J-F. [*sic*] Henner" was first published in *Le Moderniste illustré*, 1 (13 and 20 April 1889) and reprinted in *Oeuvres posthumes*, 283–89. All subsequent quotes come from the latter. See the discussion of Aurier's article in Mathews, *Aurier's Symbolist Art Criticism and Theory*, 119–21.

banal formulas. Aurier was aware that in avant-garde circles it was unacceptable to appreciate a painter like Henner. Yet he did.

Aurier went on to say that Henner was a good student who listened to his teachers but ultimately ignored them because of his own special artistic goal:

> To produce a work that would be the synthesis of the sensations, of the ideas, of the moral impressions, of the philosophies of the artist's Self; a work that would be, in all of its parts, the fatal result of all the diverse and unique functions of the Self and that therefore could never be, necessarily, that of M. Everyman, nor those of MM. the painters of the Ecole.[45]

Aurier was careful to distinguish this synthesis of the self from the "nature seen through a temperament" of the naturalists. He argued that an artist need not faithfully reproduce nature to produce sincere work; furthermore, that an artist had every right to alter nature. For him the word "sincere" could apply as much to "poets" like Puvis de Chavannes and Henner as to Courbet, whom he called a "fierce realist."

Simplification—of line, concept, and color—according to Aurier, was the essence of what made Henner a very special talent, almost without equal in the history of art. Aurier would use essentially the same argument in defense of the "deformations" and "synthesis" in Gauguin's painting, and it is signal that he found these traits first in the art of an academician. Nor was this preference a mere quirk. Aurier plainly stated that Henner's subject matter, "Nymphs, naiads . . . nude shepherdesses in the grass," was exactly what he preferred. Aurier was also quite capable of donning the mantle of a conservative religious mentality. He specifically rejected Henner's paganizing of certain Christian themes as being close to blasphemy and decried the artist's use of Christian themes as "pretext." In other words, Aurier advocated a rather traditional sense of decorum.

The Henner article is fascinating because it fills in our picture of Albert Aurier's critical personality. He was clearly prepared to stand

---

45. Ibid., 285. ("Produire une oeuvre qui soit la synthèse des sensations, des idées, des impressions morales, des philosophies du Moi de l'artiste, une oeuvre qui soit, en toutes ses parties, la résultante fatale de tous les divers fonctionnements et des seuls fonctionnements de ce Moi, et qui, partant, ne puisse jamais être, au besoin, ni celle de M. Tout-le-monde, ni celle de MM. les peintres de l'Ecole.")

independent of a strictly modernist position. In this he separated himself from a critic such as Emile Bernard. In fact, shortly after Aurier's article on Henner appeared in *Le Moderniste,* Bernard wrote a review for the same periodical, in which he included work by Henner in a list of the worst to be found at the Palais des Beaux-Arts.[46]

In the Henner article Aurier sounds like many of the critics who praised the artist throughout the 1880s in such conservative periodicals as *L'Art* and *L'Artiste.* Emile Blémont, for example, writing about Henner for *L'Artiste* in 1882 spoke, as Aurier had, of the artist's expression of his inner self.[47] He praised the painter for idealizing nature by playing down the mere accessories of the natural world and concentrating on its essence—the very synthesis of which Aurier was so fond. Blémont even stated, as Aurier would some years later, that love was the core of the artistic experience, that Henner's passion for beauty and his interpretation of reality through this passion, were central to the artist's achievement. Blémont, like Aurier, found Henner's expression to be essentially naïve and spontaneous rather than intellectual, and he compared Henner to the Italian primitives whom Aurier would later praise as examples of the naïve love of art he espoused.

The similarities between Aurier and Blémont are not mentioned as examples of direct influence but rather to indicate the nature of Aurier's interest in Henner. It was an essentially traditional view of an essentially traditional artist—an attitude not surprising for a critic who was, as Patricia Mathews has noted, just beginning to develop his critical acumen.[48] But it was also not surprising for a young critic whose introduction to the Parisian avant-garde was through literary circles—specifically decadent literary circles, as will be noted shortly. Indeed, Henner held a unique appeal for a certain literary sensibility. At their best his nymphs and bathers have about them a feeling of melancholy, and sweet, intimate reverie, suspending the viewer in a nostalgic longing

46. Emile Bernard, "Au Palais des Beaux-Arts," *Le Moderniste illustré,* i (27 July 1889), 110.

47. Emile Blémont [pseudonym of Emile Petitdidier], "Henner," *L'Artiste,* lii (January 1882), 13, 52.

48. Mathews, *Aurier's Symbolist Art Criticism and Theory,* 119–21. It might also be noted that in both the original article as presented in *Le Moderniste* and the reprint in Aurier, *Oeuvres posthumes,* Henner is incorrectly called "J.-F." rather than "J.-J." for Jean-Jacques. Was this simply a typographical error or an example of Aurier's lack of closeness to his subject? To a large extent, as Mathews notes, Aurier used Henner for his own purposes and, unlike Fénéon, for example, was not particularly interested in scrupulous attention to either the artist's intentions or, as it seems, his name.

after a lost arcadian existence. A similar golden twilight mood permeated much of the new literature. Consider, for instance, "Le Faune," from Verlaine's *Fêtes Galantes*:

> Un vieux faune de terre cuite
> Rit au centre des boulingrins,
> Présageant sans doute une suite
> Mauvaise à ces instants sereins
>
> Qui m'ont conduit et t'ont conduite,
> —Mélancoliques pèlerins,—
> Jusqu'à cette heure dont la fuite
> Tournoie au son des tambourins.[49]

The mood here is distinctly nonmodernist and Aurier's interest in Henner reflects a similar sensibility. One need not write off Aurier's defense of this conservative painter to youthful folly. An essential feature of the new literature and the new art criticism of the late 1880s was a decided traditionalism. Aurier is neither *retardataire* nor suspect in judgment here. His aggressive, purposeful defense of Henner is, however, an example of how literary tastes and a traditionalist reverie for the past were part of his critical makeup. This tendency brought him into close proximity with conservative, idealist criticism; just how close, and to what extent Aurier was actually influenced by more conservative criticism, is worth noting.

AURIER AND THE NEW IDEALISM

The very factors that separated Fénéon and Aurier served to bring Aurier closer to certain conservative thinking about art. His antimaterial-

49. An ancient faun of terracotta
    Laughs in the center of the bowling green
    Foretelling without doubt a sequel
    Inadequate to these serene moments

    Which led me and led you
    —Melancholy pilgrims,—
    To this hour of which the flight
    Turns to the sound of tambourines

ist, antiscience, and antinaturalist inclinations were manifestations of the general idealist renaissance of the period. Aurier was not only influenced by that movement; he was very much part of it. When Rémy de Gourmont penned his introduction to the posthumous publication of Aurier's writings he began by saying that he wanted to comment on Aurier's part in the renaissance of idealist art, not mentioning symbolism at all.[50] Similarly, Louis Dumur's review of 1893 of Aurier's *Oeuvres posthumes* spoke of the deceased's relationship to the idealist evolution and again made no mention of symbolism.[51] In spite of Aurier's having championed some of the most advanced painting of his time, two critics writing for the *Revue indépendante*—where Aurier himself had published—could call him reactionary and doctrinaire. The critics, Gaston and Jules Couturat, while noting Aurier's courage as an art critic, complained that his writing was spoiled by a doctrinaire, a priori tone and called him reactionary for his opposition to the scientific criticism of Hippolyte Taine.[52] Like Félix Fénéon, the Couturats feared in Aurier's writing a certain return to conservative values.

Many features of Aurier's criticism reveal how much he shared with idealist criticism of the time. His constant disparagement of Salon painting was common among progressive critics from the 1860s on. But it was also common among more conservative, idealist critics, and Aurier's specific grievances often sound like those of much less avant-garde writers. Thus, when Aurier complained that the Salon of 1891 was a "flood of purely commercial articles," he was giving voice to the same sort of criticism that the conservative Paul Lefort had made about the Salon of 1883, noting in the *Gazette des beaux-arts* that art had become a "metier, un gagne-pain."[53] When Aurier complained that Henner came close to blasphemy by using Christian subject matter as a mere pretext he echoes the sentiments of Charles Bigot, who chided modern artists for lacking "true faith" and contributing to a decline in religious painting.[54] Indeed, many of Aurier's favorite complaints fall in line with

50. *Oeuvres posthumes*, v.

51. Dumur, "G.-Albert Aurier et l'évolution idéaliste," *Mercure de France*, VIII (August 1893), 289–97.

52. Gaston Couturat and Jules Couturat, "Petites polémiques mensuelles," 62.

53. Aurier, *Oeuvres posthumes*, 346. (". . . les flots d'articles de pur commerce!") Paul Lefort, "L'Exposition nationale de 1883," *Gazette des beaux-arts*, XXVIII (1 October 1883), 274.

54. Aurier, *Oeuvres posthumes*, 287. Charles Bigot, "Le Salon de 1883," *Gazette des beaux-arts*, XXVII (1 June 1883), 457–76.

the series of relationships between symbolist and idealist criticism outlined in Chapter 2 of this book. His hatred of realism and slavish copies
of nature was quite typical among idealists. So was his anti-impressionist
stance, his hatred of Hippolyte Taine's criticism, and his desire to create
a "new" idealism. Perhaps most telling was Aurier's hatred of science.

Consider, once again, Aurier's stirring denunciation of the efficacy of
scientific investigation quoted earlier:

> After having proclaimed the omnipotence of scientific observa-
> tion and deduction for eighty years with childlike enthusiasm,
> and after asserting that for its lenses and scalpels there did not
> exist a single mystery, the nineteenth century at last seems to
> perceive that its efforts have been in vain and its boast puerile.
> Man is still walking about in the midst of the same enigmas, in
> the same formidable unknown, which has become even more
> obscure and disconcerting since its habitual neglect. A great
> many scientists and scholars today have come to a halt discour-
> aged. They realize that this experimental science, of which they
> were so proud, is a thousand times less certain than the most
> bizarre theogony, the maddest metaphysical reverie, the least ac-
> ceptable poet's dream, and they have a presentiment that this
> haughty science which they proudly used to call "positive" may
> perhaps be only a science of what is relative, of appearances, of
> "shadows" as Plato said, and that they themselves have nothing
> to put on old Olympus, from which they have removed the de-
> ities and unhinged the constellations.[55]

It is quite instructive to compare this statement with one from the idealist Ferdinand Brunetière, writing here about the philosophy of Schopenhauer:

> [T]wo things seem almost equally certain today: the one, that if
> one had been able formerly to dream of reconciling reason and
> faith, it was a beautiful dream, but it was indeed a dream that
> humanity will no longer take up again; and the other, that sci-
> ence not only will never resolve the enigma of the world and its
> destiny, but further that the very questions which interest us the

---

55. See note 142, Chapter 2.

most will forever remain beyond its grasp. Religions may therefore pass on, to the extent that their mysteries, without which they are only philosophies, are claimed submissible to reason, henceforth and forever emancipated by science. They will not pass on to the extent that there is something beyond and other than science; to the extent that they touch on those problems which, in spite of not being capable of formulation in equations, are not less real or less serious; to the extent that they respond to other needs, more universal, more profound—and perhaps more noble—than that of knowing.[56]

Brunetière's comments, published a year and a half before Aurier's, are remarkably like those of the younger critic. It is by no means impossible that Brunetière's article directly influenced Aurier. It should be remembered that Charles Morice had offered kind words for Brunetière in *La Littérature de tout à l'heure,* and we know that Aurier respected Morice's opinions.[57] Aurier was also drawn to philosophy and would have been interested in an article on Schopenhauer, who was quite fashionable in Paris at the time. The similarity in tone between these two statements by Aurier and Brunetière, however, provides the most convincing evidence of influence. There is in both a tendency toward a somewhat overstated but stirring way of making pronouncements. Both acknowledged that science had forever changed society, but they also retained a belief in something beyond what science could discover. Aurier and Brunetière shared a sense of advocacy, almost proselytizing for faith in a world of values unavailable to scientific investigation.

56. Brunetière, "La Philosophie de Schopenhauer et les conséquences du pessimisme," *Revue des deux mondes,* cii (November–December 1890), 220–21. ("Car deux choses paraissent aujourd'hui presque également certaines: l'une, que si l'on a pu jadis rêver de concilier ensemble la raison et la foi, c'était un beau rêve, mais c'était bien un rêve, que l'humanité ne recommencera plus; et l'autre, que la science, non-seulement ne résoudra jamais l'énigme du monde et de la destinée, mais encore que les questions mêmes qui nous intéressent le plus demeureront toujours en dehors de ses prises. Les religions pourront donc passer, en tant que leurs mystères, sans lesquels elles ne sont que des philosophies, prétendront s'imposer à la raison, désormais et pour toujours émancipée par la science. Elles ne passeront point, en tant qu'elles sont quelque chose de plus et d'autre que la science; en tant qu'elles touchent à des problèmes qui, pour ne pas pouvoir être mis en équations, n'en sont pas moins réels ni moins graves; en tant qu'elles répondent à d'autres besoins, plus universels, plus profonds,—et plus nobles peut-être,—que celui de connaître.)

57. Morice, *La Littérature de tout à l'heure,* 263–64. Jules Huret, *Enquête sur l'évolution littéraire,* 133, quotes Aurier noting the importance of Morice's work.

While it may seem difficult to imagine that Aurier would have been influenced by this staid old critic for the *Revue des deux mondes*—a man whom Gauguin despised—it is worth remembering that Aurier remained independent from his avant-garde artist friends on other matters (for instance, the importance of an artist like Henner). Undoubtedly Aurier would have agreed with many of the sentiments in Brunetière's article about Schopenhauer. He was also influenced by others in the idealist circle, such as Joséphin Péladan, as will be noted shortly. But Aurier's idealism requires further consideration.

The nature of Aurier's idealist theory has been analyzed recently by Patricia Mathews.[58] Aurier's writings clearly reveal his sources in German philosophy, neo-Platonism, and mystical thought. While it must be noted that idealism was only one part of Aurier's aesthetic theory, the very fact that Aurier chose sources in philosophy for any part of his artistic theory deserves recognition. The difference between Aurier and impressionist/neo-impressionist criticism here is signal. Late naturalist criticism in general sought validation for art in the art itself or in the outside world or in the temperament of the artist. Aurier formed a theory—based at least partially on the traditional realm of philosophy—and expected art to abide by it. No matter that Aurier's philosophical sources may be unusual or esoteric, and no matter how avant-garde his ideas were, the very formation of a theory based on philosophy was a return to a more traditional way of looking at art. In impressionist and neo-impressionist criticism the artists created the theory, so to speak, by creating the art. Albert Aurier was intent on something a good deal less egalitarian. Much in the mold of such late eighteenth-century theorists as Winckelmann, Lessing, and Quatremère de Quincy, he developed an idealist concept based on models from the past and looked for contemporary art that lived up to that ideal.

AURIER AND THE DECADENTS

Albert Aurier's relationship with Anatole Baju's *Le Décadent* was somewhat ambiguous. It is known that Aurier made his debut in Parisian literary circles with Baju's publication. Yet Aurier's associate and biogra-

---

58. Mathews, *Aurier's Symbolist Art Criticism and Theory*, 30–40 and elsewhere.

pher, Rémy de Gourmont, suggested he was not really one of the "shrill, myopic puppets" who wrote for Baju and that he really made fun of the whole decadent scene.[59] Similarly, Aurier's close friend, Julien Leclerc, said that the critic never reread his articles for *Le Décadent* without smiling because they had been written in a jocular vein to begin with.[60] Aurier did write a series of poems at the time of his association with Baju that he later gathered under the title "les Pourris" (rotten); certainly these were meant to satirize the decadent mentality.

On the other hand, that Aurier was associated with the publication for over two years, his name appearing among its list of principal contributors, indicates that, at least for a time, he was serious about writing for Baju. Indeed, one of the earliest studies on Aurier, that by Marcel Coulon, written in 1913 but not published until 1921, identified him as a member of decadent circles.[61] Patricia Mathews has recently noted Aurier's seriousness concerning his association with the decadents. Quoting from private letters and from an unpublished manuscript on the movement by Aurier she has shown quite conclusively that his involvement with Baju's circle was profound.[62] Indeed, as Noël Richard has noted, Aurier was second only to Baju himself in the number of his contributions to *Le Décadent*.[63]

In an 1886 article for *Le Décadent* entitled "Sensationnisme," Aurier made a serious, theoretical effort to deal with the goals of the new literature. Written just after the spate of manifestos of literary symbolism that appeared in the early months of 1886, the article was meant to clarify recent developments. Aurier, somewhat perversely, suggested that although in all their proclamations the young writers denounced naturalism and realism, the new movement could more accurately be seen as the most logical extension of realism: symbolism dealt with what was truly real, namely the ideal. The article's appearance, even though it was not particularly well written or fully developed intellectually, shows that, at least in 1886, Aurier considered Baju's publication a good forum for such discussion. But even later Aurier did not completely divorce himself from decadent circles.

Aurier's review of the Salon of 1888, which appeared in *Le Décadent*

---

59. *Oeuvres posthumes*, vi. ("fantoches, myopes et criards")
60. Leclercq, "Albert Aurier," 205.
61. Coulon, "Albert Aurier," 606ff.
62. Mathews, *Aurier's Symbolist Art Criticism and Theory*, 8–10.
63. Richard, *Le Mouvement décadent*, 51.

in May and June of that year, was by no means out of step with the decadent mentality. In one passage he praised the naïve quality of Pierre Lagarde's pastiches of Italian primitive painting. Aurier admitted the artificiality of the work but suggested that it was that very quality which constituted its appeal to "the subtle dilettantishness of a decadent critic."[64] Considering that the typical criticism published in this periodical would characteristically find a painting by the academician Benjamin Constant to be "superb, living, full of an alluringly magisterial and grandiose light," or suggest that neo-impressionist technique was "too rapid," it is not surprising that Aurier's salon would show some *retardataire* tendencies.[65] Indeed, this was the case. Aurier found Benjamin Constant to have a good deal of talent, and he praised a painting by Alfred Philippe Roll, entitled *Manda Lamétrie, fermière*, a rather blatant pastiche of the work of Jules Bastien-Lepage.[66] In spite of mixed criticism of the academician Louis Boulanger, Aurier finally came down on the side of the academic tradition:

> And, however, in spite of my antipathy for this academic painting I must acknowledge that I prefer a work such as this, sober, scrupulously honorable, of an impeccable technique, to such and such boisterous buffoonery of many of those so happily contemptuous of the Institute.[67]

At this point, then, Aurier's criticism showed much of the aggressive backwardness that was typical of *Le Décadent*. Nor would he necessarily reject the associations he made at *Le Décadent* in the future. Years later he still counted the now-forgotten Louis-Pilate de Brinn Gaubast— whom he had met at *Le Décadent* and who wrote Salon criticism in the decadent manner—among the better new writers.[68] But while such loy-

<hr>

64. "Le Salon de 1888" (June 1888), 8. (". . . le subtil dilettantisme d'un critique décadent.")

65. See Chapter 3, note 23.

66. The painting was in the exhibition, *Post-Impressionism* (London: Royal Academy of Arts, 1979–80). It is reproduced in the catalogue of that exhibition, 124.

67. "Le Salon de 1888" (June 1888), 10. ("Et cependant, malgré mon antipathie pour cette peinture académique, je dois avouer que je préfère une pareille oeuvre, sobre, scrupuleusement honnête, d'une science impeccable, à telle et telle tapageuse pitrerie de maints joyeux contempteurs de l'Institut.")

68. See Huret, *Enquête sur l'évolution litteréraire*, 133.

alty might show a circumstantial continuity between Aurier's years at *Le Décadent* and his later phase, it is in style and content that he demonstrates his debt to Baju's circle.

The general tenor of writing in *Le Décadent* can best be described as dilettantish. Its collaborators exhibited great pretension, feigning wide erudition. In a highly mannered style writers referred to philosophy, literature, and any other convenient humanist discipline, in a kind of cultural name-dropping. The periodical was also marked by a tendency toward quick pronouncements, whether pejorative or complimentary. Aurier's comments on Bouguereau in his 1888 Salon review are typical: "A canvas—not to look at: the *Premier deuil,* from Bouguereau. This is cold, unmoving, bombastic, artificially composed, and not painted."[69] This is similar in terseness—though more antagonistic and less descriptive—to a comment like the following on Georges Moreau de Tours by Louis Toche, who wrote the Salon criticism for *Le Décadent* in 1886:

> Moreau de Tours is showing . . . a painting, *La Morphine,* canvas in deliquescent note. Two women, the one twenty-five to thirty years, the other eighteen to twenty, trying to procure some sensations by injecting themselves with morphine. It is very studied as painting, very neurotic allure and, which is not bad, pleasantly situated and natural.[70]

In both cases the criticism is far from the carefully considered analyses of a Félix Fénéon.

Interestingly the closest parallel to the above quotations was to be found not in the small symbolist periodicals but rather in some of the Salon criticism of more established publications such as the *Gazette des beaux-arts,* or *L'Art,* or in newspaper supplements such as that put out by *Le Figaro.* All these showed a proclivity toward the clever phrase, colorful adjectives, and quick, erudite-sounding pronouncements. The style developed, quite naturally, in response to the overwhelming task of

69. "Le Salon de 1888" (June 1888), 10. ("Une toile—à ne pas regarder: le *Premier deuil,* de Bouguereau. —Cela est froid, inému, emphatique, artificiellement composé et pas peint.")

70. Louis Toche, "Le Décadent au Salon." ("Moreau de Tours, expose cette année . . . un tableau, la *Morphine,* toile dans un note déliquescente. Deux femmes, l'une de vingt-cinq à trente ans, l'autre de dix-huit à vingt, essayent de se procurer des sensations en se piquant à la morphine. C'est très étudié comme peinture, très névrosé d'allure, et, ce qui n'est pas mal, c'est bien planté et nature.")

writing a coherent criticism of the massive annual Salons. Critics assumed the role of the refined aesthete, gliding through the galleries, tossing off bons mots. The style, not surprisingly, appealed to Baju's circle.

While Aurier would, of course, offer much more penetrating and decisive writing in later years, he retained some of the dilettantish posturing of this early criticism throughout his career. A comment such as the following—a perfectly serious listing of symbolist sources—from his "Les Peintres symbolistes" reflects his heritage in the style of *Le Décadent*:

> They [the symbolist painters] are, properly speaking, the direct sons of the great mythological image makers of Assyria, of Egypt, of Greece of the royal epoch, the descendants of the Florentines of the XIVth century, of the Germans of the XIth, of the Gothics of the Middle Ages, a little as well the cousins of the Japanese.[71]

Much in the manner of Baju himself, Aurier was prone to spice his writing with references to ancient philosophy and culture in general. But there was more than a stylistic connection between Aurier and the decadents. Some of his most cherished ideas were nurtured in these circles.

Although superficial and at times downright silly, *Le Décadent* was infused with a sense of purpose. Even more than many of the other small literary publications of the period, there was about Baju's group a feeling of mission: they were preserving true culture in Paris. In one article Baju sought to convince the public that the highly regarded writer, Paul Bourget, was not so great as all of France seemed to think; in another, he attempted to organize the literary world against General Boulanger.[72] Whatever his cause Baju was a crusader, and this sense of crusade Albert Aurier would carry to his own work. Aurier often reads like a preacher for culture, lecturing his readers in a manner reminiscent of Baju. Consider, for example, the following from Baju:

---

71. *Oeuvres posthumes*, 304. ("Ils sont, à proprement parler, les fils directs des grands imagiers mythologistes de l'Assyrie, de l'Egypte, de la Grèce de l'époque royale, les descendants des Florentines du XIVe siècle, des Allemands du XIe, des Gothiques du moyen âge, un peu aussi les cousins des Japonais.")

72. Anatole Baju, "M. Paul Bourget," *Le Décadent*, iii (15–31 March 1888), 4–8, and Baju, "M. Boulanger c'est l'ennemi," *Le Décadent*, iii (15–31 May 1888), 14–15.

> What are these mannequins of our modern democracies up to? Poor folks, they claim that the ideal is dead and that man no longer has need of it, and they think they can explain the world with stills and retorts.[73]

In both style and subject this passage is much like that of Albert Aurier, quoted earlier this chapter:

> After having proclaimed the omnipotence of scientific observation and deduction for eighty years with childlike enthusiasm, and after asserting that for its lenses and scalpels there did not exist a single mystery, the nineteenth century at last seems to perceive that its efforts have been in vain and its boast puerile.[74]

The decadent philosophy, as articulated by Baju, contained several thoughts Aurier would later accentuate. When Baju claimed that *Le Décadent* was dedicated to pursuing, "for the benefit of pure Art, the struggle against naturalism," he gave voice to a sentiment dear to Aurier's heart.[75] In his marvelously polemical pamphlet of 1887, *L'Ecole décadent*, Baju had complained bitterly that naturalism was the "true mirror of this democratic society" because the style was absolutely devoid of high ideals.[76] Elsewhere he proclaimed that naturalism was the exact image of "this bastard society, falsely called republican."[77] His disavowal of naturalism and his consequent elitist hatred of Third Republic society were models for Aurier. So too was his desire for a higher ideal in the arts. Both Aurier and Baju sought an art that would raise the sights of the common herd and lift humanity beyond the mire of everyday reality.

Baju's program for the new decadent style also contained much that

73. Baju, "Idéal," *Le Décadent*, I (21 August 1886), unpaginated. ("Où sont ces mannequins de nos démocraties modernes? Pauvres gens, ils prétendent que l'idéal est mort et que l'homme n'en a plus besoin, et ils pensent expliquer le monde avec des alambics et des cornues!")

74. See note 142, Chapter 2. The reader might well note the similarity here between the comments of Baju and Aurier, on the one hand, and those of Ferdinand Brunetière quoted earlier in this chapter.

75. Baju, "Chronique," *Le Décadent*, III (December 1887), 3. (". . . au bénéfice de l'Art pur la lutte contre le Naturalisme.")

76. Baju, *L'Ecole décadente* (Paris: Vanier, 1887), 4. (". . . le Naturalisme, vrai miroir de cette société démocratique n'a jamais eu aucune élévation dans les idées.")

77. Ibid., 6. ("Le Naturalisme a été l'image exacte de cette société bâtarde faussement appelée républicaine.")

Aurier would adopt. He spoke of a literature without descriptions of the physical world, calling for a "rapid synthesis" conveying only "the impression of objects." He called for writers to avoid depiction and instead to "make the heart feel the sensation of things, whether by new constructions or by symbols evoking the idea."[78] All of this has a very familiar ring to those conversant with Aurier's own aesthetic program.

Throughout *L'Ecole décadent* Baju drafted various writers to the decadent cause. He called on Baudelaire, Rimbaud, Verlaine, Barbey d'Aurevilly, and Mallarmé as representatives of the cause. This name-dropping was part of Baju's effort to prove that a decadent school existed at all, and Aurier himself was part of the roll call.[79] Finally, such a marshaling of forces is not unlike what Aurier himself would later do in developing his own description of symbolism in painting. In all, Aurier owed much to Anatole Baju; although his own symbolist aesthetic was far more profound than anything his mentor produced, and his eye for painting was a good deal more educated and unconventional, his grounding in the mood of *Le Décadent* was important to his development. The same may be said for other threads of the fabric of cultural life at the time, as a few more examples will demonstrate.

AURIER AND THE CRITICISM OF PUVIS DE CHAVANNES

Albert Aurier's admiration for the art of Puvis de Chavannes is well known. In his article on Paul Gauguin he listed Puvis and Gauguin as the only great decorators of the nineteenth century. He ranked Puvis along with Gustave Moreau and the English Pre-Raphaelites as predecessors of the symbolist movement. Aurier was also influenced by the criticism of Puvis de Chavannes's painting. Although this fact has not been previously noted it was, considering the circumstances, quite natural. Puvis de Chavannes was the only artist of the late nineteenth cen-

---

78. Ibid., 10. ("Rien que une synthèse rapide donnant l'impression des objets. Ne pas dépeindre, faire sentir; donner au coeur la sensation des choses, soit par des constructions neuves, soit par des symboles évoquant l'idée avec plus d'intensité par la comparaison.")

79. Ibid., 21. Of Aurier, Baju said: "Albert Aurier, as much master of his talent for prose as for verse, has given us in these two genres some pieces where one feels an ardent breath and a powerful inspiration." ("Albert Aurier, aussi maître de son talent pour la prose que pour les vers, nous a donné dans les deux genres des pièces où l'on sent un souffle ardent et une inspiration puissante.")

tury to be almost universally admired. By the 1880s conservatives and symbolists alike championed his work, and during the eighties and nineties his career reached its apogee. It was impossible for anyone in Paris with any interest in the arts not to be aware of Puvis. In addition to long critiques of his paintings in the major Salon reviews, there were several important articles written about the artist.[80] A major retrospective of his easel paintings at the Durand-Ruel galleries during the winter of 1887–88 "set all the critics in motion," as one writer put it.[81] As a young author and art enthusiast, Aurier must have sought out everything he could read on Puvis. Not only did he read avidly, he adopted some of the ideas he found in Puvis criticism. Consider, for instance, Aurier's concentration on the "primitive" in art.

One of Albert Aurier's most cherished notions was that art must return to a more sincere and naïve expression. His favorite example of such expression was the art of the so-called Italian primitives, a term which then referred roughly to artists from Giotto's time through the late quattrocento. Aurier carefully studied the primitives in the Louvre and drew on his feeling for their work in his discussion of many contemporary artists.[82] Thus, paintings by Camille Pissarro reminded him of the "primitive Florentines," and the religious sincerity of Maurice Denis and Charles Filiger was said to be inspired more by the thirteenth century than the "insupportable religious dilettantism of today."[83]

Aurier was not alone among the symbolists in his preference for a more naïve style of painting, nor were the Italian primitives the only ones appreciated. Téodor de Wyzewa, who wrote a lengthy article on primitive German painting in 1887, noted that the "primitive masters"

80. Some of the major discussions of Puvis de Chavannes produced in the 1880s include Arthur Baignères, "La Peinture décorative au XIXe siècle, Puvis de Chavannes," *Gazette des beaux-arts*, xxiii (May 1881), 416–26; Edouard Aynard, "Les Peintures décoratives de Puvis de Chavannes au Palais des Arts," *Revue du lyonnais*, xlvii, no. 2 (1886), 241–58; André Michel, "Exposition de M. Puvis de Chavannes," *Gazette des beaux-arts*, xxxvii (January 1888), 37–44; Louis de Fourcaud, "Notes sur quelques décorateurs, Pierre Puvis de Chavannes," *Revue des arts décoratifs*, ix (1888–89), 1–10, 74–81; Gustave Kahn, "Exposition Puvis de Chavannes," *La Revue indépendante*, vi (January 1888), 142–51; Léonce Bénédite, "L'Exposition des oeuvres de Puvis de Chavannes," *L'Artiste*, lviii (January 1888), 33–37; Thiébault-Sisson, "Puvis de Chavannes et son oeuvre," *La Nouvelle revue*, xlix (November–December 1887), 643–48.

81. Bénédite, "L'Exposition des oeuvres de M. Puvis de Chavannes," 33. (". . . mettre en branle toute la critique.")

82. Noted by Leclercq, "Albert Aurier," 202.

83. *Oeuvres posthumes*, 242, 307–8. (". . . de l'insupportable dilettantisme religieux d'aujourd'hui.")

saw things not necessarily as we do but through the "precious disposition of their souls."[84] Paul Adam praised Georges Seurat for portraying modern Parisians in the manner of Memling and for rendering them "with the pure drawing of the primitives."[85] But the symbolist admiration for the painting of the Middle Ages was not new. Indeed, admiration for more naïve styles of painting continued throughout the nineteenth century. From David's followers, the Barbus, in France, to the German Nazarenes working in Rome, and the Pre-Raphaelites in England, various artists had sought purity in contact with primitive art, with art uncontaminated by a concentration on style.

To a great extent the art of Puvis de Chavannes was the culmination of such primitivist leanings in France, or at least so it was considered by many critics during the eighties and nineties. The "primitives" had been invoked in comparison with Puvis's art since the early 1880s, and it was among the idealist critics who championed Puvis that a taste for primitivism first developed as a reaction against naturalism. Gustave Ollendorff, writing in 1883, was typical of most idealists when he called Puvis the direct descendant of the primitives.[86] Edouard Aynard, in an excellent article on Puvis's Lyon murals, compared them directly to the art of the Middle Ages and stated that their naïve quality was what made them so Lyonnais, thus linking Puvis to the tradition of Hippolyte Flandrin, Louis Janmot, and other neo-primitives from that city.[87] Louis de Fourcaud, in a review of Puvis's retrospective of 1887–88 at Durand-Ruel's, made much of Puvis's "primitivism," suggesting that his naïve simplicity was the very essence of his talent. "Let the pedants and the fools smile," said Fourcaud, "this is the emotion of a child, translated by a primitive, and in this, above all, I see the quintessence of the talent of the author."[88] Such comments pervaded Puvis de Chavannes criticism at

84. The statement is from Téodor de Wyzewa, "Notes sur la peinture wagnérienne et le salon de 1886," *La Revue wagnérienne*, II (May 1886), 104–5. (". . . la disposition précieuse de leurs âmes.") The article on the German "primitives" is Téodor de Wyzewa, "Voyage aux primitifs allemands," *La Revue indépendante*, IV (September 1887), 292–323; (November 1887), 201–35.

85. Paul Adam, "Peintres impressionnistes," 550.

86. Gustave Ollendorff, "L'Exposition nationale de 1883," *Revue des deux mondes*, LIII (November 1883), 448.

87. Aynard, 248ff.

88. Fourcaud, "Notes sur quelques décorateurs," 79. ("Laissons les pédants et les niais sourire: il y a là une émotion d'enfant traduite par un primitif, et j'y vois par-dessus tout, la quintessence du talent de l'auteur.")

this time, and it is not surprising that a young critic might be stimulated by the commentary of influential writers on the work of a major artist to whom he was drawn. Aurier's interest in the primitives and his praise of simplicity and sincerity in their work developed quite naturally in the context of the new idealist criticism.

Another emphasis of Aurier's criticism—his concern for decoration— also served to link him with the writing about Puvis de Chavannes. In his article on Paul Gauguin, Aurier stated that the art of the future would be ideaist, symbolist, synthetic, subjective, and, finally, decorative. He concentrated on the decorative, he said, because "decorative painting, properly speaking, as the Egyptians and probably the Greeks and Primitives have understood it, is nothing more than a manifestation of an art at once subjective, synthetic, symbolist, and ideaist."[89] It was then that he declared Gauguin and Puvis de Chavannes to be the only great decorators of the nineteenth century. This concentration on the decorative did not originate with Aurier's discussion of Gauguin, however; it was a common theme in Puvis de Chavannes criticism. To a large extent Puvis had singlehandedly stimulated a long-dormant interest in decorative painting with his large architectural compositions of the 1880s. Thus, in his 1880 Salon review for the *Gazette des beaux-arts*, the Marquis de Chennevières made a rhetorical plea for walls for the incomparable decorator to adorn.[90] Thiébault-Sisson struck a similar chord in his review of the Durand-Ruel retrospective by suggesting that all the exigencies of Puvis's style came from a decorative aesthetic.[91] And Leonce Benédite noted that in Puvis's art "grand, ideal generalizations are necessities of decoration, which must symbolize the great stages of humanity in themselves, outside of time and place."[92] Throughout the eighties and nineties there was a tendency in Puvis de Chavannes criticism to see the artist's style as a response to the dictates of decorative art. This in turn led to discussions of that style and its deviations from

89. *Oeuvres posthumes*, 216. (". . . la peinture décorative proprement dite, telle que l'ont comprise les Egyptiens, très probablement les Grecs et les Primitifs, n'est rien autre chose qu'une manifestation d'art à la fois subjectif, synthétique, symboliste et idéiste.")

90. Marquis de Chennevières, "Le Salon de 1880," *Gazette des beaux-arts*, xxi (1 June 1880), 502.

91. Thiébault-Sisson, 643.

92. Bénédite, 35. ("Les grandes généralisations idéales sont des nécessités de la décoration qui doit symboliser les grandes étapes de l'humanité en elle-même, en dehors des temps et des lieux.")

strict naturalism, which provided a further important precedent for one of Albert Aurier's most cherished ideas. Idealist critics, writing about Puvis de Chavannes, were a major source for discussions of the concept of synthesis in the early 1880s.

"Synthesis" was nowhere more in evidence than in discussions of Puvis's paintings. Thus, when Aurier claimed that the new art would be "synthetic" or when he praised the "synthesis of drawing" in an artist's work, he was in part paying homage to a lively debate current in Puvis de Chavannes criticism. The concept of synthesis, as discussed in Chapter 2, connoted the artistic license to simplify or even deform nature in order to express an idea. In discussions of Puvis's work "synthesis" took two forms: indirect reference and actual use of the term itself.

Puvis de Chavannes was problematic for critics brought up in an era of naturalistic representation. It was obvious that Puvis did not offer photographic representations of nature, and critics favorable to his work sought to demonstrate that his style was beyond mere depiction. Thus a critic for the *Gazette des beaux-arts* in 1881 praised the *Pauvre pêcheur* for presenting an exalted reality beyond literal reproduction. In spite of some visible imperfections—this writer referred to the somewhat malformed infant in the painting—Puvis had produced an artistic work that attained the supreme goal of art, "making nature more expressive than nature itself."[93] Other critics, while praising Puvis, warned that because of his deformations from nature he made a poor example for young art students to follow. An entire generation of critics was forced to deal with Puvis's level of abstraction and they developed many different explanations for his style, ranging from the exigencies of the decorative mode to a congenital eye problem.[94] But however they explained his tendencies toward abstraction these critics were led, through Puvis's work, to accept the thought that, as André Michel put it, the ideal is "expressed by certain unconscious or systematic deformations of reality."[95] It is a concept that Albert Aurier very much took to heart. But Puvis's idealist supporters not only opened the way for accepting such artistic

93. Jules Buisson, "Le Salon de 1881," *Gazette des beaux-arts*, XXIII (1 June 1881), 491. (". . . rendre . . . la nature plus frappante qu'elle-même.")

94. Michel, "Exposition de M. Puvis de Chavannes," 40. Michel's thought that Puvis's style could be explained by an eye problem was not meant as a criticism, merely a reason. He praised Puvis highly.

95. Michel, "Le Salon de 1884," *L'Art*, XXXVI (1884), 183. (". . . exprimé par certaines déformations inconscientes ou systématiques de la réalité.")

distortion, they also made "synthesis" common language in art criticism of the period.

"Synthesis" perfectly described the style of Puvis de Chavannes. As early as 1881 a critic for *La Nouvelle revue*, recognizing the formal character of Puvis's innovations, found the *Pauvre pêcheur* to be "a complete synthesis of misery, powerfully expressed by the paintbrush, inexpressible by the pen."[96] Throughout the 1880s and 1890s the term, usually coined as *la grande synthèse*, was used to describe Puvis's large compositions. Thus, Edouard Aynard referred to "la grande synthèse artistique" of the Lyon murals.[97] The term became so connected with Puvis that Louis de Fourcaud could say, "everywhere, in everything, the desire for synthesis dominates his thinking."[98] Indeed, by 1893, a critic would use the term against Puvis, complaining about his "love of excessive synthesis."[99] For better or worse, Puvis and synthesis were irrevocably connected in art criticism of this time, and Aurier was certainly aware of the connection when he used the term in his own writing.

That some critics found Puvis overconcerned with synthesis raises an issue that should be addressed here. While the concept of synthesis again demonstrates the crossing of boundaries between advanced and conservative camps, there was a point beyond which conservative criticism was reticent to move. Albert Aurier was not so reticent. It may well be true that Aurier's discussion of the deformations in Gauguin's synthetist style owed much to discussions of synthesis in the art of Puvis de Chavannes, but it is also true that Aurier was unusual in seeing the connection between Puvis and Gauguin and in recognizing Gauguin's art as the perfect embodiment of synthesis. The difference between conservative and advanced camps here lies in the artists in whom each saw certain shared concepts manifested. Aurier was perceptive enough to see Gauguin's synthesis—a perception shared by precious few other critics.

One further aspect of Puvis de Chavannes criticism may well have influenced Albert Aurier's development as a critic. Aurier was certainly aware of the so-called renaissance of idealism, as he participated in it.

<hr>

96. Roger-Ballu, "Le Salon de 1881," 451. (". . . toute une synthèse de la misère, puissamment exprimée par le pinceau, inexprimable par la plume.")

97. Aynard, 256.

98. Fourcaud, "Notes sur quelques décorateurs," 78. ("Partout, en tout, le désir de la synthèse domine sa pensée.")

99. Henri Bouchot, "Les Salons de 1893," *Gazette des beaux-arts*, ix (1 June 1893), 477. (". . . l'amour des synthèses excessives.")

Puvis de Chavannes was also part of it and the literature on Puvis was full of reference to this revival of idealism. Advanced as well as conservative critics concerned themselves with a new ideal that differed from the tired idealism of the Academy. Puvis was the master of this new, invigorated idealism. He was consistently seen as an original artist, not copying the past but arriving at the great ideals of the past in his own manner. Maurice Hamel said Puvis's painting related to the spirit of the Renaissance and antiquity, not to academic banality.[100] Albert Aurier also sought to differentiate his brand of idealism from that of the academy by coining the term *idéiste*.[101] According to Aurier the academic idealists were producing merely another kind of realism and their art failed to deal with ideas at all. Aurier's "idées" referred to Platonic essences that he felt composed the only true existence and the only fitting subject for art. The true artist was the one who could move people to feel the great "idées." But, as was noted in Chapter 2, the attempt to distinguish between old-fashioned and new idealism was common among antinaturalists, and it was also common in the criticism of Puvis de Chavannes. The critic André Michel, for instance, in talking about Puvis's entries to the Salon of 1884, distinguished between the "*idéal*" and the "*idée*," italicizing the terms for emphasis.[102] Finally, Aurier's concentration on Platonic essences as the only fitting subject for art also resembled the line of reasoning Puvis's idealist champions used to explain the painter's simplifications of nature. Puvis rejected detailed observation, retaining only the salient features of the object in order to express the grand ideal.

In his article on the symbolist painters, Aurier declared that all the great artists of the past were symbolists—a statement designed to link the new painting with the great traditions of the Renaissance and antiquity. This may not seem so unusual until we try to imagine someone saying the same thing about impressionism. The impressionists were intent upon breaking with the tradition of the idea-oriented art of the past. Aurier was suggesting that while the form of the new symbolist art was quite unusual, its content was very much to be seen as linked to the great traditions of past art. Similarly, Edouard Aynard was referring to kinship with the very essence of past art when he said that nineteenth-

---

100. Hamel, "Le Salon de 1887," *Gazette des beaux-arts*, xxxv (1 June 1887), 492.
101. Aurier, *Oeuvres posthumes*, 211ff.
102. Michel, "Le Salon de 1884," 182.

century France could not be brought back to traditional ideas of beauty by artists who painted "correctly boring canvases according to old formulas." For Aynard, as for so many other critics at this time, the solution was the work of Puvis de Chavannes, "who proclaims the sovereign power of the idea, who guides and excites our sensibilities to that which is beautiful and worthy of loving, who thereby revives our fatigued hearts."[103] Just so, Albert Aurier sought an art that would allow the viewer to "contemplate in ecstasy . . . the radiant heavens of Ideas."[104] Once again, we gain insight into Albert Aurier's character by comparing him with the idealist champions of the art of Puvis de Chavannes, critics generally outside avant-garde circles. One final example of Aurier's dependence on traditionalist sources can be found in his relationship to one of the most conservative idealist critics of all, Joséphin Péladan.

AURIER AND PÉLADAN

It is very difficult to know just what Albert Aurier thought of Joséphin Péladan. Aurier did not choose to publish his opinions of the critic, in spite of the fact that he must have been aware of all the activity surrounding Péladan's Rose + Croix Salon in 1892. Félix Fénéon, on the other hand, did write a bitingly satirical review of Péladan's exhibition, but there are indications that Aurier might not have shared Fénéon's view.[105] For example, Aurier praised the "beautiful, mystical heads and the synthetic landscapes" of Charles Filiger, one of the artists who showed with Péladan.[106] Furthermore, Aurier's good friend and associate at the *Mercure de France*, Rémy de Gourmont, wrote a review of the Salon de la Rose + Croix for the *Mercure* in May 1892.[107] The review is

103. Aynard, 258. (". . . des tableaux correctement ennuyeux selon de vieilles formules" / ". . . qui proclament la puissance souveraine de l'idée, qui dirigent et excitent notre sensibilité sur ce qui est beau et digne d'amour, qui relèvent ainsi nos coeurs fatigués.")

104. Aurier, *Oeuvres posthumes*, 212–13.

105. Fénéon, *Oeuvres*, 210–11.

106. Aurier, "Deuxième exposition des peintres impressionnistes et symbolistes," *Mercure de France*, v (July 1892), 262. (". . . les belles têtes mystiques et les synthétiques paysages de Filiger.")

107. Rémy de Gourmont, "Les Premiers Salons: indépendants—Rose + Croix—exposition de Mme Jeanne Jacquemin," *Mercure de France*, v (May 1892), 60–66.

notable for two things: its obvious debt to Albert Aurier's thinking and its high praise of Péladan's efforts. Rémy de Gourmont preached the same antinaturalist line that Aurier had installed as the magazine's aesthetic viewpoint and he did so in support of the Rose + Croix. He suggested that it was one of the most important manifestations of the new trends that year, along with certain parts of the *Salon des indépendants* and all of the symbolist exhibitions at the gallery of Le Barc de Boutteville. He compared unfavorable criticism of the Rose + Croix Salon to the kind of criticism faced by Gauguin, and supported both Gauguin and Péladan. It was a far cry from the rousing condemnation that Fénéon had hurled at Péladan. It might also be noted that Antoine de la Rochefoucauld, who was the cofounder of the Rose + Croix Salon along with Péladan, received some very favorable commentary from Rémy de Gourmont. Later that year at Aurier's funeral, Rochefoucauld was among those paying respects.[108] However, it may be rash to assume that Aurier shared Rémy de Gourmont's opinions about Rochefoucauld or Péladan. But firmer evidence of Péladan's influence on Aurier might be found, not in any discussion of Péladan's exhibitions or his activities of the 1890s, but in a book that he published in 1888, at precisely the time when Aurier was developing his own aesthetic.

Péladan published his *L'Art ochlocratique*—from the Greek *ochlos* or "mob"—through the firm of Camille Dalou. It was a collection of his articles written from 1881 to 1883. The first two—"Le Matérialisme dans l'art" and "L'Art Mystique et la critique contemporaine"—had appeared originally in a Catholic publication, *Le Foyer, journal de famille.* Also included was his "Salon of 1882," which seems not to have appeared in any other form, as well as his long "Salon of 1883," which appeared originally in *L'Artiste.* Throughout, Péladan's criticism is strident and biased. He postures as an advocate seeking a return to traditional religious values in art, and he is fiercely antimodern. It is interesting to note just how a modernist critic like Aurier could have been influenced by the self-styled "Sâr."

Aurier shared a number of attitudes with Péladan, attitudes common to other idealist critics as well. For instance, Péladan was highly enamored of the art of the Italian primitives. He spoke with reverence of visiting the "petite salle des primitifs" in the Louvre, much as Aurier

108. See the Aurier memorial issue of the *Mercure de France*, v (November 1892), 283.

himself would do.[109] Péladan also offered high praise for Puvis de Chavannes, calling him the "most exalted individuality of our art," and specifically commended him for "having attempted, in a kind of synthetic spirit, to go as far as the simplification of technique can go."[110] Perhaps Péladan's interest in Puvis de Chavannes stimulated his spirited support of decorative painting. Péladan enthusiastically advocated a contemporary renaissance of decorative painting, noting that "all the masters were decorators."[111] Aurier, in turn, quite specifically advocated decorative painting above easel painting as the proper form for the new symbolist art.[112] Both Aurier and Péladan railed against the Salon and the general mediocrity of the academic tradition. Péladan complained of Bouguereau's "Yankee art" and suggested that his paintings were worthy of his clients, "New York salt pork merchants."[113] Aurier, for his part, would note that Europe was being decayed by a "syphilis bouguereautesque et cabanélique."[114] Péladan also hated impressionism because of its concentration on technique, and Aurier would say that neo-impressionism "trivialized" art by concentrating on technique and color.[115]

So, Aurier agreed with Péladan on certain matters. Of course it could be argued that such beliefs were not totally uncommon at this time. But the number of shared opinions between the two critics seems more than coincidental and the vehemence with which Péladan offered his pronouncements made him the most vocal advocate of positions Aurier himself would later take up. Péladan was for instance a primary anti-naturalist, hating all aspects of positivist, materialist French culture. Thus it is no surprise that he hated the positivist historian Hippolyte Taine. In fact he wrote a *Réfutation esthétique de Taine* in 1906. But even in *L'Art ochlocratique* he complained of Taine's intrusion into the world of aesthetics, suggesting that Taine's efforts were thoughtless and that he should have stayed with history, leaving aesthetics to someone more qualified.[116] Aurier also decried the influence of Taine on art and art

109. Péladan, *L'Art ochlocratique*, 20.

110. Ibid., 48 and 69. (". . . la plus haute individualité de notre art." / "M. Puvis de Chavannes, dans une espèce d'esprit synthétique, a essayé jusqu'où la simplification du procédé peut aller.")

111. Ibid., 34. ("Les maîtres étaient tous décorateurs.")

112. *Oeuvres posthumes*, 216 and 308.

113. *L'Art ochlocratique*, 54 and 28. (". . . les marchands de porc salé de New-York.")

114. *Oeuvres posthumes*, 342.

115. *L'Art ochlocratique*, 54ff. *Oeuvres posthumes*, 240.

116. *L'Art ochlocratique*, 15.

criticism. As was noted earlier, in his "Essai sur une nouvelle méthode de critique," he devoted some twenty pages to a refutation of Taine's ideas of a scientific criticism.[117]

Péladan, like Aurier, refused to accept the idea that art should copy nature: "if art is to copy nature it has no more reason to exist than any other copy when one can see the original."[118] Péladan proclaimed: "No, nature is not the goal of art, it is only the means. It is the ensemble of expressive forms, that is all! Every work is a fugue, nature furnishes the motif, the soul of the artist does the rest."[119] Aurier spoke to the same antinaturalist sentiment when he wrote that the work of art was "the synthesis of two souls, the soul of the artist and the soul of nature."[120] Like Aurier, Péladan disparaged what the naturalist mentality had done to art, noting with disgust that "anecdote, genre, and still life dominate."[121] In 1883 Péladan suggested that a large proportion of the Salon that year was no better than photography. In a humorous passage at the end of *L'Art ochlocratique* he counted 2,300 of the 2,488 paintings in the Salon that could have been accomplished better with color photography, if it had been invented, and warned painters that it soon would be.[122] Later, Aurier too would bitterly attack the naturalist inclination toward exact reproduction of visual reality by making comparisons, all unfavorable, with photography.[123]

Again, while such beliefs were common to many critics at this time, it is the vehemence with which both Aurier and Péladan expressed themselves and the number of things on which they agreed that is worth note. One must, of course, remember that Péladan never approached Aurier's vision with regard to avant-garde art, but one must also pay heed to many circumstantial similarities in their tastes. Elsewhere, we find Péladan using "idéal" and "idée" in a manner that foreshadowed Aurier's later distinction between those terms in his Gauguin article.

117. *Oeuvres posthumes,* 176–96.

118. *L'Art ochlocratique,* 52. ("Si l'art est une copie de la nature, il n'a pas plus raison d'être que toute copie, quand on peut voir l'original.")

119. Ibid., 15–16. ("Non, la nature n'est pas le but de l'art, elle n'en est que le moyen; elle est l'ensemble des formes expressives, voilà tout!

Toute oeuvre est une fugue, la nature fournit le motif, l'âme de l'artiste fait le reste.")

120. *Oeuvres posthumes,* 303. (". . . la synthèse de deux âmes, l'âme de l'artiste et l'âme de la nature.")

121. *L'Art ochlocratique,* 17. (". . . l'anecdote, le genre et la nature morte règnent.")

122. Ibid., 157.

123. *Oeuvres posthumes,* 357, for example.

Péladan proposed the following definition in his introduction to the Salon of 1883:

> Art is the effort of man to realize the ideal, to represent and depict the *supreme idea,* the idea par excellence, the abstract idea; and the great masterpieces are religious because to materialize the idea of God, the idea of an angel, the idea of the Virgin mother, demands an incomparable effort of thought and procedure. To render visible the invisible: that is the true goal of art and its only reason for existing.[124]

Or, further along he states:

> The Ideal is not some particular idea; the Ideal is *all idea sublimated* to its supreme point of harmony, of intensity, of subtlety.[125]

Aurier, for his part, would state that the new art must be "1st *Ideaist,* since its sole ideal will be the expression of the Idea."[126] Elsewhere he stated:

> The normal and last goal of painting, as I've said, like all the arts, would not be the direct representation of objects. Its finality is to express, by translating them into a special language, Ideas.[127]

To be sure Aurier did not adopt such concepts word for word from Péladan but a similarity of concentration exists here. The Sâr seems to be a source for Aurier, if not in precise specifics, certainly in mood and general concentration. Aurier's concern with the concept of synthesis provides another example.

---

124. *L'Art ochlocratique,* 52. ("L'Art est l'effort de l'homme pour réaliser l'idéal, pour figurer et représenter *l'idée suprême,* l'idée par excellence, l'idée abstraite, et les grands chefs-d'oeuvre sont religieux, parce que matérialiser l'idée de Dieu, l'idée d'ange, l'idée de Vierge mère, exige un effort de pensée et de procédé incomparable. Rendre l'invisible visible, là est le vrai but de l'art et sa seule raison d'être.")

125. Ibid., 156. (L'Idéal n'est pas telle idée; l'Idéal est *toute idée sublimée, à son point suprême d'harmonie, d'intensité, de subtilité.*")

126. *Oeuvres posthumes,* 215. (1° *Idéiste,* puisque son idéal unique sera l'expression de l'Idée.")

127. Ibid., 213. ("Le but normal et dernier de la peinture, ai-je dit, comme d'ailleurs de tous les arts, ne saurait être la représentation directe des objets. Sa finalité est d'exprimer, en les traduisant dans un langage spécial, les Idées.")

"Synthesis," as I have noted, was a common term and Péladan was one of those most addicted to its use. *L'Art ochlocratique* is sprinkled with references to "synthèse" but one passage in particular is devoted to a deeper consideration of the term. After stating that art must not copy nature, that it must concern itself with "the supreme idea," Péladan informed his readers: "If the ideal is the necessity of great art, tradition is its law. . . . The first secret of tradition is that art must be a synthesis."[128] He went on to complain that contemporary art was incapable of even plastic synthesis, which he saw as the first step toward the true goal, expressive synthesis. He also made a distinction between analytic and synthetic landscape, decrying the first and offering high praise for the second. Appearing as it did in 1888, such a discussion might well have affected the young Albert Aurier. At any rate it demonstrates once again that conservative and advanced camps shared such concepts as synthesis. Ultimately, however, no single concept in Péladan's writing would have influenced Aurier so much as the overall thrust of *L'Art ochlocratique* itself.

Joséphin Péladan's view of art was a basically romantic one. He did not expect objectivity from the art critic but felt that "the critic is a judge who should announce the law before applying it."[129] Péladan consistently applied this rule to his own criticism. He argued fiercely, at times disregarding objectivity and even truth to make his point. His polemic style and arrogant attitude flowed from this basic subjectivity, and it was Péladan's style that would have influenced Aurier most. Like Aurier, who stated that "the sole means of understanding a work of art, then, is to become its lover," Péladan argued for passionate involvement in the arts.[130] "Where are the artists who love painting and who paint for the happiness of painting?" he asked.[131] Like Aurier, he complained about the contemporary situation in which art, which should be a "vocation, like the priesthood, has become a career, like accounting, and a fashion as well."[132] His pronouncements often make more emotional

---

128. *L'Art ochlocratique*, 53. ("Si l'idéal est la nécessité du grand art, la tradition en est la loi. . . . Le premier arcane de la tradition, c'est que l'art doit être une synthèse.")

129. Ibid., 45. ("Le critique est un juge qui doit énoncer la loi, avant de l'appliquer.")

130. *Oeuvres posthumes*, 201. ("Le seul moyen de comprendre une oeuvre d'art, c'est donc d'en devenir l'amant.")

131. *L'Art ochlocratique*, 51. ("Où sont les artistes qui aiment la peinture et qui peignent pour le bonheur de peindre?")

132. Ibid., 211. ("L'art, cette vocation, comme le sacerdoce, devient une carrière, comme le notariat, et une mode aussi.")

than literal sense; as he himself said: "the first word of art is always an act of faith."[133]

Péladan's declarations certainly approached the absurd at times, but no more than Aurier's did when he carried on about the horrors of Salon naturalism or anything else that he did not appreciate. The difference was not in the spirit of the criticism but rather in the art toward which it was directed. Ultimately, Aurier was closer to Péladan's style of passionate advocacy than to the cool, rational aloofness of Félix Fénéon. Indeed, Aurier's pleading was a long way from the rational, scientific criticism of the Fénéon circle and often more in tune with the passionate beliefs of the new Catholic idealists. The following passage, with its spiritual emphasis, reference to Italian painting, focus on beauty, reference to love, its passion and, admittedly, its vagueness, is very much in the Péladan–neo-Catholic mold:

> The work of art is the translation, in a special and natural language, of a spiritual given, of varying worth, moreover, which is as minimum a fragment of the spirituality of the artist, as maximum this entire spirituality of the artist plus the essential spirituality of divers objective beings. The final work of art is then *a new being*, one could say absolutely *living*, since it has a soul to animate it that is the very synthesis of two souls: the soul of the artist and the soul of nature; I would almost write the paternal soul and the maternal soul. This new being, quasi-divine, because it is unchangeable and immortal, must be deemed capable of inspiring in those who commune with it under certain conditions, emotion, ideas, special feelings, proportionate to the purity and the depth of his soul. It is this influx, this shining sympathy felt upon viewing a masterpiece, that is called the feeling of the beautiful, the aesthetic emotion, and this feeling and this emotion, thus explained by the very communion of two souls; the one inferior and passive, the human soul, the other superior and active, the soul of the work, will appear without doubt, to whomever in good faith will want to go much deeper into things, quite analogous to what is called: Love, more truly even love than human love, which is always dirtied by some muddy sexuality. To understand a work of art is, ultimately, to love loving it, to penetrate it, I would say, at the risk of easy raillery, with

133. Ibid., 17. ("Le premier mot de l'art est toujours un acte de foi.")

immaterial kisses. I know all the ridicule that a sentimental aesthetic must evoke in this century of rude skepticism. But what of it? Who then, I ask, can boast of having truly understood *La Gioconda* or the *St. John* of Leonardo, the *Glorious Virgin* of Angelico or that of Botticelli, before having felt, in front of these mysterious and beautiful beings, the wonderful fusion of his soul, in itself, to another soul, theirs? before having felt, in sight of them, what is called the first thrill of love. And is it not solely from this unforgettable minute of intimate coming together that all of us have begun to truly learn and to truly understand the harmonious language of these sublime images, to converse with them as with divine lovers, to penetrate the intimacy of their dazzling souls, having a presentiment that they would always have revealed to us some new and miraculous joy, eternally?[134]

No one would doubt that such a passage, in its inventiveness, is superior to much of what Péladan wrote, but it is also evident that in spirit Aurier's words are reminiscent of Péladan's pronouncements.

134. *Oeuvres posthumes*, 303–4. ("L'oeuvre d'art est la traduction, en une langue spéciale et naturelle, d'une donnée spirituelle, de valeur variable, au reste, laquelle est comme minimum un fragment de la spiritualité de l'artiste, comme maximum cette entière spiritualité de l'artiste plus la spiritualité essentielle des divers êtres objectifs. L'oeuvre d'art complète est donc *un être nouveau*, on peut dire absolument *vivant*, puisqu'il a pour l'animer une âme, qui est même la synthèse de deux âmes, l'âme de l'artiste et l'âme de la nature, j'écrirais presque l'âme paternelle et l'âme maternelle. Cet être nouveau, quasiment divin, car il est immuable et immortel, doit être estimé susceptible d'inspirer à qui communie avec lui dans certaines conditions, des émotions, des idées, des sentiments spéciaux, proportionnés à la pureté et à la profondeur de son âme. C'est cet influx, ce rayonnement sympathique ressentis à la vue d'un chef-d'oeuvre, que l'on nomme le sentiment du beau, l'émotion esthétique, et ce sentiment et cette émotion, ainsi expliqués par la communion de deux âmes, l'une inférieure et passive, l'âme humaine, l'autre supérieure et active, l'âme de l'oeuvre, apparaîtra sans doute, à qui voudra de bonne foi approfondir, très analogue à ce qu'on nomme: l'Amour, plus vraiment même l'Amour que l'Amour humain toujours maculé de quelque boueuse sexualité. Comprendre une oeuvre d'art, c'est en définitive l'*aimer d'amour*, la pénétrer, dirai-je, au risque de faciles railleries, d'immatériels baisers. Je sais tout le ridicule que doit provoquer, en ce siècle de grossier scepticisme, pareille esthétique sentimentale. Mais qu'importe? Qui donc, je le demande, peut se vanter d'avoir vraiment compris la *Joconde* ou le *Saint Jean* de Léonard, la *Vierge glorieuse* de l'Angelico ou celle de Botticelli, avant d'avoir senti, devant ces êtres mystérieux et beaux, comme la délicieuse fusion de son âme, à soi, en une autre âme, la leur? avant d'avoir senti, à leur vue, comme ce qu'on nomme un premier frisson d'amour? Et ne fut-ce point seulement de cette minute inoubliée d'intime rapprochement que, tous, nous avons commencé de vraiment entendre et de vraiment comprendre l'harmonieuse langue de ces images sublimes, de converser avec elles ainsi qu'avec de divines amantes, de pénétrer en l'intimité de leurs âmes éblouissantes, pressentant qu'elles auraient toujours à nous révéler quelques nouvelles et miraculeuses joies, éternellement?")

This chapter has been devoted to a consideration of Albert Aurier's relationship to the conservative idealist criticism of his time. Aurier was certainly influenced by this body of thought in his antinaturalist position; however, we should not forget that Aurier was an inventive writer who made an original contribution to art criticism, far beyond that of any of the critics from whom he drew inspiration. Many things separated Aurier from the cultural world around him. Among these was his eloquence. One still finds Aurier's denunciations of science and his plea for spiritual ideals to be stirring and worthy of recognition. Aurier had the nerve—and perhaps the naïveté—to say exactly what he pleased. If his arguments lack the cool logic of Fénéon they still make exciting reading. Finally, although Aurier often argued like a conservative, his theories were applied to the most advanced artists of the period. As much as the vogue for Puvis de Chavannes led critics to appreciate deformations of nature, it was an exceptional critic who could relate these ideas to the art of Paul Gauguin. No matter how traditional Aurier's theories may have been, his talent for seeing the best in contemporary art was unmatched.

Finally, however, it should be understood that Aurier's connection with more conservative thought was, in a certain way, the very essence of his originality. Against the force of impressionist and neo-impressionist criticism, against the firmly antitraditional anti-idealism of a powerful figure like Félix Fénéon, against all of this Aurier was foresighted enough to recognize that the best of tradition, and the still-potent aspects of idealism, were needed to make a complete art. He performed a delicate balancing act between the conservative and the advanced and he succeeded in maintaining his position throughout his short career. Ultimately though, he must be seen as one of the last truly avant-garde symbolist art critics. Following closely on his heels was a generation of writers who would take his traditionalism even further, indeed, to the point where advanced symbolist thought was completely absorbed in conservative idealism.

5

SYMBOLISM DIVIDED:

CONSERVATIVES AMONG THE MODERNISTS

While modernism still had staunch defenders throughout the 1890s—
one thinks of such critics as Julien Leclercq at the *Mercure de France* or
Thadée Natanson at the *Revue blanche*—conservative thought was increasingly insinuated into the symbolist criticism of art during this period. An aggressive new breed of critic emerged. These critics understood the mechanics of the avant-garde. They knew the small
periodicals and the polemic style of the eighties. But, importantly, they
came to the avant-garde not out of necessity but rather desire. Desiring
an avant-garde position, rather than being forced into it by an uncomprehending establishment, the new symbolist critics took a romantic
view of their status. They wanted to be among "les jeunes" and the
"novateurs" when, in fact, they were increasingly part of a much more
accepted movement. By the nineties symbolism was no longer limited to

a scorned coterie gathering around a few "progressive" magazines. The movement had quickly gained influence in established circles and, consequently, began to lose its "advanced" cachet.[1]

Much of the new symbolist criticism was characterized by an uninitiated love of modernist painting. While critics wanted to support the very latest in art, they seemed unwilling to devote themselves to the careful study and explication of particular styles that had marked the work of writers like Félix Fénéon. Among the best critics of the period this situation was born of a fierce independence; among the worst, by a lack of depth and, perhaps, energy. Increasingly, critical writing was marked by confusion of names, movements, and styles, all in a fervent effort to toss off some quick ideas on what was new and advanced in the art world.

Finally, the nineties saw an increase in conservative theorizing. Serious discussions of painting moved steadily away from formal innovation and toward a literary idealism. The subject of paintings became more important than their form. While the critics of the nineties railed against the establishment as much as their counterparts in the eighties had—indeed at times more so—they remained remarkably unreceptive to some of the most innovative painting of the period.

The two critics discussed in this chapter, Camille Mauclair and Alphonse Germain, typify the symbolist generation of the 1890s. Their reputations were made in the nineties. Both were prolific, very much in the public eye through a wide variety of publications. Both specialized in art criticism. Most important, they were children of symbolism, as it were. While the founders of the movement had developed in a period dominated by naturalism, Mauclair and Germain were true products of the symbolist environment in which they grew to intellectual maturity. Thus, it might be argued, their attitudes reflect the central character of the period more accurately than the innovative writings of their prede-

---

1. See Lethève, *Impressionnistes et symbolistes devant la presse*, 187ff., for commentary on how soon symbolism was given serious consideration in established literary journals. Henri Mazel—who founded the second-generation symbolist periodical, *L'Ermitage*, in 1890—said that the best symbolist poetry was almost instantly admired and that the movement in general only met with token opposition, just enough to convey the impression it had triumphed over adversity. See his "Les Temps héroiques du symbolisme," *Mercure de France*, XLVII (December 1903), 670. A writer like Téodor de Wyzewa could easily move from his own short-lived *Revue wagnérienne* in 1886 to an influential position at the conservative *Revue des deux mondes* at the beginning of the nineties.

cessors.[2] For our purposes they manifest one of the most basic features of symbolist art criticism, the tendency toward tradition and literary idealism we have noted throughout this book.

CAMILLE MAUCLAIR'S ART CRITICISM

In 1895 the twenty-three-year-old critic and poet Camille Mauclair wrote two pieces on art for the established monthly *La Nouvelle revue*.[3] The articles served a twofold function. First, they introduced Mauclair as an important art critic to the readership of this respected journal. Second, they served as summation of Mauclair's ideas on painting, ideas that were the culmination of three years of intensive work for various periodicals.

Above all, Mauclair felt that France had fallen into a time of decadence in the visual arts. Although he praised many painters, he found that none of them equaled the work of the best literary men of the period, among whom he included Verlaine, Ibsen, Swinburne, and Maeterlinck. Mauclair blamed the situation in painting on what he saw as an artificial distinction between realism and idealism. For Mauclair, realism had erred not in its concentration on nature, although he expected painting to go beyond mere appearances, but rather in what he viewed as a mistaken concentration on technique. Mauclair did not criticize realism lightly. He was well aware that the realist tradition had produced the finest art of the last half of the nineteenth century, and he praised the work of realists from Courbet, through Manet, to Monet, whom he found to be "the most admirable technician of this period," technically superior to a Dürer or a Velázquez.[4] But he stopped short of placing Monet in the same rank as old masters like Dürer and Velázquez. Something was missing in Monet, a humanist idealism that Mauclair saw as the very essence of great art.

2. A. G. Lehmann, *The Symbolist Aesthetic in France* (Oxford: Basil Blackwell, 1968), 272, suggested this, specifically noting Mauclair as the sort of secondary figure that best represented symbolism, rather than the transcendent masters of the movement.

3. Mauclair, "Destinées de la peinture française," *La Nouvelle revue*, xciii (March–April 1895), 363–77; "Critique de la peinture," *La Nouvelle revue*, xcvi (September–October 1895), 314–33.

4. Mauclair, "Critique de la peinture," 323. (". . . le plus admirable exécutant de cette époque.")

At the same time Mauclair felt that idealist painters—whether the older academic idealists or the new idealists—had failed to supply the missing element in realism. Too often idealists offered a literary rather than a pictorial ideal. He complained of painters who "think in a superior manner as men and as painters think in complete stupidity."[5] Essentially, Mauclair sought the best of both sides of the realist/idealist dichotomy, a painter who could offer uplifting, grand themes as well as innovative technique. Mauclair was, if you will, and unrequited humanist. Like many of his generation he saw great humanist ideals in the art of the past, especially the Italian primitives, but also in artists like Corot, Delacroix, and Millet. But no contemporary artist, not even Monet or Puvis de Chavannes, both of whom he lavishly praised, could live up to that ideal.

Mauclair revealed much of his critical personality in these articles. He showed himself to be a traditionalist of sorts, more prone to finding greatness in the past than in the present. He was also, in spite of his recognition of some important artists, a bit blind to innovation in painting and more inclined toward contemporary literature. His ideas could sound attractive—the analysis he offered of the faults of realism and idealism was quite to the point—but too often his practical application of theory led him to champion some rather poor painters. Still, if Mauclair might be blamed for an inconsistent eye he might also be commended for taking a stand. With the *Nouvelle revue* articles Mauclair voiced, for better or worse, an aggressive independence from modernist orthodoxy.

Camille Mauclair's criticism of the 1890s presents a somewhat confusing picture to the modern historian. He has been reviled as the "archenemy" of modernist art who "viciously attacked" all new tendencies when he took over Albert Aurier's position at the *Mercure de France*.[6] He has been accused of opportunism, supporting impressionism only when the movement had gained wide popular recognition.[7] On the other hand the

---

5. Ibid., 322. (". . . pensent supérieurement comme hommes, et comme peintres ils pensent en toute stupidité.")

6. See Chipp, *Theories of Modern Art*, 53; and Rewald, *Post-Impressionism*, 492.

7. See Rewald, "Félix Fénéon," 121–22. Much of Rewald's complaint against Mauclair is based on the critic's later fanatical disavowal of modern art and modern art dealers in France, as well as his blatant anti-Semitism during the occupation. Both points are well taken. By 1930 Mauclair was ranting, in *La Farce de l'art vivant* (Paris: Editions de la nouvelle revue critique, 1929), about foreign influences despoiling French art in the form of cubism, fauvism, and

Grand Larousse lists Mauclair as a historian who, above all, fought for the impressionists. He has been lauded for his symbolist interpretation of Monet's painting and also credited by James Ensor as one of the few critics to understand and praise his art.[8] The truth, not surprisingly, is more complex than either black or white, pro or con.

Rather than turning from conservative to modernist critic opportunistically, Mauclair actually staked his early reputation on support of many new trends in painting. He was, at least in the early nineties, anything but an enemy of advanced art. Though Mauclair later did turn to a much more conservative—indeed, reactionary—attitude, the shift was the result of an avant-garde critic's emerging dissatisfaction with modernist painting, rather than a backward critic's inability to accept innovation. Mauclair, seen in this light, serves as an example of just how ingrained conservative thought was in symbolist circles. He was not an outsider who mysteriously worked himself into the position of art critic at the *Mercure*. He very much belonged there.

There can be little doubt that Camille Mauclair was a bona fide second-generation symbolist.[9] He was seven years younger than Albert Aurier and had been an intimate of Mallarmé's Tuesday afternoon gatherings. Commentary on the symbolist movement has always included Mauclair as a member. In 1898 Albert Aurier's friend Rémy de Gourmont offered an appreciative portrait of Mauclair in his *Livre des masques*.[10] André Barre included Mauclair among the "Mallarméens" in his 1911 study of the symbolist movement.[11] A. G. Lehmann used him to illustrate several themes of the symbolist aesthetic in his classic study of the movement.[12] Mauclair published widely in the symbolist periodicals of the time—indeed, his bibliography is astounding. He wrote several

---

expressionism. During the occupation he published *La Crise de l'art moderne* (Paris: C.E.A., 1944), a vituperative attack on a supposed Jewish conspiracy to promote and sell modern art. This deplorable pamphlet was clearly meant to appeal to both German Nazis and the anti-Semitic nationalist factions that permeated Vichy France. While one would not gainsay Rewald's disgust with the later Mauclair, it is the Mauclair of the 1890s that interests me in this chapter.

8. See Goldwater, *Symbolism*, 178–79; and Delevoy, *Symbolists and Symbolism*, 77.

9. For a good general view of Mauclair's relation to symbolism and an excellent bibliography, see William Clark, "Camille Mauclair and the Religion of Art" (Ph.D. dissertation, University of California–Berkeley, 1976).

10. Rémy de Gourmont, *Le Livre des masques*, ii (Paris: Mercure de France, 1898), 195–200.

11. André Barre, *Le Symbolisme*, 321.

12. Lehmann, *The Symbolist Aesthetic in France*, 142–43, 170–71, 272–80.

pieces of art criticism for the *Revue indépendante* in 1891 and 1892. The reputation he gained there for supporting advanced art was most likely what netted him a position at the *Mercure de France*. In 1893 Mauclair was also the founder, along with Lugné-Poë, of the symbolist-oriented Théâtre de l'oeuvre, where so many of the Nabis were to produce stage sets. Clearly, Mauclair played an important role in the development of the final stage of symbolism in literature. He was not an initiator nor a major theoretician of the movement—and he was at best only a minor poet—but he certainly developed as a young writer in the cradle of symbolism. He also developed as a young art critic in the cradle of avant-garde painting.

In the pages of the *Revue indépendante*, Mauclair was an enthusiastic, if somewhat uninformed, friend of advanced painting. From May 1891 until May 1892, he wrote eight articles on art for the *Revue* and none of these qualified him as a diehard enemy of the avant-garde; quite the contrary. Mauclair's first art criticism in the *Revue indépendante* was a review of an important Monet exhibition at Durand-Ruel.[13] The article began Mauclair's long commitment to Monet's work; in it he was full of praise, finding Monet to be a "magician," a "pure artist," and the "master of impressionism." He included Monet in a trinity of great artists, along with Puvis de Chavannes and Gustave Moreau. He praised other impressionists such as Degas and Pissarro, as well as the poster artist, Jules Cheret, but reserved his strongest approval for Monet.[14] One might note that this was no ordinary exhibition for Monet. It was his first showing of the grainstack series, a change in both style and exhibition practice that presented a challenge to any young critic. Mauclair responded in what would become characteristic fashion for him. His praise was enthusiastic but unsubstantial. He clearly appreciated the artist on an emotional level but did not seem to grasp the work conceptually, concerning himself with neither the question of working in series nor the growing abstraction of Monet's painting.

Mauclair's last piece for the *Revue indépendante* was also very positive about impressionism. He spoke glowingly of the great innovations of the

13. Mauclair, "Beaux-Arts," *Revue indépendante*, xix (May 1891), 267–69.

14. Pissarro's inclusion here indicates that Mauclair did not begin by attacking this painter as Rewald, "Félix Fénéon," 122, believes. Mauclair mentioned Pissarro some five times in the pages of the *Revue indépendante* (May 1891; October 1891; two times in December 1891; and May 1892), all favorably.

entire group and hoped that a coterie of equal promise might be flowering among the young painters.[15] Like so many others from this period Mauclair was cutting his critical teeth on impressionism. His wish for parallel achievement among young painters also indicates that he understood quite well that impressionism was no longer the avant-garde, and he was interested in finding out just what was. In the year he wrote for the *Revue indépendante* he championed a wide variety of contemporary painters, among them Whistler, Carrière, Toulouse-Lautrec, and Van Gogh.[16] He also offered support and encouragement to Emile Bernard and to the young Nabis painters Maurice Denis, Paul Sérusier, Edouard Vuillard, and Pierre Bonnard. Clearly, it is incorrect to call Mauclair an enemy of advanced painting at this point in his career. He is much more correctly seen as a young critic fascinated with the world of avant-garde painting and literature, trying to join in what must have seemed a highly stimulating environment.

But while Mauclair was capable of obsequious reverence for the avant-garde he also demonstrated another youthful proclivity: angry, aggressive independence. He seemed to carry on a love/hate relationship with the circles he habituated. Thus, in the same review of a suite of Odilon Redon's prints he could, on one hand, offer lavish praise and, on the other, accuse the artist of a laughable lack of intelligence.[17] He could also state that Seurat had broadened the horizons of painting greatly and then add, echoing Albert Aurier, that he was a purely technical painter who had never been able to become anything more. Concerning Paul Signac, he was less kind, saying that he was a technical painter and did not seem to aspire to anything greater.[18] Mauclair had a sharp tongue

15. *Revue indépendante*, xxiii (May 1892), 287–88.

16. On Lautrec see, for instance, *Revue indépendante*, xxii (January 1892), 143, and (March 1892), 416. This calls into question Chipp's (*Theories of Modern Art*, 53) suggestion that Mauclair was Lautrec's "archenemy." Mauclair called Van Gogh a "master" in *Revue indépendante*, xxii (January 1892), 144. In *Revue indépendante*, xxiii (April 1892) Mauclair, using a rather striking metaphor, reminiscent of Albert Aurier, said that Van Gogh was "a great incomplete artist, appearing like a meteor and disappearing too soon." (". . . grand artiste incomplet, apparu comme un météore et disparu trop tôt.") On page 136 of the same "Beaux-Arts" section he spoke of Van Gogh as one of the great strugglers, along with Manet and Renoir, teaching new forms to a new generation.

17. *Revue indépendante*, xxiii (May 1892), 286–87.

18. Mauclair, " Albert Besnard et le symbolisme concret," *Revue indépendante*, xxi (October 1891), 19.

and he demonstrated no fear of using it on modernist painters, but such petulant attacks are less important examples of his independence than his more considered disavowal of Paul Gauguin.

Mauclair's repudiation of Gauguin was not total and not the unconsidered hatred of a ranting conservative. He occasionally mentioned Gauguin favorably in the pages of the *Revue indépendante*.[19] Indeed, he described Gauguin as "a delicate luminist, and a very personal decorator, a potter, an enamelist, a completely engaging wood sculptor, in a word, indisputably an artist, and not the least grand."[20] Yet he found Gauguin's symbolism to be problematic; his reasoning here is intriguing. He specifically criticized *Jacob Wrestling With an Angel* as being "the drawn and painted realization of a sociological, humanistic, or other concept, but not at all a pictorial one."[21] He accused Gauguin of offering a translation of a text and of being a literary painter who presented either philosophical concepts or simple anecdotes. Whether or not we agree with Mauclair it is clear that he had considered Gauguin's painting quite seriously. In fact his criticism is reminiscent of Fénéon's own mistrust of the artist's literary connections. Mauclair's comments are specific, rationally presented, and no more conservative than Fénéon's in this particular regard. He seems to have been genuinely concerned with defending art against the incursions of literature and philosophy.

Mauclair could be just as independent in the tendencies he praised as in those he disparaged. Unlike most modernist critics he was able to find kind words for the Rose + Croix Salon of Joséphin Péladan.[22] He did not approve of Péladan's artistic ideas, and he recognized that many of the artists who showed with the Rose + Croix had profited greatly from the prior struggles of artists like Monet, Van Gogh, and Renoir. Yet he applauded the idealist leanings of the exhibitions and felt that many of the Rose + Croix artists displayed real merit. But while such praise of the new idealist painting might not have washed well with Félix Fénéon

19. See *Revue indépendante*, xxii (March 1892), 417 (where he told his readers that at Le Barc de Boutteville one could see two of the most beautiful works by Monticelli and Gauguin); and xxi (December 1891), 429 (where he noted two interesting lithographs by Gauguin at Boussod et Valadon).

20. Mauclair, "Albert Besnard et le symbolisme concret," 17. (". . . un luministe délicat, et un très personnel décorateur, un potier, un émailliste, un sculpteur sur bois tout à fait attachant, un artiste indiscutable en un mot, et non des moins grands.")

21. Ibid. (". . . la réalisation dessinée et peinte d'un concept sociologique, humanistique, ou autre, mais point du tout pictural.")

22. *Revue indépendante*, xxiii (April 1892), 136–39.

and his modernist colleagues it was not unheard of among the avant-garde of the nineties. Rémy de Gourmont wrote a remarkably similar review of the Rose + Croix just one month after Mauclair's offering.[23] Albert Aurier himself, as was noted in Chapter 4, was also subject to the influence of Péladan.

Again like Albert Aurier, Mauclair could find demonstration of his aesthetic principles in rather conservative artists. Thus, in a serious theoretical article, he championed the established painter Albert Besnard and defended his choice in much the same way Aurier had justified his own praise of the academic J.-J. Henner.[24] Like Aurier, he understood that his support of Besnard would surprise many in the avant-garde and much of his discussion of the painter was meant to deflect the barbs of other critics. Just as Aurier had used Henner to make a theoretical point, so Mauclair used Besnard. Although Mauclair's article often comes across as a vague amalgam of impressionist and symbolist thought—further confused by Mauclair's personal verbiage—the author's main point is clear and understandable enough. He invented the term *symbolisme concret* to describe Besnard's work. For Mauclair, Besnard represented the best tradition in modern art: that initiated by Edouard Manet, in which all sentiment and meaning in a painting derived from a personal reading of light. Besnard's symbolism began in the concrete fact of light, the realm of the painter, and not in abstract concepts, the realm of the poet.[25] Mauclair praised Besnard, then, as a nonliterary painter and condemned the intrusion of literature into the visual arts. Although his choice of Besnard may not have represented cutting-edge criticism, Mauclair's concepts—especially that rejection of the literary in painting—would have rung true with such modernists as Félix Fénéon.[26]

In all, Mauclair's tenure at the *Revue indépendante* showed him to be a young man interested in advanced art, conversant with the language and concepts of avant-garde criticism, and eager to assume the mantle of

23. Rémy de Gourmont, "Les Premiers Salons," 60–62. Both Rémy de Gourmont and Mauclair praised Antoine de la Rochefoucauld, the cofounder of the Salon, at the expense of Péladan and both appreciated the Salon's idealist bias.

24. Mauclair, "Albert Besnard et le symbolisme concret."

25. Ibid., 12ff.

26. Actually Fénéon himself had early on been highly enamored of Besnard's work. See Fénéon, *Oeuvres*, 69, for an 1887 commentary in which Fénéon felt that Besnard had become one of the most interesting figures in contemporary art.

progressive critic. He also demonstrated a certain independence, but that was not a drawback. At least in September 1892, the month Mauclair wrote his first criticism for the *Mercure de France,* he was a most likely candidate for publication in this bright, young symbolist magazine.

Mauclair wrote about the visual arts for the *Mercure* from September 1892 through September 1896, and he continued to write literary criticism for the publication after that date. During this period he submitted more than thirty-five separate entries, establishing himself as a major artistic voice of this important symbolist publication. He did not begin writing the monthly "Choses d'art" section of the periodical until January 1894, some seventeen months after Albert Aurier's death. During that interim period Yvanhoé Rambosson, Julien Leclercq—Aurier's protégé—and Rémy de Gourmont handled the arts section, and they continued to contribute to it after Mauclair began producing his short reviews of the gallery scene. His earliest articles for the *Mercure,* however, appeared before Aurier died, the first, "Notes sur l'idée pure," having been published in the September 1892 issue, along with Aurier's last "Choses d'Art" section. More important and surprising, that article seems to reflect Aurier's influence.

Mauclair's "Notes sur l'idée pure" was an eclectic bit of aesthetic theory that drew on various sources of symbolist thought.[27] He quoted Mallarmé on "pure notions" and offered comparisons from chemistry using some of the pseudoscientific language of Fénéon's circle. It was the title that indicated Aurier's influence, specifically his concern with the "idée." "The reality of an object," Mauclair began, "that is to say its sensorial relativity to the nervous centers of a conscient being, is no more than a mode of apperception and revelation of its pure idea. . . . For the idealist, the symbol is only the means to the idea."[28] One hears the echo of Aurier's comment about objects in nature merely being ideas signified—a comment made just five months earlier.[29] Elsewhere Mauclair spoke of objects as "the hieroglyphic characters wherein the

27. Mauclair, "Notes sur l'idée pure," *Mercure de France,* VI (September 1892), 42–46.

28. Ibid., 42. ("la réalité d'un objet, c'est-à-dire sa relativité sensorielle aux centres nerveux de l'être conscient, n'est qu'un mode d'aperception et de révélation de son idée" / ". . . le symbole, pour l'idéaliste, n'est que le moyen de l'idée.")

29. Aurier, *Oeuvres posthumes,* 301. ("Dans la nature, tout objet n'est, en somme, qu'une Idée signifiée.")

pure idea is complexly written."[30] This reading of objects as the elements of a special language for signifying ideas was, of course, very much a part of symbolist thought in general, but Mauclair's statement here is particularly close to Aurier:

> The strict duty of the idealist painter is, consequently, to effect a reasoned selection among the multiple elements combined in objectivity, to utilize in his work only general and distinct forms, lines and colors that serve to write forcefully the ideaic signification of the object.[31]

Finally, just as Aurier had invented the term *idéiste* to distinguish his new idealism from the old type, Mauclair spoke of idealism as the province of the new intellectualism and invented the term *idéoréalisme* to denote the "realization of ideas in a plastic medium."[32]

In all, Mauclair's "Notes sur l'idée pure" was an article very much in the spirit of the *Mercure de France* at this time, as if Mauclair were trying to please his new, more established friends. In fact, his next contribution to the magazine, "Fraternités idéales," published in February 1893, was dedicated to Rémy de Gourmont, champion of the new idealism. Mauclair affectionately addressed Gourmont as "Mon cher Gourmont" and ended his long, rambling article with an explanation of how he, a nonbeliever, could agree with Gourmont that Christ was the greatest of all artists. Permeated with references to current intellectual fads, the article shows that Mauclair was trying to please. At least at this point, he had no intention of angering the readership of this publication.

For more than a year after Aurier's death, Mauclair wrote little that might be interpreted as antagonistic toward avant-garde art. In August 1893 he praised Maurice Denis's illustrations for Gide's *Le Voyage d'Urien* but otherwise did not produce much for the *Mercure* before 1894.[33] In one article that did appear, he supported a painter who was not part of avant-garde circles, Armand Point.[34] The article, published

---

30. Mauclair, "Notes sur l'idée pure," 43. (". . . les caractères hiéroglyphiques où s'inscrit complexement l'idée pure.")

31. See, for instance, Aurier, *Oeuvres posthumes*, 215.

32. Mauclair, "Notes sur l'idée pure," 45. (". . . la réalisation des idées en un médiateur plastique.")

33. Mauclair, "Le Voyage d'Urien," *Mercure de France*, viii (August 1893), 361–65.

34. Mauclair, "Armand Point," *Mercure de France*, ix (December 1893), 331–36.

in the December 1893 issue, stands as a classic case of the confusion of idealism and symbolism that marked this period. Point was an Ecole des Beaux-Arts student whose style combined pictorial themes from Gustave Moreau and the English Pre-Raphaelites, with an overlay of Leonardo da Vinci.[35] A highly conservative painter, he prided himself on the "correctness" of his draftsmanship in renderings of sirens, nymphs, and nudes, all in the new idealist manner. He was a regular at both the annual Salons of the Société nationale and the Rose + Croix Salons of Joséphin Péladan.

Mauclair's article on Point was written in high symbolist style, filled with difficult phrases and sprinkled with the catchwords of the movement. In the manner of Puvis de Chavannes criticism, Mauclair spoke of how Point, "in painting irises, women, and swans, presents the mystery of his sensibility through essential forms."[36] And, as if recalling decadent descriptions of Gustave Moreau's painting, Mauclair discovered in Point's nudes "a precious sensuality, a singular union of chastity and perversity."[37] Finally, in the fashion of the new mystic idealists, Mauclair gushed:

> Diviner of the eyes, he paints impalpable portraits of souls with his mind, achieving a haunting quality through the inexplicable abstraction of bodies of which a single regard engenders an inquiry into life, a particular life, fluttering from perfumes to music, and only abandoning the illusion of dawn for the almost immaterial reality of a kiss.[38]

Aurier could be effusive, as we have seen, but he rarely offered such empty rhetoric—second-rate prose in praise of second-rate painting.

---

35. On Point, see Gustave Soulier, "Les Artistes de l'âme, Armand Point," *L'Art et la vie,* III (1894), 171–77. Illustrations of paintings by Point can be found in Edward Lucie-Smith, *Symbolist Art* (New York: Oxford University Press, 1972), 116. Robert Goldwater, *Symbolism,* 14. Philippe Jullian, *Dreamers of Decadence,* trans. Robert Baldick (New York: Praeger, 1971), 50, 222. Délégation à l'action artistique de la ville de Paris, *Le Symbolisme et la femme* (Paris: Délégation à l'action artistique de la ville de Paris, 1986), 114–17.

36. Mauclair, "Armand Point," 331. (". . . en peignant des iris, des femmes et des cygnes, pressent le mystère de sa sensibilité sous des formes essentielles.")

37. Ibid., 332. (". . . une sensualité précieuse, une singulière union de la chasteté et de la perversité.")

38. Ibid., 333. ("Divinateur des yeux, il peint avec son esprit d'impalpables portraits d'âmes, atteignant à la hantise par l'abstraction inexplicable de corps dont le seul regard veut s'enquérir de la vie, d'une vie particulière voletant des parfums à la musique, et n'abandonnant l'illusion de crépuscule que pour la réalité presque immatérielle d'un baiser.")

Mauclair made every attempt to link Point to the most fashionable trends of the day, comparing the artist to the all-important Italian primitives and to Moreau and Puvis de Chavannes. He found Point related to Rose + Croix painters like Fernand Khnopff and Jan Toorop and also associated his work with that of "the adorable" Maurice Denis. Elsewhere he saw Point as kin to Burne-Jones and Whistler, Renoir, and Odilon Redon—flailing about in all directions, it seems, trying to touch as many bases as possible in his praise of this odd painter.[39]

Most important for our discussion here, Mauclair also used the Point article as a forum for beginning his attacks on modernist painting. Abandoning his impartial stance with regard to the synthetists, he spoke of the "ignorant error" of Emile Bernard and—in Mauclair's first adverse comment regarding impressionism—noted that he appreciated Point's return to strict drawing of the human figure "after the marvelous debauch of impressionism."[40] What he meant by "debauch" and just how conservative he was becoming he would reveal shortly.

The year 1894, when Mauclair took over the "Choses d'art" section of the *Mercure de France,* was also the year in which he would make a major break with modernist painting.[41] He became increasingly independent of modernist orthodoxy and disenchanted with the accomplishments of painters in general, as opposed to poets. The year began calmly

39. Interestingly, Mauclair also added Jules Bastien-Lepage—the late naturalist artist who made a name for himself in Salon circles through the 1880s—to his list of sources for Point. Mauclair never explained why he thought an idealist like Point might be related to Bastien-Lepage but his reason is of less interest than the manner in which he made his assertion. Mauclair said that he knew his reference to Bastien-Lepage—whom Degas had called the "Bouguereau of the naturalists"—would astonish people but he felt the painter would soon be given more recognition. This is a surprising conclusion: at the time Bastien-Lepage, who died in 1884, was a widely imitated and popular artist. Only in avant-garde circles was he despised. Clearly, Mauclair knew that he was going against the grain of advanced thought in praising Bastien-Lepage—and Point himself for that matter. But, just as clearly, Mauclair seemed to wish to assert his independence from a pro forma avant-garde position.

40. Mauclair, "Armand Point," 335. (". . . après la débauche merveilleuse de l'impressionnisme.")

41. George Mauner, *The Nabis: Their History and Their Art, 1888–1896* (New York: Garland, 1978), 137ff., discusses Mauclair's rather remarkable turnaround. In 1893, and on two occasions in 1894, Mauclair wrote high-style appreciations of synthetist painting in catalogue prefaces for exhibitions at the galleries of Le Barc de Boutteville. But in the "Choses d'art" section of the *Mercure de France,* x (April 1894), 377–79, he attacked most of the painters in the last of these exhibitions—the very painters he had lauded so eloquently in his preface. Mauner attributes this reversal to a rift between Mauclair and Lugné-Poë of the Théâtre de l'oeuvre, for whom several of the Nabis painters showing at Le Barc de Boutteville had executed stage designs. I feel that Mauclair's disavowal of the new painting was more purposeful.

enough, with Mauclair offering strong praise for Mary Cassatt, and sounding perfectly in accord with impressionist goals.[42] But by March he began to complain severely about the detrimental effect impressionism was having on the younger generation. He reviewed three current exhibitions: Armand Guillaumin at the Durand-Ruel Gallery, Maxime Maufra at Le Barc de Boutteville, and the *Société des aquarellistes* at the Georges Petit Gallery.[43] It is the review of the Guillaumin show that is of concern here. In general Mauclair found Guillaumin to be an artist of some talent, if not quite up to the level of a Degas or a Monet, but he used Guillaumin to bring up a series of complaints concerning impressionism, complaints he had not raised before in print but had obviously considered carefully. He found impressionism to be obsessed with Japanism, overconcerned with bizarre lighting, and too much dependent on painting out-of-doors. He deplored in impressionism

> the neglect of composition and the error of consuming one's life in doing studies and fragments—studies for *what?* fragments of what?—that had led painters to neglect the figure, that is to say, to kill at least half of the plastic arts.[44]

But this was not all. Mauclair also suggested that impressionism had offered nothing to the younger generation

> aside from the idea of refining the quality of tone, and that to the detriment of style and the feeling for meaning; because the pulverization of light has produced a generation of acrobats juggling with colored brush strokes, replacing paintings formerly drowned in bitumen with multicolored fogs where line is lost, where structure and the quality of the landscape are attenuated.[45]

42. Mauclair, "Choses d'art," *Mercure de France*, x (January 1894), 92–93.

43. Mauclair, "Expositions récentes," *Mercure de France*, x (March 1894), 266–71.

44. Ibid., 266. (". . . l'oubli de la composition et l'erreur de consumer la vie à faire des études et des morceaux—études *pour quoi?* morceaux *de quoi?*—qui a mené les peintres à négliger la figure, c'est-à dire à tuer à moitié au moins l'art plastique.")

45. Ibid., 267. (". . . d'autre idée que de raffiner sur la qualité d'un ton, et cela au détriment du style et du sentiment des valeurs, car le poudroiement de lumière a produit une génération d'acrobates jonglant avec les taches colorées, remplaçant les tableaux noyés jadis dans le bitume par des brouillards multicolores où la ligne se perd, où s'atténue la structure et la qualité des terrains.")

Mauclair was quite aware that he challenged the taste of the time in criticizing impressionism but he defended himself, complaining bitterly of what he termed an "immoderate complaisance for everything that seems new and a singular propensity to believe that everything has just been invented."[46] He reminded his readers that impressionism had not invented painting. But it was not impressionism itself that posed the problem for Mauclair. He continued to praise many of the original impressionists in his writings. His complaints concerned the direction impressionist influence had taken:

> I am a little frightened to dream of the nullity into which the degenerate following of one of the most astonishing insurrections that art has seen will fall. . . . [T]he fear is that impressionism, poorly understood and poorly followed, has engulfed minds a bit more in this rut of craft for craft's sake, bogged them down in this ridiculous *fragment*, which insidiously kills the conceptual in weak brains.[47]

Mauclair's criticism was directed not only at impressionism and its following. He also attacked the concept of symbolism in painting as it had been expressed in the art of Gauguin. In a statement clearly meant to refer to Albert Aurier's use of the term in describing Gauguin, Mauclair decried the appropriation of "symbolism" from literature to painting. He worried that painters did not understand the term and that it was ruining them. He complained about the deformations of Gauguin and his followers and specifically condemned their interest in equating fresco with easel painting, as well as their concentration on the decorative—all concerns which Aurier had praised. He berated young painters for pretending to express the inexpressible without knowing first how to draw. In essence, Mauclair offered a very conservative line and—for whatever reasons—it was with this article that he declared war on certain aspects of advanced painting.

46. Ibid. (". . . une complaisance déréglée pour tout ce qui semble nouveau et une singulière propension à croire que tout vient d'être inventé.")

47. Ibid., 267–68. ("Je m'effraie un peu de songer à la nullité où tombera de suite la dégénérescence d'une des plus étonnantes insurrections d'art qu'ait vues l'art pictural . . . il est à craindre que l'impressionnisme, mal compris et mal suivi, ait encore enlisé un peu plus les esprits en cette ornière du métier pour le métier, en cette glu dérisoire du *morceau*, qui tue tout doucement les conceptions dans des cerveaux mal affermis.")

It was also in the March 1894 issue of the *Mercure de France,* in the review of the *Société des aquarellistes* at the Georges Petit Gallery, that Mauclair compounded his conservatism by declaring that the painter Georges-Antoine Rochegrosse exemplified the move back to the true roots of art. The more common view of Rochegrosse—whose *Knight Among the Flowers* (Fig. 11) of 1894 has become a minor classic of kitsch—was as an academic painter who distorted the aims of impressionism. Mauclair's championing of this weak artist could only have served to further alienate the writer from avant-garde artistic circles. But Mauclair was unapologetic for his interest in Rochegrosse. In a later article he specifically praised *The Knight Among the Flowers,* suggesting that its author was

> a man who has no reason to envy the best of the impressionists and has, in addition, a true intellectualism. M. Rochegrosse is one of the rare spirits of these times, one of the very rare plasticians for whom form is not the goal but the means. . . . I say this because I think it and I am not concerned with the advice of revolutionary critics, who are as "pompier" as anyone, and who only discern certified talents after having consulted the latest fashion.[48]

In short, by 1894 Mauclair had made sweeping changes in his critical position. He was apparently no longer concerned about associating himself with the avant-garde and certainly willing to attack facets of modernism in order to express his own emphasis on figure drawing. Initially it was the deformations of Gauguin and his followers that elicited his attack, but then his own prejudice spurred him on to denounce the influence of impressionism itself.

Evidently Mauclair's open attack on modernist painting generated swift response from the community of advanced artists in Paris. By July 1894 he was defending himself in print against painters who had called for his dismissal from the *Mercure de France* and who "were scandalized

---

48. Mauclair, "Les Salons de 1894," *Mercure de France,* xi (June 1894), 162. (". . . un homme qui n'a rien à envier aux meilleurs des impressionnistes, et il a, en plus, une intellectualité réelle. M. Rochegrosse est un des rares esprits de ce temps, un des très rares plasticiens pour qui la forme ne soit pas le but, mais le moyen . . . je dis ceci comme je le pense et je me soucie peu d'être de l'avis des critiques révolutionnaires, qui sont tout aussi 'pompiers' que les autres, et ne décernent des brevets de talent qu'après avoir consulté la mode.")

that a simple *littérateur* would dare to deny them genius."[49] But Mauclair was far from cowed. He lashed back at his assailants, suggesting that painters "are and always will be imbeciles."[50] He also went beyond his earlier attacks, boldly stating:

> *The impressionists are the naturalists of art,* and I don't understand at all the contemporary poets who are tender toward them. These are the same theories, the same vacuity of mind, the same virtuosity for its own sake.[51]

The pages of the *Mercure de France* were soon ablaze with invective. Julien Leclercq—Aurier's friend at the *Mercure* and staunch supporter of Gauguin—wrote a long and careful response to Mauclair's repeated attacks.[52] His article was a classic statement of the differences between modernist and idealist positions in art criticism. He countered Mauclair's insistence on intellectualism in painting, suggesting, much as Albert Aurier had a few years earlier, that intelligence was only half of what an artist needed. The artist must also put theories in movement, make things live.[53] Leclercq also ridiculed Mauclair's taste in painting—especially his support for Rochegrosse, Besnard, and Point—wondering if it was so intellectual to paint "a ponderous Parsifal among dense flowers and characterless nudes."[54] Leclercq defended Gauguin's draftsmanship by carefully outlining the modernist position that skill in drawing is not related to trompe l'oeil realism. Throughout his article Leclercq insisted that Mauclair's rhetoric was without substance, that his pronouncements carried the weight of polemic, not knowledge.

49. Mauclair, "Lettre sur la peinture," *Mercure de France,* xi (July 1894), 270. (". . . se scandalisent qu'un simple littérateur s'avise de leur refuser du génie.") The article was addressed to a M. Raymond Bouyer, art critic at the symbolist *L'Ermitage,* and represents another attempt on Mauclair's part to engage in a dialogue through his articles. As will be seen, the other critic to be discussed in this chapter, Alphonse Germain, was fond of the same ploy to gain recognition in symbolist circles.

50. Ibid. (". . . ce sont et ce seront toujours des imbéciles par grâce d'état.")

51. Ibid., 271. (*"Les impressionnistes sont les naturalistes de l'art,* et je ne comprends nullement que les poètes actuels leur soient tendres, eux qui éreintent la reproduction de la nature de Zola. Ce sont les mêmes théories, la même vacuité d'esprit, la même virtuosité pour elle même.")

52. Julien Leclercq, "La Lutte pour les peintres," *Mercure de France,* xii (November 1894), 254–71.

53. Ibid., 255. Aurier offered a long and elegant argument for the passionate, emotional side of art in his article on Gauguin, *Oeuvres posthumes,* 216ff.

54. Leclercq, "La Lutte pour les peintres," 256. (". . . un Parsifal lourd parmi des fleurs épaisses et des nus sans caractère.")

Mauclair responded in the next issue of the *Mercure de France*.[55] He, in turn, suggested that Leclercq was the ignorant one, not knowing what he was talking about, especially concerning the Pre-Raphaelites. His reference to Leclercq's "friends" then showing at *Le Barc de Boutte-ville* sounded like Leclercq's own comment on Mauclair: "lots of words, a doctoral air, hatred of known artists, the secret desire for money, and empty heads."[56]

Not surprisingly, the *Mercure de France* played up the debate. It made for spicy reading. Leclercq's attack on Mauclair was followed by an article on Flemish painting by Roland de Marés dedicated, affectionately, to Mauclair, indicating apparently that the editors were not taking sides.[57] In his "Choses d'art" section for the month, Mauclair greeted the new art season in Paris by complaining that painting was sick, that artists had yet to solve the realist/idealist "problem," and that poets had given them too much credit.[58] Adolphe Retté joined the fray in the December 1894 number with a short letter that simultaneously attacked and defended both Mauclair and Leclercq.[59] Retté praised Mauclair for "courageously" speaking out against Gauguin and his followers and then chided Leclercq for supporting them. On the other hand Retté agreed with Leclercq that Mauclair's fondness for Rochegrosse, Point, and Besnard was ridiculous, and he attacked Mauclair's interpretations of German philosophy, noting ruefully that Mauclair was "very young."

Mauclair's response to Retté and further comments on Leclercq were published in the January 1895 issue, as was a Julien Leclercq review of a small Gauguin exhibition. Then, in February, perhaps at the behest of the editors, Mauclair wrote an "apology."[60] He admitted that his tone may have at times been too aggressive, but insisted that he always tried to remain impartial and treated artists with the courtesy and respect they deserved. Far short of being contrite, however, Mauclair turned his apology into a manifesto of his own ideas. He stated plainly that he had attempted to judge art according to a specific set of aesthetic considerations, which he outlined as follows:

55. Mauclair, "Choses d'art," *Mercure de France*, xii (December 1894), 384–86.
56. Ibid., 386. (". . . des mots, des mots, un air doctoral, la haine des artistes connus, le désir secret de l'argent, et la tête creuse.")
57. *Mercure de France*, xii (November 1894), 271.
58. *Mercure de France*, xii (November 1894), 284–86.
59. Adolphe Retté, *Mercure de France*, xii (December 1894), 390–91.
60. Mauclair, "Choses d'art," *Mercure de France*, xiii (February 1895), 235–38.

Necessity of drawing, suspicion of color for itself, constant search for character, union of the conceptual to the painting of the fragment, infirmity of plastic art without a cerebral motif as of cerebration without sufficient expressive resources, vanity of deformed drawing, optical error of pointillism, lack of aptitude of the neo-impressionist painters for any symbolism, aesthetic dissociation of the sense of synthesis in the mind and on the canvas, insufficience of anatomical study, lack of works truly composed, plethora of studies, exaggeration of taste for decoration in paintings, arrogance towards the masters, ignorance of the history of art, desire for the bizarre in place of the original—all these matters have passed through my articles.[61]

He also took advantage of the opportunity to redouble his attack on the new painting. Claiming that his close friendships with many of the symbolist painters allowed him to examine their works intimately, he called their paintings "little nothings" and noted that everywhere among connoisseurs their work was losing ground. He suggested that he could shock the naïve defenders of these painters if he related what the masters who had paved the way for them were saying about them. "I could astonish," he continued, "if I wrote certain confessions of the painters themselves, I would sadden, if I transcribed the incredible witnesses to ignorance and of candid fatuity that I have collected from them. One could make a lamentable and laughable document of stupidity from what is said among these newcomers."[62] Such tabloid-level comments were hardly apologetic in tone. Mauclair obviously relished being the center of controversy.

The warfare continued with the June 1895 issue of the *Mercure de*

61. Ibid., 235. ("Nécessité du dessin, défiance de la coloration pour elle-même, recherche constante du caractère, union d'une conception à la peinture de morceau, infirmité de l'art plastique sans motif cérébral comme de la cérébralité sans ressources d'expressions suffisantes, vanité du dessin déformé, erreur optique du pointillisme, inaptitude des peintres néo-impressionnistes à tout symbolisme, dissociation esthétique du sens de la synthèse dans l'esprit et sur la toile, insuffisance d'études anatomiques, manque d'oeuvres réellement composées, pléthore d'esquisses, exageration du goût pour la décoration dans les tableaux, arrogance envers des maîtres, ignorance de l'histoire de l'art, désir au bizarre au lieu de l'original—toutes ces constatations ont passé dans mes articles.")

62. Ibid., 237. ("J'éttonerais, si j'écrivais certains aveux de ces peintres eux-mêmes, j'attristerais, si je transcrivais les incroyables témoignages d'ignorance et de candide fatuité que j'en recueillis. On ferait un sottisier lamentable et risible de ce qui se dit entre 'novateurs.'")

France, in which Emile Bernard published an open letter to Mauclair.[63] Bernard took the opportunity to outline his history as an artist, to explain that he had introduced Albert Aurier to modern art, and to demonstrate that Gauguin had benefited from his own early work. He took issue with Mauclair's suggestion that the young modernists were insincere and generally offered an explanation for the new painting, or at least for the new painting as he saw it. Mauclair responded in the July issue of the *Mercure* with his own open letter to Bernard.[64] He stated that he had followed a specific aesthetic program and complained about the abuse he had suffered for his candor. Mauclair admitted that his ideas had undergone an evolution, that he had in fact changed his opinion from the days when he ardently defended the new painting, and that his old friends did not understand his change. Mauclair went on to argue for more open criticism, less programmatically in favor of everything new, and claimed he still very much felt these new painters were his "comrades." His tone was conciliatory but he conceded nothing. He ended by agreeing to disagree with the new work and asserting his right to do so. Again, such comments were not designed to make friends among the avant-garde.

Some fourteen months later Mauclair wrote his last entry for the arts section of the *Mercure de France.*[65] In it he once again noted the controversy his articles had stirred up, adding that he regretted nothing. With a note of sadness he admitted that he wished the attacks on him had taken another tone and concluded, magnanimously, that it was time for him to move aside and let someone more favorably inclined toward newer painting have the field. One wonders if the editors had asked Mauclair to leave. Regardless, he certainly remained active as a critic, now writing for the more conservative, and bigger, *La Nouvelle revue.* The transformation from the Camille Mauclair who offered such praise of advanced painting in the pages of the *Revue indépendante* to the conservative who "viciously attacked all new tendencies" seemed to be complete. Indeed, one cannot discount a certain opportunism in Mauclair's turn from his earlier views. Mauclair had clearly attempted to write in the style of the *Mercure de France* in his first months with that publica-

---

63. Emile Bernard, "Lettre ouverte à M. Camille Mauclair," *Mercure de France,* xiv (June 1895), 323–39.

64. Mauclair, "Réponse à M. Emile Bernard," *Mercure de France,* xv (July 1895), 91–96.

65. Mauclair, "Art," *Mercure de France,* xix (September 1896), 562–64.

tion, and his new association with the mainstream *Nouvelle revue* might have given rise to a similar "house" style of criticism. While writing for the *Nouvelle revue* he continued the polemic mood of his earlier work but he supported more "palatable" artists. The pattern, one might say, was much the same for symbolism itself—the more accepted the movement, the more diluted was its statement. But such a view is not only too cynical, it is also too simplistic. Several mitigating facts prevent drawing such a clear-cut picture of this critic.

First of all, as has already been noted, Mauclair's general view that impressionism had led French painting in problematic directions was not unique in symbolist circles. When, for instance, Mauclair praised Monet as a great master of the brush but lamented his lack of ideas, he echoed Albert Aurier's criticism.[66] What brief comments Mauclair made about neo-impressionism were also similar to Aurier's negative view of the style.[67] Mauclair's comments on Gauguin had been foreshadowed by Félix Fénéon's; even if, typically, Mauclair carried the invective to extremes, his attacks merit no more condemnation than those of Fénéon himself.[68]

Second, some of Mauclair's changing attitude toward modernist painting was due to his own political evolution. Early in his career Mauclair had been a typical symbolist/anarchist, generally disdainful of bourgeois society but not active in either the political or social realm. By the midnineties all of this would change.[69] In quick succession Mauclair became a political activist and a former symbolist. His 1897 "Souvenirs sur le mouvement symboliste en France, 1884–1897"—written, once again, for the *Nouvelle revue*—was meant as an epitaph for the movement.[70] Offering an objective view of symbolism's achievements Mauclair sug-

66. Compare, for instance, Mauclair, "Critique de la peinture," 323ff., with Aurier, "Claude Monet," *Oeuvres posthumes*, 221–25.

67. Mauclair, "Choses d'art," *Mercure de France*, xvii (February 1896), 269, even used the same term as Aurier—"sealing wafers"—to describe neo-impressionist dots. In "Choses d'art," *Mercure de France*, x (March 1894), 284–86, Mauclair offered the standard complaint that neo-impressionist technique was mechanical and boring, and he leveled harsh criticism at Paul Signac, whom Aurier also disliked.

68. One might also add that like Fénéon, Mauclair had praised Gauguin's earlier style but reviled the newer symbolist work.

69. On Mauclair's changing political beliefs and his disavowal of symbolism, see Clark, "Camille Mauclair and the Religion of Art," 88ff.

70. Mauclair, "Souvenirs sur le mouvement symboliste en France, 1884–1897," *La Nouvelle revue*, cviii (September–October 1897), 670–93, (November–December 1897), 79–100.

gested that new directions were necessary for French literature, directions that were less obscure, less concentrated on the esoteric fine points of writing: in short more engaged.

Part of Mauclair's new feeling toward symbolism was due to the simple truth that the movement was running out of steam, but it was also based on his changing view of the artist's role in society, an attitude caused by his own active support of Alfred Dreyfus. Indeed, Mauclair's "Souvenirs sur le mouvement symboliste en France" appeared at precisely the time when the Dreyfus case was heating up. The "affair," of course, galvanized French society and Mauclair was not immune to its influence. His political position became consciously socialist and more concerned with the plight of the worker; he began to call for a socially responsible art. This attitude, combined with his feeling that symbolism as a movement was finished, may well have stimulated his disavowal of much contemporary painting. Central to his complaints about impressionism, neo-impressionism, and the art of Gauguin had been a mistrust of art that concentrated so heavily on technique, on "virtuosity for its own sake." Thus he could, along with Joséphin Péladan, complain that painting had become decadent.[71] However wrongheaded, Mauclair's reaction to modernist painting was not simply based on an opportunistic transfer to an established publication. His attitude may well have been motivated by his socialist sensibilities.

Finally, the element of independent personal taste must be considered in relation to Mauclair's disavowal of modernist painting. This does not simply mean that Mauclair was entitled to his personal opinions. Of course he was, but the fact that personal opinion is so often the focus of Mauclair's art criticism is in itself signal. In the last two chapters we observed a shift in critical attitudes toward painting. Fénéon was neo-impressionism's patient explicator, while Aurier was more independent of the artists he championed. Mauclair was more independent yet. Not only was his criticism removed from the careful explanation of Fénéon, it had, indeed, come to be at odds with painting itself. Increasingly, symbolist criticism revolved around the critic's own aesthetic program, concentrating, significantly, on written theory rather than painted object. Such, finally, was inherent in the fact that symbolism was a literary

71. For the comment about virtuosity for its own sake, see note 51, this chapter. For the thought that painting had become decadent, see Mauclair, "Destinées de la peinture française," 375–76.

movement before it was a factor in painting. Mauclair's aggressive, no-holds-barred attitude toward modernist painting serves then as metaphor for the profound differences between a literary movement and the efforts of painters.

THE ART CRITICISM OF ALPHONSE GERMAIN

In a period rife with astonishing characters Alphonse Germain's criticism can still be surprising. Germain was pompously erudite and arrogantly opinionated; he wrote in a flamboyant style reminiscent of Joséphin Péladan. He can appear, at least from the perspective of late twentieth-century art history, to be wildly inconsistent in both aesthetic judgment and theoretical acumen. At times he seems to have been at the cutting edge of modernist thought. At other times his opinions were deeply conservative. In reality he was quite typical of his period, both in his egotistical posturing and his inconsistent attitude toward avant-garde art. He was that remarkable sort of critic we have been noting, that phenomenon peculiar to the 1890s, a conservative who thought himself to be in the forefront of the avant-garde.[72]

Germain, who was the same age as Félix Fénéon, was born in Lyon in 1861. But while Fénéon was active in Paris from the early 1880s, Germain only began to make a name for himself there in the late eighties and, especially, the early nineties. Although he remains virtually unknown today his art criticism and theory were much in evidence in late symbolist circles. He published various books on art and art history well into the twentieth century, but it is his critical work in the short period from 1889 through 1894 that is of most interest here.[73] It was during

72. Very little has been written about Germain. An early article about Germain is by Armand Praviel, "Un ecrivain d'art, Alphonse Germain," *L'Occident*, IV (December 1903), 281–85. Elizabeth Martin, "The Symbolist Criticism of Painting," 140–41, discusses him merely as a follower of Péladan. His name appears most often in bibliographies of neo-impressionism but occasionally makes it into discussions of other subjects—especially the art of Alexandre Séon, as will be noted shortly. He was recently mentioned in connection with the art and theory of Paul Sérusier. See Caroline Boyle-Turner, *Paul Sérusier* (Ann Arbor: UMI Research Press, 1983), 64–65, 98–99. Also see Constance Naubert-Riser, "La Critique des années 1890."

73. Among Germain's many publications on art are *Pour le beau* (Paris: E. Girard, 1893); *Notre art de France* (Paris: E. Girard, 1894); *Comment rénover l'art: l'art chrétien en France des origines au XVIe siècle* (Paris: Bloud, 1906); *L'Influence de Saint François d'Assise sur la civilisation*

these five years that he formed his personality as a critic and demonstrated the conservative/progressive mixture that is our concern.

Like many of his colleagues in nineteenth-century French intellectual
circles Germain published often. From 1889 to 1894 he produced two
books—*Pour le beau* (1893) and *Notre art de France* (1894)—and more
than forty articles in more than ten different periodicals. His affiliations
were, also, wide-ranging. Thus his writing could be found in the ultraconservative *Moniteur des arts*, or the mystical Catholic *Le Saint-Graal*,
as well as the anarchist-oriented *Entretiens politiques et littéraires*, or that
bastion of Belgian modernism, *L'Art moderne*. His appearance in *L'Art
moderne* was based on his expertise in neo-impressionist style, and it was
as an enthusiastic friend of Seurat's group that Germain began his career
as an art critic.

Germain's first article on painting was a laudatory review of the 1889
Salon des indépendants.[74] In a manner reminiscent of Félix Fénéon,
Germain set about patiently explaining the goals of the neo-impressionists, noting their sources in contemporary color theory and their artistic
heritage from Corot through impressionism. He quoted from Georges
Vanor, author of *L'Art symboliste*, in praise of the neo-impressionists and
argued against the then-current notion that the group lacked identifiable
personalities, noting: "they are not the students of any pontiff; each of
them has his own aesthetic just as each of them has his own originality."[75]
He concluded by saying that no matter how much the public might
scoff, the new movement would take its place in the Louvre; he claimed
that the neo-impressionists would achieve fame by combining the brush
stroke of Monet and the linear control of Poussin.[76]

Two years later, for an important issue of *La Plume* focused on the
newest movements in painting, Germain wrote the section on neo-impressionism.[77] Here he once again carefully explained the theoretical

---

et les arts (Paris: Bloud, 1903); *Les Artistes lyonnais du XIIIe siècle à nos jours* (Lyon: H. Lardauchet, 1910).

74. Germain, "Beaux-Arts, l'exposition des indépendants," *Art et critique*, i (15 September
1889), 250–52.

75. Ibid., 251. (". . . il ne se font les lévites d'aucun pontife, chacun d'eux a son esthétique
comme chacun d'eux a son originalité.")

76. This thought is reminiscent of Maurice Denis's comments on Cézanne, *Du symbolisme au
classicisme, théories*, 171.

77. Germain, "Théorie chromo-luminariste, exposé et critique," *La Plume*, iii, no. 57 (1
September 1891), 285–87. For more on this issue of *La Plume* and Germain's role in it see my
"In 1891."

basis of the movement. He also noted that he preferred the term *chromo-luminariste*, as Seurat himself did, thereby revealing a degree of closeness to the painters. He offered long quotes from Chevreul, Goethe, and Ogden Rood along with citations from Charles Henry and Félix Fénéon, all in praise of the neo-impressionists, whom he called courageous seekers after harmony itself. Earlier that year Germain had published two articles in *L'Art moderne,* which the editors found to be a clear and succinct setting-forth of neo-impressionist theory.[78] Germain understood the patient, studious attitude of Seurat and his followers and their concern with matters relating solely to painting. Thus he began the first of his articles in *L'Art moderne:* "It is not in the goal of being *realist* that the young innovators concern themselves so much with scientific observation, but to arrive methodically at Harmony in painting, through painterly means—exclusively."[79] On the surface, then, Germain appeared to be an intimate of neo-impressionist circles and a strong supporter of their painting, a logical successor to Félix Fénéon. But, although Germain did have relatively intimate contact with neo-impressionist circles and was quite supportive of their paintings, he was not temperamentally attuned to their painting style and eventually turned away from the movement.

Even in his praise of neo-impressionism in the September 1891 issue of *La Plume* Germain voiced certain reservations about divisionist technique. He warned against a too-ardent love of physics and scientific experimentation and suggested that their fear of literary sources might impel the neo-impressionists toward a dryly mathematical style. His warning was not without precedent. Félix Fénéon's protégé, Georges Lecomte, who actively supported the movement, had said as much, and Vincent van Gogh had also warned against too much concentration on technique.[80] But Germain's tack was somewhat more conservative. Germain expressed concern that neo-impressionist technique made difficult the rendering of modeling and relief. Again, in his article for *L'Art*

78. Germain, "Théorie des néo-luminaristes," *L'Art moderne,* xi (12 July 1891), 221–22, (26 July 1891), 239–40.

79. Germain, "Théorie des néo-luminaristes," 221. ("Ce n'est pas dans le but de faire *réaliste* que les jeunes novateurs se passionnent pour les observations scientifiques, mais pour arriver méthodiquement à l'Harmonie en peinture par des moyens peintres,—exclusivement.")

80. Georges Lecomte, "Salon des XX, conférence de M. Georges Lecomte," *L'Art moderne,* xii (28 February 1892), 66. Van Gogh's comment can be found in Norma Broude, *Seurat in Perspective,* 49.

moderne, he worried not only about relief and modeling but also about accurate aerial perspective and a true sense of depth in neo-impressionist painting. He hoped that in their next exhibition these painters would indicate a solution to the problem.

Two years later Germain was even more skeptical. In an article entitled "Pour le beau," eventually published in book form, he reviewed the current movements in painting.[81] He once again recognized the historical import of neo-impressionism. But, after carefully outlining the sources and goals of the movement, he more strongly disparaged neo-impressionist technique. No longer hopeful of a solution to their "problems," he suggested that the technique, while good for effects of color and light, destroyed perspective and gave no sense of relief or modeling. Echoing an old complaint, he suggested that Seurat's style was fine for landscape or decorative efforts but unsuitable for the human figure. He argued that the neo-impressionists were passionately enamored with theorems and that their paintings had degenerated into little more than intellectual experimentation. Germain stopped short of totally rejecting the movement, allowing that it had been a step in the right direction, and that Seurat himself had been turned toward a new style when he died. But, finally, Germain felt that only one painter was on the right path: Alexandre Séon. His reasons for choosing this little-known painter are of interest in revealing his attitude toward events in contemporary painting, especially his changing view of neo-impressionism.

It is quite possible that Germain was introduced to advanced painting by Alexandre Séon. He did not write art criticism prior to the time he began associating with Séon and others around the office of *L'Ermitage.*[82] Séon was particularly concerned with drawing technique—he was professor of drawing for the schools of the city of Paris—and was also a follower of Puvis de Chavannes, having worked with the master for

<hr>

81. Germain, "Pour le beau," *Essais d'art libre,* iii (February–March 1893), 1–120. It is in chapter 2, "le Chromo-luminarisme," 13–20, that he discusses neo-impressionism.

82. Adolphe Retté, *Le Symbolisme,* 120–21, related how Germain and Séon could always be found conversing about art off in one corner of Henri Mazel's apartment during the Wednesday afternoon receptions of *L'Ermitage.* It appears that Germain may have dabbled in producing art himself, perhaps through his friendship with Séon. Camille Mauclair, "Choses d'art," *Mercure de France,* x (March 1894), 286, commented, negatively, about a contribution Germain made to the Salon des cent at the gallery of the publication *La Plume.* Mauclair also derided Séon, calling him "un Cabanel des pauvres."

many years.[83] Just so, Germain accentuated "proper" drawing in his criticism and continuously extolled Puvis's murals. Whether or not Séon actually was responsible for Germain's interest in the visual arts, the critic never resisted an opportunity to include the painter's name among the leaders of the avant-garde. For Germain, Séon was the incarnation of the new symbolist aesthetic in painting, and he devoted several articles to careful analysis of his work.[84]

For his part, Séon seems to have been in close contact with neo-impressionist circles for a time. Séon and Seurat were in Henri Lehmann's studio at the Ecole des Beaux-Arts together and they evidently became friendly.[85] They were both interested in Puvis de Chavannes, and Séon might have introduced Seurat to the master, as he had been working in Puvis's studio since 1881. Both Seurat and Séon were attracted to color theory and developed extensive aesthetics based on careful study of the physics of color. Indeed, Séon's theory—very much in evidence in symbolist periodicals of the early nineties through Germain's articles—closely resembles that of Seurat. The following quotation from an article written by Germain in 1892 serves as an excellent example. Speaking of Séon, Germain noted:

> Posing as postulate that each color of the spectrum and white, which contains all color, corresponds to one or more of our primordial perceptions, this cerebral artist deduced that their thou-

83. See the exhibition catalogue, *French Symbolist Painters* (London: Arts Council, 1972), 145.

84. See, for instance, Germain, "Du symbolisme dans la peinture," *Art et critique*, II (5 July 1890), 417; "Alexandre Séon," *La Plume*, III (1 September 1891), 303; "Critique d'art, sur un tableau refusé," *La Plume*, III (15 May 1891), 171–72; "Le Désespoir de la chimère," *La Plume*, IV (1 June 1892), 244; "Un peintre idéaliste-idéiste, Alexandre Séon," *L'Art et l'idée*, I (February 1892), 107–12. A recent source on Séon is Delphine Montalant, "Alexandre Séon, peintre symboliste," *L'Oeil*, no. 362 (September 1985), 40–45.

85. Philippe Jullian, *Dreamers of Decadence*, 81, even suggested that Séon brought Seurat under the influence of Péladan just before Seurat's death. It has also been suggested that in the year 1889 Seurat would see no one but Séon. The statement, a quotation from a letter from Dubois-Pillet to Signac was made by the collector Elie-Charles Flamand in the exhibition catalogue, *French Symbolist Painters*, 145. Flamand owned Séon's *Désespoir de la chimère* among other symbolist paintings. François Cachin has informed me that the letter, now in the Signac archive, simply says, in reference to Seurat, "il ne cause qu'avec Séon . . . ," and nothing more. Richard Thomson, *Seurat* (Oxford: Phaidon, 1985), 189, quoted Flamand and also Charles Angrand to the same intent. For more on the relationship between Seurat and Séon, see my "Seurat et ses amis de l'Ecole des Beaux-Arts."

sand nuances are suited to complementarize the iconic symboliz-ation of a state of soul or abstract ideas. And he schematizes his theory in the following rules:

Corporealize, *by lines*, a symbol into a type amplified to the archetype; homogenize this symbol, by means of hues, with the character of a being, or better his substratum.

Observe all, everywhere, preferably in people, but CHOOSE.

Everything comes down to style, idealize everything. Style is, he recognized along with Charles Blanc, "truth aggrandized, sim-plified, stripped of all superfluous detail, rendered to its original essence, its typical aspect." The ideal, he understands, according to the definition of Joséphin Péladan: "all idea sublimated, to its point of supreme harmony, intensity, subtlety."

Then, MEASURE shape and form, enshrine their composition in a frame of decorative arabesques; choosing light and hue *in rap-port* with the subject to be treated, and make their infinite tonal values (have they not a soul!) concur with some aesthetic emo-tion, some sensation of the passions, without which the most knowledgeable harmonic chromatization is only a romance with-out words. The idea which gives rise to a deed, *expletivize* by a concordance of *expressive* linear directions, and a dominance of *pertinently* symbolic colorations.

Consider finally as a duty the respect of the law of harmony that governs all of nature, proceed by analogy and enclose its fiction in true resemblance; then take science as a guide without being rendered a slave of a system.[86]

86. Germain, "Un peintre idéaliste-idéiste, Alexandre Séon," 109–10. ("Posant comme pos-tulat que chaque couleur spectrale et le blanc qui les contient toutes correspondent à une ou plusieurs de nos perceptions primordiales, ce cérébral en déduit que leurs mille nuances sont aptes à complémentariser la symbolisation iconique d'un état d'âme ou d'idées abstraites. Et il schématise sa théorie en les règles suivantes:

Corporéiser, *par les lignes*, un symbole dans un type amplifié à l'archétype; homogénéiser ce symbole, *au moyen des teintes*, avec le caractère d'un être ou mieux son substratum.

Observer tout et partout, de préférence en le peuple, mais CHOISIR.

Tout monter au style, idéaliser tout. Le style, c'est, reconnaît-il avec Charles Blanc, 'la vérité agrandie, simplifiée, dégagée de tous les détails insignifiants, rendue à son essence ori-ginelle, à son aspect typique.' L'idéal, il le comprend, selon la définition de Joséphin Péladan, 'tout idée sublimée, à son point suprême d'harmonie, d'intensité, de subtilité.'

Donc, MESURER figure et forme, enchâsser sa composition dans une ossature d'arabesques décoratives; élire luminosités et teintes *en rapport* avec le sujet à traiter, et faire concourir leurs infinies valeurs de tons (n'ont-elles pas une âme!) à quelque émotion esthétique, quelque

A good deal of what is offered here can be attributed to the influence of Seurat. The insistence on the "cerebral" nature of the artist, the scientific interest in color, the quote from Charles Blanc, and the final concentration on harmony all hark to Seurat's theory. Séon also developed a symbolism of lines—vertical lines symbolized elevated thoughts; oblique lines to the left evoked sadness; lines to the right, joy—that is heavily indebted to Seurat.[87]

Just as Séon seems to have drawn extensively from Seurat's theory, Germain was deeply influenced by the man who published that theory, Félix Fénéon. The passage above shows Germain to have been, as Fénéon was, quite fond of scientific-sounding terms, like "expletivize" and "homogenize."[88] The manner in which Germain carefully analyzes Séon's thoughts and is at pains to say exactly what the artist himself wanted is also analogous to Fénéon's writing, as is the generally detached tone of Germain's style. Nor should one be surprised that Germain was influenced by a recognized leader of the avant-garde like Fénéon. What is surprising—and, one supposes, disconcerting to champions of modernism—is how temperamentally unsuited Germain, and Séon as well, were to neo-impressionism. They were more attuned to the style of the criticism—that superior, distant attitude so typical of Fénéon—than the style of the painting. It comes as no surprise that their brief espousal of modernism quickly evaporated in a conservative symbolism, more to their liking and more in the manner of the 1890s.

For all the modernist ring to his theory Séon's paintings never participated in neo-impressionist style nor, for that matter, any modernist

---

sensation passionnelle, sans quoi la plus suave chromatisation harmonique n'est qu'une romance sans paroles. L'Idée que suscite un geste, *l'explétiver,* par une concordance de directions linéaires *expressives,* et une dominante de colorations *pertinemment* symboliques.

Considérant enfin comme un devoir le respect de la loi d'harmonie qui régit la nature entière, procéder par analogie et enclore sa fiction dans la vraisemblance; donc, prendre la science pour guide sans se rendre l'esclave d'un système.")

87. See Fernand Weyl, "Alexandre Séon," *L'Art et la vie,* IV (1894), 406–13. One might add that Séon's very concentration on drawing is reminiscent of Seurat's interests during the 1880s. Germain thought that Séon's theory of lines was his own unique invention. In "Du symbolisme dans la peinture," 418, he stated—reversing the proper order of importance—that Seurat's theory of line was "almost identical to that of Séon" ("presque identique à celle de Séon").

88. Retté, *Le Symbolisme,* 121, noted Germain's proclivity for inventing new and different terms and suggested that he would have been a lot more interesting to read if he had been less creative.

style. He was also, it seems, a slow study. During the 1880s, while Seurat demonstrated steady development with *Bathing at Asniers* and *A Sunday Afternoon on the Island of La Grand Jatte,* Séon was deeply involved with a project for the city hall of Courbevoie—close, incidentally, to the island where Seurat was working. The paintings (Fig. 12) are quite fine but too heavily influenced by Puvis de Chavannes to support the color theory and language of lines that Germain claimed began with these murals.[89] Séon's *Despair of the Chimera* (Fig. 13)—produced the year Seurat completed *Le Chahut* and *Circus*—was also supported by theoretical references to "cold hues" and "broken verticals" but is equally derivative.[90] Here it was Puvis de Chavannes, Gustave Moreau, and literary symbolism in general that Séon drew from. Few paintings show a more jarring mixture of modernist theory and traditionalist sensibilities.

Séon did not really hit his stride until later in the decade, when he became involved with Péladan's Rose + Croix Salons. His portrait of Péladan (Fig. 14), with its rich purples and golds and static linearity, displays an aggressive traditionalism in style—one wants to call it reactionary—that is the painted equivalent of the Sâr's ideas about art.[91] Here, and in other work of the mid to late nineties (Fig. 15), Séon developed a hard, linear style, cold, distant, and unashamedly literary, that stands with some of the best products of the late symbolist manner in Paris. Alphonse Germain developed an equally traditionalist criticism to complement Séon's painting.

Germain's criticism became increasingly conservative under the influence of Joséphin Péladan. His description of Séon's Courbevoie murals as "the act of faith from a worshipper of the Beautiful" certainly sounds like Péladan.[92] In 1889 Germain had praised Manet as one of the sources

89. Germain, "Pour le beau," 24.

90. Germain, "Un peintre idéaliste-idéiste, Alexandre Séon," 111.

91. Weyl, "Alexandre Séon," 406, did call it reactionary but he meant the term as a compliment, noting that Séon was "basically a reactionary: he wants to go back to the study of the great masters of Greece and Italy." (". . . au fond un réactionnaire: il veut revenir à l'étude des grands maîtres de la Grèce et de l'Italie.")

92. Germain, "Du symbolisme dans la peinture," 419. (". . . l'acte de foi d'un adorateur de Beau.") This is similar to Péladan's, "The first word of art is always an act of faith," *L'Art ochlocratique,* 17. ("Le premier mot de l'art est toujours un acte de foi.") Péladan, ibid., 58–59, also noted that any beautiful work of art was automatically Catholic, "the elevation and beauty of a work constituting an implicit Catholicism." (". . . la hauteur et la beauté d'une oeuvre

of modern art, but by 1893 he chided Renoir and Degas, among others, for following Manet in limiting themselves to the anecdotal side of French life—Péladan had said much the same.[93] Germain was also sympathetic to other Rose + Croix artists, among them Fernand Khnopff and Carlos Schwabe. He was not, however, uncritical of the Sâr's exhibitions, complaining that the quality of paintings was not sufficiently high to support the noble sentiments of the enterprise.[94]

A picture of Germain as critic emerges now. He was both influenced by some of the stronger voices of the time yet unwilling to be a mere follower. He seemed to admire, even copy, Fénéon's critical style yet developed an aesthetic that radically diverged from neo-impressionist orthodoxy. Just so he took Fénéon's criticism of Gauguin to new extremes, complaining not only of the "ugliness" of the deformations of the synthetists but also viewing the problem as a breach with the Greek ideal of beauty.[95] Though he was influenced by Péladan—they were, after all, both Lyonnais Catholics—he rejected the trendy nature of Péladan's mystical religiosity. Instead, Germain was a defender of absolute, traditional, orthodox Catholicism. In a clear reference to Péladan, he warned young Catholics of the "sophism" of the occult and theosophy, and pleaded against "renascent Magianism" and "impious initiation."[96]

Engaged, yet disengaged from the avant-garde, Germain could entitle an article—a few months before Albert Aurier's similar move—"Du symbolisme dans la peinture," emphasizing, as would Aurier, "l'Idée." But while Aurier's symbolist painter was Gauguin, Germain's was Séon. Germain could entrain Maurice Denis in a published dialogue on the subject of neo-traditionism, agreeing on most theoretical points but ultimately and absolutely disagreeing on the artists representative of the new trends.[97] At least in the early nineties, Germain fulminated against

---

constituent un catholicisme implicite.") Germain made a similar argument at the beginning of "Pour le beau," 1–3.

93. The praise of Manet was in "Beaux-Arts, l'exposition des indépendants," 251. The attack on Renoir, Degas, and Manet came in "Pour le beau," 11, but he also made similar comments in "Un peintre idéaliste-idéiste, Alexandre Séon," 108.

94. Germain, "Salon de la Rose + Croix," L'odéal et l'idéalisme, I (May 1892), 176–80.

95. "Pour le beau," 30–31.

96. Germain, "L'Art et l'apologétique," Mercure de France, VII (March 1893), 224, 228.

97. Germain's "Beaux-Arts, du tempérament peintre," Art et critique, II (27 September 1890), 618–20, was a response to Denis's "Définition du néo-traditionnisme," which appeared in the same periodical a month previously. Denis responded in the next issue, "A M. Alphonse

precisely the artists Denis upheld: Cézanne, Van Gogh, Gauguin and his followers.

Germain was simply unable to recognize how fully Gauguin and the Nabis embodied the new symbolist ideas in painting. While he railed against naturalism and the academic style he could complain that the "deformers," as he called Gauguin's group, had abandoned perspective and modeling. "Nothing," he said, "justifies the exclusion of perspective and the suppression of relief, nothing, not even this style of high tapestry design dear to the traditionists."[98] Elsewhere he argued that "because everything is geometry in space, in matter, in the human body, the work of art must take into account perspective shading and the structure of relief, even in its most idealized and dreamlike manifestations."[99] The standard academic battery of "sound" drawing, perspective, and modeling were, for Germain, the armaments for defending art from the barbaric onslaught of the dreaded "deformers."

But two of Germain's complaints against the synthetists are, in particular, significant to this discussion. The first was religious, the second political. Germain managed to combine orthodox Catholicism with an orthodox desire for plastic beauty in art. "To suppress plastic beauty!" he pontificated, "is to prostitute the FORM by which divine Revelation incarnates the invisible SUBSTANCE of the Father!—impiety, illogicality."[100] For Germain, beauty was a reflection of God, and the artist—whose duty was leading souls to the faith through art—must re-create the image of exterior beauty "piously, according to the natural order and the divine informing principle."[101] To a critic like Germain, devoted to reviving religious art, "deforming" nature was not only bad artistic form, it was sacrilege.

As was noted in Chapter 1, the new Catholicism of the later nineteenth century in France was highly conservative politically. So too was

---

Germain," *Art et critique*, II (18 October 1890), 667–68. The discussion here is indicative of the differences between two basically traditionalist approaches.

98. Germain, "Théorie des déformateurs, exposé et réfutation," *La Plume*, III, no. 57 (1 September 1891), 290. ("Rien ne justifie l'exclusion de la perspective et la suppression des reliefs, rien, pas même cette recherche de haute tapisserie chère aux traditionnistes.")

99. "Pour le beau," 33. (". . . parce que tout est géométrie dans l'espace, dans la matière, dans le corps humain, l'oeuvre d'art doit tenir compte des dégradations perspectives et de la structure des reliefs, même dans ses manifestations les plus idéalisées, les plus *rêve*.")

100. Ibid., 48. ("Supprimer la beauté plastique! c'est-à-dire prostituer la FORME par laquelle le divin Révélateur incarna l'invisible SUBSTANCE du Père!—impiété, illogisme.")

101. Ibid., 52. (". . . pieusement d'après l'ordre naturel et le divin principe informant.")

Alphonse Germain. He denounced modern democratic societies, equating the loss of faith with the rise of the masses:

> In losing the Faith, a race loses the notion of Art and Beauty, the coming to power of the Voltairean bourgeoisie has materialized the spirit, the laicization of instruction has prosaicized souls, the invasion of the termites of mediocrity has lowered sentiments, logical consequence: intellectualism is being banned from society.[102]

What a remarkable turnabout this statement represents! The positivists of the sixties and seventies could not have imagined that faith and intellect might be combined in the same paragraph. Germain not only combined the two; he clearly saw Catholicism as responsible for the intellectual health of France. He echoed here the conservative Catholic political agenda, making reference to the gargantuan struggle between the church and the Third Republic for control of education (a struggle to be dealt with more fully in Chapter 6). He also reflected, with that reference to race, the party line of the nationalists.

Nationalism was an important factor in French politics from the later days of the Boulanger episode at the end of the eighties until well into the twentieth century.[103] Although nominally beginning as a socialist cause, nationalism evolved—much as did its Nazi counterpart in Germany—into a marked rightist fanaticism. Though never dominant, the movement gained adherents all across French society during the Dreyfus affair, through passionate anti-Dreyfussard fulminating. In this, nation-

---

102. Germain, "Aux intellectuels," *Entretiens politiques et littéraires*, ii (February 1891), 40. ("En perdant la Foi, une race perd la notion de l'Art et du Beau, l'avènement au pouvoir de la bourgeoisie voltairienne avait matérialisé l'esprit, la laïcisation de l'enseignement a prosaïsé les âmes, l'envahissement des termites de la médiocrité achève de mesquiniser les sentiments conséquence logique: l'intellectuel mis au ban de la société.")

103. On nationalism and the political situation in France at the end of the nineteenth century see, for example, the following sources in English: William Curt Buthman, *The Rise of Integral Nationalism in France* (New York: Columbia University Press, 1939); Stephen Wilson, *Ideology and Experience: Antisemitism in France at the Time of the Dreyfus Affair* (Rutherford N.J.: Fairleigh Dickinson University Press, 1982); Robert F. Byrnes, *Antisemitism in Modern France* (New York: Howard Fertig, 1969); Samuel M. Osgood, *French Royalism Under the Third and Fourth Republics* (The Hague: Martinus Nijhoff, 1960); Robert L. Hoffman, *More Than a Trial* (New York: Free Press, 1980); Jean-Denis Bredin, *The Affair*, trans. by Jeffrey Mehlman (New York: George Braziller, 1986); Theodore Zeldin, *France, 1848–1945*, vol. 1, *Ambition, Love and Politics* (Oxford: Clarendon Press, 1973). See also Zeev Sternhell, *La Droit révolutionnaire, 1885–1914: les origines françaises du fascisme* (Paris: Editions du Seuil, 1978).

alism and Catholicism combined forces. The radical Catholic Edouard Drumont became one of the bulwarks of French nationalism and was largely responsible for the anti-Semitic tone of the movement. Charles Maurras, who would later establish the reactionary *Action française*, was another major early voice of nationalism. While nationalism itself was a complex force that can hardly be outlined in a few short sentences, one nationalist concentration is important for us: the theme of Latinity. It was a concept dear to both Drumont and Maurras.

The nationalist concern for Latinity was both anti-Semitic and patriotic. Great stock was put in continuation of the accomplishments of the classical world, as embodied in the Latin race and, importantly, Christian art. Asian, African, and, especially, Jewish cultures were excluded. So too, for that matter, was northern European culture. A highly traditionalist Latin aesthetic developed, emphasizing rational order, truth, and beauty as the attributes of Latinity.[104] Alphonse Germain's criticism was rife with the catchwords and themes of nationalist Latinity. Thus he spoke of how Christian art had enlarged upon the classical tradition.[105] He sought out racial characteristics in art, looking for those physiognomic features that a nation retained across the centuries and demanding works that "nationalized" rather than modernized.[106] He specifically decried the "sophistry" of Cézanne, Gauguin, and Van Gogh, whom he found to be "intensive temperaments, but disequilibriated and in no way Latin."[107] This is a direct echo of Charles Maurras's theories. Indeed, Maurras published an article putting forth his Latinist aesthetic in *L'Ermitage*—according to Adolphe Retté, he caused quite a controversy among the symbolists who gathered around the offices of the periodical.[108] Evidently Germain was swayed by Maurras's argument. Not only, then, were the artistic "deformations" of the synthetists bad art and sacrilegious, they were, somehow, to the distorted nationalism of the Dreyfus affair years, unpatriotic.

104. Charles Maurras condemned the French romantic movement on nationalist grounds as being outside the Latin character of the French race. He said the same about democracy, "Kantianism," and Protestantism. See Buthman, *The Rise of Integral Nationalism in France*, 151–62.

105. Cf., "Pour le beau," 114.

106. Germain, "Un fragment de *Notre art de France*," *Essais d'art libre*, v (June–July 1894), 99.

107. Germain, "Théorie des déformateurs, exposé et réfutation," 290.

108. The article, "Repentir de Pythéas," appeared in the January 1892 issue of *L'Ermitage*. See Retté, *Le Symbolisme*, 114–19, for an interesting discussion of its effects.

Both Alphonse Germain and Camille Mauclair turned away from modernist painting, albeit for different reasons. That they could each sermonize about "proper" draftsmanship indicates less a shared theoretical foundation than a shared reaction to the "deforming" synthetist style of the time—the style of the avant-garde. As such they represent one major trend in the symbolist art criticism of the 1890s: a rejection of modernist painting by critics literally raised in a modernist milieu. One final conservative turn in symbolist art criticism is of interest now, not a rejection of modernism but, rather, a modification of its goals. No one represents this better than the painter—and critic—Maurice Denis.

6

MAURICE DENIS'S CONSERVATIVE MODERNISM

In 1898 the painter Maurice Denis received his first commission for a large-scale religious ensemble. The Congregation of the Brothers of the Holy Cross, an order headquartered at Neuilly, selected the painter to decorate the chapel in their Collège de Sainte-Croix at Le Vésinet, across the Seine from the painter's hometown of St. Germain-en-Laye. Denis settled on the theme of "The Exaltation of the Holy Cross" and produced one of the true masterpieces of late nineteenth-century religious art (Figs. 16, 17a–f). In a setting magically both interior and exterior, a religious drama of disarming naturalness and ethereal spirituality is played out. Charmingly "ordinary" young altar boys—certainly meant to evoke *collège* students—go about their ritual celebrations flanked by a choir of angels, singing from hymnals. Above, floats a visionary, seraphic presentation of the Holy Cross itself. Around the infinitely sweet, ordered landscape are the traditional symbols of Christianity: the grapes and wheat, roses and cypresses. The entire scene, from the soft violet columns, the cool mint-green trees, to the rich white and red vestments of angels and boys, is suffused in a glowing, devotional light. Like so much of the traditional ritual of this ancient religion, the painting is solemn, spiritual, comforting, and fine.

The *Exaltation of the Holy Cross* is also, on the very eve of the twentieth century, unapologetically conservative and traditional. Gone, it seems, to all intents and purposes, are the flat, brilliant colors of Nabis cloisonism.[1] If Denis's painting of the early nineties, such as *Sunlight on the Terrace* (Fig. 18) can be seen as providing a bridge from Gauguin's synthetist style to the fauve abstractions of Matisse, this decoration appears more like a barrier between the two. The past, not the modernist present, dominates here. The artist's increasing interest in Ingres is evident in the sharp, linear definition of faces and details of costume. Denis himself noted in his journal a similarity between the pleated tunics worn by altar boys and the drapery folds in archaic Greek statuary—a similarity he called upon to give the Sainte-Croix murals an architectonic spine.[2] One especially feels the influence of Denis's beloved Italian primitives, above all, Fra Angelico. That slightly tilted floor—the perspective lines receding to the point where the priest at mass would raise the Host—as well as the soft color harmonies and the general feeling of humble, reverential silence, all pay homage to "Beato" Angelico.

For all of the traditional aspects of the Sainte-Croix decorations, however, Denis did not produce a standard pastiche of older styles. Comparison with Bouguereau's *Annunciation*, of 1888 (Fig. 19)—also meant as a chapel decoration—reveals the modernity of Denis's conception. Against the minute, photographic detail of the Bouguereau, the *Exaltation of the Holy Cross* now seems more abstract, flatter. Bouguereau's careful, subtle shadow modeling gives way to patches of color juxtaposed to lend the effect of roundness. Denis's color now seems lighter, more brilliant—indeed, more impressionist.

This shifting view of Denis's painting seems appropriate enough. Like one of those perceptual illusions that lend opposed images of the same silhouette, Denis's art changes aspect. Blink and it is modernist; blink

1. There is, however, in the green, violet, red harmonies here, a certain reminiscence of Edouard Vuillard.

2. Maurice Denis, *Journal*, vol. 1, 1884–1904 (Paris: La Colombe, 1957), 147–48.

again and it is all homage to the past. Finally, of course, this split view of Denis is based on a fallacy, that conservative and modernist styles are exclusive. As we have seen, in 1890s Paris this was far from the case. What I propose in this chapter is a demonstration of just how well Denis, in criticism and practice, could combine tradition and modernism. Remarkably, Denis was the embodiment of all of the trends we have discussed in previous chapters. Too often, survey-level studies of the nineteenth century stress only Denis's famous statement about battle horses, nudes, and flat surfaces covered with arranged areas of color. Too often, this statement is seen as a prophetic foreshadowing of twentieth-century abstraction. Such an interpretation is incorrect in terms of the general course of art history and a disservice to Denis. Far from mere prologue to modernist abstraction, Denis's art and criticism—intelligent, sensitive, and intensely personal—deserve study as expressions exquisitely attuned to the conservative mood of the nineties.

MODERNISM

Denis's contribution to the modernist tradition in painting should not be neglected. Denis was a major transmitter of postimpressionist style to the avant-garde of the early twentieth century. Such daring paintings as his *Sunlight on the Terrace* of 1890 are important visual manifestations of the lessons of Gauguin as translated by his young Nabis followers. In the early 1890s Denis produced a series of such works, all tiny paintings, gems of brilliant color and abstract pattern. In terms of criticism even a partial listing of Denis's articles from the early twentieth century reveals the magnitude of his contribution to the new generation's knowledge of the masters of modernism. By 1909 Denis had produced important articles about Maillol, Pissarro, Cross, Cézanne, Redon, Van Gogh, Sérusier, and, especially, Gauguin. At the end of the first decade of the twentieth century, when the idea of "avant-garde" painting was still somewhat novel, very few critics—and certainly no painter—could claim to have published such a wide modernist repertoire.

In his youth Denis seems to have reveled in taking revolutionary stances and making bold pronouncements about art. That battle horse/flat surface statement at the beginning of his "Définition du néo-traditionnisme" was meant to sound radical—never mind that it was based on long-standing naturalist, or even academic, teaching.[3] The article itself, published when the painter was just twenty years of age, is punctuated throughout with short, aphoristic declarations. Specific contemporary artists are named, either in praise or denegration. Each of the sections, headed with Roman numerals, reads like a proposition in a manifesto, and that is certainly what Denis intended.

Much like Alphonse Germain and Camille Mauclair, Denis loved associating himself with the avant-garde. His writing of the early nineties is filled with defensive attacks against an uncomprehending and barbaric public. "It has been just four years now," he began his preface to the ninth exhibition of symbolist and impressionist painters, "since some young unknown men took it into their heads to exhibit, with the disinterested and audacious Le Barc de Boutteville, some canvases that the public was then in the habit of mocking ruthlessly."[4] In January 1889 Denis noted in his journal the formation of the Nabi group with Paul Sérusier, calling himself and his friends, "young men, devotees of the Symbol, misunderstood by the world, which mocks us."[5] Denis clearly enjoyed "admitting" to such raillery from the public. Indeed, his use of pseudonyms in early articles permitted him to refer to himself as one of

3. The statement, which is the opening line of the "Définition du néo-traditionnisme," is translated in Chipp, *Theories of Modern Art*, 94: "It is well to remember that a picture—before being a battle horse, a nude woman, or some anecdote—is essentially a plane surface covered with colors assembled in a certain order." In spite of the fact that Chipp noted the similarity between Denis's statement and one made by Charles Blanc, then professor at the Ecole des Beaux-Arts—"Painting is the art of expressing all of the conceptions of the soul by means of all the realities of nature, represented on a single surface in their forms and in their colors"—there is still a tendency to see Denis's pronouncement as revolutionary. Ultimately Denis's words ring truest as an art student's restatement of a classroom maxim, as valid in classic theory as it was in naturalist thought. Twenty years earlier Emile Zola had noted that in Manet's painting "a head placed against a wall is nothing but a more or less white spot against a more or less gray background, and the clothing juxtaposed to the face becomes merely a more or less blue spot placed next to the more or less white spot" ("Une nouvelle manière en peinture: Edouard Manet," *Revue du XIXe siècle* [1 January 1867]; as translated in Nochlin, *Realism and Tradition in Art*, 72.)

4. Denis, *Du symbolisme au classicisme*, 46. ("Voici quatre ans à peine que quelques jeunes gens inconnus se sont avisés de montrer, chez le si désintéressé et audacieux Le Barc de Boutteville, des toiles qu'on avait coutume alors, dans le public, de blaguer impitoyablement.") In quoting from Denis's writings I have first gone to this source because it is most widely available. However, many sections of Denis's original *Théories* were cut from this edition. Where necessary I have quoted from Denis, *Théories, 1890–1910, Du symbolisme et de Gauguin vers un nouvel ordre classique*, 4th ed. (Paris: L. Rouart and J. Watelin, 1920).

5. *Journal*, I, 73. ("Seigneur, nous sommes quelques Jeunes, dévots du Symbole, incompris du monde qui nous raille.")

the misunderstood young generation. In an exchange of commentary with Alphonse Germain published in *Art et critique* Denis—signing himself Pierre Louis—cited among the youngest new talents, one "Maurice Denis, the author of the drawings for 'Sagesse.'"[6] Denis's famous *Homage to Cézanne* (Fig. 20) from 1900, with its careful depiction of sources, influences, and practitioners of the very latest art of the nineties, was certainly meant to define an avant-garde. In this Denis clearly evoked Henri Fantin-Latour's equally illustrational, programmatic paintings of the naturalist and impressionist avant-garde of the sixties and seventies.

But Denis's modernism was, of course, based on more than the simple desire to be associated with an "advanced" and "despised" minority. He understood, supported, and publicized core theories of the modernist tradition. In his preface to the Le Barc de Boutteville exhibition of 1895, Denis argued vehemently against the idea that art was a copy of something else. He spoke of the necessity for art to develop its expression from its own formal means rather than through subject. In a manner reminiscent of Félix Fénéon he championed an art "without affectation and without literature."[7] He condemned the efforts of "literary" painters, whom he saw as drawing too much of their expression from subject, and not enough from form. Much like the twentieth-century historian Robert Goldwater, Denis was aware of the similarities between idealist and symbolist thought and sought to differentiate between the two. While praising symbolism for being "a light for spirits deeply grieved by naturalism," he added that "at the same time [symbolism was] too much taken with painting to fall into idealist reveries."[8] He insisted symbolism was not an idealist theory, even suggesting it was initiated by landscape painting—in particular, Cézanne—and that its roots were in positivist philosophy and the scientific age.[9] In support of this thought he noted not only the psychological theories of Hippolyte Taine and Herbert Spencer but also the psychophysical researches of Seurat and Pissarro.

Denis was trying to create a sort of textbook modernism, and he sounds convincing in his rejection of "literary" idealist painting; it is

6. "A M. Alphonse Germain," 668. (". . . et Maurice Denis, l'auteur des dessins de 'Sagesse.'")

7. *Du symbolisme au classicisme,* 49. (". . . sans mièvrerie et sans *littérature.*")

8. Ibid., 72. ("C'était vraiment une lumière pour des esprits navrés de naturalisme, et en même temps trop épris de peinture pour donner dans les rêveries idéalistes.")

9. Ibid.

thus no surprise that the twentieth-century scholars of late nineteenth-century art history owe much to Maurice Denis. He could picture a seamless avant-garde, developing from impressionist landscape style to the decorative aesthetic of the Nabis. In the above quotations he managed a kind of balancing act: on the one hand he noted the reaction against naturalism that dominated the eighties; on the other, he saved impressionism from condemnation by suggesting that somehow the reaction against naturalism was based in positivist philosophy, thereby avoiding association with idealist "excesses." But something isn't quite right. Maybe that personal notion about Cézanne and landscape painting being the beginning of symbolism is the indication; or perhaps the idea that symbolism was based in positivist science is the problem. But one has the uncomfortable sense of square pegs placed in round holes here.

One explanation for the disjunction in Denis's statements about modernist art is the reactive and self-oriented quality of some of his writing. Often Denis's commentary was stimulated by what others had said. Sometimes Denis cited the catalyst, as when he wrote in response to published articles by other critics or when he made direct reference to a particular statement. Sometimes his allusions to fellow writers were more oblique, requiring knowledge of articles little known today. Such is the case with that attempt at making Cézanne the father of symbolism. The argument came from an article published in Maurice Pujo's aggressively idealist *L'Art et la vie*. It was the first and last time Denis published in this journal, and he was partially responding to a series of articles—and an exhibition sponsored by the periodical—entitled "Les Artistes de l'âme."[10] The "artists of the soul" under consideration included such idealists as Edmond Aman-Jean, Armand Point, Alexandre Séon, Alphonse Osbert, and Andhré des Gachons—all of whom exhibited at one time or another with Péladan's Rose + Croix. Denis took pains to distinguish the efforts of the Nabis avant-garde from this group as a way of establishing prior claim to symbolism in painting. He specifically stated that landscape and still life had inaugurated the symbolist

10. Among the articles in the "Les Artistes de l'âme" series: Henry Béranger, "Edmond Aman-Jean," *L'Art et la vie*, i (1893), 33–37; Gustave Soulier, "Armand Point," iii (1894), 171–77; Gustave Soulier, "Andhré des Gachons," iv (1894), 479–84; Gustave Soulier, "Alphonse Osbert," iv (1895), 502–5; Fernand Weyl, "L. Lévy-Dhurmer," v (1896), 120–30; Maurice Pujo, "Réponse à M. Octave Mirbeau," v (1896), 186–89.

movement and not the "peintres de l'âme." He saw the young idealists as partaking in an old variety of allegory and allowing literature, rather than painting, to dominate their work.[11] To separate himself from such painters Denis emphasized the contribution of Cézanne to symbolism and underplayed the similarities between idealist and symbolist reactions to naturalism, even suggesting that somehow symbolism was based in positivist philosophy. Of course it was only in Denis's personal brand of symbolist history that Cézanne was the dominant influence, not necessarily in the actual development of the movement. This is not to say that Denis was not being forthright. He meant what he said, but he meant it in reaction, as a way of differentiating himself from a tendency he mistrusted, not specifically upon reflection concerning the general history of the symbolist movement.[12]

This reactive, shoot-from-the-hip style, though not a constant in Denis's criticism, could and did force him to contradict himself and in this one begins to find demonstration of a less than "pure" modernism. In 1892 Denis listed Aman-Jean and "other ideaists who show at the Rose + Croix" among the artists demonstrating a new artistic evolution.[13] This time he was reacting against naturalist subject matter in painting, and those "painters of the soul" provided the proper foil. Also in 1892 Denis complained of the "rather mathematical" propensities of certain neo-impressionists (he specifically mentioned Signac) who used science to research color, thus producing a style of disconcerting dryness and coldness.[14] Denis seems to counter here his own avowal that symbolism was based partially on certain scientific discoveries of the positivist age; furthermore his criticism of Signac would later be reversed. By 1910 he could speak favorably of the "precise mind and vigorous will" that Signac had brought to neo-impressionism.[15] Denis might, on the one hand, laud the "free, supple impressionist technique" of Monet, Sisley, Renoir,

---

11. *Du Symbolisme au classicisme*, 75.

12. Elsewhere he offered a more balanced view of the beginnings of symbolism in painting. See, for instance, *Du symbolisme au classicisme*, 165, where he notes the importance of Redon in the development of one aspect of symbolist style.

13. Pierre L. Maud [pseudonym of Denis], "Notes d'art et d'esthétique," *La Revue blanche*, II (May 1892), 364–65. (". . . autres idéistes qui exposaient aux Rose-Croix.")

14. Pierre Louis [pseudonym for Denis], "Notes sur l'exposition des indépendants," *La Revue blanche*, II (April 1892), 233. (". . . plutôt mathématiques.")

15. *Théories*, 162. (". . . esprit précis et d'une volonté vigoureuse.")

or Pissarro, and, on the other, praise the symbolists for knowing "how to distinguish a painting from a study."[16]

One could, of course, argue that such "contradictions" are minor inconsistencies in a long career devoted to proselytizing for modernist art, but there is a good deal more evidence to suggest that Denis's devotion to modernism was limited. In the early nineties he was most certainly influenced by some of the very same idealists he so vehemently denounced in that 1896 article in *L'Art et la vie*. Like so many of his generation Denis was influenced as a young man by Joséphin Péladan's traditionalist idealism.[17] Certainly some of the fire behind Denis's "neo-traditionnisme" is a reminiscence of Péladan's proclaimed belief, republished in 1888, in "the Ideal, Tradition, Hierarchy." Denis was also influenced by the conservative Alphonse Germain, not only to the extent of borrowing some of the older critic's terminology—such as *ipséité*—but also in theory, particularly classical theory.[18]

While Denis disavowed some of his early idealist leanings later in life, he would never get all that idealism out of his system, as it were. Nor should we expect him to have done so. What makes Denis such a model product of the nineties is that mixture of the conservative/idealist and the avant-garde/symbolist permeating everything he did. The Sainte-Croix murals may reflect the influence of cloisonist patterning in such details as the face of the angel on the right of one of the lateral panels (Fig. 17e) but the very traditional composition of the whole mitigates this touch of modernism. Ten years earlier, the *Catholic Mystery* (Fig. 9)

16. The first quote is from an article about Pissarro, written in 1903, *Du symbolisme au classicisme*, 151. ("La libre, la souple technique impressionniste.") The second quote is from the 1895 "Préface de la IXe exposition des peintres impressionnistes et symbolistes," *Du symbolisme au classicisme*, 50. ("Ils savent distinguer un tableau d'une étude.")

17. In his 1903 article, "L'Influence de Paul Gauguin," *Du symbolisme au classicisme*, 51, Denis noted how the students at the Académie Julian spoke often about Péladan. In his *Journal*, 37, he noted an article by Péladan on Fra Angelico, and elsewhere he could sound quite like Péladan in speaking of painting as an essentially religious act, *Journal*, 63. Matthew Herban III, "Maurice Denis' 'Nouvel ordre classique,' As Contained in His 'Théories' (1890–1910)" (Ph.D. dissertation, University of Pennsylvania, 1972), 59ff, also discusses Denis's relationship to Péladan.

18. Denis used the term *ipséité* in the "Définition du néo-traditionnisme," *Du symbolisme au classicisme*, 35. Denis and Germain exchanged letters in *Art et critique* in 1890. See Germain, "Beaux-Arts, du tempérament peintre," and Pierre Louis [pseudonym of Denis], "A M. Alphonse Germain." Elsewhere, *Du symbolisme au classicisme*, 75, Denis noted Germain as one of the important young critics. As will be noted later in this chapter, Denis shared the Latinist sentiment of Germain as well.

demonstrated a similar combination. Undertaken after the formation of the Nabis group and clearly influenced by the Pont-Aven style of Gauguin, the painting is, just as clearly, far from Gauguin in subject matter. As noted in Chapter 2, Gauguin could derive much from observing the simple faith of Breton peasants but he could never be called a religious painter. Denis's orthodox Catholicism made him exactly that. Again, he offered a mitigated modernism. Ten years after the Sainte-Croix murals Denis produced an astounding article, "De Gauguin et de Van Gogh au classicisme," in which he saw Gauguin and Van Gogh showing the way to a revival of classicism.[19] In it, as will be noted in detail a bit further on, the modernist tradition is altered to fit Denis's own evolved artistic sensibilities.

Art historians are well aware that Maurice Denis's style became increasingly conservative throughout his life. By the 1940s his paintings seem hopelessly outdated, buried, as it goes, by the modernist lineage of Matisse, Picasso, and Miró. But one would be hard-pressed to determine the turning point, the point at which Denis seems to give up on the modernist tradition. Was it the ascendency of Matisse and the fauve painters that turned Denis away from the avant-garde? Even earlier, in 1898, while in Rome with André Gide, Denis spoke of the "error" of an "exaggerated reaction" against academic decadence and the wrong-headedness of an art—the reference was to impressionism—based on immediate sensory pleasure.[20] But even in the early nineties Denis sounded a conservative note. The twenty-fifth proposition of his "Défi-nition du néo-traditionnisme" proudly proclaimed: "In this epoch of decadents, who—I hope—are the primitives of a laborious preparation of something new, those of us who look backwards are still the most complete."[21] This is not the statement of a devout follower of Gauguin. Already the call of the past, of tradition, attracted the young avant-gardist.

Indeed, long before Denis knew of the work of Gauguin or the im-

---

19. The article, reprinted in both *Du symbolisme au classicisme* and *Théories*, was originally published in Adrien Mithouard's *L'Occident* in May 1909.

20. *Journal*, i, 133. The seems to conflict with a statement made three years earlier, *Du symbolisme au classicisme*, 48, in which Denis preferred an art that achieved its expression through formal means rather than subject and offered purely visual pleasure.

21. *Du symbolisme au classicisme*, 46. ("A cette époque de décadents, qui sont des primitifs—je l'espère—en cette laborieuse préparation de quelque chose, ceux de nous qui retardent sont encore les plus complets.")

pressionists, or anything of the avant-garde, he was devoted to the masters of the past. When he encountered the art of Gauguin in 1889 Denis had already formed a permanent attachment to tradition, most significantly to the art of Fra Angelico. Denis learned much from Gauguin, from Cézanne, from the entire impressionist, postimpressionist legacy. But he was selective in what he drew from modernism. For him it was one style of many to choose from. His devotion to the avant-garde was sincere and strong but not single-minded. While it is true that Denis remained adamantly opposed to the incursion of "literary" thought in painting, and while his picture of the development of the symbolist avant-garde art in the nineties has many affinities with modernist art history, one must also recognize that Denis saw the theories of the nineties as best expressed in the "renaissance of religious art."[22] This is not an orthodox modernist view. Ultimately it mattered not at all to Denis that modernist style had largely disavowed religious art. He felt no compunction whatsoever in using the style to support his staunch Catholicism. Factors other than strict adherence to avant-garde doctrine determined Denis's artistic vocabulary: his devotion to tradition, his religion, his conservative politics and life-style. Each of these deserves special notice because each demonstrates how profoundly Denis was enmeshed in the tendencies discussed in previous chapters.

TRADITION

In February 1891, Maurice Denis summarized the goals of symbolist art as follows:

> For some excellent reasons the symbolist painters have forbidden themselves documentary study and impressionist notation, which is precisely what interests art lovers today. It seems to me that they have everything to gain from this abstention: they avoid being facile, vulgar, and insignificant. They have no "morceaux" to sell. They search out, above all, the great aesthetic results and this with the distinctness and concision of architects.

22. See Denis's 1934 article, "L'Epoque du symbolisme," *Du symbolisme au classicisme*, 57–67.

It is the theory of the "plane surface covered with colors assembled in a certain order."[23]

He swept aside both naturalist subject matter and impressionist style in favor of "les grands résultats esthétiques," and in utilizing such a heavily laden term indicated his own desire to link the new art with the great achievements of the past, with "Tradition." Indeed, no critic or painter of the nineties rivaled Denis in his profound respect for tradition.

Perhaps one of the most telling aspects of Denis's relationship to the past is how well he knew it. Had he not been a painter Denis might well have made a career for himself as an art historian. His writings indicate familiarity with a wide range of historical material, from Vasari to Winckelmann, from Delécluze to Charles Blanc. Denis produced studies of art—one might note, as example, his excellent article on the students of Ingres—that were models in sensitivity to both the development of style and intellectual history.[24] As a critic Denis was aware of the past and greatly influenced by it, drawing on the styles and theories of such important French predecessors in the discipline as Diderot and Baudelaire and Zola.[25] Denis's very method of dealing with contemporary art demonstrated his concern for tradition. He explained the influence of Paul Gauguin. He discussed Gauguin and Van Gogh in terms of a developing classical school. He was, in other words, seeking to identify— indeed, to create—a new tradition. In whatever he did Denis consulted the past, borrowing where desirable, rejecting when necessary.

As we have seen, a traditionalist bias was not unusual for a young French artist/critic in the 1890s. While the seventies had been concerned with "la vie moderne" of the impressionists and in the eighties one might praise Seurat as a "Puvis modernisant," the nineties were less enthusiastic about the modern world, more inclined toward a revival of

23. Pierre Louis [pseudonym of Denis], "Pour les jeunes peintres," *Art et critique*, III (20 February 1891), 94. ("Pour d'excellentes raisons, les peintres symbolistes s'interdisent l'étude documentaire et la notation impressionniste, qui intéressent précisément les amateurs d'aujourd'hui. Il me semble qu'ils ont tout à gagner à cette abstention: ils évitent d'être faciles, vulgaires, insignifiants. Ils n'ont pas de 'morceaux' à vendre. Ils recherchent avant tout les grands résultats esthétiques, et cela avec une netteté et une concision d'architectes. C'est la théorie de la 'surface plane recouverte de couleurs en un certain ordre assemblées.'")

24. Denis's "Les élèves d'Ingres," *Théories*, 89–127, was originally published in *L'Occident* in 1902.

25. Herban, "Maurice Denis' 'Nouvel Ordre Classique,'" notes these and other sources for Denis's criticism.

the past.[26] Denis's love of tradition fit well with the mood of the decade. Just as Alphonse Germain had called for a return to the firm artistic foundations of traditional art, so too Denis would talk of the need for a return to discipline.[27] But Denis not only fit the revivalist spirit of his time, he helped to create it. Consider this from the twenty-fourth proposition of his "Définition du néo-traditionnisme":

> The grand art, that is called decorative, of the Hindus, the Assyrians, the Egyptians, the Greeks, the art of the Middle Ages and of the Renaissance, and the decidedly superior works of modern art, what are these? if not the transformation of vulgar sensations—of natural objects—into holy icons, hermetic and imposing?[28]

How close this is, in mood, pace, and style, to Albert Aurier's later proclamation about the symbolist painters:

> They are, properly speaking, the direct sons of the great mythological image makers of Assyria, of Egypt, of Greece of the royal epoch, the descendants of the Florentines of the XIVth century, of the Germans of the XIth, of the Gothics of the Middle Ages, a little as well the cousins of the Japanese.[29]

Denis's pronouncements on tradition were central to the development of symbolism in the 1890s and such was only proper. Even at the tender age of twenty, when the above statement was written, Denis had already been steeping himself in the art of the past for some five years.

The very first journal entry of the thirteen-year-old Maurice Denis was a list of proposed summer vacation activities, among them "promenades aux musées."[30] The serious young student was to make many such visits over the following years. On August 18 he happily noted receipt of his museum card, authorizing entry to Versailles, the Louvre, the Luxembourg, and the museum at Saint-Germain-en-Laye. At first the young

26. Fénéon's famous statement about Seurat being a "Puvis modernisant," from "Les Impressionnistes en 1886," is in *Oeuvres plus que complètes*, 37.

27. See, for instance, Denis's comments about Matisse, *Théories*, 232ff. and 196–98.

28. *Du symbolisme au classicisme*, 45. ("Le grand art, qu'on apelle décoratif, des Indous, des Assyriens, des Egyptiens, des Grecs, l'art du moyen âge et de la Renaissance, et les oeuvres décidément supérieures de l'art moderne, qu'est-ce? sinon le travestissement des sensations vulgaires—des objets naturels—en icônes sacrées, hermétiques, imposantes.")

29. Aurier, *Oeuvres posthumes*, 304. (See Chapter 4, n. 71, for the original French.)

30. *Journal*, 1, 9.

Denis merely delighted in seeing the art of the masters but he quickly developed strong opinions. He confessed to not liking Rubens and boldly preferred the academic Bouguereau to the then-popular naturalists, Roll and Beraud—an early bow to "correct" style that would have repercussions much later.[31] But such snap judgments are of little import except as indications of selectivity, a trait of Denis's traditionalism better shown in his early and continued interest in the art of Fra Angelico.

Through 1890 no artist had greater influence on Denis than Fra Angelico. After that time, even when under the spell of Gauguin and Cézanne, Denis remained faithful to the monk/painter. Again, this is not surprising for an aspiring young French artist in the late 1880s. We have already specified the importance of the Italian primitives to the developing symbolist and idealist styles. Denis himself noted an article about Fra Angelico—a "superb study"—by Joséphin Péladan in an 1885 journal entry.[32] But with a good deal more intensity than most, Denis studied "mon Angelico" carefully, reading all he could find, lovingly examining every detail of the master's work in the Louvre. In his youthful enthusiasm Denis prayed to "Beato Angelico" and spoke of the painter and Jeanne Dufour, his first childhood love, as the two models for his life.[33]

As he had fixated on Fra Angelico so would Denis later focus on other artists from the past, developing a personal artistic pantheon as guide for both art and theory. Over the years these personal choices would develop into an expansive aesthetic based on a revived and revised classicism. Toward this goal the art of the Italian primitives and the Greeks served as successive models, along with such classical masters as Ingres, Poussin, and Puvis de Chavannes. Denis's classical theory developed over a long period of time—indeed it began while he was studying classics at the Lycée Condorcet—changing in contact with various influences, from Albert Aurier to the novelist André Gide, to the poet/politician Adrien Mithouard. Denis's theory was too evolutionary in character to submit to facile explication, yet several key points—aside, of course, from the simple fact of its classical orientation—demonstrate just how traditional it was.[34]

The very formation of a theoretical support system was, to be sure,

31. Ibid., 18, 42.
32. Ibid., 37.
33. Ibid., 57, 59, 68.
34. The only extensive treatment of Denis's theory is Herban, "Maurice Denis' 'Nouvel Ordre Classique.'"

traditional in mood. Denis could, in fact, echo such academicians as Ingres himself when he assumed the role of pedagogue. On his first trip to Rome in 1898 Denis came under the spell of the classical school. He spoke of long conversations with André Gide and how the two of them would "become classicists together."[35] It was under these circumstances that he wrote to Vuillard about the "error" of an "exaggerated reaction against academic decadence."[36] In the article summing up his theories in light of his Roman experience, "Les Arts à Rome, ou la méthode classique" of 1898, Denis argued against the "stupid vanity that makes searching out apparent originality a condition sine qua non of the work of art."[37] He praised the solid methods of the classical school for saving generations of secondary talents by transmitting the lessons of the past. Even among poorer painters the school was able to preserve something of the soul of the great masters of classical style.

Denis's 1902 article on "Les Elèves d'Ingres," with its manifesto-like promulgation of sound academic method, would have pleased the old master himself. Denis began by suggesting that the arts were poised on the eve of a new classical period, "the necessary reaction against excess, whether the frivolities of impressionism, or against the vain theories that hold up any expression of individual emotion for a manifestation of beauty."[38] Such statements reverberate with the force of Ingres's own denunciations of the exaggerated individuality of a Delacroix. Against such "excess of individualism" Denis found the pupils of Ingres to be demonstration of "the advantages of strong academic discipline, which improves the strongest, and confers, in subordinating them, a usefulness to mediocre artists."[39] What Denis advocated here, in simple terms, was the academic principle that a sound traditional education is necessary for all those who would seek to produce art.

Later, in 1908, Denis would back up such support for academic method by signing on as teacher at the Académie Ranson in Venice. He

35. *Journal*, I, 134.

36. Ibid., 133–34. ("Il y a là une erreur, une mode, une réaction exagérée contre une décadence académique.")

37. *Du symbolisme au classicisme*, 99. (". . . cette vanité stupide qui fait rechercher l'originalité apparente comme une condition *sine qua non* de l'oeuvre d'art.")

38. *Théories*, 89. (". . . la réaction nécessaire contre les excès ou les frivolités de l'Impressionnisme, ou contre ces vaines théories qui tiennent toute expression d'une émotion individuelle pour une manifestation de Beauté.")

39. Ibid., 90. (". . . les avantages de la forte discipline classique qui améliore les forts, et confère, en les subordonnant, une utilité aux médiocres.")

continued to teach there occasionally through 1919, when he founded his own Ateliers d'art sacré. Denis himself was well aware of the irony of his involvement with the teaching of art, which was so opposed to the avant-garde notion of unteachable artistic genius.[40] However, his inclination toward the academic was no mere product of Denis's later "ultraconservative" phase.[41] We have already noted his youthful preference for the "correct" method of Bouguereau. This, coupled with early thoughts about the symbolists' ability to distinguish paintings from studies, or his praise of Puvis de Chavannes as conserving "misunderstood tradition," gives rise to a more complete view of Denis.[42] There was never a time, either as older painter or avid young student at the Académie Julian, when Denis wholly rejected the efficacy of academic teaching.[43]

Central to Maurice Denis's new classical theory was something equally important to older classical theory, the artist's relationship with nature. His first publication, that "Définition du néo-traditionnisme," was intimately concerned with the question of nature in painting. Threading his way past naturalism, Denis noted that nature was never the same, not only in and of itself but also in the way that artists revealed it. He moved, eventually, toward a more traditional view, stating—and again one hears the echo of Ingres—that "Art is the sanctification of nature."[44] Over the years Denis developed his conception of the artist's relationship to nature, a conception tempered equally by contact with Cézanne and with classical tradition. For Denis the goal of

40. See, for instance, *Du symbolisme au classicisme,* 117, where he admits that he had once been opposed to academies but had come to understand the import of sound instruction.

41. Chipp, *Theories of Modern Art,* 53–54, stated that Denis wrote perceptive symbolist theory but only "for a few years, until he turned ultraconservative like others of the Nabis and began to apply doctrinaire religious interpretations to the idealist principles of Symbolism." In truth Denis was always conservative and certainly always ready to apply religion to his art. His style certainly evolved but it is well to note that some of his most perceptive studies of symbolism were written long after his style had become highly conservative.

42. See *Journal,* i, 42; *Du symbolisme au classicisme,* 50; and, for the comment on Puvis de Chavannes, Pierre Louis [pseudonym of Denis], "A blanc et noir," *Art et critique,* ii (8 November 1890), 717.

43. Denis certainly reacted against "decadent" academic teaching, namely the idea that art should copy nature. See, for instance, *Du symbolisme au classicisme,* 49, where he spoke of academic propagation of the idea that art is the copy of something else. Yet even this statement, made in his preface to the Le Barc de Boutteville exhibition of symbolists in 1895, was followed by a paragraph in which Denis specified that the problem was that rules were badly taught and badly defended. Rules, and therefore academic teaching, were not the problem. Poor academic method was.

44. *Du symbolisme au classicisme,* 45. ("L'art est la sanctification de la nature.")

the artist would be to produce a parallel to nature, not a copy of it. In the early nineties, when opposed to the popular view of naturalism as concerned with slavish copies of nature, this goal could sound radical. Later in the decade the same antinaturalist sentiment, explicating the classical method, could sound much more traditional. In 1902 he could carefully quote Ingres's aphorisms about nature and the harmony of the ideal. In all, from avant-garde synthetist to conservative classicist, Denis expounded a similar, traditionalist view of the artist and nature, at once as staid as Ingres and as avant-garde as any of the antinaturalist generation.

Just so, Denis sought to grapple with issues central to earlier nineteenth-century art and theory, concepts such as the rational versus the sensual, the classic versus the romantic. Denis's "subjective and objective deformation" of nature, in spite of the clear reference to Gauguin and Aurier, still have about them much of the standard debate between classic and romantic temperaments.[45] In Denis's view Gauguin represented the "objective deformation" of nature, a cerebral, rational alteration of the natural world for decorative purposes. Van Gogh, on the other hand, subjectively deformed nature according to more emotional dictates. Denis finally saw the two types of deformation, or synthesis, as integrally linked in the art of Cézanne, who for him represented the sense of balance and equilibrium necessary for the highest art. What impresses most throughout such discussions is the "standard" quality—in the best sense of that term—of Denis's arguments. His classical theory was formed of the same elements as the earliest classical theory and, for all of his references to and support of modernist artists, it is tradition that dominated his thought.

In a very real way tradition was the young Maurice Denis's first badge of identification. The "Définition du néo-traditionnisme" proclaimed support of the art of the past in a world led astray by naturalism. Both early and late in his career, Denis used tradition in reaction to the "excesses" of the modern school, and in this he would slowly but surely divorce himself from modernism. Thus while both Denis and Albert Aurier came to attack impressionism, Aurier did so because he found the movement too wrapped up in the real world, not abstract or sufficiently emotional. Denis, in contrast, found the style too disorderly. If confirmation were needed of how Denis's concern for tradition could

45. Ibid., 113ff.

estrange him from agreement with some of the modernists he most respected, one could do no better than compare his fulsome praise for
Ingres with Odilon Redon's forthright denunciation of everything for
which the master stood.[46]

In seeking to cure the excesses of overindulgent youth—both his own
and that of others—Denis, as neo-traditionalist, could construct his
own Gauguin, much as had Albert Aurier. While Aurier and Denis
shared a general symbolist view of Gauguin's work, Denis formulated a
rather opposite portrait of the artist. Aurier's Gauguin was decidedly
mystical, a passionate, exotic, indeed, romantic character. When, in his
1891 article on Gauguin, Aurier finally got down to talking about the
painter he used such charged terms as "esotericism," "enigma," "savage,"
and "troubling."[47] Denis, in discussing the influence of Gauguin in 1903,
specifically noted that the young artists of the nineties scarcely felt
Gauguin's exoticism.[48] For Denis (although he pretended to speak for
the generation of the nineties, using collective pronouns, one doubts
that all of the Nabis would have agreed with his reading) Gauguin was
primarily an example of "expression by decor."[49] Seeing only classical,
"objective deformation" in Gauguin he tried to make of him a sort of
Poussin without classical culture. Denis's Gauguin became the transmitter
of the ideas of Cézanne, continuing Cézanne's reconstruction of art not in
esoteric mystification but with more theoretical rigor.[50] While one allows
the critic latitude in interpretation, one must realize that Denis was finally
talking as much about his own traditionalism as he was about Gauguin.

Tradition was, then, a major focus for Maurice Denis. It served to
differentiate him from the naturalist world around him and to mitigate
the influence of modernist art on him. In the form of a lifelong concern
for sound method, tradition would lead him to reject one of modernism's
most fruitful directions, the art of Henri Matisse. Denis would berate the
young fauve painters, Braque, Van Dongen, and Derain, for having "evidently little concern for nature and a horror of Greco-Latin beauty."[51]

46. See Odilon Redon, A soi-même (Paris: Librairie José Corti, 1961), 146–47.

47. Aurier, Oeuvres posthumes, 218–19.

48. Théories, 170. The transcription of the article on Gauguin in Du symbolisme au classicisme
ends just before this statement.

49. Ibid.

50. Du symbolisme au classicisme, 121.

51. Théories, 233. (". . . évidemment peu de souci de la nature, et horreur de la beauté
gréco-latine.")

He complained that the "school" of Matisse ignored "material practice," and believed that "inspiration or sensitivity completely make up for ineptitude of the hand."[52] Maurice Denis, card-carrying member of the avant-garde of 1890, was too much the traditionalist to countenance the "audacities" of the avant-garde of 1905.

RELIGION

It would be difficult to overestimate the importance of religion in Maurice Denis's life and work. Any visitor to the Musée du Prieuré at Saint-Germain-en-Laye will understand this immediately. Home, studio, place of worship, the Prieuré was a virtual monastery for this man who held up the monk/painter Fra Angelico as model. Fragments of religious decorative projects line the walls of the atelier. A few yards from the door of his studio stands the entrance to the private chapel, dedicated in 1922, where Denis could attend mass daily. The combination of art and religion that the Prieuré represents formed the very core of Denis's career desires. As early as 1885, the fourteen-year-old Denis had written in his journal of wanting to raise up in "profane Paris" a chapel decorated by the new artistic-religious organization of which he dreamed.[53] By May 1885 Denis had already spoken of his chosen vocation as "Christian artist," worrying that there seemed to be no place at the Salon for someone who wished to celebrate the miracles of Christianity.[54] He never wavered from this childhood commitment. Indeed, paintings such as *Catholic Mystery* are, in their devout, humble piety, the rule rather than the exception in Denis's work.

Throughout the earliest journal entries Denis demonstrated how intimately entwined religion and art were for him. He could describe a procession of the Blessed Sacrament in loving detail, noting the gripping effect of the ritual, the smoke rising from extinguished candles held by marching women, "dark shadows stirring in the blue vapor."[55] Elsewhere he might describe the chanting of the Credo at mass as "a sublime and

52. Ibid., 232. (". . . elle croit que l'inspiration ou la sensibilité suppléent à toutes les maladresses de la main.")

53. *Journal*, i, 40.

54. Ibid., 59, or 52, for another indication of the artist's vocation.

55. Ibid., 35. (". . . ce sont des ombres noires qui s'agitent dans de la vapeur bleue.")

beautiful poetry which makes one tremble."[56] Or his journal entries might take the form of a prayer, such as the following from 27 December 1885: "That I might only have the time, Jesus! I would make an image of your adorable Heart, and I would put all of my love and all of my art into it. But no . . . school keeps me far from Painting, just when I need it most intensely."[57] The sentiment, indeed the very capitalization, of such statements indicates well enough the confluence of art and religion in Denis's mind. Religious needs played a dominant role in his art theory as well.

One of the key motivations for Denis's rejection of naturalism was his faith. "The Church," he wrote, "the holy souls, must finally understand that realism, naturalism, even the most pure, are not capable of satisfying them." What the church needed was a painter/monk, "called by God" to lead a revolt against the naturalist "impiety and impurity that degrade art."[58] A similar sentiment led Denis, in his 1896 "Notes sur la peinture religieuse," to uphold the Byzantine tradition of Christian art against the naturalist exercises of the Renaissance—and at this point before his trip to Rome and conversion to classical theory, against the Greco-Roman tradition as well.[59] Just so Denis praised the hieratic manner of Egyptian art which, he reasoned, refined itself by developing away from the naturalism of the old kingdom through a system of formulas imposed by religion.[60] Certainly part of Denis's love for Fra Angelico and the Italian primitives was their freedom from absolute visual realism, which he felt better allowed them to evoke religious sentiments.

Astoundingly—for someone who once suggested that landscape painting had initiated the symbolist movement in painting—Denis's religious antinaturalism also led him to bemoan the way impressionism and neo-impressionism had concentrated on light. In "Le Soleil" of 1906 he wrote of the passion in modernist art for capturing effects of sunlight.

56. Ibid., 45. ("C'est une poésie sublime et belle qui fait trembler.")

57. Ibid., 63. ("Que n'ai-je le temps, Jésus! Je vous ferais une image de votre Coeur adorable, et j'y mettrais tout mon amour, tout mon art. Mais non, le lycée me tient loin de la Peinture, alors que j'en ai le plus vivement besoin.")

58. Ibid., 64. ("L'Eglise, les âmes saintes doivent fatalement comprendre que le réalisme, le naturalisme, même les plus purs, ne sont pas capables de les satisfaire." / "Il faut un homme appelé par Dieu, un moine, un ascète, un mystique, un saint qui lève aux yeux du siècle l'étendard de la révolte contre l'impiété et l'impureté qui avilisent l'art, suivies de la médiocrité et de la décadence.")

59. *Théories*, 36ff.

60. Ibid., 174.

Tracing impressionism through Monet, and then neo-impressionism through the theories of Charles Henry, Denis finally settled on what he saw as the great wrong in both movements: "The error of each, the error of us all, has been to seek out light above everything. One must first search out the kingdom of God and his justice, that is to say the expression of our souls in beauty, and the rest will be given to us in the bargain."[61] Denis went on from this statement to offer a more conventional (or at least more modernist) conception of the development away from naturalism but not without leaving the distinct impression that religion colored every aspect of his thinking.

Much of what Denis understood as tradition was, at first, conditioned by his Catholicism. Above all, his interest in Fra Angelico stemmed as much from religious sentiment as from artistic inclination. In 1885 he noted in his journal a project for writing a life of the "holy artist," vowing that he would "ask Our Holy Father the Pope for official beatification of the Dominican."[62] In a solemn, worshipful description of Angelico's *Coronation of the Virgin* in the Louvre, Denis focused on the diffuse light, which he called "holy," and the religious ideal of this "painted prayer."[63] Some fourteen years later, in the *Exaltation of the Holy Cross*, he would recall that "holy" light to a similarly pious effect. Much like Joséphin Péladan, Denis spoke of a return to the style of Angelico as a way of reviving religious art: "Painting is an essentially religious and Christian art. If this character has been lost in our impious century, it must be rediscovered. And the means is to restore to honor the aesthetic of Fra Angelico, who alone is truly Catholic; who alone responds to the aspirations of the pious, mystic souls who love God."[64]

Denis's profound Catholicism also influenced his commitment to

61. *Du symbolisme au classicisme*, 176. ("L'erreur des uns et des autres, notre erreur à tous, ç'a été de chercher avant tout la lumière. Il fallait chercher d'abord le royaume de Dieu et sa justice, c'est-à-dire l'expression de notre âme en beauté, et le reste nous eût été donné par surcroît.")

62. *Journal*, 1, 40. ("Et plus tard j'irai demander à Notre Saint-Père le Pape la béatification solennelle du dominicain.")

63. Ibid., 42. ("C'est vraiment une prière peinte.") Denis's description of Fra Angelico's painting, with its emphasis on shadowless, sanctified light, might well be applied to Denis's own *Exaltation of the Holy Cross*.

64. Ibid., 63. ("La peinture est un art essentiellement religieux et chrétien. Si le caractère s'est perdu dans notre siècle impie, il faut le retrouver. Et le moyen, c'est de remettre en honneur l'esthétique de Fra Angelico, qui seule est vraiment catholique; qui seule répond aux aspirations des âmes pieuses, mystiques, aimant Dieu.")

modernism. The very nature of the Nabis movement—to the extent that it stressed group activity and decorative emphasis—might be seen as fulfillment of the dream of an artistic-religious community of decorators the fourteen-year-old Denis had confided to his journal in 1885. The statement quoted above concerning the impressionists' error in concentrating on light certainly demonstrates a willingness to discard modernist style in favor of a religious ideal. Eulogizing Renoir in 1919, Denis took the occasion to add a religious gloss to the painter's nudes. Praising Renoir's respect for religious tradition he spoke of the artist's women as transformed by painting into something chaste, "exempt from perversity."[65] The article, mixing classical theories concerning the ideal in sensual beauty and religious concepts of propriety, is an excellent example of Denis's personal reading of impressionist style, and Catholicism was key to that reading.

Denis would also come to interpret the symbolist style of the 1890s as finding fulfillment in religious art. Even the "Définition du néo-traditionnisme" of 1890 suggested an underlying religious motive for symbolism. Calling art a "sanctification of nature," Denis spoke of the "moral order" that came from the arrangement of shapes and colors in Gauguin's art.[66] Read thus, Gauguin's synthesis could serve the purposes of religion as much as art. Certainly *Catholic Mystery* put synthetist style at the service of Catholic doctrine. By the 1930s Denis saw synthetist theory as preparation for the revival of religious art that he had undertaken. His "L'Epoque du symbolisme," written for the *Gazette des beaux-arts* in 1934, was meant to outline briefly the important events, artists, and accomplishments of the nineties. In it Denis remained faithful to the modernist interpretation of artistic style in which "literary abuses" were to be avoided. He even suggested that the platonic theories of Albert Aurier were not suitable to the best painters of the period because the artists were too concerned with painting itself to be caught up in philosophical speculation. Yet this art-for-art's-sake sentiment did not prevent Denis from finally seeing the mood of the nineties as having led to the renaissance of religious art in which "the theories of 1890 have found their greatest collective flowering."[67] In his *Histoire de l'art religieux*

---

65. *Du symbolisme au classicisme*, 127. (". . . exempte de perversité.")

66. Ibid., 45, 43.

67. Ibid., 66. ("Qu'il suffise de rappeler que c'est dans ce qu'on a appelé la renaissance de l'art religieux que les théories de 1890 ont trouvé leur épanouissement le plus collectif.")

of 1939 Denis again would press the modernist tradition to serve the goals of a Catholic artistic revival.[68] In Chapters 1 and 2 we noted some of the features of French Catholicism in the latter half of the nineteenth century. Maurice Denis's position with regard to the mood of the religious revival needs to be considered now. What kind of Catholic was Maurice Denis?

One is most inclined to answer that Denis was conservative and ultramontane, along with Léon Bloy, a "Catholic of the Syllabus."[69] Yet, as with almost any observation about Denis, contradictory evidence can be found. Like many of his generation Denis read and appreciated the writings of Ernest Renan and, indeed, quoted the historian often. This was not the act of a dyed-in-the-wool conservative Catholic; as noted in Chapter 1, Renan was one of the most hated figures among the ultramontane writers of the period. Denis certainly knew the Catholic criticism of Renan, and often tempered his mention of the writer by disclaiming some of his ideas. But whether he recognized in Renan the "devil" seen by men like Barbey d'Aurevilly and Léon Bloy, he retained positive opinions of the historian.[70] Similarly, Denis could praise the liberal Catholicism of Lamennais, Lacordaire, and Montalembert, writers out of favor among the most radical members of the conservative ultramontane faction of the later nineteenth century.[71]

But if Denis appreciated liberal Catholic writers he could also be impressed by their opposites. Early on he had been given a copy of Veuillot's *Çà et là*. He was impressed by the lively style of this fierce ultramontane polemicist, although he disagreed heartily with many of the writer's opinions about literature. Not surprisingly for a dedicated young painter, he was most taken with a statement by Veuillot concerning the vocation of the Christian artist, "working for the glory of that which one loves."[72] Finally, however, none of Denis's published remarks about

68. Denis, *Histoire de l'art religieux* (Paris: Flammarion, 1939), 283ff.

69. Sellière, *Léon Bloy, psychologie d'un mystique*, 127.

70. See, for instance, Denis, *Journal*, i, 44, where he noted some reservations about Renan's opinions on other matters but specifically appreciated the historian's attachment to Brittany.

71. *Théories*, 91, and *Journal*, i, 161.

72. *Journal*, i, 52. (". . . travailler pour la gloire de celui qu'on aime.") Although Denis's tastes would run to less controversial writers later in life he still seems to have continued reading Veuillot and discussing the ultramontane writer with friends such as Gide. See *Journal*, i, 142.

the religious writers he appreciated provides for any definitive conclusions concerning his Catholicism. But the general tenor of his voluminous commentary on religion itself is more revealing. In his journals and in his formal articles Denis often demonstrated a conservative turn that would have appealed to Pius IX himself.

A worshipful and contrite humility marked much of the fervent new Catholicism of the later nineteenth century in France. The authoritarian papacy of Pius IX had called for humble obedience on the part of the faithful, and there was much in Maurice Denis that fit the desired model. The lowered heads and silent demeanor of his human figures— saints and laypersons as well—combined with the purity of both color and light in their rendering yields a mood of submissive reverence to much of his work (Figs. 9, 16, and 17c–f). Indeed, few artists were better suited temperamentally than Denis to illustrate Paul Verlaine's devout *Sagesse,* those pious professions of faith from the old decadent poet.

Something of the fanaticism of writers like Léon Bloy could, at times, rear up in Denis's writings. He might, like Bloy, rail against "indifferent" Catholics.[73] With similar intolerance he would note in his journal that Catholicism was the only viable religion and that no other could possibly appear to replace it.[74] A few years later he could reduce the Islamic faith to "Christianity as understood by the Arabs."[75] When he called painting "an essentially religious and Christian art," he clearly echoed the ideas of Joséphin Péladan, a writer easily Bloy's equal in fanatical religiosity.[76] Péladan's influence on the youthful Denis has already been noted, but even after his encounter with Gauguin and the formation of the Nabis group Denis could sound like Péladan. In "Notes sur la peinture religieuse" of 1896, for example, he stated that "the Christian spirit is perpetuated in all very beautiful works," and proclaimed symbolism itself "a Christian theory."[77]

Evidently Denis's devout personality led his parents to worry about his mental health. On 8 January 1886, he noted in his journal that his

---

73. Ibid., 41.

74. Ibid., 115.

75. Ibid., 148. (". . . le christianisme compris par des Arabes.")

76. Ibid., 63. ("La peinture est un art essentiellement religieux et chrétien.")

77. *Théories,* 41–42. ("Mais comme l'esprit chrétien s'est perpétué dans toutes les oeuvres très belles!" / "Or le symbolisme est une théorie chrétienne.")

mother and father thought "an exaggerated religiosity would consume my brain and render me mad."[78] While it was most assuredly a youthful phase that Denis's parents noted, some of the fervor of the artist's childhood carried over past adolescence. The "Notes sur la peinture religieuse" began with a purposefully reactionary and excessive profession of faith:

> If God had given for me to be born some centuries earlier, in Florence at the time of Brother Savonarola, certainly I would have been among those who defended the aesthetic of the Middle Ages with a puerile and violent ardor, against the invasion of classical paganism. I would have been one of those pious reactionaries, faithful to the hieraticism of the past, for whom the new ideas announced immediate decadence. Humble student of Angelico descending on holidays from San Marco to the Signoria, among the penitent painters, among the believing masses, I would have decried the Renaissance.[79]

Much of Denis's religious personality is revealed in such a statement. As his later theory would reveal, Denis was not willing to reject either the Renaissance or classical paganism totally. But he most assuredly would allow his Catholic faith to temper his interest in both.

Denis was, quite clearly, aware of the more fanatical side of the new Catholicism and not averse to professing a faith sympathetic to some of its more excessive aspects. He was not, however, a Léon Bloy. But neither was he a freethinker, which forces an issue. Statements like the one above could not be made from a neutral position in the charged political atmosphere of late nineteenth-century France. The "progressive," "liberal" cachet of the naturalist avant-garde, the multitude of conversions

---

78. *Journal*, 1, 64. ("Mes chers parents craignent qu'une religiosité exagérée n'use mon cerveau et me rende fou.")

79. *Du symbolisme au classicisme*, 69. ("Si Dieu m'avait donné de naître quelques siècles plus tôt, à Florence au temps de frère Savonarole, certainement j'aurais été de ceux qui défendaient, avec une ardeur puérile et violente, contre l'envahissement du paganisme classique, l'esthétique du moyen âge. J'aurais été de ces pieux retardataires, fidèles au hiératisme du passé, pour qui les idées nouvelles annonçaient la prompte décadence. Petit élève de l'Angelico en descendant les jours de fête de San Marco à la Signoria, parmi les peintres repentis, parmi la foule croyante, j'aurais conspué la Renaissance.") Charles Chassé, *Le Mouvement symboliste dans l'art du XIXe siècle* (Paris: Librairie Floury, 1947), 160, quoted this same passage and, throughout his chapter on Denis, noted the importance of religion in the painter's life.

among the young symbolist avant-garde, the church's position in relation to the republican government, the government's own hostility to the church, and most poignantly, the Dreyfus affair, all conspired to make neutrality impossible where such devout Catholicism was concerned.

CONSERVATISM

In 1904 Anatole France posted a scathing account of the debris of the Dreyfus affair in a long and bitter preface to Emile Combes's *Une campagne laïque*.[80] Combes, the socialist who then headed the Third Republic, had written his history of the government's recent anticlerical campaign in an effort to explain—and to garner popular support for—his policies with regard to the role of the Catholic church in the French educational system. France, who was then a highly respected man of letters and member of the Académie française, used his preface to detail the position of the church in the politics of the "affair." He did not paint a pretty picture. In much the tone of Zola's famous "J'accuse" of 1898, France singled out the fomenters of anti-Dreyfus agitation. Politically he condemned the ultraconservative, nationalist organizations— the *Ligue de la patrie française* and the *Ligue des patriotes* were among the most active—for stirring up ancient racial hatreds. He spoke of a clerical "armée noire," allied with the nationalists against not only Dreyfus but the republican government as well. He cited several religious orders—Jesuits, Dominicans, and especially the Assumptionists with their radical rightist journal, *La Croix*—for inciting antirepublican, anti-Semitic and, ultimately, seditious sentiment among the people. France complained bitterly of churchmen who thought that God had sent them the Dreyfus affair in order to lead the nation back to the Catholic faith. He also briefly referred to the history of church-state relations after the French Revolution.

The Catholic church and the French government were often at odds during the nineteenth century. The church lost too much property under the Revolution and suffered too many "martyrdoms" at the hands of

---

80. Emile Combes, *Une campagne laïque* (Paris: H. Simonis Empis, 1904), v–xxxvi. An excellent recent source on the politics of this period is Malcolm O. Partin, *Waldeck-Rousseau, Combes and the Church: The Politics of Anticlericalism, 1899–1905* (Durham: Duke University Press, 1969).

the Jacobins to trust fully any government calling itself "republican." The government, on the other hand, recalled the monarchist connections of the church, the vast wealth of many religious orders, and the "defiant" papal allegiances of ultramontane Catholics. As early as 1794, the French government had enacted laws meant to regulate religious orders, especially with regard to their expansive control of education. Legislation designed to wrest educational power from the church would appear often throughout the century. Anatole France spoke to the primary reason for such legislation when he condemned the Jesuits for specializing in educating the sons of the bourgeoisie, jealously monitoring the young men throughout their early careers, and continuing to exercise influence over them when they became powerful in commerce, the military, and politics.[81] Control of education was the focal point not only for Anatole France's attack against the church but for the Third Republic as well. The "campagne laïque" referred to in Emile Combes's title was the republican government's six-year struggle—from 1899 to 1905—to disenfranchise all of the religious teaching orders in France.

While several laws regulating the existence of educational orders were already on the books in France, enforcement had been haphazard throughout most of the nineteenth century. By the end of the century as many as half the congregations of the various teaching orders existed without government approval.[82] As long as relations between the church and the Third Republic remained on a relatively smooth course no action was taken against the unauthorized congregations. But there was nothing smooth about church-state interaction in the wake of the Dreyfus case. Anatole France was largely correct in his assessment of Catholic anti-Dreyfus fulminating. Many of the congregations were openly politicized and audaciously attacked the government. Vocal young Catholics and vociferous young nationalists—the fanatical Edouard Drumont and Charles Maurras were prime movers—allied in a reactionary "patriotic" front against the republic. The government, in the hands of the successive socialist cabinets of Pierre Waldeck-Rousseau and Emile Combes, fought back. Beginning in 1899 the coalition of "radical" socialists in control of the republic launched an all-out campaign to control the teaching activities of the congregations. Salaries of

81. Combes, *Une campagne laïque*, xiv–xv.
82. Partin, *Waldeck-Rousseau*, 24–25.

priests who had become too political were suspended.[83] At first regulation was the main goal, but hostile anticlerics such as Georges Clemenceau soon called for revocation of all religious teaching rights and, eventually, destruction of the orders themselves. The wave of anticlericalism that swept the country during these years would not subside until 1905 with abrogation of the formal relationship between church and state in France.

Finally—to return to the subject—it is only within the charged political climate of these years that one can accurately gauge Maurice Denis's conservatism. While Denis was never an activist, he was political. If his Catholicism alone had not politicized him it certainly would have done so in the divisive atmosphere of the Dreyfus case. Neutrality was not a favored position with regard to Dreyfus, and it was certainly not in vogue among the fervent young Catholics of the 1890s. The times forced a political stance. Religion, and personal predilection, dictated conservatism for Denis.

Maurice Denis was, to the extent that personality might determine political preference, a born conservative. Forget, for a moment, the "revolutionary" Nabis painter, and consider instead the young man from a modest but comfortable bourgeois family, living the greatest part of his life in his comfortable hometown of Saint-Germain-en-Laye. No spirit of revolution against the artistic establishment would lead him from his quiet, respectable home. As a youth he confided to his journal a wish to retire from the world—after winning the Prix de Rome to be sure, but retirement nonetheless. At this particular stage Brittany was the focus of the dream:

> I would live there, friend of the curé and the mayor, and of everyone, in a village of fishermen. I would have my little house and my little garden and my little studio and my little chapel and my little rabbits. I would live, poor, humble, peaceful, and content under the eyes of God, far from noisy and rich Tout-Paris, which besets me.
>
> I would interest myself in all the good work of my village; I would search only to be loved.

83. The French government had paid the salaries of bishops and pastors since the Concordat of 1801 between Napoleon and the Catholic church.

> Then, for a few sous, I would paint the poor churches of the region and, not to be forgotten completely, each Salon would see me bring my canvas, a design bursting with the perfumed air of Brittany, of the land of prayer.
>
> Is this not a thing to be envied, to live thus, without ambition, without money, without care?[84]

While Denis was never so reclusive as this simple dream suggests, the Prieuré and Saint-Germain-en-Laye would serve as refuge for him throughout his life. Home and family were always central themes in his painting. Thus, his *Sunlight on the Terrace* of 1890 and the *Exaltation of the Holy Cross,* so different in conception and style, share location. The terrace of the earlier painting is the famous wooded park adjacent to the royal chateau at Saint-Germain-en-Laye, where Denis often made evening promenades with his family. The Sainte-Croix murals (Fig. 17b) present another view of the terrace—this time from the main route between Le Vésinet and Saint-Germain-en-Laye—rising up like a new Fiesole in the background of this modern-day Angelico's celebration of faith.

Home, family, religion, and tradition were all inextricably linked in Denis's art. His *Dessert in the Garden* (Fig. 21) of 1897 shows the painter and his wife Marthe in the garden of their home next to the Prieuré. Everything in the painting, from the gentle fullness of line to the warm, sanctified glow of the setting sunlight, or the emulation of traditional portraiture as sign of fidelity, speaks of conservation in the best sense. It is a painting of values to be preserved and cherished, by an artist unabashedly willing to promote such sensibilities at a time when many of the avant-garde considered themselves to be anarchists.

Denis often populated his religious paintings with family members.

---

84. *Journal,* I, 44–45. ("J'aurais vécu là, ami du curé et du maire, et de tout le monde, dans un bourg de pêcheurs; j'aurais eu ma petite maison et mon petit jardin et mon petit atelier et ma petite chapelle et mes petits lapins. J'aurais vécu pauvre, humble, paisible et content sous le regard de Dieu, loin de ce bruyant et riche Tout-Paris qui m'obsède.

Je me serais intéressé à toutes les bonnes oeuvres de mon village, j'aurais cherché à être aimé.

Puis, pour quelques sous j'aurais peint les églises pauvres d'alentour, et pour ne pas être oublié tout à fait, chaque Salon m'aurait vu apporter ma toile, conception éclose à l'air parfumé de la Bretagne, de la terre où l'on prie.

Est-ce que cela ne vous fait pas envie, de vivre ainsi sans ambition, sans argent, sans soucis?")

The Virgin Mary could bear a striking resemblance to Marthe, the Denis children could become the Christ child or the infant John the Baptist. Nor was this merely a matter of convenience, of models readily at hand. Religion and art were intensely personal matters to Denis. Much like a medieval Christian, Denis saw religion in every aspect of life. His family became the Holy Family, his world a place of religious symbols as rich as any fifteenth-century Netherlandish painting might depict. A sense of containment, of religion contained within the family environment, of values necessitating protection, of a life to be preserved, permeated Denis's work and personality.

Above all, however, the political situation remains the key to understanding Denis's conservatism. The sense of order and rationality that dominated his painting and life would lead him to become a royalist.[85] The opposition of nationalists and Catholics to the Third Republic exercised a good deal of influence on Denis. Religion would certainly have led him to oppose the policies of both Waldeck-Rousseau and Emile Combes. The government of Combes, in particular, was extremely prejudiced against both the church and its teaching orders. No Catholic, either liberal or reactionary, could have supported the anticlerical campaigns of 1899–1905. In November 1902 Denis confided to his journal concern over the "lois Combes," a reference to Combes's enforcement of the laws regulating the existence and right to teach of all religious orders.[86] At stake was the immediate closing of 125 religious educational establishments and the proposed shutdown of some 3,000 more. In apparent reaction to this attack on religious education Denis conceived a painting to be entitled *Our Lady of the Schools*—the Virgin Mary as protectress of the private Catholic schools under fire from the government. According to his journal entry a rough sketch for the painting had been completed on 26 November 1902.

Our Lady of the Schools (Fig. 22), shown in the Salon of the Société Nationale in 1903, bears all the earmarks of Denis's increasingly traditionalist style at the turn of the century. The tight linear control and the "perfect," rounded features of all the figures suggest the influence of Ingres. The generally humble attitude of the children, as well as the Madonna, certainly evoke Denis's favored "Beato" Angelico. The crowded, airless, grouping of kneeling children on the right derives from

85. Ibid., 222, where Denis noted, "Je deviens royaliste."
86. Ibid., 182.

any number of primitive sources, perhaps Flemish painting in this instance. Aside from the stark differences between this and such Nabis works as *Sunlight on the Terrace*, there is nothing startling about *Our Lady of the Schools*. It is a quiet painting, but its appearance in 1903 made a statement in direct opposition to the anticlerical policies of the republic. It is not a radically reactionary manifesto, but Denis's affiliations are clear enough. The conjunction of the Virgin's head with the map of France in the background, typical prop in any French school, allegorizes the artist's message to his country. Just so, Denis accentuated a favorite nationalist cause in the northeast sector of the map, the provinces of Alsace and Lorraine, lost to the Germans in 1870.

Denis's associations during these years also suggest a conservative political viewpoint. He had become close friends with Denys Cochin, rightist member of the Chamber of Deputies and one of the staunchest opponents of Waldeck-Rousseau and Combes. Cochin had led the Catholic opposition to the anticlerical campaign with impassioned addresses before the chamber and had published many of the speeches in a book clearly meant to counter Emile Combes's *Une campagne laïque*.[87] Denis also rallied to support two publications that voiced opposition to the government's "priest eating," as it was termed in some circles. He became a regular correspondent of Adrien Mithouard's *L'Occident*, a publication that was not overtly political, yet did not hide its disapproval of Emile Combes's policies. Denis was also close to a much more politically oriented publication, the *Echo de Seine-et-Oise*, which combined a concentration on the local news of such suburban enclaves as Le Vésinet and Saint-Germain-en-Laye with antigovernment rhetoric. Like any Catholic of the time, Denis opposed governmental attacks on his religion. His reaction, though conservative, is not surprising considering the battering religious orders were taking. One is surprised, however, at the extent to which Denis seems to have mixed Catholic loyalty with reactionary nationalist sentiment.

The development of nationalist sentiment was, of course, a factor not only in France but in much of Europe as well. Love of nation, rather than specific locality, had developed throughout the nineteenth cen-

---

87. Denys Cochin, *Ententes et ruptures* (Paris: Calmann-Levy, 1906). Both books are composed of transcriptions of speeches made by their authors, mainly before the legislature. The intention of each was to present the author's side of the argument under the guise of documentary reporting of legislative discourse.

tury, often accompanied by pride in racial characteristics and national/ racial cultural accomplishments. Often, as the twentieth century has shown only too well, excessive nationalism could lead to bitter racial hatreds—especially, but not exclusively, anti-Semitism—and war. The nationalist sentiment alive in France from the late 1880s often tended toward reactionary political stances. No single opposition group was more aggressive in condemnation of the Third Republic than the nationalists. Militarism was reflected in a strong desire for revenge against Germany for the humiliation of the Franco-Prussian War. The favored nationalist theme of "Latinity," espoused by Charles Maurras and many Catholics as well, also suggested an orientation away from northern Europe, while at the same time serving the needs of anti-Semitism. Reactionaries, such as the fanatical Catholic polemicist Edouard Drumont, railed against the Jews economically, socially, and culturally. The Dreyfus affair greatly stimulated the nationalist cause.[88] Anti-Semitic hatred of the Jewish officer, who had "betrayed" the nation, was an early concentration. When it became clear to all but the most rabid nationalists that Dreyfus was innocent, a reactionary support of military dignity prevented conservatives from admitting to the army conspiracy that had convicted the man in the first place. Guilt or innocence quickly became a minor issue. To the nationalist right the Dreyfus case was an affront to national pride and the military, and therefore a security risk. To the left the case was a matter of social justice (and, on a more cynical level, a platform for launching political careers).

Denis began his 1904 article, "De la gaucherie des primitifs," with a series of ironical comments about the new nationalist sentiment leading to double attributions of the work of primitives—so that a particular painter listed among the "Flemish school" in Bruges might be categorized as "French" in Paris.[89] It was one of the few times he published any comment capable of being called antinationalist. Denis read and respectfully quoted some of the chief nationalist politicians—men such as Charles Maurras and Maurice Barrès—and his writing during the key years of the Dreyfus affair reflects distinct sympathy with the nationalist cause.

88. On the Dreyfus affair see Chapter 5, note 103, and for an important recent source on the effect of the case on art see the catalogue of the Jewish Museum's exhibition, *The Dreyfus Affair: Art, Truth and Justice*, ed. by Norman Kleeblatt (Berkeley and Los Angeles: University of California Press, 1987).

89. *Théories*, 172.

He was, for instance, anti-Dreyfusard. Writing to Vuillard from Rome in February 1898, just a month after Zola's "J'accuse," Denis spoke of being "heartbroken" over Zola's action and "angry" that the *Revue blanche* had decided to intervene in the affair.[90] Indeed, the *Revue blanche*, so supportive of the Nabis painters, was to become one of the staunchest Dreyfusard sympathizers. As he turned more deeply conservative, Denis began to take attacks on his ideas as being stimulated by pro-Dreyfus factions—meaning, by this, liberal factions. Thus, in 1905, he could complain of the "vengeful Dreyfusist thunderbolts of the Institute" being hurled at him for "conspiring" against modern art.[91] Writing about Cézanne, in 1907, Denis equated Dreyfusism with young modern artists' too-liberal acceptance of the "negligences and imperfections" in Cézanne's work.[92] Such a direct connection between liberal artistic practices and liberal political positions suggests the depth of Denis's anti-Dreyfus sentiment. It also suggests the nature of those sentiments. Like so many others Denis was not necessarily concerned with the guilt or innocence of Dreyfus himself but rather with the wider implications of the case. Thus, in Rome, he worried about the effect foreign journalists discussing the case might have on French national pride, or, back in Paris, tossed around the term *dreyfusistes* as a general condemnation of liberal attitudes.[93]

Although he could make fun of excessive nationalist pride in art, Denis was also prone to promote specifically French art with specifically French characteristics. He argued in his journal that the French owed very little to English sources in the development of landscape painting during the nineteenth century.[94] He sought out "unknown" works of

90. *Journal*, I, 134.

91. *Théories*, 188. (". . . les foudres vengeresses des dreyfusistes de l'Institut!")

92. Ibid., 255. To quote more fully: "But it would also be as puerile to glorify Cézanne for his negligences and imperfections. Let's try to escape the prejudices which breed Dreyfusism and neurasthenia. Let us not be the dupes of the spirit of paradox, disorder, and subtlety." ("Mais il serait tout aussi puéril de faire gloire à Cézanne de ses négligences et de ses imperfections. Essayons d'échapper aux préjugés qu'engendrent le dreyfusisme et la neurasthénie; ne soyons pas dupes de l'esprit de paradoxe, de désordre et de subtilité.") The paragraph containing these sentences was the only paragraph deleted from the original 1907 article when it was reprinted by Olivier Revault D'Allonnes in *Du symbolisme au classicisme*. As the article runs to seventeen pages in reprinted form the deletion was apparently not made for reasons of space.

93. See *Journal*, I, 135, for Denis's fears that newspaper accounts of the case would have an adverse effect on French national pride.

94. Ibid., 37.

French masters and wrote enthusiastic descriptions of his "finds."[95] But ultimately Denis preferred a wider definition of nationalist sentiment, and this came in the form of a modified version of the Latinity so prized by men like Charles Maurras. Following Adrien Mithouard, who had founded the journal *L'Occident* in 1901 to promote a specifically Western ideal, Denis believed in the occidental world as the culmination of all the great cultural currents of the past. Denis's classical aesthetic was the artistic theory underlying his occidentalism. Like Maurras, Denis celebrated the order, clarity, and rationality of the Latin tradition. Like Maurras, Denis felt that the romantic movement contained the seeds of decadence in its self-indulgence—he referred specifically to Delacroix—and praised the neo-classical school for its "truly French qualities of precision and clarity."[96] The nationalist movement was, for Denis, confirmation of his own interest in tradition and gave political body to what might otherwise have been only an artistic theory. In his "De Gauguin et de Van Gogh au classicisme" of 1909, Denis linked the new artistic interest in classical order with the integral nationalism of Maurice Barrès precisely because both concentrated on tradition.[97]

Unfortunately Denis drew more than tradition from nationalist thought. Like Maurras and Drumont and so many other nationalists, Denis allowed his love of Latin culture to lead him to make anti-Semitic statements. In his journal Denis mentioned a conversation with Gide "à propos des Juifs." He spoke disparagingly of science, internationalism, and modern pantheism as the "goal or means of Jewish expansion."[98] Elsewhere he dismissed the Roman newspaper *La Tribuna* for being "un

95. See, for instance, "La Peintre de Beaune," *Théories*, 133–35; "La Père Besson," *Théories*, 152–57; "Exposition de François Vernay," *Théories*, 135–36. Also see *Journal*, i, 172–75, 180–81, for more of Denis's enthusiasm for "rediscovering" French art.

96. *Théories*, 92. ("Il apportait donc avec des qualités vraiment françaises de précision et de clarté un double idéal de vérité et de beauté.") Denis was so taken with Maurras that he founded and served as honorary president of the St. Germain-en-Laye chapter of Maurras's *Action française*. See *Journal*, iii, 64–67, for Denis's letter of resignation from the *Action française* in 1927, just after the pope had condemned the organization. Even then Denis deeply regretted having to sever ties with the group.

97. Ibid., 267. Interestingly, the three sentences in which Denis spoke favorably of integral nationalism were deleted from the reprint of the article in *Du symbolisme au classicisme*. See note 92 above.

98. *Journal*, i, 130. ("En effet, ce que les libres-penseurs appellent la science, l'internationalisme, le surhomme [accompagné d'esclaves de Nietzsche], le panthéisme moderne [de Spinoza], tout cela est le but ou le moyen de l'expansion juive.")

journal israélite."[99] In 1899 Denis commented on the Nabis exhibition at Durand-Ruel, noting a division between Latin and Semitic characteristics in the group of exhibiting artists.[100] He included Edouard Vuillard, Pierre Bonnard, and Félix Vallotton in the latter category and Paul Sérusier, Paul Ranson, and himself in the former. Although he made no direct pejorative comments, it is clear which Denis preferred. The Semitic taste placed little importance on figures and, therefore, drawing. It was a style suited for small apartments. The Latin, on the other hand, concentrated on large paintings in which the human figure and symbolism played an important part. Simplification and unity were central to this aesthetic. Standing alone, such classifications need not be taken too seriously, but within the context of nationalist anti-Semitism they take on a chilling dimension.[101]

While no excuses should be made for such sentiments one must understand the position from which Denis operated. First and foremost, Maurice Denis was a Catholic and an artist. Those two loves dominated his life and his political position as well. That Latin sensibility was artistic with Denis before it became political. In January 1905 Camille Mauclair, by then a dyed-in-the-wool socialist and staunch supporter of Dreyfus, wrote an article accusing Denis, along with many others, of promoting nationalist sentiment in art.[102] Denis responded with an article of his own, published in *L'Ermitage* in May 1905.[103] Denis would set a rightist tone when he dedicated a reprint of the article to Adrien Mithouard, "who had the pride to found, in the midst of the Dreyfusist crisis, *L'Occident.*"[104] Throughout the article Denis argued that a return to tradition, to order and stability, was at the heart of the generation of

---

99. Ibid., 135. ("La *Tribuna* est un journal israélite.")

100. Ibid., 150.

101. It should be understood that each of the statements by Denis noted here was from his private journal. Many years later, Thadée Natanson—the Jewish editor of the *Revue blanche* who angered Denis when he "intervened" in the Dreyfus affair—praised the painter for being one of the first to "hold out his hand" to the Jews just when they were being persecuted. See Natanson, *Peints à leur tour* (Paris: Albin Michel, 1948), 302. Yet Denis, like so many others, did not denounce the vocal anti-Semitism of nationalists like Barrès and Maurras. Indeed, as stated in note 96 above, Denis founded the Saint-Germain-en-Laye chapter of Maurras's blatantly anti-Semitic *Action française.*

102. Camille Mauclair, "La Réaction nationaliste en art et l'ignorance de l'homme de lettres," *La Revue*, LIV (15 January 1905), 151–74.

103. "La Réaction nationaliste," *Théories*, 187–98.

104. Ibid., 187. ("A Adrien Mithouard, qui eut la fierté de fonder, en pleine crise dreyfusiste, *L'Occident.*") The original article, entitled "Peinture," was not dedicated to Mithouard, who published the first three editions of Denis's *Théories.*

the 1890s. He suggested that impressionism had led to a style too much concerned with medium and too free. He stated that the young generation—specifically meaning Matisse in this case—would benefit from a strong dose of tradition, be it French or nationalist. In essence he argued for the nationalist artistic agenda: a Latin aesthetic of order, clarity, and stability. Elsewhere Denis argued that a democratic liberalism was destroying the arts through an exaggerated emphasis on individuality over strong formal training. The result, in the art of Matisse and others, was a "sterile and empty liberty."[105]

This, of course, is far indeed from the liberated mood of the early symbolist avant-garde, just as Denis's politics were far from those of anarchists/symbolists like Félix Fénéon. One wants, at first, to argue with Denis—to say that the spirit of 1890 had very little to do with the conservative position he had assumed. But the evidence is on Denis's side. As we have seen throughout this book, conservative sensibilities, be they political, social, or artistic, could be found at the very heart of the evolving symbolist criticism of art and, as Denis shows, of symbolist painting as well. Denis became conservative because he read conservatism in the mood of the nineties and because he felt tradition to be the best path for his artistic sensibilities. Many modernists would say that his art suffered from too much emphasis on the past, yet both his art and his criticism are rich and fascinating, if for nothing else than for his unique interpretation of the events we all feel we know so well. There is certainly no reason to regret Denis's love of tradition, or his conservative temperament, when confronted with such paintings as the *Exaltation of the Holy Cross*. Here the best of Denis's Catholicism, traditionalism, and Latin sense of order produce a magical effect, timeless and perfect. Ironically, however, Denis's art did suffer once from being on the "wrong" political side. In 1906, following enforcement of the laws so aggressively pursued by Emile Combes, the Congregation of the Brothers of the Holy Cross at Le Vésinet was disbanded and their property auctioned off.[106] Denis's paintings were saved, eventually passing into the hands of the Musée des Arts Decoratifs. Today, owing no doubt to their size and their late date in the career of this painter recognized most for his Nabis work, they remain in storage at the Musée d'Orsay.

105. See Denis's article, "Liberté épuisante et stérile," *Théories*, 225–34. The article was originally published in *La Grande revue*, 10 April 1908.

106. See Patrick Vazeilles, "De Saint-Rémy au collège du cédre," *Revue municipale du Vésinet*, no. 56 (September 1987), 66.

CONCLUSION

Throughout this book I have noted some of the ways in which the avant-garde symbolist criticism of art was influenced by various factions, more conservative and more established. No one should be surprised that avant-garde movements tend increasingly toward conservatism as they mature. A pattern of progressive artistic movements becoming established and recalcitrant in terms of newer movements has been the norm rather than the exception in Western art. The symbolist criticism of art was unusual, however, in terms of the rapidity with which it was accepted in conservative circles, and in terms of the speed of its own conversion to conservative thought. As I have suggested, the central reason for this state of affairs was the shared hatred of naturalism in both traditional and avant-garde camps. Antinaturalism served to bring together, if only briefly, such divergent critics as Péladan and Aurier, just as Aurier's hatred of naturalism and the invasion of science in the arts tended to draw him away from a perspicacious avant-garde critic like Fénéon.

Again, it is by no means surprising that one artistic movement might reject some of the tenets of a previously dominant form. Cubism would, by and large, reject symbolism just as symbolism had rejected naturalism. Disavowals of established styles, whether once avant-garde or not, have been as important as continuity in the development of modern art. What distinguished symbolism in this ebb and flow of artistic movements was the way in which its complaints about the past—the naturalist past—were so like the complaints made in conservative circles. A few reasons can be proposed for what might be termed the conservative core of the symbolist criticism of art.

First and foremost, symbolism was basically a literary movement. The poems of Mallarmé predated by several years the painting of Gauguin. When Albert Aurier entitled his article about Gauguin "Symbolism in Painting," the inference of the movement's prior literary beginning was clear enough. Virtually all of the critics who wrote about avant-garde painting in the 1880s and early 1890s were members of the symbolist literary movement before they turned to criticism, and they brought literary tastes to painting. This literary association, on occasion, gave rise to traditional, even trite, pronouncements on the nature of painting. This was certainly the case with Alphonse Germain and Camille Mauclair. The symbolist criticism of painting tended to be more concerned with subject than formal analysis: Moreau and Redon appealed more than Seurat; Gauguin, even when understood, as by Aurier, never enjoyed the careful analysis Fénéon gave Seurat. The positive aspect of symbolist criticism's literary bias was its invigorated, passionate language of criticism (Aurier is the prime example). On the negative side, there was a tendency toward blindness to the subtleties of painting; Seurat's rejection by the second wave of symbolist critics was a central failing. Whether positive or negative, however, the literary nature of symbolist criticism functioned as a conduit to conservative thought about art. Idealist and symbolist critics alike called for a return to more noble, important, mysterious subjects in reaction to the ignoble, ordinary, quotidian subject matter of naturalism.

The French political climate of the 1880s and 1890s also played a role in the conservative turn of symbolist art criticism. While it is dangerous to assume a one-to-one relationship between political and artistic philosophies it is clear that France was witness to a rising tide of conservative thought at the end of the nineteenth century. Many factions of French society were skeptical of modern, democratic mores and sought a return to the monarchist and religious values of the past. Fundamental, traditional concepts were praised and supported against the progressivist thought of the positivist and naturalist past. Again, the symbolist criticism of art, because of its opposition to naturalism, often found itself in alliance with conservative, even reactionary, political forces.

Revolutions are limited by their context. The revolutionary strives against an existing order and the struggle is couched in terms of opposi-

tion to that order and is, thereby, inextricably related to it. So too with
the literary and artistic revolution known as symbolism. In this case the
context was a cultural world dominated by naturalism, and the revolt
was primed by a widespread desire to go beyond what existed. If naturalism had not been there first to provide such a strong force to oppose,
avant-garde and conservative antinaturalists might never have agreed.
They might well have fought each other even more than, in fact, they
did. But the differences between symbolist and idealist criticism should
not go unremarked. At risk of oversimplification, the differences might
be reduced to two: effectiveness and visual acuity.

As is fitting, the best symbolist critics deserve praise for the effectiveness of their writing as much for their prescient recognition of artists we
now appreciate. While Aurier and Péladan may have shared ideas about
art, Aurier's writing was a good deal more effective than the Sâr's. Péladan was a forceful stylist, especially in the context of publications like
L'Artiste, but he was no match for Aurier at his best. On the other hand
Alphonse Germain, even when he supported Seurat, simply did not pos-
sess the literary skills to carry it off. A primary contribution of the symbolist criticism of art was its effective and cogent proselytizing for avant-
garde painting. While it may seem obvious to say so, it is important to
draw attention to the writers themselves and away from the artists they
wrote about. Indeed, effectiveness and visual acuity are, in a sense, opposites—the ability of the writer not necessarily corresponding with the
eye of the critic. Thus Fénéon could be sensational in his condemnation
of Gauguin, and Aurier could praise Henner with considerable flair.

Yet the sensitive eye of the best symbolist critics deserves recognition.
To call for synthesis and a return to ideals was one thing, but to see
Gauguin or Seurat or Redon as manifesting traits that so many critics
sought was signal and daring. Only the most informed and up-to-date
critics could see Seurat as the "modernizing Puvis" that he was, or
Gauguin as master of the decorative tradition everyone praised in Puvis.
Aurier, Fénéon, Huysmans, and Denis put the avant-garde art of the
eighties and nineties to words, and in doing so offered an incomparable
literary record to the future. Throughout this book I have noted that the
ability to see the ideals of many antinaturalists in the avant-garde artists
of the period was central to symbolist criticism. But something else is
equally clear: no critic from this period supported all of the painters that
are now considered the most advanced. Generally those critics who appreciated Seurat were antagonistic toward Gauguin, and the reverse.

Factionalism characterized symbolism and it could cloud the judgment of even the best critics.

Finally, I have spoken of the symbolist criticism of painting and symbolist critics but it must be clear by now that the profile of the "typical" symbolist critic was never clear-cut. If Fénéon figured as the prime example at one time, Aurier did so later; and these two could be as different from each other as they were from more established critics. My contention here has been that an increasing conservatism marked symbolist criticism and, thereby, distinguished its practitioners. Yet such conservatism was not a retreat. It was aggressive and, ironically, modern. Symbolist critics, in spite of their desire to seek out the latest in painting, also demonstrated a marked proclivity for going against the grain. Thus Huysmans, who began by supporting impressionist painting, found himself enchanted with Gustave Moreau, the very antithesis of impressionism. When Camille Mauclair so vocally promoted the art of Georges Rochegrosse he was taking part in the essentially symbolist attraction for that which was unusual. He was well aware of his choice and enjoyed the notoriety it caused. The same was true with Albert Aurier's championing of Jean-Jacques Henner. The very spirit that led symbolist critics to challenge popular opinion in praising avant-garde art could also edge them toward opposition to group avant-gardism. Reacting against established tastes, whether avant-garde or those of the common herd was part of the very cachet of symbolist criticism, resisted by none of its masters.

SELECTED BIBLIOGRAPHY

Adam, Paul. "L'Art symboliste." *La Cravache* (23 March 1889), unpaginated.

———. "Les Artistes indépendants." *La Vogue*, II (30 August–6 September 1886), 260–67.

———. "Avertissement aux prolétaires." *Entretiens politiques et littéraires*, III (December 1891), 196–203.

———. "Critique des moeurs." *Entretiens politiques et littéraires*, VI (February 1893), 135–37.

———. "Eloge de Ravachol." *Entretiens politiques et littéraires*, V (July 1892), 27–30.

———. "Peintres impressionnistes." *Revue contemporaine*, IV (April 1886), 541–51.

———. "La Presse et le symbolisme." *Le Symboliste*, I (7–14 October 1886), unpaginated. Reprinted in Jean Moréas. *Les Premièrs armes du symbolisme*. Paris: Vanier, 1889, 59–64.

———. "Souvenirs sur les hommes et sur l'apparence de Dieu." *Entretiens politiques et littéraires*, IV (March 1892), 116–28.

———. "Le Symbolisme." *La Vogue*, II (October 1886), 397–401.

Alsberg, John. *Modern Art and its Enigma*. London: Weidenfeld and Nicolson, 1983.

Aman-Jean, Edmond. "Jean Bellegambe (1475–1540)." *L'Art dans les deux mondes* (31 January 1891), 118–20.

———. "Puvis de Chavannes." *L'Art dans les deux mondes, no. 172* (29 November 1890), 10–11.

Anderson, R. D. *France 1870–1914: Politics and Society*. London: Routledge and Kegan Paul, 1977.

Arguëlles, Jose. *Charles Henry and the Formation of a Psychophysical Aesthetic*. Chicago: University of Chicago Press, 1972.

Arnal, Oscar L. *Ambivalent Alliance: The Catholic Church and the Action Française 1899–1939*. Pittsburgh: University of Pittsburgh Press, 1985.

Arnason, H. H. *History of Modern Art*. New York: Abrams, 1968.

Arnaud, Noël. "Aurier aux savantes ailées et Irénée." *Dossiers du collège de pataphysique, no. 15* (1961), 51–62.

Art Journal. Special issue. "Symbolist Art and Literature." xlv (Summer 1985).

Aurier, G.-Albert. "Deuxième exposition des peintres impressionnistes et symbolistes." *Mercure de France,* v (July 1892), 260–63. This article is basically a reprint of Aurier's preface to the second Le Barc de Boutteville exhibition. The article is also reprinted in *Modern Art in Paris: Post-Impressionist Group Exhibitions.* New York: Garland, 1982, unpaginated.

———. *Oeuvres posthumes.* Paris: Mercure de France, 1893.

———. [Marc d'Escaurailles, pseud.]. "Le Salon de 1888." *Le Décadent,* iii (15–31 May 1888), 9–14; (1–15 June 1888), 8–12.

———. [Jacques Lelong, pseud.]. "Salon de 1889." *Le Moderniste illustré,* i (June 1889), 54–55, 63.

———. [Albert d'Escorailles, pseud.]. "Sensationnisme." *Le Décadent,* i (13 November 1886), unpaginated.

Aynard, Edouard. "Les Peintures décoratives de Puvis de Chavannes au Palais des Arts." *Revue du lyonnais,* xlvii, no. 2 (1886), 241–58.

B., William. "Les Expositions du mois." *La Revue blanche,* i (April 1891), 16–22.

———. "Les Salons." *La Revue blanche,* i (August 1891), 216–30.

Babbitt, Irving. *The Masters of Modern French Criticism.* Boston: Houghton Mifflin, 1912.

Baignères, Arthur. "La Peinture décorative au XIXᵉ siècle, Puvis de Chavannes." *Gazette des beaux-arts,* xxiii (May 1881), 416–26.

Baju, Anatole. *L'Anarchie littéraire.* Paris: Vanier. 1892.

———. "Chronique." *Le Décadent,* i (21 August 1886), unpaginated.

———. "Chronique." *Le Décadent,* iii (December 1887), 1–3.

———. "Décadents et symbolistes." *Le Décadent,* iii (15–30 November 1888), 1–2.

———. *L'Ecole décadente.* Paris: Vanier, 1887.

———. "Idéal." *Le Décadent,* i (21 August 1886), unpaginated.

———. "M. Boulanger c'est l'ennemi." *Le Décadent,* iii (15–31 May 1888), 14–15.

———. "M. Paul Bourget." *Le Décadent,* iii (15–31 March 1888), 4–8.

———. *Principes du socialisme.* Paris: Vanier, 1895.

———. [Un Bourgeois Lettré, pseud.]. *La Verité sur l'école décadent.* Paris: Vanier, 1887.

Barazetti-Demoulin, Suzanne. *Maurice Denis.* Paris: Editions Bernard Grasset, 1945.

Barbey d'Aurevilly, Jules. *Les Philosophes et les écrivains religieux.* Paris: Quantin, 1887.

———. *Philosophes et écrivains religieux et politiques.* Paris: A. Lemerre, 1909.

Barre, André. *Le Symbolisme.* Paris: Jouve, 1911.

Barrès, Maurice. "M. le Général Boulanger et la nouvelle génération." *La Revue indépendante,* vii (April 1888), 55–63.

Baudelaire, Charles. *Les Fleurs du mal, précédées d'une notice par Théophile Gautier.* Paris: Calmann-Levy, 1883.

Baume, Jean de la. "Albert Aurier." *La Revue indépendante,* xxv (October 1892), 130–40.

Bénédite, Léonce. "L'Exposition des oeuvres de M. Puvis de Chavannes." *L'Artiste,* lviii (January 1888), 33–37.

Béranger, Henry. "L'Art, la science et la démocratie." *Essais d'art libre,* i (February 1892), 1–10.

———. "Les Artistes de l'âme, Edmond Aman-Jean." *L'Art et la vie,* i (1893), 33–37.

Bergeron, Francis, and Philippe Vilgier. *Les Droits dans la rue: nationaux et nationalistes sous la troisième république.* Paris: DMM, 1985.

Bergson, Henri. *Essai sur les données immédiates de la conscience.* Paris: F. Alcan, 1889.

Bernard, Emile. "Au Palais des Beaux-Arts." *Le Moderniste illustré,* i (27 July 1889), 108–10.

———. "Lettre ouverte à M. Camille Mauclair." *Mercure de France,* xiv (June 1895), 323–39.

———. "Louis Anquetin, artiste peintre." *Mercure de France,* ccxxxix (November 1932), 590–601.

Bibliothèque Nationale. *Le Mouvement symboliste, études bibliographique et iconographique.* Paris: Bibliothèque Nationale, 1936.

Bigot, Charles. "Le Salon de 1883." *Gazette des beaux-arts,* xxvii (1 June 1883), 457–76.

Blanc, Charles. *Grammaire des arts du dessin, architecture, sculpture, peinture.* Paris: Librairie Renouard, 1883 [originally published 1867].

Blavatsky, Helena Petrovna. *Isis Unveiled: A Master Key to the Mysteries of Ancient and Modern Science and Theology.* New York: J. W. Bouton, 1877.

———. *The Secret Doctrine: The Synthesis of Science, Religion and Philosophy.* New York: W. Q. Judge, 1888.

Blémont, Emile [pseudonym of Emile Petitdidier]. "Henner." *L'Artiste,* lii (January 1882), 5–14, 50–59.

Bloy, Léon. "A propos de *Souvenirs d'enfance et de jeunesse* de M. Renan." *Le Chat noir,* ii (1 September 1883), 134.

———. *Le Désespéré.* Paris: Tresse and Stock, 1887.

———. *Le Révélateur du globe.* Paris: A. Sauton, 1884.

Boime, Albert. *The Academy and French Painting in the 19th Century.* London: Phaidon, 1971.

Bouchot, Henri. "Les Salons de 1893, premier article." *Gazette des beaux-arts,* ix (1 June 1893), 441–83.

Bougot, A. *Essai sur la critique d'art.* Paris: Hachette, n.d. [1875].

Bourget, Paul. *Essais de psychologie contemporaine.* Paris: Plon, 1901 [originally published Paris: Plon-Nourrit, n.d. (1881)].

Boyle-Turner, Caroline. *Paul Sérusier.* Ann Arbor: UMI Research Press, 1983.

Brady, Sister Mary Rosalie. *Thought and Style in the Works of Léon Bloy.* Washington, D.C.: Catholic University of America Press, 1945.

Bredin, Jean-Denis. *The Affair.* Translated by Jeffrey Mehlman. New York: George Braziller, 1986.

Brinn Gaubast, Louis-Pilate de. "L'Exposition des artistes indépendants." *Le Décadent,* i (18 September 1886), unpaginated.

Brookner, Anita. *The Genius of the Future, Studies in French Art Criticism.* London: Phaidon, 1971.

Broude, Norma. *Seurat in Perspective.* Englewood Cliffs, N.J.: Prentice-Hall, 1978.

Brücke, Ernst Wilhelm Ritter von. *Principes scientifiques des beaux-arts suivies de l'optique et la peinture par H. Helmholtz.* Paris: G. Baillière, 1878.

Brunetière, Ferdinand. "La Critique scientifique." *Questions de critique.* Paris: Calmann-Levy, n.d., 297–324.

———. "Le Faux naturalisme." *Revue des deux mondes,* xlix (15 February 1882), 932–43.

———. "Les Origines du roman naturaliste." *Revue des deux mondes,* xlvii (15 September 1881), 438–50.

———. "La Philosophie de Schopenhauer et les conséquences du pessimisme." *Revue des deux mondes,* cii (November–December 1890), 210–21.

————. *La Renaissance de l'idéalisme.* Paris: Librairie de Firmin-Didot, 1896.

————. *Le Roman naturaliste.* Paris: Calmann-Levy, 1893.

Brunius, Teddy. *Mutual Aid in the Arts from the Second Empire to the Fin de Siècle.* Stockholm: Almquist and Wiksell, 1972.

Buisson, Jules. "Le Salon de 1881, premier article, M. Puvis de Chavannes." *Gazette des beaux-arts,* XXIII (1 June 1881), 490–94.

Burhan, Filiz Eda. "Vision and Visionaries: Nineteenth Century Psychological Theory, the Occult Sciences and the Formation of the Symbolist Aesthetic in France." Ph.D. dissertation, Princeton University, 1979.

Buthman, William. *The Rise of Integral Nationalism in France.* New York: Columbia University Press, 1939.

Byrnes, Robert. *Antisemitism in Modern France.* New York: Howard Fertig, 1969.

Canaday, John. *Mainstreams of Modern Art.* New York: Holt, Rinehart and Winston, 1959.

Caramaschi, Enzo. *Essai sur la critique française de la fin-de-siècle: Emile Hennequin.* Paris: Nizet, 1974.

Caro, Elme Marie. *Littré et le positivisme.* Paris: Hachette, 1883.

————. "La Philosophie positive, ses transformations, son avenir." *Revue des deux mondes,* LI (May 1882), 5–46.

————. "Le Prix de la vie humaine et la question du bonheur dans le positivisme." *Revue des deux mondes,* LII (August 1882), 481–520.

Cartault, A. "Beaux-arts, l'art et la science dans la peinture, d'après MM. Brücke et Helmholtz." *La Revue politique et littéraire,* VIII (21 June 1879), 1202–8.

Charlton, Donald Geoffrey. *Positivist Thought in France During the Second Empire, 1852–1870.* Oxford: Clarendon Press, 1959.

Chassé, Charles. *Gauguin et le group de Pont-Aven.* Paris: H. Floury, 1921.

————. *Gauguin et son temps.* Paris: Bibliothèque des Arts, 1955.

————. *Le Mouvement symboliste dans l'art du XIXe siècle.* Paris: Librairie Floury, 1947.

————. *Les Nabis et leur temps.* Paris: Bibliothèque des Arts, 1960.

Chennevières, Marquis de. "Le Salon de 1880." *Gazette des beaux-arts,* XXI (1 June 1880), 393–407, 499–524.

Cherbuliez, Victor. "L'Art et la nature." *Revue des deux mondes,* LXI (1 July 1891), 5–42 (15 July 1891), 241–86 (1 August 1891), 481–520 (15 August 1891), 721–55.

Chesneau, Ernest. "Philosophie de l'art, par H. Taine." *L'Art,* XXX (1882), 258–60.

Chipp, Hershel. *Theories of Modern Art.* Berkeley and Los Angeles: University of California Press, 1971.

Chiron, Yves. *Maurice Barrès, le prince de la jeunesse.* Paris: Perrin, 1986.

Clark, John. *La Pensée de Ferdinand Brunetière.* Paris: Nizet, 1954.

Clark, William. "Camille Mauclair and the Religion of Art." Ph.D. dissertation, University of California–Berkeley, 1976.

Cochin, Denys. *Ententes et ruptures.* Paris: Calmann-Levy, 1906.

Combes, Emile. *Une campagne laïque.* Paris: H. Simonis Empis, 1904.

Cornell, Kenneth. *The Symbolist Movement.* New Haven: Yale University Press, 1951.

Coulon, Marcel. "Une minute de l'heure symboliste, Albert Aurier." *Mercure de France,* CXLV (February 1921), 599–640.

Couturat, Gaston, and Jules Couturat. "Petites polémiques mensuelles: *Feu,* M. G.-Albert Aurier." *La Revue indépendante,* XXVI (February 1893), 45–66.

Curtis, Michael. *Three Against the Third Republic: Sorel, Barrès, Maurras*. Princeton: Princeton University Press, 1959.

Decaudin, Michel. "Albert Aurier. De l'esprit décadent à l'esprit symboliste." *Bulletin de la société toulousaine d'études classiques*, no. 136 (February–March 1962), 1–4.

———. "Aurier l'ignoré." *Dossiers du collège de pataphysique*, no. 15 (1961), 41–46.

Délégation à l'action artistique de la ville de Paris. *Le Symbolisme et la femme*. Paris: Délégation à l'action artistique de la ville de Paris, 1986.

Delevoy, Robert. *Journal du symbolisme*. Geneva: Skira, 1977.

———. *Symbolists and Symbolism*. Translated by Barbara Bray. Geneva: Skira, 1978.

Delsemme, Paul. *Téodor de Wyzewa*. Brussels: Presses universitaires de Bruxelles, 1967.

———. *Un théoricien du symbolisme, Charles Morice*. Paris: Nizet, 1958.

Denis, Maurice [Pierre Louis, pseud.]. "A M. Alphonse Germain." *Art et critique*, II (18 October 1890), 667–68.

———. *Histoire de l'art religieux*. Paris: Flammarion, 1939.

———. *Journal*. Vols. 1–3. Paris: La Colombe, 1957.

———. [Pierre L. Maud, pseud.]. "Notes d'art et d'esthétique." *La Revue blanche*, II (May 1892), 360–66.

———. [Pierre Louis, pseud.]. "Notes sur l'exposition des indépendants." *La Revue blanche*, II (April 1892), 232–34.

———. *Nouvelles théories sur l'art moderne et sur l'art sacré*. Paris: Rouart et Watelin, 1921.

———. [Pierre Louis, pseud.]. "Pour les jeunes peintres." *Art et critique*, III (20 February 1891), 94.

———. *Du symbolisme au classicisme, théories*. Paris: Hermann, 1964.

———. *Théories, 1890–1910, Du symbolisme et de Gauguin vers un nouvel ordre classique*, 4th ed. Paris: L. Rouart and J. Watelin, 1920.

Desjardins, Paul. "Sur M. E. Melchior de Vogüé, a propos de sa réception académique." *Revue bleue*, XXVI (8 June 1889), 713–19.

Dorra, Henri. "Extraits de la correspondance d'Emile Bernard des débuts à la Rose-Croix (1876–1892)." *Gazette des beaux-arts*, XCVI (December 1980), 235–42.

———. "Le Portrait de Péladan par Séon." *Bulletin des musées et monuments lyonnais*, VI, no. 3 (1977), 55–67.

———. "La Symbolique du chemin et de l'arbre chez Maurice Denis." *La Revue du Louvre et des musées de France*, no. 4 (1982), 254–59.

Doty, Stewart. *From Cultural Rebellion to Counterrevolution: The Politics of Maurice Barrès*. Athens: Ohio University Press. 1976.

Drumont, Edouard. *La France juive, essai d'histoire contemporaine*. Paris: Librairie Blériot, 1887 [originally published in a two-volume edition by E. Dentu, Paris, 1886].

———. *Le Testament d'un anti-sémite*. Paris: E. Dentu, 1891.

Dumur, Louis. "G.-Albert Aurier et l'évolution idéaliste." *Mercure de France*, VIII (August 1893), 289–97.

Duret, Théodore. *Les Peintres impressionnistes*. Paris: Librairie parisienne, 1878.

Duval, Elga Liverman. "Téodor de Wyzewa: Critic Without a Country." Ph.D. dissertation, Columbia University, 1960.

Fénéon, Félix. *Au-delà de l'impressionnisme*. Paris: Hermann, 1966.

———. *Oeuvres plus que complètes*. Geneva: Librairie Droz, 1970.

Fontainas, André. *Mes souvenirs du symbolisme.* Paris: La Nouvelle revue critique, 1928.

Fouillée, Alfred. *Le Mouvement idéaliste et la réaction contre la science positive.* Paris: Félix Alcan, 1913 [originally published in 1896].

Fourcaud, Louis de. "Notes sur quelques décorateurs, Pierre Puvis de Chavannes." *Revue des arts décoratifs,* ix (1888–89), 1–10, 74–81.

———. "Le Salon de 1884." *Gazette des beaux-arts,* xxix (June 1884), 465–92.

Fraser, Elizabeth M. *Le Renouveau religieux d'après le roman français de 1886 à 1914.* Paris: Société d'édition "Les belles lettres," 1934.

French Symbolist Painters. London: Arts Council, 1972.

Gaigalas, Vytas V. *Ernest Renan and His French Catholic Critics.* North Quincy, Mass.: Christopher Publishing House, 1972.

Gautier, Théophile. *Portraits contemporains.* Paris: Charpentier, 1881.

Germain, Alphonse. "A travers les jurys des Salons." *Entretiens politiques et littéraires,* ii (June 1891), 206–9.

———. "Alexandre Séon." *La Plume,* iii, no. 57 (1 September 1891), 303.

———. "L'Art et l'apologétique." *Mercure de France,* vii (March 1893), 224–28.

———. "L'Art et l'état." *Entretiens politiques et littéraires,* i (1 November 1890), 274–76.

———. "L'Art et les pouvoirs publics." *L'Ermitage,* iv (December 1893), 340–43.

———. "L'Art religieux." *Le Saint-Graal,* i (May 1892), 150–57.

———. *Les Artistes lyonnais du XIIIe siècle à nos jours.* Lyon: H. Lardauchet, 1910.

———. "Aux intellectuels." *Entretiens politiques et littéraires,* ii (February 1891), 40–44.

———. "Du beau moral et du beau formel." *L'Ermitage,* vi (April 1895), 193–97.

———. "Beaux-Arts, du tempérament peintre." *Art et critique,* ii (27 September 1890), 618–20.

———. "Beaux-Arts, l'exposition des indépendants." *Art et critique,* i (15 September 1889), 250–52.

———. "Ceux de l'école." *Entretiens politiques et littéraires,* ii (October 1891), 136–41.

———. *Comment rénover l'art: l'art chrétien en France des origines au XVIe siècle.* Paris: Bloud, 1906.

———. "Considérations esthétiques sur l'évolution picturale." *L'Ermitage,* ii (July 1891), 398–404.

———. "Contre le japonisme." *L'Ermitage,* iii (July 1892), 24–28.

———. "Cri d'alarme." *L'Ermitage,* iv (August 1893), 94–96.

———. "Critique d'art, sur un tableau refusé." *La Plume,* iii (15 May 1891), 171–72.

———. "De la critique en art figuratif." *Essais d'art libre,* ii (January 1893), 266–70.

———. "Le Désespoir de la chimère." *La Plume,* iv (1 June 1892), 244.

———. "Un fragment de *Notre art de France.*" *Essais d'art libre,* v (June–July 1894), 97–104.

———. "L'Idéal au Salon de la Rose + Croix." *L'Ermitage,* iii (April 1892), 210–16.

———. "L'Idéal et l'idéalisme." *L'Art et l'idée,* i (April 1892), 176–80.

———. *L'Influence de Saint François d'Assise sur la civilisation et les arts.* Paris: Bloud, 1903.

———. "Jean Pézieux." *L'Ermitage,* v (July 1894), 1–3.

———. "Joséphin Péladan." *Art et critique,* ii (11 January 1890), 17–20.

————. "M. Meissonier et la peinture de genre." *L'Ermitage*, ii (May 1891), 273–75.

————. "Le Modernisme et le Beau." *La Plume*, iii (15 March 1891), 115–16.

————. *Notre art de France*. Paris: E. Girard, 1894.

————. "Un peintre idéaliste-idéiste, Alexandre Séon." *L'Art et l'idée*, i (February 1892), 107–12.

————. "Pour le beau." *Essais d'art libre*, iii (February–March 1893), 1–120.

————. *Pour le beau*. Paris: E. Girard, 1893.

————. "De Poussin et des bases de l'art figuratif." *L'Ermitage*, iv (February 1893), 101–6.

————. "Les Préraphaélites et l'esthétique de M. Ruskin." *L'Ermitage*, iii (December 1892), 364–72.

————. "Un projet." *Entretiens politiques et littéraires*, ii (February 1892), 80–83.

————. "Puvis de Chavannes et son esthétique." *L'Ermitage*, ii (March 1891), 140–44.

————. "Salon de la Rose + Croix." *L'Idéal et l'idéalisme*, i (May 1892), 176–80.

————. "Du symbolisme dans la peinture." *Art et critique*, ii (5 July 1890), 417–20.

————. "Théorie chromo-luminariste, exposé et critique." *La Plume*, iii, no. 57 (1 September 1891), 285–87.

————. "Théorie des déformateurs, exposé et réfutation." *La Plume*, iii, no. 57 (1 September 1891), 289–90.

————. "Théorie des néo-luminaristes (néo-impressionnistes)." *L'Art moderne*, xi (12 July 1891), 221–22; (26 July 1891), 239–40.

————. "La Vrai Renaissance." *L'Ermitage*, v (June 1894), 341–43.

Gibson, Michael. *Les Symbolistes*. Paris: Nouvelle éditions française, 1984.

Gibson, Ralph. *A Social History of French Catholicism 1789–1914*. London: Routledge, 1989.

Goldwater, Robert. "Symbolic Form: Symbolic Content." *Problems of the Nineteenth and Twentieth Centuries, Acts of the Twentieth International Congress of the History of Art*, iv (Princeton: Princeton University Press, 1963), 111–21.

————. *Symbolism*. New York: Harper and Row, 1979.

Goncourt, Edmond de. *Paris and the Arts, 1851–1896: From the Goncourt Journal*. Edited and translated by George J. Becker and Edith Philips. Ithaca: Cornell University Press, 1971.

Gourmont, Rémy de. "Les Premiers Salons: indépendants—Rose + Croix—exposition de Mme. Jeanne Jacquemin." *Mercure de France*, v (May 1892), 60–66.

————. *Promenades philosophiques*. Paris: Mercure de France, 1905.

————. *Le Livre des masques*. Vols. i–ii. Paris: Mercure de France, 1898.

Griffiths, Richard. *The Reactionary Revolution, The Catholic Revival in French Literature, 1870–1914*. London: Constable, 1966.

Guéroult, Georges. "Du rôle du mouvement des yeux dan les émotions esthétiques." *Gazette des beaux-arts*, xxiii (June 1881), 536–42; xxiv (July 1881), 82–90.

————. "Formes, couleurs et mouvements." *Gazette des beaux-arts*, xxv (February 1882), 165–79.

Guyau, Jean Marie. "L'Antagonisme de l'art et de la science." *Revue des deux mondes*, lx (15 November 1883), 356–86.

Haftmann, Werner. *Painting in the Twentieth Century*. New York: Praeger, 1965.

Halperin, Joan U. *Félix Fénéon, Aesthete and Anarchist in Fin-de-Siècle Paris*. New Haven: Yale University Press, 1988.

————. *Félix Fénéon and the Language of Art Criticism*. Ann Arbor: UMI Research Press, 1980.

———. "Scientific Criticism and *le beau moderne* of the Age of Science." *Art Criticism*, I, no. 1 (Spring 1979), 55–71.

Hamel, Maurice. "Le Salon de 1887." *Gazette des beaux-arts*, XXXV (1 June 1887), 473–511.

Hamilton, George Heard. *Manet and His Critics*. New Haven: Yale University Press, 1954.

———. *Painting and Sculpture in Europe, 1880–1940*. Harmondsworth, Middlesex: Penguin, 1967.

Helmholtz, Hermann von. *Optic physiologique*. Translated by Emile Javal and N. Th. Klein. Paris: V. Masson et fils, 1867.

Hennequin, Emile. *La Critique scientifique*. Paris: Perrin, 1888.

———. "La Critique scientifique des oeuvres d'art." *La Revue contemporaine*, IV (January 1886), 449–88; V (May 1886), 3–39, 197–215.

———. "L'Esthétique de Wagner et la doctrine Spencérienne." *La Revue Wagnérienne*, I (8 November 1885), 282–86.

———. *Etudes de critique scientifique: écrivains francisés*. Paris: Perrin, 1889.

———. *Etudes de critique scientifique: quelques écrivains français*. Paris: Perrin, 1889.

———. "Homage à Goya. " *Revue contemporaine*, I (January–April 1885), 307–8.

———. "Notes d'art, de la peinture, à propos d'une lettre de M. J.-F. Raffaëlli, I." *La Vie moderne*, VIII (1886), 724.

———. "Notes d'art, de la peinture, à propos d'une lettre de M. J.-F. Raffaëlli, II." *La Vie moderne*, VIII (1886), 746–47.

———. "Notes d'art, l'exposition des artistes indépendants." *La Vie moderne*, VIII (1886), 581–82.

———. "Notes d'art, l'exposition internationale, encore le Salon." *La Vie moderne*, VIII (1886), 499–500.

———. "Notes d'art, les impressionnistes." *La Vie moderne*, VIII (1886), 389–90.

———. "Notes d'art, le Salon." *La Vie moderne*, VIII (1886), 290–91.

———. "Notes d'art, le Salon, II." *La Vie moderne*, VIII (1886), 340–41.

———. "Notes d'art, oeuvres de Paul Baudry, les pastellistes, le musée du Luxembourg, soixante-cinq aquarelles de Gustave Moreau." *La Vie moderne*, VIII (1886), 242–43.

———. "Odilon Redon." *Revue littéraire et artistique*, V (4 March 1882).

Herban, Mathew, III. "Maurice Denis' 'Nouvel Ordre Classique' As Contained in His 'Théories' (1890–1910)." Ph.D. dissertation, University of Pennsylvania, 1972).

Herbert, Eugenia. *The Artist and Social Reform: France and Belgium, 1865–1898*. New Haven: Yale University Press, 1961.

Herbert, Robert L., and Eugenia W. Herbert. "Artists and Anarchism: Unpublished Letters of Pissarro, Signac and Others." *Burlington Magazine*, CII (November 1960), 473–82.

Hermann, Fritz. *Die Revue blanche und die Nabis*. Vols. I–II. Munich: Mikrokopie, 1959.

Hoffman, Robert. *More Than a Trial*. New York: Free Press, 1980.

Holt, Elizabeth. *From the Classicists to the Impressionists*. New York: Anchor, 1966.

Homer, William I. *Seurat and the Science of Painting*. Cambridge: MIT Press, 1964.

Houssaye, Henry. "Le Salon de 1882." *Revue des deux mondes*, LXI (1 June 1882), 561–92.

———. "Le Salon de 1884." *Revue des deux mondes*, LXIII (1 June 1884), 560–95.

Hughes, Robert. "Old Masters of the Modern." *Time* (14 January 1980), 73.

Humbert, Agnès. *Les Nabis et leur époque.* Geneva: Editions Pierre Cailler, 1954.

Huret, Jules. *Enquête sur l'évolution littéraire.* Paris: Charpentier, 1891.

Huysmans, Joris-Karl. *Against Nature.* Translated by Robert Baldick. Harmondsworth, Middlesex: Penguin, 1959.

———. *L'Art moderne.* Paris: Plon, 1883.

———. *Certains.* Paris: Tresse and Stock, 1889.

———. "Chronique d'art: les indépendantes." *La Revue indépendante,* III (April 1887), 51–57.

———. "La Genèse du peintre." *La Revue indépendante,* I (May 1884), 22–27.

Irvine, William. *The Boulanger Affair Reconsidered.* New York: Oxford University Press, 1989.

Jewish Museum. *The Dreyfus Affair: Art, Truth and Justice.* Edited by Norman Kleeblatt. Berkeley and Los Angeles: University of California Press, 1987.

Jirat-Wasiutynski, Vojtech. *Paul Gauguin in the Context of Symbolism.* New York: Garland, 1977.

Jullian, Philippe. *Dreamers of Decadence.* Translated by Robert Baldick. New York: Praeger, 1971.

———. *The Symbolists.* Translated by Mary Anne Stevens. Oxford: Phaidon, 1977.

Jullian, René. *Le Mouvement des arts du romantisme au symbolisme.* Paris: Albin Michel, 1979.

Kahn, Annette. *J.-K. Huysmans, Novelist, Poet and Art Critic.* Ann Arbor: UMI Research Press, 1987.

Kahn, Gustave. "De l'esthétique du verre polychrome." *La Vogue,* I (18 April 1886), 54–65.

———. "Exposition Puvis de Chavannes." *La Revue indépendante,* VI (January 1888), 142–51.

———. *Symbolistes et décadents.* Paris: Vanier, 1902.

Lafenestre, Georges. "Le Salon de 1887." *Revue des deux mondes,* LXXXI (1 June 1887), 604–39.

Larkin, Maurice. *Church and State After the Dreyfus Affair.* London: Macmillan, 1974.

Leclercq, Julien. "Albert Aurier." *Essais d'art libre,* II (November 1892), 201–8.

———. "Aux indépendants." *Mercure de France,* II (May 1891), 298–300.

———. "Beaux-Arts." *Mercure de France,* I (May 1890), 174–76.

———. "La Lutte pour les peintres." *Mercure de France,* XII (November 1894), 254–71.

Lecomte, Georges. "L'Esthopsychologie." *La Cravache parisienne,* no. 359 (15 September 1888), unpaginated.

———. "Salon des XX, conférence de M. Georges Lecomte, des tendances de la peinture moderne." *L'Art moderne,* XII (14 February 1892), 49–51; (21 February 1892), 57–58; (28 February 1892), 65–68.

———. "Le Salon du Champ-de-Mars." *L'Art dans les deux mondes,* no. 26 (16 May 1891), 309.

Lefort, Paul. "L'Exposition nationale de 1883." *Gazette des beaux-arts,* XXVIII (1 October 1883), 273–78.

Lefranc, F. "Le Naturalisme contemporain d'après une conférence de M. Brunetière." *L'Art,* XLVIII (1890), 201–5.

Lehmann, A. G. *The Symbolist Aesthetic in France.* Oxford: Basil Blackwell, 1968.

Lemonnier, Camille. "Une tentation de St. Antoine de Félicien Rops." *La Revue indépendante,* I (June 1884), 125–31.

Lethève, Jacques. *Impressionnistes et symbolistes devant la presse.* Paris: Armand Colin, 1959.

Levin, Miriam. *Republican Art and Ideology in Late Nineteenth-Century France.* Ann Arbor: UMI Research Press, 1986.

Levine, Steven Z. *Monet and His Critics.* New York: Garland, 1976.

Lövgren, Sven. *The Genesis of Modernism.* Bloomington: Indiana University Press, 1971.

Lucie-Smith, Edward. *Symbolist Art.* New York: Oxford University Press, 1972.

Lunn, Margaret. "G.-Albert Aurier, Critic and Theorist of Symbolist Art." Ph.D. dissertation, Massachusetts Institute of Technology, 1982.

McConkey, Kenneth. "The Bouguereau of the Naturalists: Bastien Lepage and British Art." *Art History,* I (September 1978), 371–82.

McElrath, Damian, O.F.M. *The Syllabus of Pius IX, Some Reactions in England.* Louvain: Bibliothèque de l'université, Bureau de la Revue, 1964.

Maingon, Charles. *L'Univers artistique de J.-K. Huysmans.* Paris: Nizet, 1977.

Mallock, William Hurrell. *Is Life Worth Living?* Chicago: Belford, Clarke, 1879.

Marlais, Michael. "In 1891: Observations on the Nature of Symbolist Art Criticism." *Arts Magazine,* LXI (January 1987), 88–93.

———. "Seurat et ses amis de l'Ecole des Beaux-Arts." *Gazette des beaux-arts,* CXIV (October 1989), 153–68.

Martin, Elizabeth. "The Symbolist Criticism of Painting." Ph.D. dissertation, Bryn Mawr College, 1948.

"Matérialisme." *La Revue indépendante,* I (May 1884), 1–4.

Mathews, Patricia. "Aurier and Van Gogh: Criticism and Response." *Art Bulletin,* LXVIII (March 1986), 94–104.

———. *Aurier's Symbolist Art Criticism and Theory.* Ann Arbor: UMI Research Press, 1986.

Mauclair, Camille. "Albert Besnard et le symbolisme concret." *La Revue indépendante,* XXI (October 1891), 6–30.

———. "Armand Point." *Mercure de France,* IX (December 1893), 331–36.

———. "Art." *Mercure de France,* XVIII (April 1896), 157–59.

———. "Art." *Mercure de France,* XVIII (May 1896), 314–19.

———. "Art." *Mercure de France,* XVIII (June 1896), 465–68.

———. "Art." *Mercure de France,* XIX (July 1896), 186–89.

———. "Art." *Mercure de France,* XIX (August 1896), 379–80.

———. "Art." *Mercure de France,* XIX (September 1896), 562–64.

———. "Beaux-Arts." *La Revue indépendante,* XXI (December 1891), 428–29.

———. "Beaux-Arts." *La Revue indépendante,* XXII (January 1892), 143–44.

———. "Beaux-Arts." *La Revue indépendante,* XXII (March 1892), 415–18.

———. "Beaux-Arts." *La Revue indépendante,* XXIII (April 1892), 136–42.

———. "Beaux-Arts." *La Revue indépendante,* XXIII (May 1892), 283–88.

———. "Beaux-Arts, l'exposition Claude Monet." *La Revue indépendante,* XIX (May 1891), 267–69.

———. "Choses d'art." *Mercure de France,* X (January 1894), 92–93.

———. "Choses d'art." *Mercure de France,* X (February 1894), 189–90.

———. "Choses d'art." *Mercure de France,* X (March 1894), 284–86.

———. "Choses d'art." *Mercure de France,* X (April 1894), 377–79.

———. "Choses d'art." *Mercure de France,* XI (May 1894), 92–95.

———. "Choses d'art." *Mercure de France,* XI (July 1894), 300–301.

———. "Choses d'art." *Mercure de France,* XII (September 1894), 91–93.

———. "Choses d'art." *Mercure de France,* XII (October 1894), 189–91.

————. "Choses d'art." *Mercure de France,* xII (November 1894), 284–86.

————. "Choses d'art." *Mercure de France,* xII (December 1894), 383–86.

————. "Choses d'art." *Mercure de France,* xIII (January 1895), 118–21.

————. "Choses d'art." *Mercure de France,* xIII (February 1895), 235–38.

————. "Choses d'art." *Mercure de France,* xIII (March 1895), 358–59.

————. "Choses d'art." *Mercure de France,* xIv (April 1895), 100–101.

————. "Choses d'art." *Mercure de France,* xIv (May 1895), 242–44.

————. "Choses d'art." *Mercure de France,* xIv (June 1895), 357–59.

————. "Choses d'art." *Mercure de France,* xvI (November 1895), 253–55.

————. "Choses d'art." *Mercure de France,* xvI (December 1895), 410–13.

————. "Choses d'art." *Mercure de France,* xvII (January 1896), 129–31.

————. "Choses d'art." *Mercure de France,* xvII (February 1896), 265–69.

————. "Choses d'art." *Mercure de France,* xvII (March 1896), 418–20.

————. *Claude Monet.* Paris: F. Rieder, 1924.

————. "Critique de la peinture." *La Nouvelle revue,* xcvI (September–October 1895), 314–33.

————. "Destinées de la peinture française." *La Nouvelle revue,* xcIII (March–April 1895), 363–77.

————. *Eleusis, causeries sur la cité intérieure.* Paris: Perrin, 1894.

————. "Expositions récentes." *Mercure de France,* x (March 1894), 266–71.

————. *La Farce de l'art vivant.* Paris: Editions de la nouvelle revue critique, 1929.

————. "Fraternités idéales." *Mercure de France,* vII (February 1893), 129–35.

————. "Lettre sur la peinture." *Mercure de France,* xI (July 1894), 270–75.

————. "Maurice Beaubourg." *Mercure de France,* Ix (October 1893), 139–43.

————. "Notes simples sur Paul Vogler." *Essais d'art libre,* III (April–May 1893), 128–32.

————. "Notes sur l'idée pure." *Mercure de France,* vI (September 1892), 42–46.

————. "La Peinture musicienne et la fusion des arts." *Revue bleue,* xvIII (23 August 1902), 297–303.

————. "Pour l'idéalisme." *Essais d'art libre,* I (July 1892), 251–58.

————. "Préface." *Quatrième exposition des peintres impressionnistes et symbolistes.* Paris: Galerie Le Barc de Boutteville, 1893, 3–8. Reprinted in *Modern Art in Paris: Post-Impressionist Group Exhibitions.* New York: Garland, 1982, n.p..

————. "Préface." *Cinquième exposition des peintres impressionnistes et symbolistes.* Paris: Galerie Le Barc de Boutteville, 1893, 3–6. Reprinted in *Modern Art in Paris: Post-Impressionist Group Exhibitions.* New York: Garland, 1982, n.p..

————. "Préface." *Sixième exposition des peintres impressionnistes et symbolistes.* Paris: Galerie Le Barc de Boutteville, 1894, 3–6. Reprinted in *Modern Art in Paris: Post-Impressionist Group Exhibitions.* New York: Garland, 1982, n.p..

————. "La Réaction nationaliste en art et l'ignorance de l'homme de lettres." *La Revue,* LIv (15 January 1905), 151–74.

————. "Réponse à M. Emile Bernard." *Mercure de France,* xv (July 1895), 91–96.

————. "Le Salon du Champs-de-Mars." *La Revue indépendante,* xxIII (May 1892), 193–208.

————. "Les Salons de 1894." *Mercure de France,* xI (June 1894), 157–62.

————. "Le Snobisme et le néo-mysticisme." *La Nouvelle revue,* xcv (July–August 1895), 141–51.

————. "Souvenirs sur le mouvement symboliste en France, 1884–1897." *La Nouvelle revue,* cvIII (September–October 1897), 670–93; (November–December 1897), 79–100.

————. "Le Voyage d'Urien." *Mercure de France,* vIII (August 1893), 361–65.

Mauduit, Anne-Marie, and Jean Mauduit. *La France contre la France: la séparation de l'Eglise et de l'Etat, 1900–1906.* Paris: Plon, 1984.

Mauner, George. *The Nabis: Their History and Their Art, 1888–1896.* New York: Garland, 1978.

Mazel, Henri. "Le Problème religieux." *L'Ermitage,* i (May 1890), 59–69.

———. "Les Temps héroiques du symbolisme." *Mercure de France,* xlviii (December 1903), 666–74.

Mellerio, André. *Le Mouvement idéaliste en peinture.* Paris: H. Floury, 1896.

Mercure de France, vi (November 1892). Memorial issue containing several articles on Albert Aurier.

Michaud, Guy. *Message poétique du symbolisme.* Paris: Nizet, 1947.

Michel, André. "Exposition de M. Puvis de Chavannes." *Gazette des beaux-arts,* xxxvii (January 1888), 37–44.

———. "Le Salon de 1884." *L'Art,* xxxvi (1884), 161–67, 181–86, 201–13, 227–37; xxxvii (1884), 9–16, 31–39.

———. "Salon de 1888." *Gazette des beaux-arts,* xxxvii (June 1888), 441–54; xxxviii (July 1888), 21–31; (August 1888), 137–53.

Mirbeau, Octave. "Paul Gauguin." *L'Art moderne,* xi (22 March 1891), 92–94.

Montalant, Delphine. "Alexandre Séon, peintre symboliste." *L'Oeil,* no. 362 (September 1985), 40–45.

Monteil, Edgar. "*Le Manuel d'instruction laïque* et la critique." *La Revue indépendante,* i (May 1884), 9–21.

Moréas, Jean. *Les Premières armes du symbolisme.* Paris: Vanier, 1889.

Morice, Charles. *Du sens religieux de la poésie.* Geneva: Eggimann, 1893.

———. *Lettre à mes amis sur quelques points de durable actualité, I—Le Retour ou: mes raisons.* Paris: Messein, 1913.

———. *La Littérature de tout à l'heure.* Paris: Perrin, 1889.

Natanson, Thadée. *Peints à leur tour.* Paris: Albin Michel, 1948.

Naubert-Riser, Constance. "La Critique des années 1890, impasse méthodologique ou renouvellement des modèles théoriques?" *La Critique d'art en France, 1850–1900,* ed. Jean-Paul Bouillon. Saint-Etienne: Université de Saint-Etienne, Centre Interdisciplinaire d'Etudes et de Recherches sur l'Expression Contemporaine, 1989, 193–204.

Nochlin, Linda. *Impressionism and Post-Impressionism, 1874–1904.* Englewood Cliffs, N.J.: Prentice-Hall, 1966.

———. *Realism and Tradition in Art, 1848–1900.* Englewood Cliffs, N.J.: Prentice-Hall, 1966.

Ollendorff, Gustave. "L'Exposition nationale de 1883." *Revue des deux mondes,* liii (November 1883), 436–53.

Orton, Fred, and Griselda Pollock. "Les Données bretonnantes: la prairie de répresentation." *Art History,* 3 (September 1980), 314–43.

Orwicz, Michael. "Confrontations et clivages dans les discours des critiques du salon, 1885–1889." *La Critique d'art en France, 1850–1900,* ed. Jean-Paul Bouillon. Saint-Etienne: Université de Saint-Etienne, Centre Interdisciplinaire d'Etudes et de Recherches sur l'Expression Contemporaine, 1989, 177–92.

Osgood, Samuel. *French Royalism Under the Third and Fourth Republics.* The Hague: Martinus Nijhoff, 1960.

Paradise, Jo Anne Culler. *Gustave Geffroy and the Criticism of Painting.* New York: Garland, 1985.

Partin, Malcolm. *Waldeck-Rousseau, Combes and the Church: The Politics of Anti-Clericalism, 1899–1905.* Durham: Duke University Press, 1969.

Péladan, Joséphin. *L'Art idéaliste et mystique.* Paris: E. Sansot, 1909.

———. *Le Décadence esthétique, l'art ochlocratique, Salons de 1882 et de 1883.* Paris: Camille Dalou, 1888.

———. "L'Esthétique à l'exposition nationale des beaux-arts." *L'Artiste,* LIII (October 1883), 257–304; (November 1883), 353–86; (December 1883), 433–75.

———. *Réfutation esthétique de Taine.* Paris: Mercure de France, 1906.

Petit, Jacques. *Léon Bloy.* Paris: Desclée de Brouwer, 1966.

Peyre, Henry. *Qu'est-ce que le symbolisme?* Paris: Presses Universitaires de France, 1974.

Peyrot, Maurice. "Symbolistes et décadents." *La Nouvelle revue,* XLIX (November–December 1887), 122–46.

Pickvance, Ronald. *Van Gogh in Saint-Rémy and Auvers.* New York: Metropolitan Museum of Art, Abrams, 1986.

Pierrot, Jean. *The Decadent Imagination, 1880–1900.* Chicago: University of Chicago Press, 1981.

Pincus-Witten, Robert. *Occult Symbolism in France, Joséphin Péladan and the Salons de la Rose-Croix.* New York: Garland, 1976.

Pissarro, Camille. *Letters to His Son Lucien.* Ed. by John Rewald. New York: Pantheon, 1943.

Praviel, Armand. "Un ecrivain d'art, Alphonse Germain." *L'Occident,* IV (December 1903), 281–85.

Pujo, Maurice. "Les Artistes de l'âme, réponse à M. Octave Mirbeau." *L'Art et la vie,* V (1896), 186–89.

Raynaud, Ernest. *La Mêlée symboliste.* Paris: La Renaissance du livre, 1920.

Redon, Odilon. *A soi-même.* Paris: Librairie José Corti, 1961.

Retté, Adolphe. Letter to the Editor. *Mercure de France,* XII (December 1894), 390–91.

———. "L'Art et l'anarchie." *La Jeune belgique,* XII (March 1893), 104–7. Originally published in *La Plume,* V (1 February 1893), 45–46.

———. *Le Symbolisme, anecdotes et souvenirs.* Paris: Vanier, 1903.

Rewald, John. "Félix Fénéon." *Gazette des beaux-arts,* XXXII (July–August 1947), 45–62; XXXIII (February 1948), 107–26.

———. "Odilon Redon." *Odilon Redon, Gustave Moreau, Rodolphe Bresdin.* New York: Museum of Modern Art, 1961.

———. *Post-Impressionism.* 3d ed. New York: Museum of Modern Art, 1978.

Rey, Robert. *La Renaissance du sentiment classique dans la peinture française à la fin du XIXe siècle.* Paris: Les Beaux-Arts, 1931.

Richard, Noël. *A l'aube du symbolisme.* Paris: Nizet, 1961.

———. *Le Mouvement décadent.* Paris: Nizet, 1968.

Rod, Edouard. *Les Idées morales du temps présent.* Paris: Perrin, 1911.

———. *Nouvelles études sur le XIXe siècle.* Paris: Perrin, 1899.

Roger-Ballu. "Le Salon de 1881." *La Nouvelle revue,* X (May–June 1881), 450–51.

Rood, Ogden. *Modern Chromatics.* New York: Appleton, 1879.

Rookmaaker, H. R. *Gauguin and 19th-Century Art Theory.* Amsterdam: Swets and Zeitlinger, 1972.

Roskill, Mark. *Van Gogh, Gauguin, and the Impressionist Circle.* Greenwich, Conn.: New York Graphic Society, 1970.

Royal Academy of Fine Arts, London. *Post-Impressionism*. London: Harper and Row, 1979–80.

Rusic, Svetozar. "Biographie d'Albert Aurier." *Dossiers du collège de pataphysique*, no. 15 (1961), 47–51.

Seager, Frederick. *The Boulanger Affair*. Ithaca: Cornell University Press, 1969.

Seillière, Ernest. *Léon Bloy, psychologie d'un mystique*. Paris: Editions de la nouvelle revue critique, 1936.

Shiff, Richard. *Cézanne and the End of Impressionism*. Chicago: University of Chicago Press, 1984.

———. "The End of Impressionism." In *The New Painting, Impressionism 1874–1886*. San Francisco: The Fine Arts Museums of San Francisco, 1986, 61–89.

———. "The End of Impressionism: A Study in Theories of Artistic Expression." *Art Quarterly*, n.s. I (Autumn 1978), 338–78.

Signac, Paul. *D'Eugène Delacroix au néo-impressionnisme*. Paris: Collection Savoir, 1978.

———. "Extraits du journal inédit de Paul Signac, I, 1894–95." *Gazette des beaux-arts*, XXXVI (July–September 1949), 97–128.

[———.] "Variétés, impressionnistes et révolutionnaires." *La Revolte*, IV (June 1891), 3–4.

Sloane, Joseph. *French Painting, Between the Past and the Present*. Princeton: Princeton University Press, 1951.

Smith, Paul. "Paul Adam, *Soi* et les 'Peintres impressionnistes': la genèse d'un discours moderniste." *Revue de l'art*, no. 82 (1988), 39–50.

Soulier, Gustave. "Les Artistes de l'âme, Alphonse Osbert." *L'Art et la vie*, IV (1895), 502–5.

———. "Les Artistes de l'âme, Andhré des Gachons." *L'Art et la vie*, IV (1894), 479–84.

———. "Les Artistes de l'âme, Armand Point." *L'Art et la vie*, III (1894), 171–77.

Sternhell, Zeev. *La Droit révolutionnaire, 1885–1914: les origines françaises du fascisme*. Paris: Editions du Seuil, 1978.

Symons, Arthur. *The Symbolist Movement in Literature*. New York: Dutton, 1919.

Taine, Hippolyte. *Philosophie de l'art*. 6th ed. Paris: Hachette, 1893.

Thiébault-Sisson. "Puvis de Chavannes et son oeuvre." *La Nouvelle revue*, XLIX (November–December 1887), 643–48.

Thomson, Belinda. "Camille Pissarro and Symbolism: Some thoughts prompted by the recent discovery of an annotated article." *Burlington Magazine*, CXXIV, no. 946 (January 1982), 14–23.

———. *The Post-Impressionists*. London: Phaidon, 1989.

Thomson, Richard. *Seurat*. Oxford: Phaidon, 1985.

Tissot, Ernest. *Les Evolutions de la critique française*. Geneva: H. Georg, 1890.

Toche, Louis. "Le 'Décadent' au Salon." *Le Décadent*, I (9 May 1886), unpaginated.

Tucker, Paul. *Monet in the Nineties*. New Haven: Yale University Press, 1989.

L'Université de Saint-Etienne. *La Critique d'art en France, 1850–1900*. Ed. by Jean-Paul Bouillon. Saint-Etienne: Centre Interdisciplinaire d'Etudes et de Recherches sur l'Expression Contemporaine, 1989.

L'Université d'Orléans. *Les Ecrivains et l'affaire Dreyfus*. Paris: Presses Universitaires de France, 1983.

University of Kansas Museum of Art. *Les Mardis: Stéphane Mallarmé and the Artists of His Circle*. Lawrence, Kans.: University of Kansas Museum of Art, 1965.

Vanor, Georges. *L'Art symboliste*. Paris: Vanier, 1889.

Vazeilles, Patrick. "De Saint-Rémy au collège du cèdre." *Revue municipale du Vésinet*, no. 56 (September 1987), 60–67.

Venturi, Lionello. *Les Archives de l'impressionnisme*. Paris: Durand-Ruel, 1939.

Véron, Eugène. *L'Esthétique*. Paris: C. Reinwald, 1878.

———. "Salon de 1885." *L'Art*, xxxviii (1885), 193–203.

Vogüé, Eugène Melchior, vicomte de. "A travers l'exposition, IX, dernièrs remarques." *Revue des deux mondes*, xcvi (1 November 1889), 173–95.

———. "La Littérature réaliste." *Revue des deux mondes*, lxxv (15 May 1886), 288–313.

Weber, Eugen. *Action Française, Royalism and Reaction in Twentieth-Century France*. Stanford: Stanford University Press, 1962.

Weisberg, Gabriel P. "From the Real to the Unreal: Religious Painting and Photography at the Salons of the Third Republic." *Arts Magazine*, lx (December 1985), 58–63.

———. "P.A.J. Dagnan-Bouveret and the Illusion of Photographic Naturalism." *Arts Magazine*, lvi (March 1982), 100–105.

———. "P.A.J. Dagnan-Bouveret, Jules Bastien-Lepage, and the Naturalist Instinct." *Arts Magazine*, lvi (April 1982), 70–76.

———. *The Realist Tradition: French Painting and Drawing, 1830–1900*. Cleveland: Cleveland Museum of Art, 1980.

———. "Vestiges of the Past: The Brittany Pardons of Late Nineteenth-Century French Painters." *Arts Magazine*, lv (November 1980), 134–38.

Weyl, Fernand. "Alexandre Séon." *L'Art et la vie*, iv (1894), 406–13.

———. "Les Artistes de l'âme, L. Lévy-Dhurmer." *L'Art et la vie*, v (1896), 120–30.

Wilson, Stephen. *Ideology and Experience: Antisemitism in France at the Time of the Dreyfus Affair*. Rutherford, N.J.: Fairleigh Dickinson University Press, 1982.

Wyzewa, Téodor de. "Une critique." *La Revue indépendante*, i (November 1886), 49–78.

———. "Notes sur la peinture wagnérienne et le Salon de 1886." *La Revue wagnérienne*, ii (May 1886), 100–113.

———. "Voyage aux primitifs allemands." *La Revue indépendante*, iv (September 1887), 292–323; (November 1887), 201–35.

Zeldin, Theodore. *France, 1848–1945*. Vols. i–ii. Oxford: Clarendon Press, 1973–77.

Zemel, Carol M. *The Formation of a Legend, Van Gogh Criticism, 1890–1920*. Ann Arbor: UMI Research Press, 1980.

Zola, Emile. *Le Bon combat*. Paris: Collection Savoir Hermann, 1974.

———. "M. H. Taine, artiste." *Oeuvres complètes, x, oeuvres critiques*. Paris: Circle du livre précieux, 1968.

INDEX

Académie française, 7, 14, 41
Action française, 182
Adam, Paul, 27, 53, 65, 79, 85
    preface to Georges Vanor's *L'Art symbol-iste*, 67–68
Aman-Jean, Edmond, 69–70, 190
    St. Geneviève Before Paris, 49, 51, Fig. 8
    St. Julian the Hospitator, 49, Fig. 7
anarchism, 53
antinaturalism, 5–9, 26–41
antipositivism, 58–65
anti-Semitism, 15, 22–23, 103, 182, 217–18
L'Art, 35, 121, 129
art criticism
    antinaturalism in, 30–41
    antipositivism in, 58–65
    Catholic revival in, 44–52
    conservative turn of, 149–51
    Maurice Denis's, 187–202, 205–6, 215, 218–19
    determinist, 60–65
    Alphonse Germain's, 171–82
    Joris-Karl Huysmans's, 86–91
    Camille Mauclair's, 151–71
    new idealism in, 41–44
    Joséphin Péladan's, 139–45
    and politics, 55–58
    scientism and, 65–72
    symbolism in, 77–80
    "synthèse" in, 72–76, 136–37

Art et critique, 189
L'Art et la vie, 190, 192
L'Artiste, 35, 56, 121, 140
"Les Artistes de l'âme," 190–91
L'Art moderne, 172, 173
Aurier, Albert, 26, 32, 72, 73, 78, 97, 107, 122, 205
    attacks materialism, 68–69, 112–14, 116–17
    and determinist art criticism, 61, 64, 113–14
    and Félix Fénéon, 108–19
    on Paul Gauguin, 40, 106, 135, 137
    on Jean-Jacques Henner, 119–22
    and idealism, 41, 43, 122–26, 137–39
    and impressionism, 39–40
    influences on, 126–47
    on Claude Monet, 39–40
    and neo-impressionism, 109–12
    as symbolist art critic, 105–6
    on Hippolyte Taine, 61, 113–14
    on Vincent van Gogh, 115–16
Aynard, Edouard, 137, 138–39

Baju, Anatole, 43, 54, 83–84, 85, 126–32
Barbey d'Aurevilly, Jules, 15–16, 19
Barre, André, 153
Barrès, Maurice, 102, 215, 217
Bastien-Lepage, Jules, 6, 35
Baudelaire, Charles, 30, 83

Bénédite, Léonce, 135
Bergson, Henri, 11
Bernard, Claude, 8
Bernard, Emile, 57, 107, 168
Bigot, Charles, 46, 123
Blanc, Charles, 33, 66, 74
Blavatsky, Helena Petrovna, 12n. 14
Blémont, Emile (Emile Petitdidier), 121
Bloy, Léon, 19, 20, 45, 52, 53, 206, 207
   and Catholicism of the Middle Ages, 21–22
   and Rodolphe Salis, 16–18
Bougot, A., 62
Bouguereau, William, 129
   Annuniciation, 186, Fig. 19
Boulanger, General Georges, 23, 53, 102
Boulanger, Louis, 128
Bourget, Paul, 45–46, 62, 81–82
Breton, Jules, 6
Brinn Gaubast, Louis-Pilate de, 90n. 38, 128
Brittany pardon paintings, 47
Bruckë, Ernst Wilhelm Ritter von, 66
Brunetière, Ferdinand, 19, 29, 46, 64
   and Aurier, 70, 124–26
   and idealism, 42
   and Hippolyte Taine, 63
   and Emile Zola, 27–29
Bussy, Charles de, 15

Cabanel, Alexandre, 82
Café Volpini exhibition, 93
Caro, Elme Marie, 12
Carrière, Eugène, 117–18
Cartault, Augustin, 66
Catholic Church
   and Leo XIII, 14, 18–19, 20
   and Pius IX, 13–14, 20, 207
   and positivism, 12
   and Ernest Renan, 14–17
   and the Third Republic, 209–10
Catholicism
   anti-intellectualism in, 19–22
   and art criticism, 44–52
   and *Le Chat noir*, 17–18
   Maurice Denis's, 202–9
   Alphonse Germain's, 180–81
   revival of, 8, 19–20, 103
   and symbolism, 51–52
Cazin, Jean-Charles, 47–48

Hagar and Ishmael, 47, Fig. 5
Tobias and the Angel, 47, Fig. 4
Cézanne, Paul, 102, 180, 182, 190–91, 194, 216
Champfleury (Jules Husson), 8
Chat noir, Le, 16, 17–18, 94, 100
Chennevières, Marquis de, 135
Cherbuliez, Victor, 73
Chesneau, Ernest, 62
Chevreul, Michel-Eugène, 65
Claudel, Paul, 19
Clemenceau, Georges, 211
Cochin, Denys, 214
Combes, Emile, 209, 210, 213
Comte, Auguste, 9, 10
Constant, Benjamin, 86, 128
Coulon, Marcel, 127
Couturat, Gaston, 123
Couturat, Jules, 123
Cravache parisienne, La, 64, 75, 78, 84, 103

Dagnan-Bouveret, Pascal-Adolphe-Jean, 34, 118
   Pardon in Brittany, 47, Fig. 3
   Wedding at the Photographer's, 31, Fig. 2
Darwin, Charles, 8
Daudet, Léon, 19
decadence, 80–84, 126–32
Décadent, Le, 85, 106, 109, 118, 126–32
decoration, 135–37
Denis, Marthe, 212–13
Denis, Maurice, 2, 59, 72, 78
   and anti-Semitism, 217–18, 218n. 101
   art and nature in theory of, 199–200
   "Les Arts à Rome, ou le méthode classique," 198
   and Albert Aurier, 196
   on Paul Cézanne, 190–91, 194, 216
   conservative style, 193–94
   and Dreyfus affair, 211
   "Les Elèves d'Ingres," 198
   and Fra Angelico, 197, 203, 204
   and Greco-Latin beauty, 201–2
   and idealism, 192
   and Camille Mauclair, 218–19
   as modernist, 187–90
   and Joséphin Péladan, 192
   and the prieuré, 202, 212
   and religion, 202–9
   as royalist, 213

and tradition, 6, 194–202
Catholic Mystery, 51, 192–93, 205, Fig. 9
Dessert in the Garden, 212, Fig. 21
Exaltation of the Holy Cross, 185–86, 192,
    204, 212, 219, Figs. 16, 17 a–f
Homage to Cézanne, 189, Fig. 20
Our Lady of the Schools, 213–14, Fig. 22
Sunlight on the Terrace, 186, 212, 214, Fig.
    18
Desjardins, Paul, 7–9
Dreyfus affair, 181, 209–11, 215–16
Drumont, Edouard, 22–23, 23 n. 37, 53, 182
Dumas, Alexandre, 8
Dumur, Louis, 43, 123
Dupanloup, Monsignor, 14, 15

L'Echo de Paris, 106
L'Echo de Seine et Oise, 214
Ecole des Beaux-Arts, 31, 41, 175
Enquête sur l'évolution littéraire, 29
Entretiens politiques et littéraires, 172
L'Ermitage, 52, 103, 182, 218
d'Escaurailles, Albert. *See* Aurier, Albert
d'Escaurailles, Marc. *See* Aurier, Albert
des Esseintes, Duc Jean Floressas, 81

Fénéon, Félix, 32, 34, 53, 61–62, 116
    and Albert Aurier, 108–19
    and Paul Gauguin, 91–102, 104
    and Alphonse Germain, 177
    and Joris-Karl Huysmans, 87–91
    and impressionism, 38–39
    Les Impressionnistes en 1886, 1–2
    and scientific jargon, 65, 67, 114–15
Figaro, Le, 129
Filiger, Charles, 139
fin de siècle, 5–6, 52
Flaubert, Gustave, 8
Fouillée, Alfred, 11
Fourcaud, Louis de, 137
Foyer, journal de famille, Le, 140
France, Anatole, 29, 209–10
France juive, La, 22

Gallicanism, 13
Gauguin, Paul, 2, 6, 26, 156, 163, 205
    and Albert Aurier, 40, 106, 135, 137
    and Félix Fénéon, 91–102, 104
    and synthesis, 72, 75–76, 137
Gautier, Théophile, 83

Gazette des beaux-arts, 123, 129, 135, 136
Germain, Alphonse, 171–72
    and Albert Aurier, 179
    and conservative Catholicism, 180–81
    and Félix Fénéon, 177, 179
    on Paul Gauguin, 75–76, 180
    and nationalist themes, 182
    on neo-impressionism, 172–74
    and Joséphin Péladan, 178–79
    and Alexandre Séon, 174–79
Gide, André, 198
Gogh, Vincent van, 2, 115–16, 155 n. 16,
    180, 182
Goldwater, Robert, 25–26
Goncourt, Edmond de, 23 n. 37
Gourmont, Rémy de, 71, 123, 127, 139–40
Guéroult, Georges, 66
Guyau, Jean Marie, 67

Hamel, Maurice, 138
Helmholtz, Hermann von, 66
Hennequin, Emile, 61, 63–64, 79
Henner, Jean-Jacques, 35, 118, 119–22
    Nymph by a Fountain, Fig. 10
Henry, Charles, 41, 66, 67, 68, 112–13
Houssaye, Henry, 34, 35
Huret, Jules, 29, 106, 109
Huysmans, Joris-Karl, 27, 48, 56, 62
    and Léon Bloy, 18, 52
    and Catholicism, 19, 21, 51, 103
    and Félix Fénéon, 87–91
    on naturalism, in painting, 31–32, 37–38
    as symbolist art critic, 78
    and the symbolists, 86–87

idealism, 2, 25, 26, 27
    Edmond Aman-Jean and, 69–70
    and antinaturalism, 6–7
    Albert Aurier and, 41, 43, 122–26, 137–
        39
    Anatole Baju and, 43, 84
    Ferdinand Brunetière and, 42
    new, 41–44
    Joséphin Péladan and, 142–43
    and politics, 53–58
idéiste, 138
impressionism, 6, 35–41, 154, 161–63, 191
Ingres, Jean-Auguste-Dominique, 186, 198
Italian primitives, 50, 133–35, 186

Journal des débats, Le, 8

Kahn, Gustave, 53, 65, 79, 80, 83
  attacks decadents, 85
  "De l'esthétique du verre polychrome," 67
  on Joris-Karl Huysmans, 86
  interviewed by Jules Huret, 109

Lafenestre, Georges, 36
Lagarde, Pierre, 128
Latinity, nationalist theme of, 182, 217
Laurens, Jean Paul, 83
Le Barc de Boutteville gallery, 111
Leclerq, Julien, 111, 127, 165–66
Lecomte, Georges, 64, 75, 98, 99
Lefort, Paul, 123
Lehmann, A. G., 153
Lelong, Jacques. *See* Albert Aurier
Lemaitre, Jules, 29
Lemonnier, Camille, 89
Leo XIII, Pope, 14, 18–19, 20
literary influence in painting and art criticism, 97–99, 189, 222
Littré, Emile, 9, 14, 15

Mallarmé, Stéphane, 58, 222
Manet, Edouard, 6, 35–36, 37
Mathews, Patricia, 126, 127
Matisse, Henri, 201–2, 219
Mauclair, Camille
  and Albert Besnard, 157
  conservatism of, 152–53, 152n. 7
  and the Dreyfus affair, 170
  and Paul Gauguin, 156, 163
  on impressionism, 152, 154, 161–63
  and Julien Leclerq, 165–67
  at the *Mercure de France*, 158–68
  on nationalism, 218
  "Notes sur l'idée pure," 158–59
  and Armand Point, 159–61
  at the *Revue indépendante*, 154–57
  and Georges-Antoine Rochegrosse, 164
  and the Rose + Croix Salon, 156
  and socialism, 170
  and symbolism, 153–54, 169–70
Maurras, Charles, 182, 215, 217
Mazel, Henri, 52
Mellerio, André, 1–2, 43–44
Mercure de France, 78, 103, 106, 109, 139, 149, 152, 154
  Camille Mauclair at, 158–68
Michel, André, 33–34, 42, 46, 49–50
  on Puvis de Chavannes, 75n. 160, 136n. 94, 138

Middle Ages, 21–22, 50
Mirbeau, Octave, 98n. 61, 100–101
Mithouard, Adrien, 214, 217, 218
Moderniste illustré, Le, 78, 106, 119, 121
Monet, Claude, 39–40, 152, 154
Moniteur des arts, Le, 172
Monteil, Edgar, 44
Moréas, Jean, 8, 85
Moreau, Gustave, 8, 38, 82
Moreau de Tours, Georges
  A *Stigmatization in the Middle Ages*, 48, Fig. 6
Morice, Charles, 8, 27–29, 42, 51, 52, 59, 64, 72, 103, 125

Nain jaune, Le, 15
nationalism, 181–82, 209, 214–18
naturalism, 5–9, 26, 30–31, 47–48, 99–101, 165
neo-impressionism, 86, 87, 90, 91, 100, 109–12, 172–79
Nouvelle revue, La, 29, 137, 151, 152, 168–69

L'Occident, 217, 218

Péladan, Joséphin, 24, 33, 48, 50, 54, 63, 69, 79, 90
  L'Art ochlocratique, 140
  and Albert Aurier, 139–47
  on Catholicism in art, 44–45
  on democracy's effect upon art, 55–56
  and Maurice Denis, 192, 204, 207
  and Alphonse Germain, 178–79
  idealism, 42, 142–43
  on impressionism and Edouard Manet, 35–36
  his romanticism, 144–45
  on synthesis, 73–74, 144
Pissarro, Camille, 6, 98, 99, 106, 154n. 14
Pius IX, Pope, 13–14, 20, 207
Pléiade, La, 106
Plume, La, 52, 78, 103, 106, 172
Point, Armand, 190
positivism, 9–12, 14–17, 58–65
Punch, 13
Puvis de Chavannes, Pierre, 2, 6, 8, 50
  Albert Aurier influenced by criticism of, 132–39
  synthesis in criticism of, 74–75

Ravachol (François Claudius Koenigstein), 53n. 90
Redon, Odilon, 38, 64, 88
Renan, Ernest, 14–17, 47
Renoir, Auguste, 106, 205
Rerum Novarum, papal encyclical, 18
Retté, Adolphe, 19, 51, 56–57, 108, 166
Révolte, La, 100
Revue blanche, 103, 149, 216
Revue bleue, 7, 8
Revue contemporaine, 63, 102
Revue des deux mondes, 27, 30, 36, 103, 126
Revue encyclopédique, 106
Revue indépendante, 27, 51, 56, 78, 79, 84, 86, 87, 91, 102, 103, 106, 109, 116, 123
   Camille Mauclair and, 154–58
Revue wagnérienne, 56, 79, 102
Rochefoucaud, Antoine de la, 140
Rochegrosse, Georges-Antoine
   The Knight Among the Flowers, 164, Fig. 11
Roger-Ballu, 74, 137n. 96
Roll, Alfred Philippe, 128
Rood, Ogden, 66
Rookmaaker, H. H., 72–73
Rops, Félicien, 38, 82
Rose + Croix Salon, 101–2, 139–40, 156

Saint-Graal, Le, 172
Salis, Rodolphe, 16–18
Salon, 30–34, 46–51, 82–83, 101, 107, 142
   Albert Aurier and, 118–19, 127–28, 129–30
Salon, Rosicrucian. *See* Rose + Croix Salon
scientism and art criticism, 65–72
Second Empire, 10
Séon, Alexandre, 174–79, 190
   Despair of the Chimera, 178, Fig. 13
   Holiday, 178, Fig. 12
   Portrait of Joséphin Péladan, 178, Fig. 14
   The Return Home, 178, Fig. 15
Sérusier, Paul, 71
Seurat, Georges, 2, 87, 114–15, 175–77
Signac, Paul, 98, 100, 111
Sutter, David, 66
Syllabus of Errors, papal encyclical, 13–14, 16, 206
symbolism, 25–26, 40, 51–52, 84–91, 175, 222
   and antinaturalism, 5–7, 25
   in art criticism, 78–80, 105

   and the establishment, 29–30, 149–50
   and politics, 53–58
Symboliste, Le, 84, 85, 86, 102
synthesis, 72–76, 136–37, 144

Taine, Hippolyte, 10, 33, 47
   criticism of, 8, 14, 15, 59–63, 113–14
Tardieu, Charles, 35
Thiébault-Sisson, 135
Third Republic, 6, 53, 54, 209–11
Toche, Louis, 86n. 23, 129
Toulmouche, Auguste
   Forbidden Fruit, 31n. 15, Fig. 1

ultramontane Catholics, 13, 54, 206–7
Union pour l'action morale, 8

Vanor, Georges, 8, 51, 84–85
Verlaine, Paul, 8, 19–20, 51, 122
Véron, Eugène, 33, 49
Veuillot, Louis, 15, 206
Vie de Jésus, 15
Vie moderne, La, 79, 106
Vignier, Charles, 41
Vogüé, Eugène Melchior, vicomte de, 7, 42, 45, 63
Vogue, La, 27, 67, 79, 85, 86, 91, 92, 102

Waldeck-Rousseau, Pierre, 210, 213, 214
Wyzewa, Téodor de, 51, 55, 61, 64, 103

Zola, Emile, 26–28, 37, 60–61, 69